FULTON-MONTGOMERY COMMUNITY COLLEGE
JX1995.F36 1994
Feld, Werner J. International organi
[redacted]

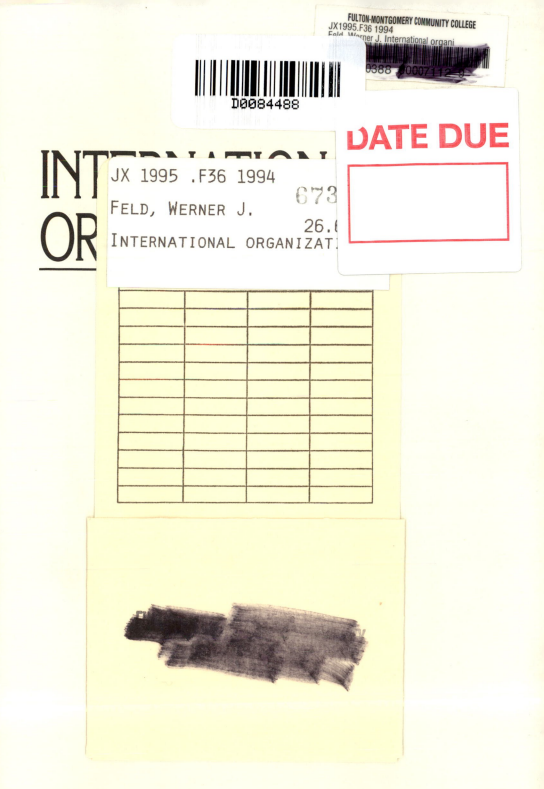

D0084488

INT

OR

JX 1995 .F36 1994
FELD, WERNER J.
673
26.
INTERNATIONAL ORGANIZATI

DATE DUE

[redacted]

INTERNATIONAL ORGANIZATIONS

A Comparative Approach

THIRD EDITION

WERNER J. FELD and
ROBERT S. JORDAN
with LEON HURWITZ

PRAEGER

Westport, Connecticut
London

67375

[redacted]

Library of Congress Cataloging-in-Publication Data

Feld, Werner J.
International organizations : a comparative approach / Werner J. Feld and Robert S. Jordan with Leon Hurwitz.—3rd ed.
p. cm.
Includes bibliographical references and index.
ISBN 0-275-94342-9 (HB). — ISBN 0-275-94702-5 (PB)
1. International agencies. I. Jordan, Robert S., 1929– . II. Hurwitz, Leon. III. Title.
JX1995.F36 1994
341.2—dc20 93-17663

British Library Cataloguing in Publication Data is available.

Copyright © 1994 by Werner J. Feld and Robert S. Jordan

All rights reserved. No portion of this book may be reproduced, by any process or technique, without the express written consent of the publisher.

Library of Congress Catalog Card Number: 93-17663
ISBN: 0-275-94342-9 (HB)
0-275-94702-5 (PB)

First published in 1994

Praeger Publishers, 88 Post Road West, Westport, CT 06881
An imprint of Greenwood Publishing Group, Inc.

Printed in the United States of America

The paper used in this book complies with the Permanent Paper Standard issued by the National Information Standards Organization (Z39.48–1984).

10 9 8 7 6 5 4 3 2 1

This book is dedicated to our many students, some of whom have gone on to careers in diplomacy or in international administration, or who are themselves teachers. We hope that they and those other students who will read this book can appreciate the following sentiment by the late Barbara Ward:

> The two worlds of man, the biosphere of his inheritance and the technosphere of his creation, are out of balance, indeed, potentially in deep conflict. And man is in the middle. This is the hinge of history at which we stand. The door of the future opening onto a crisis more sudden, more global, more inescapable, more bewildering than any ever encountered by the human species. And one which will take decisive shape within the life span of children who are already born. No problem is insoluble in the creation of a balanced and conserving planet, save humanity iteself. Can it reach in time the vision of joint survival? Can its inescapable physical interdependence, the chief new insight of our century, induce that vision? We do not know. We have the duty to hope.
>
> Barbara Ward, *Only One Earth*

We cannot do without force. . . . You cannot establish freedom, my fellow citizens, without force, and the only force you can substitute for an armed mankind is the concerted force of the combined action of mankind.

President Woodrow Wilson, 1919
Speech at Sioux Falls, Iowa
September 18, 1919

CONTENTS

FIGURES AND TABLES

FIGURES

TABLES

ACRONYMS

ADB	Asian Development Bank
AEC	African Economic Community
AFL-CIO	American Federation of Labor—Congress of Industrial Organizations
AFSC	American Friends Service Committee (Quakers)
AID	Agency for International Development (US)
AMC	American Mining Congress
ANCOM	Andean Common Market
APEC	Asia-Pacific Economic Cooperation Forum (ASEAN)
ASEAN	Association of Southeast Asian Nations
BENELUX	Belgium, The Netherlands, Luxembourg (in re the EC, etc.)
BIS	Bank for International Settlements
BTO	Brussels Treaty Organization
CACM	Central American Common Market
CAM	Central American Market
CAP	Common Agricultural Policy (EC)
CARICOM	Caribbean Community and Common Market
CBM	Confidence-Building Measures (i.e., Helsinki Accords and CSCE)
CBW	Chemical-Biological Warfare (in re treaties to prohibit)
CCISUA	Coordinating Committee for Independent Staff Unions and Associations of the UN System

CENTO	Central Treaty Organization (also known as the Baghdad Pact)
CFE	Conventional Forces in Europe Treaty
CIS	Commonwealth of Independent States (in re the former Soviet Union)
COMECON or CMEA	Council for Mutual Economic Assistance (defunct with the demise of the Soviet bloc)
COMSAT	Communications Satellite Corporation
COSPAR	Committee on Space Research (UN)
CPR or COREPER	Council/Committee of Permanent Representatives (NATO/EC)
CSCE	Conference on Security and Cooperation in Europe
CTC	Centre on Transnational Corporations (UN)
CWC	Conventional Weapons Convention
D-G	Directorate-General
DPC	Defense Planning Committee (NATO)
EAC	East African Community
EACSO	East African Common Services Organization (EAC)
EAGGF	European Agricultural Guidance and Guarantee Fund
EC	European Communities
ECA	Economic Commission for Africa (UN)
ECLA	Economic Commission for Latin America (UN)
ECOMOG	Economic Community Monitoring Group (ECOWAS)
ECOSOC	Economic and Social Council (UN)
ECOWAS	Economic Community of West African States
ECSC	European Coal and Steel Community (EC)
ECU	European Currency Unit
EDC	European Defense Community
EEC	European Economic Community (EC)
EFTA	European Free Trade Association
EIB	European Investment Bank
EMCF	European Monetary Cooperation Fund
EMF	European Monetary Fund
EMS	European Monetary System
EMU	Economic and Monetary Union (EC)
ENDC	Eighteen-Nation Disarmament Committee (UN)
EP	European Parliament (EC)
EPC	European Political Cooperation (EC)

ERDF	European Regional Development Fund (EC)
ERM	Exchange Rate Mechanism (EC)
EURATOM	European Atomic Energy Community (EC)
FAO	Food and Agriculture Organization (UN)
FCCD	Fund for Cooperation, Compensation, and Development
FFH/AD	Freedom from Hunger Campaign/Action for Development (FAO)
FICSA	Federation of International Civil Servants Associations
GATT	General Agreement on Tariffs and Trade
GCC	Gulf Cooperation Council
GDR	German Democratic Republic (the former East Germany)
GIEWS	Global Information and Early Warning System (FAO)
GNP	Gross National Product
IACHR	Inter-American Commission on Human Rights
IAEA	International Atomic Energy Agency
IATA	International Air Transport Association
IBRD	International Bank for Reconstruction and Development (World Bank Group)
ICA	International Commodity Agreement (UNCTAD)
ICAO	International Civil Aviation Organization
ICDA	International Coalition for Development Action
ICJ	International Court of Justice
ICNAF	International Commission for North Atlantic Fisheries
ICRC	International Committee of the Red Cross
ICSC	International Civil Service Commission (UN)
ICSU	International Council for Scientific Unions
IDA	International Development Association (World Bank Group)
IDB	Inter-American Development Bank
IFAD	International Fund for Agricultural Development
IFC	International Finance Corporation
IGO	Intergovernmental Organization
IGY	International Geophysical Year
ILO	International Labour Organization (UN)
IMF	International Monetary Fund (World Bank Group)
IMO	International Maritime Organization
INFCE	International Nuclear Fuel Cycle Evaluation
INGO	International Nongovernmental Organization

INPFC	International North Pacific Fisheries Commission
INTERPOL	International Criminal Police Organization
IOC	Intergovernmental Oceanographic Commission
IPRA	International Peace Research Association
IRC	International Rescue Committee
ISA	International Seabed Authority
ISPA	International Scientific and Professional Association
ITC	International Trade Centre (UN-GATT)
ITO	International Trade Organization
ITU	International Telecommunications Union
IVC	Index of Voting Cohesion
IVL	Index of Voting Likeness
LAFTA	Latin American Free Trade Association
LAIA	Latin American Integration Association
LDC	Less Developed Country
MEP	Member, European Parliament (EC)
MNC	Multinational Corporation
MNE	Multinational Enterprise
MTCR	Missile Technology Control Regime
NAFTA	North American Free Trade Agreement
NATO	North Atlantic Treaty Organization
NGO	Nongovernmental Organization
NIC	Newly Industrialized Country
NIEO	New International Economic Order
NORAD	North American Defense Command
NPG	Nuclear Planning Group (NATO)
NPT	Nuclear Non-Proliferation Treaty
NSG	Nuclear Suppliers Group
NTB	Non-Tariff Trade Barrier (GATT)
NWFZ	Nuclear Weapons–Free Zone
NWICO	New World Information and Communication Order (UNESCO)
OAS	Organization of American States
OAU	Organization of African Unity
OCAM	African and Malagasy Common Organization
OECD	Organization for Economic Cooperation and Development
OEEC	Organization for European Economic Cooperation
ONUC	UN Congo Force

OPEC	Organization of Petroleum Exporting Countries
PLO	Palestine Liberation Organization
PPE	European Peoples Party
PRC	People's Republic of China
PRCT	Regional Scientific and Technological Development Program
PTVA	Professional, Technical, and Voluntary Associations
SCOPE	Scientific Committee on Problems of the Environment
SCOR	Scientific Committee on Oceanic Research
SDR	Special Drawing Rights (IMF)
SEA	Single European Act (EC)
SEATO	Southeast Asia Treaty Organization
SELA	Latin American Economic System
SPID	Sectoral Program of Industrial Development
STABEX	Commodity Export Earnings Stabilization Scheme
START	Strategic Arms Reduction Talks
TAB	Trade and Development Board (UNCTAD)
TCDC	Conference on Technical Cooperation among Developing Countries (UN)
TNC	Transnational Corporation
UK	United Kingdom (Great Britain)
UN	United Nations
UNCED	UN Conference on Environment and Development (also called "Earth Summit" and "Rio Conference")
UNCLOS	UN Conference on the Law-of-the-Sea
UNCTAD	UN Conference on Trade and Development
UNDOF	UN Disengagement Observer Force
UNDP	UN Development Program
UNEF	UN Emergency Force (Suez Crisis)
UNEP	UN Environment Program
UNESCO	UN Educational, Scientific, and Cultural Organization
UNFICYP	UN Peacekeeping Force in Cyprus
UNFPA	UN Fund for Population Activities
UNHCR	UN High Commissioner for Refugees
UNICEF	UN Children's Fund
UNIDO	UN Industrial Development Organization
UNIFIL	UN Interim Force in Lebanon
UNITAR	UN Institute for Training and Research
UNMOGIP	UN Military Observer Group in India and Pakistan (Kashmir)

UNPROFOR	UN Protection Force (Croatia)
UNRWA	UN Relief and Works Agency
UNTSO	UN Truce Supervision Organization (Palestine)
UNU	United Nations University
UPU	Universal Postal Union
USDA	U.S. Department of Agriculture
USSR	Former Union of Soviet Socialist Republics
WCARRD	World Conference on Agrarian Reform and Rural Development
WFC	World Food Council (UN)
WFP	World Food Program (UN)
WHO	World Health Organization (UN)
WIPO	World Intellectual Property Organization (UN)
WMO	World Meteorological Organization (UN)
WTO	Warsaw Treaty Organization (now dissolved)

PREFACE TO THE THIRD EDITION

Since the second edition of this text appeared, the Cold War has come to an end. To some historians this represents the recreation of the pre-Cold War world or, perhaps even more apposite, the international system that antedated World War I. By this is meant that particularistic national self-interest governs individual state actions, without necessary regard to the ideological or national interests of previous over-arching superpower rivalries that were built around the mutual threat of nuclear annihilation.

One significant difference from either of these earlier periods, however, has been the phenomenal growth of both governmental and nongovernmental international organizations before, during, and after the Cold War. More recently, they have been used either to be of assistance when called upon in the settlement of disputes or, more particularly, to provide social and humanitarian aid when the consequence of either interstate or intrastate violence becomes intolerable to the international community at large.

With the demise of the Cold War, which was brought on by the failure of communist single-party "command" economies to compete successfully with democratic "demand" economies, almost the entire world economy now is shaped significantly by the market-oriented deflationary policies of the World Bank (IBRD) and the International Monetary Fund (IMF) and by the tariff-reducing and trade-promoting policies of the General Agreement on Tariffs and Trade (GATT). These organizations are guided by the experience derived from the Depression and World War II. It is a widely held belief that runaway inflation and the consequent degradation of a state's money, coupled with restraints on the free flow of goods and services across national boundaries (in a policy of "beggar thy neighbor"), can lead to domestic impoverishment that, in turn, may bring on political extremism.

It was feared that "cheap money" and "protectionism" could result in the rise of hypernationalistic or militaristic governments, or of communistic dictatorships.

What has happened instead is that the reunification of Germany and the dissolution of the Eastern bloc and then Soviet Union, followed by the former Yugoslavia and then Czechoslovakia, have brought about a revival of ancient ethnic feuds that are being played out within the confines of the modern territorial state, but whose territorial objectives are not confined by the borders established at the end of World War II. In other words, the erstwhile *evolution* of the modern territorial state is being accompanied, in some instances, by the *devolution* of the state. In this respect, some of the developed states of Europe are now behaving no differently than the so-called developing, or even the less-developed, states of Africa and Asia.

Ironically, economic motivations are being subordinated to these other motivations which have brought on terrible suffering in Europe as well as in Africa, Asia, and the Middle East. Equally significant is the fact that the assumption that lay behind creating dispute settlement and peacekeeping machinery through the United Nations and through such regional international organizations as the Organization of American States (OAS), the Organization of African Unity (OAU), and the Economic Community of West African States (ECOWAS), is not holding up either in Europe (e.g., the Balkans) or in Africa (e.g., Liberia, Angola, Sudan, and Somalia).

What is to be done? Can the hasty coalition of states acting in 1991 to counter the invasion of Kuwait by Iraq, which was motivated by economic concerns (oil) as well as by issues of national self-governance and human rights and led by the United States with the legitimization of the UN Security Council, be seen as a model? Can the members of the Security Council, and especially the Permanent Members who possess the veto, continue to find it advantageous to subordinate their respective national interests in the cause of a common interest? Even if they can, evidence suggests that achieving peace through the collective use of force may prove elusive.

Despite the many factors that affect the making of intergovernmental organization (IGO), as well as international nongovernmental organization (INGO), decisions, and the recognition that international action involves not only a single decision to be analyzed but also a continuum of interrelated (and often contradictory) options, the decision-making approach to the study of IGOs and INGOs can provide significant insights into the dynamics of their activities and the bureaucratic and political processes used to obtain national and international objectives. Indeed, movement in the international arena flows from hundreds of decisions made, not only in IGOs and INGOs, but also in national institutions and enterprises around the world. The new illustrative cases written for this third edition focus on these aspects of the contemporary international system.

We would like to acknowledge the many, very useful comments by our students at the Graduate School of International Studies at the University of Denver and the University of New Orleans. In fact, in some cases, research by some of the students found direct application in the development of the text, for which we are very grateful. Our thanks also go to Janet Davis and Jane Jordan for their dedicated service in assisting in the preparation of this manuscript for the publisher. Dan Eades, Political Science Editor at Praeger, has been extraordinarily patient as the manuscript has undergone a fundamental revision, and to the publisher for excellent copyediting.

INTERNATIONAL ORGANIZATIONS

INTRODUCTION: AN OVERVIEW

BRIEF HISTORICAL BACKGROUND

It is commonplace to date the beginning of the contemporary system of sovereign territorial states from the end of the Thirty-Years War in 1648, concluded by the Peace of Westphalia. During the seventeenth and the greater part of the eighteenth centuries, interactions between states in Europe were determined primarily by the interests of dynastic rulers who reigned as absolute monarchs over such states as France, Russia, Austria, and Prussia. Their concerns were prestige, military power, and territorial security, and therefore, many of their interactions dealt with the formation of military or dynastic alliances. But as the agrarian economies of Western Europe began to respond to the impact of the Industrial Revolution, international economic relations assumed greater importance. Consequently, by the nineteenth century, interstate relations increasingly embraced matters of commerce and trade in manufactured goods.[1]

This growth of manufacturing capacity in the rising industrial states of Western Europe and North America rapidly altered traditional distribution and consumption patterns throughout the world. With rapid industrialization came revolutionary improvements in the facilities of travel, transportation, and communication within and between states. These improvements offered opportunities, but also generated new problems for governments.

The sheer complexity of these developments led governments to seek new forms of interstate cooperation which resulted, by the nineteenth and early twentieth centuries, in what used to be known generally as international organizations, but which we now call intergovernmental organizations (IGOs) since their members are sovereign nation-states. Some of the earlier IGOs, many of which are examined in this text, had limited purposes, both in time and in function (e.g., perhaps providing nothing more than secretariat support for a meeting of heads of government or their representatives, as was the case for the periodic gatherings that grew out of the Congress of Vienna in 1815 and became known as the "Congress System"). Other early IGOs were somewhat more elaborate, such as the *Zollverein,* a customs union of Germanic states set up in 1819 with Prussia as the leader. After World War II, this notion of a customs union was revived with the 1957 Treaty of Rome, which brought into existence the European Economic Community, or common market. Still others, which were created near the end of the nineteenth century, included the Universal Postal Union (UPU) and the International Telegraphic (now Telecommunications) Union (ITU).

It is in this century that IGOs have proliferated, some possessing extensive and intricate bureaucratic structures. The League of Nations (created in 1919 after World War I) and the United Nations (established in 1945 after World War II) are, of course, prime examples of attempts to create IGOs based on what were hoped would be universal concepts that would provide the normative basis, as well as operational guidelines, to regulate the problems of conflict between or among states. But the European Communities (EC), the North Atlantic Treaty Organization (NATO), the Organization of American States (OAS), and the Organization of African Unity (OAU) are also important examples of the proliferation of regional IGOs dedicated to promoting cooperation on various issues or resolving conflict situations. Their performance is assessed so that comparative conclusions can be drawn in the chapters which follow.

As the IGOs proliferated, another kind of international organization, which was composed of nongovernmental organizations interested in the promotion of a variety of goals in the international arena, grew by leaps and bounds. These organizations, known as international NGOs or INGOs, play increasingly important roles in international politics and cannot be ignored in a comparative study of IGOs.

The tremendous political and economic transformations in Central and Eastern Europe, not least of which was German reunification, along with the disintegration of the Soviet Union in the beginning of 1989, not only ushered in extraordinary changes in intergovernmental relations, but also had an impact on INGOs as well, just as the United Nations came to play an increasingly important role in dealing with post-Cold War disputes and conflicts. The UN Security Council has acted with greater authority in dealing with various civil conflicts because the five Permanent Members, led by the United States, have authorized the Secretary-General to assume responsibilities that transcend any previous precedents. This point is discussed throughout this revised text, and in particular in Chapter 5. The extent of the involvement of the Security Council in various crises is shown

Table I.1
United Nations Peacekeepers: The Forces until Now

Mission		U.N. Personnel
Angola	Angola Verification Mission	479
Arab-Israeli Conflict	Truce Supervision Organization	272
Balkans	Protection Force	22,500
Cambodia	Transitional Authority in Cambodia	17,531
Cyprus	Peacekeeping Force in Cyprus	2,197
El Salvador	Observer Mission in El Salvador	595
Goland Heights	Disengagement Observer Force	1,350
India and Pakistan	Military Observer Group	38
Iraq and Kuwait	Iraq-Kuwait Observation Mission	409
Lebanon	Interim Force in Lebanon	5,805
Somalia	Operation in Somalia	550
Western Sahara	Mission for the Referendum in the Western Sahara	365

Source: Report of the Secretary General on the Work of the Organization (GA Document A 47/1, September 11, 1992)

in Table I.1. Additionally, the International Monetary Fund (IMF) lent its considerable expertise to efforts made by various Western industrial powers to put what was left of the Soviet Union, now called the Commonwealth of Independent States (CIS), back on its economic feet, certainly a difficult and complex task.[2]

APPROACHES TO THE STUDY OF INTERNATIONAL ORGANIZATION

As in the study of international relations in general, a number of approaches can be taken in the study of the academic field known as international organization. Since both IGOs and INGOs comprise this field of study, this text focuses on both because the current configuration of global politics, although continuing to rest on the notion of territorial sovereignty, is now combining with ethnic particularism, at one level, and "globalism," at another level, to weaken the force of territorial nationalism.[3]

One of the possible ways of conducting this study is through the *historical approach,* which is especially important because, as has been implied, international organization (used in its collective sense) has a clearly defined history marked by institutional successes and failures. However, as Inis Claude aptly remarks, "The unpredictable history of the future, no less than the ineradicable history of the past, is a factor in the shaping of political institutions."[4] Nevertheless, it is generally accepted that the contemporary world can be better understood, and future trends more clearly perceived and assessed, if one possesses some familiarity with the past. In particular, the pages that follow reflect our belief that the future of international organization may indeed be more successfully perceived if the experiences of the last century, in particular, are kept in mind, without neglecting, of course, the new political realities brought on by the demise of the Cold War.

Another well-recognized approach to the study of international organization consists of the *analysis of the international legal norms and treaties* underlying the establishment of particular IGOs, and of the competences that the bureaucracies and other organs of these organizations possess, both in the international arena and vis-à-vis their respective member states. While legal analysis and codification have a definite place in the understanding and evaluation of particular IGOs, they provide only partial insights into the actual political dimensions that define the effectiveness of contemporary universal or regional IGOs.[5]

Another approach has to do with the *structural-functional analysis* of institutions created by particular IGOs. In a broad sense, as one scholar suggests, functions refer to "what must be done" while structures refer to how what must be done is to be done.[6] *Structure* means a pattern—that is, observable uniformity—of institutional actions and operations. A main purpose of *function* in a very abstract sense is the maintenance of the larger, or transcendent, unit within which the structure is embedded.[7] This approach, therefore, focuses on both the formal (i.e., legal) and informal (i.e., political) manner in which the pertinent institutional bureaucracies perform their assigned functions.

This form of analysis can also provide an understanding as to how these institutional bureaucracies function in the larger context of international politics and to what extent the expectations of the states founding the IGOs are being fulfilled. The analysis must take into account how demands (inputs) by the various constituencies of IGOs are being processed, the particular end products of the function performance process (output), how feedbacks are monitored by the IGO to determine how well it fulfills its purpose, and how satisfactorily the interests of member states are being promoted and safeguarded.[8] In this connection, it should be emphasized again that INGOs are becoming increasingly salient actors in the field of international organization, both in their own right and as interacting agents with governments at the national or subnational levels, with IGOs at the international level, with each other, or perhaps with some mix of all these.[9]

Another useful approach to the study of IGOs (and, to a lesser degree, INGOs) is *decision-making analysis*. International bureaucracies, with their intergovernmental political organs, have various competences for decision making conferred on them by their governing charters or statutes. The nature and consequences of these competences vary from one IGO to another; in some cases, decisions may be directly binding on the member states as well as on the international bureaucracy. Occasionally, decisions can directly affect persons residing in the member states as, for example, under certain circumstances in the European Communities (EC). In more cases, however, the decisions are nonbinding or nonself-enforcing, with compliance or noncompliance depending on the perceptions of member state governments concerning the best way to serve their respective national interests. The contemporary "energizing" of the United Nations Security Council in peacekeeping, peacemaking, and related issues of compliance has created a new dimension of IGO intervention in what otherwise would be considered violations of the principle of domestic jurisdiction.

Another aspect of IGO decision making is its *locus*. In our complex world, the effect of decisions made by an IGO may well depend on whether a particular decision can be taken exclusively within the institutional apparatus of the IGO or whether national organs of the member states must participate in the decision-making process. What, then, is the impact of the participating member states on IGO decision making, and which functional areas of national governments have the greatest influence on multilateral decision making? What is the interplay between IGO institutions and national governments with respect to the decision-making process, and what effect does this have on the functions to be performed by the IGO? What are the domestic policymaking dynamics in national governments that explain their voting behavior in IGOs? When humanitarian-oriented IGOs—such as UNICEF, UNHCR, WHO, or WFP—are directly involved in dealing with the consequences of internal civil disorder that necessitate the use of armed forces mobilized under IGO auspices, then the interaction of domestic with international loci of decision making becomes more complex and more diffuse. If INGOs are also included, the multiplicity of interests, bureaucracies, and missions can create an intolerable strain on established processes of international decision making.

This leads to another aspect of decision-making analysis (often considered the core), that is, the inquiry into the *motivations, attitudes, and behavior* of the decision makers who give particular decisions their shape, scope, and direction. Seen from this perspective, decision making refers to the act of choosing among available alternatives.

However, this simple statement conceals the difficulty of such analysis.

Problems abound, including the insufficiency of information available to decision makers, uncertainty about alternatives and their consequences, and manifold pressures exerted on policymakers to accommodate, at times, both domestic interest groups and foreign governments. These problems make it very difficult for a decision maker to reach a rational decision: one directed toward the attainment of a clearly defined goal that would reflect the highest preference. Presumably, this preference should be based on the assumption that comprehensive, relevant information on all alternatives is available and is used, that the consequences of all alternative courses can be fully established, and that the selected alternative will possess the highest utility in reaching the goal desired. Such conditions are not, however, always attainable.

Social scientists must assume, nevertheless, that in all human relations, the rational elements that go into a decision will tend to predominate over the nonrational components.[10] These elements must be discovered rather than taken for granted, and their discovery requires an assessment of the various influences bearing on every decision made. They include the social and economic backgrounds of the decision makers; their personal goals, interests, and aspirations; their prior commitments; and specific motivations that may stem from the bureaucratic position they hold.

Despite the many factors that affect the making of IGO (and INGO) decisions and the recognition that international action involves not only a single decision to be analyzed, but also a continuum of interrelated (and often contradictory) decisions, the decision-making approach to the study of IGOs can provide significant insights into the dynamics of IGO activities and the bureaucratic and political processes used to obtain national and international objectives. Indeed, movement in the international arena flows from hundreds of decisions made in IGOs and INGOs, and also in national institutions and private enterprises around the world.

THE FOCUS OF THIS TEXT

While the commitment in this textbook is to a comparative analysis, the historical, legal, structural/functional, and decision-making approaches are also employed as appropriate. They focus, however, more on relevant formal and informal circumstances of decision making than on the idiosyncratic attributes of decision makers with respect to particular decisions. Furthermore, no text dealing with international organization in a collective sense can limit itself to an analysis of the United Nations and its specialized and affiliated agencies, even if one were to accept the premise that there exists an incipient "world organization" that might lead eventually to some form (or forms) of world government. On the contrary, we are impressed with the increasing *pluralism* of the world community, its *decentralized* nature, and its *resistance to system and order* in either theory or practice. However, it is not entirely accurate to characterize what goes on as reflective of an essentially chaotic "state of nature" (to recall Thomas Hobbes); there are a few normative, constitutional, legal, functional, or power/political levers that can be pulled by one or more decision makers that can effectively and systematically determine the course of human history.

It is very important, therefore, to measure *task performance* as a primary criterion of IGOs. Any assessment of the quality of IGO task performance in the past, present, or future suggests that international organizations have a long way to go before they can meet the needs and the aspirations of the world community; nonetheless, there is, in fact, no more effective way to understand comparatively their increasingly valuable, yet diversified, roles. They are integrated as much as possible in the theoretical framework.[11]

We have set up broad categories of organizations to be examined throughout the text. In this third edition, more inclusive illustrative cases have been included to reveal the interinstitutional complexity, as well as the task-performance relevance, of our major categories of IGOs. Thus, a clearer comparison can be derived from our more generalized analyses and descriptions under each major chapter heading. One category of organizations, the "UN Family," will present an overview of the great variety of functions carried out by this wide-flung assembly although the main emphasis is on the major organs that comprise of UN Headquarters. The second category is called "Major Regional Organizations in the Euro-Atlantic World" and will concentrate on the European Community (EC), the North Atlantic Treaty Organization (NATO), the Organization of Economic Cooperation and Development (OECD), and the Conference on Security and Cooperation in Europe (CSCE) without neglecting other organizations. "Major Non-European Regional Organizations" will emphasize the Latin American Free Trade Association (LAFTA) and its regional counterparts, the Economic Community of West African States (ECOWAS) and the Association of Southeast Asian Nations (ASEAN). Other regional organizations, such as the OAU, and economic and trade organizations, such as the General Agreement on Tariffs and Trade (GATT), are also examined.

NOTES

1. For a good historical overview, see Paul Reuter, *International Institutions* (London: George Allen and Unwin, 1958). Also see Robert S. Jordan and Werner J. Feld, *Europe in the Balance: The Changing Context of European International Politics* (London: Faber and Faber, 1986), esp. ch. 1.

2. Taken from the *New York Times,* December 1, 1992, p. 5.

3. See, for example, Georges Abi-Saad, ed., *The Concept of International Organization* (Paris: UNESCO, 1981).

4. Inis Claude, *Swords into Plowshares,* 4th ed., rev., (New York: Random House, 1984), p. 17 For an analytical discussion of the nature and evolution of the state

system, see Seyom Brown, *International Relations in a Changing Global System: Toward a Theory of the World Polity* (Boulder, CO: Westview Press, 1992).

5. For an elaboration of this approach, see Stephen M. Schwebel, *The Effectiveness of International Decisions* (Dobbs Ferry, NY: Oceana, 1971). See also Thomas Franck, *Political Questions/Judicial Answers: Does the Rule of Law Apply to Foreign Affairs?* (Princeton, NJ: Princeton University Press, 1992).

6. Marion J. Levy, Jr., *The Structure of Society* (Princeton, NJ: Princeton University Press, 1951), p. 64.

7. Ibid., pp. 57–62.

8. For an elaboration of the functional approach to the study of IGOs, see Thomas George Weiss, *International Bureaucracy* (Lexington, MA: D. C. Heath, 1975).

9. For a preliminary and tentative discussion of possible new combinations, see the symposium issue, "Multilateralism" in *International Organization* 46 (Summer 1992).

10. For a good general analysis of decision-making behavior in international politics, see John Spanier, *Games Nations Play*, 8th ed. (Washington, DC: Congressional Quarterly Press, 1991).

11. One way of defining and measuring task performance is through the theoretical framework of functionalism. See A. J. R. Groom and Paul Taylor, eds., *Functionalism: Theory and Practice in International Relations* (New York: Crane, Russak and Co., 1975).

1 CHANGING CONCEPTUALIZATIONS

Although the subject of international organization has been studied intensively for decades, it has been only fairly recently that careful distinctions began to be made between international organizations whose constituent members were nation-states and those composed of private citizens organized in the manner of interest groups. The former, as mentioned in the Introduction, are known as intergovernmental organizations (IGOs); the latter are termed international nongovernmental organizations (INGOs), examples of which are the International Chamber of Commerce, the World Confederation of Labor, and such more recent INGOs as Bread for the World and Amnesty International. In some instances, mixed governmental-nongovernmental units have been formed, such as, for example, the Communication Satellite Corporation (COMSAT).

The number of IGOs and INGOs has grown tremendously since World War II. This should not be surprising when one considers that the number of nation-states has more than tripled since World War II, largely as a consequence of decolonization and, more recently, as the result of the fragmentation of the Soviet Union, Czechoslovakia, and Yugoslavia. The number of nation-states, as measured by the membership of the United Nations, now approaches 200. The number of active IGOs in 1991 was 297.[1]

The growth of INGOs also has been spectacular. In 1991 a total of 4,620 INGOs was listed by the Union of International Associations; their number was estimated in the early 1980s by the Union to exceed 10,000 by the year 2000, although this figure is now considered to be optimistic, despite the increasing globalization of international communications.[2] It should be noted, however, that not all INGOs are still actively pursuing their original objectives; however, even the dormant INGOs may retain their institutional structures and thus can be reactivated to pursue either the same or different objectives. Chapter 6 deals in greater detail with different aspects of INGO operations, especially in the context of the post-Cold War period.

Concomitant with their growth, IGOs and INGOs have become increasingly significant actors in world politics. We are well acquainted with some of the larger IGOs such as the United Nations, NATO, EC, IMF, OAS, and the Organization of Petroleum Exporting Countries (OPEC). However, there are also many smaller IGOs that have various impacts on what happens in the international arena, especially at the regional level, such as ASEAN and the Economic Community of West African States (ECOWAS). This is discussed in chapter 5. INGOs can affect the behavior of states, although generally, the power of individual INGOs is relatively limited.

THE NATURE OF IGOs

Basically, IGOs are set up by three or more states to fulfill common purposes or attain common objectives.[3] In most instances, they constitute the framework for political and military alliances or economic cooperation schemes. IGOs possess a number of particular features that are examined briefly:

1. The purposes and objectives pursued by IGOs reflect common or converging national interests of the member states and, therefore, are normally long-range in nature.

2. The achievement of IGO goals is theoretically carried out with the equal participation of all states, although in practice, this is often not the case. The process of achieving IGO goals is best described as a roundtable, or brokerage, operation. This is in contrast to normal one-on-one diplomacy under bilateral treaties, through which two states may also pursue common purposes but which are based on trade-offs of advantages and disadvantages between the two governments.

3. The most distinguishing feature of an IGO is its institutional framework. This framework may be very simple, consisting of nothing more than a lightly staffed secretariat, as used to be the case in the Congress of Vienna, or it may be complex and comprehensive, approximating the legislative, executive, and judicial branches of a national government, as is seen in the EC. In most instances, however, the legislative functions are quite limited. Representatives of the member states of the IGO normally meet in an annual plenary conference that can last over several weeks or even months and at which general policy is laid down. Decisions often require a two-thirds majority and, on major issues, unanimity. In some of the more political IGOs, "consensus formation" is utilized to avoid isolating a major power or a significant minority. A council (usually composed of the permanent representatives of the member governments) is frequently

entrusted with supervising the day-to-day executive functions of the IGO. It meets more often than the conference and frequently decides questions by unanimous vote. The performance of judicial functions is normally carried out by selected international tribunals, such as the Court of Justice of the European Communities or the International Court of Justice (ICJ), which is a principal organ of the United Nations, but to which other IGOs may also assign jurisdictional competences. In internal personnel matters, Administrative Tribunals are formed to apply the growing body of staff rules and regulations and other forms of law-making instruments to individual cases.[4] The variations in institutions and their functions are examined in detail in Chapter 3.

4. IGOs are always established by a multilateral international treaty. This treaty is often called a convention, charter, or constitution. It stipulates the competences of the intergovernmental or bureaucratic organs of the IGO and the interrelations among them, and it sets up the basic norms and operational principles of the organization.[5]

5. IGOs are considered to have an "international legal personality" which means that, under international law, they can act in some ways similarly to a state; some (i.e., the United Nations), have standing to sue or may be sued in the International Court of Justice. They can conclude international treaties in their own name, and diplomatic missions can be accredited to them from their own member states as well as from other nations.

CLASSIFICATION OF IGOs

IGOs are classified by the Union of International Associations into various categories based on geographic and constitutional considerations.[6] In addition to the *global* and *regional* categories, which are based on their geographic scope, several new categories have been added.

An *intercontinental* IGO is one whose membership and preoccupations exceed that of a particular continental region. A good example is the OECD headquartered in Paris; its members come from North America (the United States and Canada), Asia (Japan), Australia, New Zealand, and Europe. Another example of this type of IGO is GATT.

The *universal* classification is applied to IGOs that have a minimum of sixty members. This would apply to the United Nations. Other IGOs may be considered in this classification if the distribution of at least thirty members is well balanced among the various continents. These include GATT, UNESCO, IAEA, FAO, ICAO, IFAD, and IMO. CSCE, the Conference for Security and Cooperation in Europe, may also now be an example as it reaches close to sixty members. These IGOs are discussed in the various illustrative cases in the text. Also see Figure 2.1, "The Structure of the United Nations."

Another category is entitled *federation of international organizations*. The only IGO that currently fits this category is the United Nations because of the focal role of the New York headquarters in relation to its specialized agencies that are members of the UN system.

It should be noted that these categories also apply to INGOs, and we will return to this subject when we discuss the nature of these international organizations later in this chapter.

The function or functions that an IGO is designated to perform may include the *enhancement* of the member states' security by adding collective military strength to their political power, the *advancement* of their economic performance in order to raise the economic well-being of their people, or *improvement* of their scientific and technological capabilities as well as technical cooperation.[7] In some cases, IGOs are assigned more than one function. The main functions of the United Nations, for example, embrace security but also include economic, social, and cultural responsibilities on a global basis. These are laid out in Article 1 of the UN Charter. (See Appendix B.) Humanitarian activities (e.g., care of refugees, children, acquired immune deficiency syndrome or AIDS, starvation), which have taken up much of UN resources in the 1980s and 1990s, have tended to merge the security function into their economic, social, and cultural responsibilities. We discuss this transformation in Chapters 5 and 6. In the Americas, the OAS performs as an IGO and is composed of most of the states in the Western hemisphere with the same range of basic functions. In Africa, ECOWAS began as an economic organization but later assumed political and security functions.

Figure 1.1 provides a matrix showing possible combinations of functions. Perhaps the largest number of IGOs falls in category II, which would include the whole array of the specialized and affiliated agencies of the United Nations. However, the number of IGOs in category I also is significant, considering the high level of interest of states in both economic and security regional organizations.

There are several IGOs in category III: the OAU and the OAS are examples. Obviously, however, only one global, multifunctional IGO exists at present: the United Nations.

Other possible categories are the scope of an IGO's competence and its degree of integration (also shown in Figure 1.1). The competence may be either general or limited. For example, the European Coal and Steel Community (ECSC) is a regional IGO of the EC with a competence that is limited to the coal and steel sectors of its member states. On the other hand, the European Economic Community (EEC) of the EC, also a regional IGO, has a nearly general competence in all the economic sectors of the member states, including agriculture, but excepting coal and steel. NATO and OPEC are also examples.

In terms of degree of integration, IGOs may be judged as being either very loosely integrated, with a minimal institutional structure and a minimum of powers conferred upon them by their member states, or as falling

Figure 1.1
Classification of IGOs

By Scope

Functional Scope	*Geographic Scope*	
	Regional	*Global*
Monofunctional	I	II
Multifunctional	III	IV

By Competence and Function

Competence	*Function*				
	Security	Economic	Political	Social	Cultural
General	NATO OAS UN	EEC ANCOM	Arab League		UNESCO
Limited	OAU	ECSC	Council of Europe	OAS	OAS

By Integration

Low	Alliance without institutional framework
	Intergovernmental relationship with institutional framework
	Independent IGO decision making
	Supranational organization
High	World government

at the other end of the spectrum. The highest level of integration exists when an IGO approaches supranational status. The term *supranational* means that the member states of the IGO have transferred to the organs of the organization some of the powers of decision making and implementation usually exercised only by sovereign states. The organs or institutions of the IGO may be given the authority to issue certain legal rules that are binding on the populations of the member states without requiring the endorsement of national legislation. A supranational IGO, then, would be the nearest international unit of governance analagous to a state, which is the primary national unit of governance. Lying somewhere in between are regimes, which we discuss in Chapter 7.

The most useful classification scheme for purposes of comparative analysis may involve a focus on the prime organizational tasks to be carried out by IGOs, namely, the *management of cooperation,* taking into account the skills employed in the coordination of organizational activities and in the achievement of necessary political compromises. Most economic IGOs clearly are task-oriented because they are propelled by some combination of economic interests. Security IGOs, for which the management of cooperation by political compromise may be more difficult, may experience greater disharmony among their member states over defining the tasks to be performed. Political IGOs, such as the Council of Europe or military alliances, are subject to this difficulty as well. Conflict resolution is the foremost task of the United Nations, the OAS, and the OAU, as is clearly indicated by their constituent treaties. In the post-Cold War era, conflict prevention, as well as conflict resolution (i.e., peacekeeping, peacemaking, and even peacebuilding), are acquiring added interest as national units are being torn asunder as much by internal conflict as by interstate violence.

However, these IGOs, and especially the United Nations, also perform significant economic coordinating tasks, and these indeed are the main missions for many of the UN specialized and affiliated agencies.

Attempts have been made to introduce organization theory into explaining, and perhaps predicting, the behavior of IGOs, but so far, these efforts have not been very comprehensive.[8] Nevertheless, an evaluation of task performance by individual IGOs provides an important criterion for comparative analysis and assessment. Such evaluation would include; (1) *the degree of need satisfaction achieved as related to the attainment of the purposes for which the IGO was created;* (2) *judgments on the capacity of the IGO to solve functional problems;* (3) *examination of the quality of the IGO's executive leadership and its ability to maintain institutional effectiveness;* and (4) *the leadership's capacity to shape the IGO's overall functional environment.*

The degree of success of an IGO's task performance depends to a large extent on *the effectiveness of its international bureaucracy.* To make judgments on the civil servants composing the bureaucracy requires evaluations of bureaucratic autonomy and morale, of the existence of strong or weak organizational ideologies, and of the prospects for needed institutional change, reinforcement, or perhaps merely survival.

Another important aspect in comparing IGOs' task performances is their *ability to develop policies and to implement them.* Success in this area depends on the IGO's autonomy and the confidence of member governments in its political leadership. Even more important, however, are the perceptions of member governments as to how closely policies developed by the IGO will match their respective national interests. Hence, member governments may encourage or discourage policy development by the IGO in accordance with their judgments regarding national benefits and costs. If the development by an IGO of particular policies is viewed as useful by member governments, or if an IGO has acquired such a high measure of autonomy in a specific (usually functional) policy area that it can go ahead with policy formulation without the specific blessing of the member governments, then its success at implementation will depend on how well flows of constituency demands and the efforts to support these demands are continually processed into policy outputs. In turn, the IGO's capacity to influence the behavior of governmental (and nongovernmental) constituencies and its actual exercise of this influence will be enhanced. The illustrative cases in chapters 5 and 6 are designed to reveal these interactions.

Task performance evaluation must also take into account policy outcomes, especially how far these outcomes differ from policy intent and what the unintended direct or indirect effects of these policies have been. The various efforts at conflict resolution in the post-Cold War period, discussed later in this volume, address this point.

Finally, the saliency to the member states of issues that are the potential objects of IGO policies is a significant variable for policy development and successful task performance. This is particularly the case when policy implementation requires action by the member states of the organization. Good examples here are the implementation of the EC's Common Agricultural Policy (CAP) and its Regional Development Fund (ERDF). The greater the saliency of the issues to the member states, the greater are the chances that they will want to exercise control over IGO policy development or perhaps assume policy formulation themselves. Such circumstances might lead to the redefinition of IGO goals by the member governments, the reduction of IGO autonomy, the request for changes in IGO operational or bureaucratic modes (such as the ongoing restructuring effort in the United Nations), and maybe the need for the renewed justification of the IGO's existence.[9] Effort is being exerted at present by some interest groups in the EC to modify the CAP in order to make it possible to find a compromise solution with the United States for a successful Uruguay Round of GATT-sponsored trade negotiations, but many European agricultural interests, which are beginning to organize themselves transnationally, oppose these efforts. The Somalia peacekeeping/peacemaking effort is a final example.

According to Anthony Judge, a number of IGOs (and INGOs as well) may also be usefully characterized according to the peculiarities in their structure.[10] One such category could be the intergovernmental profit-making corporation; another could include the various regional development banks such as the Asian Development Bank (ADB), the Inter-American Development Bank (IDB), or the International Finance Corporation (IFC) component of the World Bank Group. Other characteristics of IGOs may refer to their mode of action; for example, the Permanent Court of Arbitration, whose sole purpose is to provide the means for the settlement of international disputes through arbitration, and the Bank for International Settlements (BIS), which concentrates on facilitating bank clearings of accounts across national boundaries.

In our view, task performance and the evaluation of its quality provide the most significant criteria against which to compare IGOs, and perhaps even large INGOs. Figure 1.2 offers a graphic overview of basic tasks to be performed and a number of variables that may explain high or low success of task performance in individual IGOs. However, a note of caution

Figure 1.2
Organizational Tasks and Evaluation

	Management Evaluation	
Task Performance	*High Success*	*Low Success*
Cooperation	I	II
Conflict resolution	III	IV

Explanatory Variables for IGO Management Evaluation

Degree of need satisfaction
Quality of IGO policy development, implementation, and outcomes
Issue saliency for member-states
Executive leadership quality
Management and problem-solving skills of IGO executives and administrators
Nature and capabilities of civil servants (IGO and nationals seconded to the organization)

is in order here. It is often easier to set up the comparative criteria than to develop the empirical evidence regarding particular variables. In other words, we may observe the results of IGO activities and policy outcomes without having sufficiently precise evidence to attribute particular results or outcomes to specific actions or operations. For example, we can draw comparisions of United Nations peacekeeping activities to reveal both operational and political constraints, thereby relating policy initiatives to policy outcomes. The illustrative cases provide indications that suggest the influence and effects of certain variables.

IGOs: PATTERNS OF GROWTH

In the beginning of this chapter, we pointed to the remarkable growth of IGOs. Table 1.1 shows the pattern of growth from 1909 to 1991, relating it to the expansion of the number of states during that time and providing information on the mean number of states per IGO and the mean number of IGO members per state.

From an inspection of this table, it is clear that the growth of IGOs was steady until 1985, when the mean number of states had reached 19.1 per IGO and the mean number of shared memberships, 33.9. It is evident that during the past hundred years, an international network-building process has occurred among states. Furthermore, it is obvious that most states belong to a number of IGOs, either global or regional. (For further illustration, see Appendix A, "Membership of the United Nations and Its Specialized and Related Agencies").

Returning to Table 1.1, it is interesting to note certain spurts in the creation of IGOs. A noticeable acceleration took place during the 1905–1909 period which may have been caused by increasing economic trans-

Table 1.1
Evolution of IGOs and INGOs, 1909–1991

	IGOs	INGOs
1909	37	178
1956	132	973
1960	154	1,255
1964	179	1,470
1968	229	1,899
1972	280	2,173
1976	252	2,502
1981	337	4,265
1984	365	4,615
1985	378	4,676
1986	369	4,649
1988	309	4,518
1990	293	4,646
1991	297	4,620

BREAKDOWN BY CATEGORIES 1991

	IGOs		INGOs	
	#	%	#	%
Federation of International Organizations	1	0.3	39	0.9
Universal Membership Organizations	34	11.5	427	9.2
International Membership Organizations	40	13.5	773	16.7
Regional-Oriented Membership Organizations	222	74.7	3381	73.2
Total	297	100.0	4620	100.0

Source: *Yearbook of International Organizations*. Vol. 1 (Brussels: Union of International Associations, 1991–1992) p. 1667.

actions across national boundaries (which needed regulation) and by technological developments (which required coordination). However, it was clearly the periods immediately following World Wars I and II that witnessed the greatest proliferation of new IGOs. Various means for the settlement of disputes through conflict resolution measures (better organizational tools and management techniques to enhance international cooperation and improved border-crossing defensive arrangements) were put in place to prevent a repetition of the destructive havoc of life and property that were the result of the two world wars. Table 1.1 shows IGO-INGO trends of growth.

It may be interesting to speculate on the decline of IGOs that began in 1978. The low point in total IGO numbers was in 1990 (223). The trend of the future is uncertain, but there is no doubt that some IGOs were discontinued because they were unsuccessful in their assigned task perfor-

Table 1.2
Location of IGO and INGO Secretariats, 1991

Countries in which the greatest number of principal secretariats of intercontinental and universal membership organizations are located (includes INGOs).

Country	Total Secretariats
United Kingdom	206
France	200
United States of America	163
Switzerland	142
Belgium	123
Netherlands	64
Germany	60
Canada	39
Italy	35
Austria	26
Sweden	25
Japan	20
Australia	20
Denmark	18
Spain	16
Finland	13
Czechoslovakia	11

Source: *Yearbook of International Organizations*. Vol. 1 (Brussels: Union of International Associations, 1991–1992) p. 1599.

mance. The East African Community (EAC) is an illustrative case in point; it was dissolved in 1977 after increasingly severe problems in the management of the IGO could not be corrected. A similar fate befell the Central American Common Market (CACM), but efforts to reestablish the organization eventually may prove successful. With the demise of the Cold War, the Warsaw Treaty Organization (WTO) disappeared and perhaps eventually NATO will follow suit. In 1985, France ranked first in number of IGO memberships (275), followed by Britain (247) and Denmark (233). The US held 195 memberships and ranked eleventh. Table 1.2 shows the location of the various IGO and INGO secretariats.

HISTORICAL FLASHBACKS

The first IGO to be established was the Congress of Vienna which attempted to institutionalize regular consultations among the Great Powers of that era. It was convened in 1815 to lay the diplomatic foundations for a new European order amid the ruins left by the Napoleonic Wars. Although four major conferences were held between 1815 and 1822, severe differences in policies and objectives among the Great Powers made it clear that the time had not arrived for institutionalized collaboration and management in

Europe. Nevertheless, the leaders of the major states involved had constituted themselves as the Concert of Europe, which continued to meet sporadically for the rest of the century to deal with pressing political issues.

The Rhine Commission

The Congress of Vienna established a subordinate organization, the Rhine Commission, whose purpose was to regulate traffic and trade along the Rhine River. The members of this Commission were the littoral states of the Rhine, each of which had one vote. The Commission was given considerable powers to amend its own rules and to act as a court of appeals for the decisions of local courts regarding river problems or issues. Similar commissions were established later for the Danube, Elbe, Douro, and Po rivers.

Public International Unions

While the various river commissions dealt at times with politically sensitive issues, another type of IGO sprang up in the middle of the nineteenth century which was concerned primarily with nonpolitical, technical matters. These IGOs were known as public international unions, and the most important of these were the ITU (1865), the UPU (1874), and the International Union of Railway Freight Transportation (1890). Other IGOs of a very nonpolitical nature that were established during that period dealt with such diverse fields as agriculture, health, standards of weights and measurements, patents and copyrights, and narcotics and drugs. Some of these IGOs had elaborate institutional frameworks: for example, the Universal Postal Union had a Congress of Plenipotentiaries that met every five years, a Conference of Delegates of Administrations, and a Permanent International Bureau. The Conference had amendment powers and frequently used majority voting.

The *Zollverein*

The first attempt at economic integration in Europe came with the establishment of the German *Zollverein* in 1834. This organization was a loosely joined customs union and lasted until 1867. Initially, only eighteen of the thirty-eight German states—kingdoms, duchies, and free cities—participated, but by 1867, almost all states had become members. Prussia was the moving spirit and overall manager of the *Zollverein*. The General Congress was the chief organ; decisions were made by unanimity.

The League of Nations

The first major effort to organize a global security IGO for the peaceful settlement of disputes through mechanisms for conflict resolution was the creation of the League of Nations. It was established in 1919 by the victorious nations of World War I led by U.S. President Woodrow Wilson, but the U.S. did not join. The principle underlying the League of Nations was the notion of collective security, under which all member states of this IGO were obligated to come to the aid of a member state that was the victim of military aggression. A more vague but, in the long run, just as consequential, principle was that of national self-determination and political independence. The two principles appear to both complement and contradict each other in the post-Cold War period. Successor states to the Soviet Union face internal pressures that threaten their integrity and the fate of the post-USSR Confederation of Independent States.

The United Nations

The creation of the United Nations in 1945 is the culmination of the global IGO. It represents not only a single IGO, derived from the precedent of the League (although the International Labour Organization was associated with it), but also a whole family of global IGOs that includes the International Labour Organization (ILO) as well as the UN Educational, Scientific, and Cultural Organization (UNESCO), the World Health Organization (WHO), the Food and Agriculture Organization (FAO), and many others. Indeed, over the years there has been a continuing proliferation of UN specialized and affiliated agencies, many of which were created during the Cold War period to deal with the problems of Third World development. Hence, the classification of the United Nations as a federation, or perhaps more accurately a confederation, seems well justified.

Regional IGOs

The rapid increase of regional IGOs followed the conclusion of World War II when economic cooperation schemes were seen as providing solutions for the ravages of the war in Western Europe, and led to the establishment of the EC and the European Free Trade Association (EFTA). The Benelux Convention, in fact, was signed as early as 1944 but did not come into force until 1948. The Council for Mutual Economic Assistance, better known as COMECON or CMEA, was the Soviet bloc's response to the EC. It was dissolved in 1991.

Many regional economic IGOs were also set up as a consequence of decolonization, with the rationale to accelerate the development process of these new states. Noteworthy, in this respect, are the regional development banks. (Some older underdeveloped states, such as those in central and Latin America, were also beneficiaries.) In spite of many failures, this rationale has continued to provide the major justification for creating new regional IGOs or expanding their functions.

A number of regional security IGOs also sprang up following World War II. However, their establishment was primarily in response to the bipolar competition of the Cold War that had evolved between the two superpowers and which had global ramifications. Hence, by the 1950s, NATO and WTO had come into being; NATO (but not WTO) continues to this day. Two security IGOs that were created under U.S. leadership in Southeast Asia and in the Middle East to contain the Soviet Union and the People's Republic of China (PRC)—SEATO and CENTO, respectively—have since disappeared. The disintegration of the Soviet Union and the establishment of the Commonwealth of Independent States (CIS), covering most but not all of the former area, has radically altered the security concerns of the world. From a bipolar world, international politics finds itself now in a new world with the United States as the only superpower, albeit not entirely without constraints on the use of its power. Existing and, perhaps, new security IGOs may have to be given changed or new task performances to cope with the multiplicity of regionally-based conflicts that may have internal ethnic origins, and also cross-border consequences. These range from Central Asia through the Balkans to Africa and hence to Southeast Asia.

THE NATURE OF INGOs

In the early pages of this chapter we commented briefly on the rapid rise in the number of INGOs and provided estimates of how many of these nongovernmental organizations might be operating by the year 2000. Naturally, such estimates are risky and the reliability of such predictions depends on many circumstances, including how an INGO is defined. Indeed, although the number of INGOs has fallen slightly, from 4,676 in 1985 to 4,620 in 1991, their intervention in international politics—especially by humanitarian INGOs—has probably increased.

The variety of objectives pursued by INGOs is extensive, including the International Chamber of Commerce, representing business and trade interests, and the World Confederation of Labor, consisting mainly of Catholic unions and promoting their goals. Other examples are the International Union of Architects, the International Federation of Teachers, Bread for the World, Amnesty International, Doctors without Borders, International Rescue Committee (IRC), and the International Committee of the Red Cross (ICRC).

The Union of International Associations has set up a number of criteria for defining INGOs, covering aims, membership, governance, and financing. The aims must be genuinely international in character and manifest the intention to engage in activities in at least three states, the membership must be drawn from individuals or collective entities of at least three states and must be open to any appropriately qualified individual or entity in the organization's area of operations, the constitution must provide for a permanent headquarters and make provisions for the members to periodically elect the governing body and officers, the headquarters and the officers should be rotated among the various member states at designated intervals, the voting procedure must be structured in such a way as to prevent control of the organization by any one national group, and substantial financial contributions to the budget must come from sources in at least three states. As a consequence, many international societies and unions in North America are excluded since their funds are usually derived wholly from U.S. members. Furthermore, no attempt must be made to make profits from direct distribution to the members of the INGOs, but this does not mean that members may not be helped to increase their profits or better their economic organization through the activities of the INGOs.[11]

A resolution by the UN Economic and Social Council (ECOSOC) in 1968 (No. 1296–XLIV) appears to broaden the above criteria. It defines an INGO as follows: "Any international organization which is *not* established by intergovernmental agreements shall be considered as a nongovernmental organization . . . , including organizations which accept members designated by government authorities, provided that such membership does not interfere with the free expression of views of the organization." Kjell Skjelsbaeck has expanded the definition of INGOs even further by considering the representation of members from only two states to be sufficient if at least one of the representatives is not a governmental official.[12]

Why is it important to worry about these differences in definition? To some extent, they change the nature of INGOs. Moreover, they affect their ability to interact with such UN bodies as ECOSOC and UNESCO (depending on whether they are recognized by these bodies as legitimate INGOs) and they have an effect on what entities are construed as INGOs in statistical as well as functional comparisons.

INGOs carry out a variety of border-crossing activities to attain their goals in the pursuit of the interests for which they have been created. These activities include setting up relationships of the INGOs with both governmental and nongovernmental entities and actors; such relations have been labeled transnational in contrast to traditional international relations, which are generally understood to apply only to activities and contacts between governmental actors.

The objectives of transnational INGO initiatives can be broken down into three groups: 1) *to promote their own interests in the international and national arenas;* 2) *to promote, modify, or oppose the goals of the United Nations, its specialized agencies and affiliates, and regional IGOs,* and; 3) *to support, modify, or oppose the goals of national governments.* All three of these groups of initiatives apply, for example, to the illustrative case in Chapter 6 concerning the UN Conference on Environment and Development (UNCED).

The objectives under the latter two categories are likely to be functions of the specific objectives in the first, but this is not necessarily the case when it comes to general, often ideological, goals. This observation is related to the case in Chapter 5 about the U.S. withdrawal from UNESCO. It is also quite conceivable that a particular INGO will support specific IGO goals but oppose national goals of a particular government. Therefore, IGOs and national governments may perceive an individual INGO as either friendly or hostile, and these perceptions may differ from case to case. Consider, for example, the work of the ICRC and humanitarian INGOs in civil wars, of Amnesty International's activities in cases where government takeovers are disputed, of various other human rights "watchdog" groups, and of INGOs that engage in monitoring such disparate activities as drug trafficking, arms sales transfers and, environmental degradation.

The capability of INGOs to mount effective transnational initiatives depends on the strength and distribution of their membership, their organizational effectiveness and financial resources, and their institutionalized and informal contacts with governmental and IGO agencies. Some of the criteria for evaluation discussed earlier with respect to IGOs may also be applicable to INGO assessment. We examine these issues further in Chapter 6.

CLASSIFICATION OF INGOs

The functional breakdown of INGOs provided in Appendix C shows the various ways in which INGOs are classified by the Union of International Associations. Moreover, the task is becoming more complex all the time, in part because of the changing definition of security in the post-Cold War period.

Two features of this appendix should be noted. First, in 1976 the criteria for inclusion in the INGO statistics were broadened, and this allowed the addition of borderline cases. Apparently, the arguments put forth by scholars such as Kjell Skjelsbaeck for expanding the INGO description have been effective. Second, a relatively large number of INGOs (close to 30 percent of the total) are defunct or dormant. It is interesting to find that, according to figures for 1970–1971, a high ratio of groups pursuing interests involving politics, such as international relations, law, and administration, fall in the defunct or dormant category, while the percentage of defunct or inactive economic and health care groups is relatively small.

The *Yearbook of International Organizations* identifies other classifications that are only indirectly related to the general functional purposes of Appendix C, although all ultimately seek to promote specific causes.[13] One such category is characterized by its hybrid nature; this involves mixtures of IGOs and INGOs. Some INGOs have government-related memberships, such as the International Criminal Police Organization (INTERPOL) and the International Union of Official Travel Organizations. Other INGOs have special status in international law: the best known is the ICRC, which is recognized by the Geneva Convention.

We should note that political parties may also develop into transnational organizations, for example, the European Peoples Party, the European Christian Democratic Union, and the Socialist International. All three organizations are INGOs with a special relationship to a number of national governments, and the first two are also specially related to the EC, a regional IGO. Also considered to be INGOs are opposition bodies to established governments, such as the Palestine Liberation Organization (PLO) before it assumed territorial governing responsibilities.

While, as we have seen, INGOs are basically nonprofit-making entities, many transnational activities with powerful effects on international politics and decision making are carried out by another type of INGO: the profit-oriented multinational corporation (MNC), which is now more frequently referred to as the transnational corporation (TNC). Although it would be tempting to include TNCs in our comparative analysis of the field of international organization because they contribute in interesting and important ways to the web of economic and political interdependence, their nature and structure are quite different from those of IGOs and INGOs. This seriously hampers any meaningful comparison. Moreover, a vast literature exists on TNCs that would have to be considered carefully if we were to make them part of our analytical efforts. Hence, TNCs will generally be omitted from our study, except where references to them might offer special insights, as in the illustrative case in Chapter 6 on the attempt by the Centre for Transnational Corporations to devise a code of conduct for TNCs.

In the same way as with IGOs, it is useful to distinguish between global or universal INGOs and regional organizations. INGOs often have sprung up or are related to regional IGOs. The number of European INGOs expanded rapidly after the establishment of the three IGOs comprising the EC, especially the EEC. However, regional INGOs also exist and operate outside the context of regional IGOs.

Finally, INGOs can be classified in terms of their task performance. Since most INGOs pursue particular interests, their foremost task is the attainment of specific goals for the promotion of their interests. Successful goal attainment requires the design of appropriate strategies and the effective execution and implementation of the strategies devised. In turn, the competent performance of these tasks depends on the management of cooperation among members of the INGO, including the careful coordination of aspirations and the achievement of necessary compromises. In some cases, this will require expertise in conflict resolution. INGO participation in Somalia is an example. For some INGOs whose primary concern is the maintenance of peace or the arbitration of disputes, conflict resolution is likely to be the central task, although the management of cooperation may be equally important. As in the Balkans, the management of cooperation of INGOs in civil or ethnic situations in which the United Nations and/or regional IGOs are also deeply involved can become very difficult to maintain.

INGO GROWTH PATTERN AND DISTRIBUTION

International NGOs, as delineated above, are generally assumed to date back to 1846, when the World's Evangelical Alliance was founded.[14] The dramatic growth of INGOs from 1909 to 1991 is illustrated in Table 1.1. The number of INGOs founded increased sharply in the periods immediately following major wars (for example, the Russo-Japanese War and World Wars I and II) and decreased during periods of rising international conflict and wars, such as the time spans 1911–1920 and 1931–1940. This suggests that international strife and turmoil impede the growth of INGOs.[15] In contrast, the settlement of devastating wars, coupled with the bitter memories of their misery and deprivation, seems to stimulate the formation of INGOs, reflecting a revived spirit of border-crossing cooperation. In the post-Cold War period, in which intra-state warfare has become as prevalent—if not more so—as inter-state warfare, INGOs have become caught up in situations involving levels of conflict that defy easy classification, as well as in those situations concerned only with economic and social development as such. The two types of situations are often, of course, intertwined, especially if economic sanctions or blockades are imposed on a warring state or faction.

It is interesting to note that a very similar situation prevailed in the growth pattern of IGOs since 1860, also shown in Table 1.1. Expanding international cooperation after World Wars I and II is clearly evidenced by the sharp increases in the founding of IGOs during the periods 1921–1930 and 1941–1960. Equally visible is the distinct drop in increases between 1931 and 1940.[16] Periods of relative harmony, as existed between 1981 and 1991, may have stabilized their number, but post-Cold War conflicts have tested the usefulness of IGOs established to deal with post-World War II or Cold War political/security conditions. These conditions have been accompanied by the sharp increases in international trade and in the transnational movements of people, whether as a consequence of war or poverty, or both.

Between 1954 and 1976 the number of INGOs nearly tripled, and most of the functional categories shared in this rise. However, there are some notable exceptions, based primarily on the nature of the groups. For example, the number of trade unions increased by only about 15 percent, while sports and recreation groups increased by about 90 percent. Some groups, such as agriculture and transport, nearly quintupled. The drop of INGO numbers, or perhaps their stabilization since 1985, may also be explained by a more interdependent world arena and by existing networks. Advanced telecommunications also play a part.

The largest representation in INGOs came from Europe, followed by North and South America; however, the highest growth rates in national representation were found in Africa, Asia, and the Pacific, where national representation more than tripled. Nevertheless, in net numbers of representation, the European states and the other Western-oriented industrial states predominate, with France, Britain, and the former Federal Republic of Germany holding top honors. As for IGO and INGO secretariats, Britain and France provided most of the locales, followed by the United States and other West European countries.

Finally, using the current terminology developed by the Union of International Associations for "conventional" IGOs and INGOs, we present the latest comparative figures in Appendix C. Not surprisingly, regionally oriented organizations predominate, comprising 74 percent of the IGOs and 73.3 percent of the INGOs.

INTERNATIONAL ORGANIZATION AND INTERDEPENDENCE

From our discussion of the growth and geographic distribution pattern of IGOs and INGOs, there is a clear indication that the web of international and transnational contacts and relationships between governments and nongovernmental actors has grown immensely and has become increasingly close-knit. It is fair to assume that as a result of this development, the number of border-crossing interactions, such as diplomatic intercourse; commercial, trading, and financial transactions; employment and migratory shifts for economic, humanitarian, or political causes; and various lobbying efforts, has also increased. However, it will require further investigation to determine the full meaning of these interactions. Do they signify the increased creation of interdependence among states, with varying welcome or unwelcome effects on the international system, as it often seems fashionable to assert? Alternately, are these border-crossing activities merely a reflection of an expanding world population trying to manage its affairs within an increasingly complex political, economic, and social environment? When we note such recent transnational problems as refugee migrations, drug trafficking, and arms transfers, the world indeed appears to be changing into a "global village." Electronics and computer technology have also transcended the notion of border crossing.

To answer these questions, we need to explore briefly the nature and effects of interdependence, a term that came into vogue during the 1970s and has generated a vast literature.[17] It would exceed the scope of this text to evaluate critically this literature in its totality. Instead, we will present here a description and definitions of interdependence and an examination of its effects on national governments. In addition, the role that IGOs and INGOs might play within the operational context of interdependence will be examined. The concept of interdependence should also be related to that of multilateralism, as discussed in Chapter 7.

The basis for global and regional interdependence is the *differential distribution of needs, aspirations, and capabilities of states, of their peoples, and of other international actors,* including such IGOs as the EC. William Coplin and Michael O'Leary describe interdependence as the existence of conditions in which the perceived needs of some individual groups in one state are satisfied by the resources or capabilities that exist in at least one other state. Thus, *patterns of transnational interdependence are a product of the interface between needs and capabilities across national boundaries.*[18]

Interdependence is manifested by flows of people, of civilian and military goods and services, of capital, and of information across national boundaries in response to needs in one or more states and in accordance with the capabilities of others. These flows are often referred to as *transactional flows,* and they can be quantitatively measured. Depending on their particular interests, a variety of governmental groups and national NGOs, such as particular bureaucracies or economic pressure groups, may be involved in these flows. The existence of similar needs may lead to formal and informal coalitions among states, among states and IGOs, and among governmental and nongovernmental actors. Current global problems, such as those of health and disease, refugees, transfers of arms and nuclear/ballistic missile technology, and food are attracting such formal and informal coalitions. Complementary capabilities may also produce alliances. On the other hand, the unequal distribution of capabilities may conjure up perceptions of dependence and, indeed, actual dependency by less favored states on economically and politically more powerful states. This is why the dangers of the spread of biological, chemical, and nuclear weapons technology have attracted so much international attention. Similar capabilities, coupled with unequal resources, may also sharpen economic competition in international trade and in the search for (or control over) sources of raw materials, with oil being a clear case. The competition between the United States and Japan is one example, that between the United States and the EC is another, and the Gulf War between a U.S.-led UN coalition and Iraq is a third.

From the foregoing discussion it is evident that the different capabilities possessed by governmental and nongovernmental actors play a crucial role, not only for present and future interdependence relationships in regional and global contexts, but also for the successful pursuit of the satisfaction of needs and aspirations of individual states. Such capabilities as the quality and quantity of military forces, economic and financial means, and industrial and technological proficiency can be translated into international power and influence, while their absence may signal serious vulnerability. Hence, small states usually must be more modest in their policy aspirations than the big powers because they have control over more limited resources, although the skillful exploitation of a larger state's weaknesses may compensate for limitations in resources. The international politics of oil comes to mind again as one example, while terrorism as a policy instrument is another. If the hostilities in Vietnam have proved anything, it is that even the greatest military power on earth, the United States, does not possess unlimited resources or sufficient means to achieve all its desires, especially in the face of internal political dissent. The former Soviet Union learned the same lesson in its military intervention in Afghanistan.

Given that the conditions exist that can produce interdependence, what actually triggers such a relationship and what are the effects on, and consequences for, the states involved in interdependence relationships, and their governments?[19] A broad notion of interdependence has been put forth by Oran Young, who defines it as "the extent to which events occurring in any given part or within any given component of a world system affect (either physically or perceptually) events taking place in each of the other parts or component units of the system."[20] When directed primarily to economics, interdependence is considered to be present when there is an increased sensitivity to external economic developments.[21] According to Robert Keohane and Joseph Nye, sensitivity "involves degrees of responsiveness within a policy framework—how quickly do changes in one country bring costly changes in another, and how great are the costly effects?"[22] The problems of the oil price increases that began in 1973 for Western Europe, Japan, and the United States come to mind, and the troublesome economic and financial relations between the United States and Japan offer another example. Still another case in point is the political and economic interdependence of the advanced Western and West Asian countries during the 1991 Gulf War against Iraq.

A second dimension of interdependence is "vulnerability," which "rests on the relative availability and costliness of the alternatives that various actors face."[23] In other words, vulnerability reflects the varying inability of a state, IGO, or private actor to accept and cope with the economic, political, and social costs imposed by external events, even if policies have been, or will be, changed. The different effects of the actions of OPEC on consumer states in both the industrially advanced and the developing countries constitute a good example of varying degrees of vulnerability.

The emphasis on vulnerability is also a criterion in Kenneth Waltz's definition of interdependence which focuses on the cost of disentanglement from an interdependent relationship.[24] For Waltz, then, a country or an IGO may be affected by what another actor does, or may be sensitive to the border-crossing actions of other actors, but the relationship would not necessarily be interdependent unless there is a definitive cost to the country or IGO for extracting itself from the interdependent relationship, and here, the economic and other capabilities of different actors are likely to be decisive.

What are the consequences for participants of an interdependent relationship? Keohane and Nye observe that such relationships may produce benefits, but costs are also incurred because interdependence restricts the autonomy of the participants in this relationship. Whether the benefits exceed the costs depends on the values of the actors as well as the nature of the relationship.[25] Obviously, it is very rare that, in terms of benefits and costs, a truly reciprocal, symmetric relationship exists anywhere. Indeed, it is the asymmetries in interdependence caused by differing economic, political, and, perhaps, military capabilities of the actors that are the normal circumstances in their relationships and provide sources of influence for governmental and nongovernmental actors in their dealings with each other. A dramatic example of this point is the withdrawal in 1992 of Britain, Italy, Sweden, and other EC member states from the European Exchange Rate Mechanism (ERM) when their national efforts to stabilize their currencies against the German mark were, in effect, bleeding them of their foreign exchange reserves.

As already pointed out, it is the inequality of capabilities within interdependent relationships that at times evokes fears of dependence on the part of both governmental and nongovernmental actors. Unequal capabilities among states, instead of producing perceptions of reciprocal dependence that might induce governments to treat the actions of other governments or IGOs as though they were events within their own borders and might be seen within the context of converging, if not identical, interests, are more likely to lead to suspicion, envy, and tensions.[26] The differing conceptions in mid-1993 of Italy and the U.S. over the means to achieve the UN's objectives in Somalia, and in particular in Mogadishu, perhaps can be seen as an example. The Italians stressed negotiations with the dominant warlord, assuming converging interests, whereas the U.S. favored capturing him, confiscating his weapons, and disarming his followers, assuming divergent interests. Hence, governmental leaders may feel called upon to resort to national means and solutions as a countervailing force against the real or imagined threat of dependence on other states or private entities. Such actions harm the prospects of useful collaboration among states and are likely to undermine, if not destroy, the benefits that interdependence networks may produce. For example, the tendency to resist reciprocity in trade relations because of suspicions of unequal costs and benefits has been a constant feature of the GATT negotiations.

Perceptions of this dependence have aggravated all the other problems that many leaders of the developing states have faced in the high-priority task of nation building and their consequent preoccupation with sovereignty and autonomy of choice. While these leaders may perceive various degrees of dependence and restrictions on their autonomy (this is sometimes called neocolonialism), there is also a reverse dependence on certain developing states exhibited by some industrial states. This dependency stems from the need for certain fuel raw materials, especially oil, and a number of nonfuel strategic raw materials, such as bauxite, manganese, tungsten, and zinc, among others. The disposal of uranium is also playing an increasingly important international role as nuclear weapons are dismantled. However, the interdependence pattern that flows from dependence on minerals is subject to modification as new technologies are developed, substitutes for minerals that are in short supply are found, and industrial needs change. The growing interdependency in food is only too obvious, and will be discussed later in this text. The possible accessibility of manganese and other mineral resources on the seabed also threatens to one day alter this dependency relationship. Additionally, problems of debt management have underscored the high degree of interdependence that this can create between, for example, U.S. banks and Latin American countries.

Many governmental and private analysts look at interdependence as creating undesirable dependence, and some think it is a code word for economic bondage.[27] They see a widening economic gap between affluent and poor societies. For these analysts, the process of interdependence escalates tensions over the restrictions of national or societal autonomy; threatens the achievement of national economic, social, and political objectives; and may produce violent nationalist and interstate conflict. The deflationary policies of the International Monetary Fund (IMF) are feared to be destabilizing by many, especially those responsible for economic policy-making in the successor states of the former Soviet Union and in the post-Cold War governments of the former Soviet bloc.

Is interdependence increasing or declining? After engaging in a very careful and thoughtful study based on statistical data ranging from 1880 to the present, Richard Rosecrance and five collaborators came to the following conclusion: "The pattern of contemporary interdependence is much more mixed than many have believed. The amplitude of economic change has increased, and the response of one economy to another has become more unpredictable. Relationships no longer appear to be stable across time. Interdependence may be becoming unstable."[28]

Rosecrance and his colleagues state that data from recent years indicate a gradual and progressive detachment of individual national policies from the general trend toward interdependence. Since their study concentrates on the advanced industrial states, perhaps this conclusion may not be generally applicable to all states. Moreover, they acknowledge that the decline in the relationship among the industrialized states may have led to a more intimate relationship of these states with outside states, such as the oil producers, other developing states, and the former communist bloc.[29]

Nonetheless, whatever the thrust and the outcome of these developments, we agree that continuing linear increases in interdependence may occur, not only among the industrially advanced states, but also in the remainder of the world where, in fact, interdependence may be actively resisted. Much will depend on the future organization and structure of economic, political, and military cooperation among states and nongovernmental actors, and it is here that IGOs and INGOs can play an important role.

It seems to us that the mere increase in the number of IGOs and INGOs, and the resulting proliferation of border-crossing contacts and relations by itself, have little effect on the intensification of regional and global interdependence. Only when IGOs and INGOs become involved in the *management* of existing interdependencies or in the purposeful creation of new interdependencies can we speak of their positive contribution. This brings us back to our discussion of IGO and INGO organizational tasks, which include the management of cooperation through coordination measures, the achievement of compromise, the selection of appropriate goal-attaining strategies, and the resolution of conflicts. The effective execution of all these tasks can produce or maintain beneficial interdependence relationships, accomplish a more adequate distribution of costs, resolve perceptions of dependency, and initiate new interdependence arrangements that maximally promote the interests of all participants.

It is in Europe that we find the best examples of the enhancement of regional interdependence through the management of cooperation by IGOs and INGOs. The EEC, the ECSC, the OECD, and NATO are cases in point. However, there have also been management failures. The attempt to move from the Soviet Union to the Commonwealth of Independent States is an exercise in interdependence management whose full success remains doubtful. In all cases, attempts at the management of cooperation can diminish as well as enhance interdependence.

Another instance of less-than-successful management of cooperation is the inability of the OECD to obtain the collaboration of its member states in the full coordination of their economic policies, despite the annual economic summit meetings of the so-called G-7, largest OECD states. In Eastern Europe, the desire for maximum national autonomy, democracy, and a free market system, especially in Poland, Hungary, and the former Czechoslovakia, has resulted in difficulties for economic policy. In the case of Czechoslovakia, these difficulties contributed to its dissolution into Czech and Slovak units. The efforts at coordination by the EC and other Western countries have been less than successful in creating positive interdependence, and the creation by NATO of the so-called North Atlantic Cooperation Council with "partners" consisting of the former members of the Soviet bloc, has thus far not proven to be an avenue for eventual full membership in NATO.[30] The bitter arguments over farm export policies between the

United States and the EC and between France and its fellow EC members are also cases in point. Forging a common policy regarding Bosnia-Herzegonia between the United States and its chief NATO allies has not been easy.

Security IGOs in Europe also have encountered problems in the management of cooperation. While NATO wants to retain its preeminent position among the IGOs, the CSCE and the Western European Union (WEU) are competitors for this position. Cooperation among them in a period of a rapidly dissolving perception of threat to Europe has been a difficult task, although both the Balkan situation and the ethnic unrest in the former Soviet Central Asian republics have engendered collaboration among these groups and between them and the United Nations, as well.

Selected INGOs in Western Europe also have contributed to the enhancement of interdependence, especially in the economic sector. A large number of regional business and agricultural interest groups have been established at the Brussels headquarters of the EC, which have assisted the EC institutions in their cooperation management tasks. However, the effectiveness of these INGOs has been spotty, depending very much on the objectiveness of national interest groups that often proved more attuned to the promotion of their more parochial national, rather than broader regional, interests.

The management of cooperation has been much more difficult, and much less successful, in other regions. The main reasons have been differing perceptions of benefits and costs that might be derived from the enhancement of regional interdependence by regional IGOs, as well as the lower management skills of many IGO civil servants. Few INGOs directly related to IGO objectives have been formed outside the areas of Japan, North America, and Western Europe, and whatever influence they may have been able to exert has been minimal.[31]

Globally, the United Nations (with its many specialized and affiliated agencies, conferences, and other units) has the potential of increasing economic and political interdependence. Although the initial inspiration for the creation of that body was the peaceful settlement of disputes, it was not until 1990 and Operation Desert Shield that the United Nations was able to overcome its earlier inability to manage the needed cooperation required to provide or enhance the kind of interdependence that would impose compelling constraints on states to refrain from the use of force. However, during the last few years, the use of the UN Security Council has been greatly expanded with the active concurrence of the permanent members, suggesting a positive shift in the management of cooperation in a crucial area of interdependence. Proposals for reform of the UN machinery for peacekeeping and peacemaking are reflective of this enhancement of utilizing multilateral means to deal with real or potential conflicts.

In the economic and political sectors, during the 1970s, North-South issues became a major preoccupation of the United Nations and, theoretically at least, the effective management of cooperation, including the application of planning, programming, and budgetary tools, could have made contributions to the enhanced and beneficial interdependence of the member states. However, while on lower, mostly technical levels, some positive interdependence arrangements have been engineered (for example, increased opportunities for loans for development or preferential treatment of imports), the great issue of the North-South dialogue such as the implementation of components of the largely unsuccessful New International Economic Order (NISO)—the attempt in the 1970s by the Third World to obtain more favorable terms of the trade and other concessions from the industrialized states—have not been resolved.[32] The UN had become the most important forum for the so-called "Group of 77," block of Third World states to promote a thoroughgoing rearrangement of trade and other relationships. However, such a wide gap existed in terms of cost benefit perceptions that successful reform was impossible to achieve.

The ability of universal INGOs to contribute effectively to enhanced interdependence has also been problematical. In the post-Cold War areas of conflict, ranging from the exodus of Haitian and Vietnamese refugees to the human suffering experienced in such places as the Balkans and the Horn of Africa, clear limits to effective action have emerged.

The foregoing discussion of interdependence underscores the role that IGOs and INGOs can play in the process of redressing the asymmetries of the capabilities that national governments and nongovernmental actors have at their disposal. This process depends on the quality with which IGOs perform (or are allowed to perform) their assigned tasks, and on the skills with which they use their organizational tools.

A comparative analysis as to how these tasks are performed will give us greater insight into how IGOs and the various clusters of INGOs participate in the international system than would a sequential study of individual IGOs and INGOs. In addition, it may aid us in making a reliable assessment of the impact that these organizations may achieve on continuity or change in the global political system and subsystems.

INTERNATIONAL ORGANIZATIONS AND INTERNATIONAL REGIMES

However, before embarking further on our comparative analysis, it is important to comment briefly on the conceptual differences in the field of international organization between particular IGOs, on the one hand, and international regimes, on the other. Basically, both entities deal with the management of cooperation for various purposes, but they differ in a number of aspects.

The term *international regime* is of relatively recent vintage (early 1970s), and therefore has come into vogue. It applies to arrangements involving mostly governmental actors but affecting also nongovernmental forces in a wide variety of issue areas, including fisheries conservation, international food production and distribution, international trade issues, telecommunications policy, and meteorological coordination across national boundaries. In some cases, regimes may be formal, as was the case with the Bretton Woods monetary arrangement, which was based on an interstate agreement and resulted in the IMF, or they may be informal, where the regime may be merely implicit from the actions of the states involved.[33] They are global (e.g., the International Atomic Energy Agency or IAEA and the fisheries conservation regimes), or they may be regional. An example of the latter is the European Monetary System (EMS), which is based on an agreement among the EC member states and for which the EC Treaty provides overall legitimacy. The European Monetary and Economic Union (EMU) will become part of the EC structure in the second half of the 1990s.

Definitions for international regimes vary. According to Keohane and Nye, they involve regulations and control of transnational and interstate relations by governments through the creation or acceptance of procedures, rules, and institutions for certain kinds of activity.[34] Ernst B. Haas defines regimes as "norms, rules, and procedures agreed to in order to regulate an issue area."[35] The most comprehensive concept of international regimes comes from Oran Young. He regards them as social institutions governing the actions of those interested in "specifiable" or meaningful sets of activities. As such, they are recognized patterns of practice around which expectations converge.[36] Young views regimes as structures that may be more or less formally articulated and may or may not be accompanied by explicit organizational arrangements, although the core of every regime is "a collection of rights and rules."[37] He also asserts that in formal terms, "the members of international regimes are always sovereign states, though the parties carrying out the actions governed by international regimes are often private entities (for example, fishing companies, banks or private airlines)."[38] The number of regime members may vary from a very few to several hundred if the nongovernmental participants are included. Finally, the various actions of states flowing from any given regime will often shape further the regime's contents, especially if clear-cut goals are kept in mind.

From this discussion, a picture emerges of international regimes as goal-oriented enterprises whose participating members seek benefits through explicit or tacit authoritative allocations of values (e.g., the conservation of fish, nonproliferation of nuclear weapons, or the profits from deep-seabed mining). Nongovernmental actors, including transnational or multinational corporations, are often participants, and it is not inconceivable that the latter may be, at times, the instigators or proponents for the creation of regimes. In any event, they are likely to participate assiduously in the negotiations and bargaining that may lead up to the formation of international regimes, as the many sessions of the UN Conference on the Law-of-the-Sea (UNCLOS) clearly demonstrated.

While both IGOs and international regimes are designed to pursue goals in the international arena and both may be based on international accords that set up institutions, assign rights and obligations, and provide for particular procedures, the issue and issue areas addressed by regimes appear to be narrower and to lack the comprehensive nature of most IGO concerns. Regime structures also are more fluid and more subject to evolutionary developments than those of IGOs. As Keohane and Nye point out (correctly in our view), IGOs "in the broad sense of networks, norms, and institutions" may include the norms associated with specific international regimes, but they belong to a broader category than regimes because they encompass patterns of elite networks and (if relevant) a range of formal institutions.[39]

There are also important voices that oppose the term *international regime*. For example, Susan Strange, formerly of the London School of Economics and Political Science, argued that the concept is pernicious because it obfuscates the interests and power relationships that are the cause of behavior in the international system. "All those international arrangements dignified by the label regime are only too easily upset when either the balance of bargaining power or the perception of national interest (or both together) change among those states who negotiate them."[40]

We sympathize with Strange's arguments, and because of the vast literature on regimes, we feel it is appropriate to discuss and illustrate them in subsequent chapters, and especially in Chapter 7.

NOTES

1. See Union of International Associations, *Yearbook of International Organizations,* vol. 1 (Brussels: Union of International Associations, 1991–92), App. 5.
2. Ibid.
3. This is part of the conventional definition. Michael Wallace and J. David Singer argue that bilaterally created IGOs should not be excluded; otherwise, an organization such as the North American Defense Command (NORAD), which is composed of the U.S. and Canada, would be excluded. See their "Intergovernmental Organizations in the Global System, 1815–1964: A Quantitative Description," *International Organization* 24 (Spring 1970): 239–87.
4. For an elaboration on this point, see Robert S. Jordan, "Law Relating to the International Civil Service," in *The Role of the United Nations in the International Legal Order,* ed. Christopher Joyner and Oscar Schachter (Cambridge: Grotius Publications for the American Society of International Law, in press).
5. Ibid.
6. See Union of International Associations, *Yearbook,* vol. 1, App. 5, pp. 1647–48.
7. See also Ephraim Been-Baruch, "An Examination of Several Classifications

of Organizations," *International Review of History and Political Science* 17 (May 1980): 1–19. A useful compendium of IGOs is contained in Arthur S. Banks, eds., *The Political Handbook of the World* (Binghamton, NY: CSA Publications 1991), and also *The Economic Handbook of the World.*

8. See Leon Gordenker and Paul R. Saunders, "Organization Theory and International Organizations," in *International Organization,* ed. Paul Taylor and A. J. R. Groom (London: Frances Pinter, 1978), pp. 84–110, and the works cited therein.

9. Much of the preceding discussion leans heavily on the excellent analysis by Lawrence S. Finkelstein, "International Organizations and Change," *International Studies Quarterly* 8 (December 1974): 485–519. See also Robert W. Cox, "The Executive Head," *International Organization* 22 (Spring 1968): 205–30.

10. Anthony J. N. Judge "International Institutions: Diversity, Borderline Cases, Functional Substitutes and Possible Alternatives," in Taylor and Groom, *International Organization,* pp. 28–83.

11. See Union of International Associations, *Yearbook,* regarding the types of organization included.

12. Kjell Skjelsbaeck, "The Growth of Intergovernmental Organizations in the Twentieth Century," *International Organization* 25 (Summer 1971): 420–42.

13. For these categories, see *Yearbook of International Organizations: 1978 Supplements. An Overview.*

14. According to Lyman C. White, the first international NGO was the World Alliance of the YMCAs, founded in 1855. White contends that the Evangelic Alliance was not a truly international NGO because "its so-called members . . . were mere subscribers to its publications, without any voting rights." *International Non-Governmental Organizations* (New York: Greenwood Press, 1968), p. 279, n. 5. Others believe that the Rosicrucian Order, founded in 1674, was the first international NGO. See Skjelsbaeck, "Intergovernmental Organizations," p. 424.

15. Skjelsbaeck, "Intergovernmental Organizations," p. 425.

16. We should note that J. David Singer and Michael Wallace used slightly different data for IGOs founded from those used in Figure 1.3 of this volume. "Intergovernmental Organization and the Preservation of Peace, 1816–1864: Some Bivariate Relationships," *International Organization* 24 (Summer 1970): 520–47. These disparities, which may be due to definitional differences, do not, however, affect the general growth trend.

17. See, for example, Robert O. Keohane and Joseph S. Nye, *Power and Interdependence: World Politics in Transition* (Boston: Little Brown, 1977); and Richard Rosecrance et al., "Whither Interdependence," *International Organization* 31 (Summer 1977): 425–71.

18. William D. Coplin and Michael K. O'Leary, "A Policy Analysis Framework for Research, Education and Policy-Making in International Relations" (paper delivered to the 1974 International Studies Association convention, St. Louis, Missouri). See also Robert S. Jordan, "The Role of Actors in Global Issues," in *The Politics of Global Resources,* ed. James E. Harf and B. Thomas Trout (Durham, NC: Duke University Press, 1987). For a more general discussion, see Hoyt Purvis, *Interdependence: An Introduction to International Relations* (New York: Harcourt Brace Jovanovich College Publishers, 1992).

19. Edward L. Morse, "Transnational Economic Processes," *International Organization* 25 (Summer 1971): 373–97. See also Guy F. Erb and Valeriana Kallab, eds.,

Beyond Dependence: The Developing World Speaks Out (Washington, DC: Overseas Development Council, 1975).

20. Oran R. Young, "Interdependence in World Politics," *International Journal* 24 (Autumn 1969): 726. For a later survey of various aspects of interdependence, see Bruce Russett, Harvey Starr, and Richard J. Stall, eds., *Choices in World Politics: Sovereignty and Interdependence* (New York: W. H. Freeman, 1989). The pervasiveness of Ted Turner's Cable News Network (CNN) is another example.

21. Richard N. Cooper, *The Economics of Interdependence* (New York: McGraw Hill, 1968), pp. 3–8. See also Jeffrey A. Frieden and David A. Lake, eds., *International Political Economy: Perspectives on Global Power and Wealth* (New York: St. Martin's Press, 1991).

22. Keohane and Nye, *Power and Interdependence,* p. 12.

23. Ibid., p. 13.

24. Kenneth F. Waltz, "The Myth of Interdependence," in *The International Corporation,* ed. Charles P. Kindelberger (Cambridge, MA: MIT Press, 1970), pp. 205–23.

25. Keohane and Nye, *Power and Interdependence,* pp. 9–11. See also Michael Brenner, "Multilateralism and European Security," *Survival* 35 no. 2 (Summer 1993): pp. 138–155.

26. An extensive literature on the issue of dependency evolved during the 1970s. For example, the entire issue of *International Organization* 32 (Winter 1978) is devoted to dependency and dependence, with five articles focusing on theoretical aspects and four dealing with regional problems. See also Richard B. Fagan, "Studying Latin American Politics: Some Implications of a Dependence Approach," *Latin American Research Review* 12 (1977): 3–26; Robert R. Kaufman, Harry I. Chermotsky, and Daniel S. Geller, "A Preliminary Test of the Theory of Dependence," *Comparative Politics* 7 (April 1975): 303–30; Benjamin Cohen, *The Question of Imperialism* (New York: Basic Books, 1973), which is a critical analysis of dependency theory; and Thomas Moran, *Multinational Corporations and the Politics of Dependence* (Princeton, NJ: Princeton University Press, 1974).

27. See Hayward R. Alker, Lincoln P. Bloomfield, and Nazli Choucri, *Analyzing Global Interdependence,* vol. 2 (Cambridge, MA: Massachusetts Institute of Technology, Center for International Studies, 1974). Another widely recognized discussion of the theory and practice of interdependence in the 1970s and later is Joan Edelman Spero, *The Politics of International Economic Relations,* 3rd ed. (New York: St. Martin's Press, 1985).

28. Rosecrance et al., "Whither Interdependence," p. 441.

29. Ibid., p. 442.

30. The Work Plan for the NACC "involved intensified contacts and consultations with Cooperation Partners by NATO's various specialised committees and the Military Committee." *NATO Press Release* (92) 85, October 16, 1992. The EFTA-EC agreement on free trade can be seen as a positive example.

31. See W. Andrew Axline, "Underdevelopment, Dependence, and Integration: The Politics of Regionalism in the Third World," *International Organization* 31 (Winter 1977): 83–105.

32. See Robert S. Jordan, "Why an NIEO: The View from the Third World," in *The Emerging International Economic Order: Dynamic Processes, Constraints, and Opportunities,* ed. Harold Jacobson and Dusan Sidjanski (Beverly Hills, CA: Sage, 1982).

33. See Keohane and Nye, *Power and Interdependence,* p. 20.
34. Ibid., p. 5.
35. Ernst B. Hass, "Why Collaborate? Issue Linkage and International Regimes," *World Politics* 32 (April 1980): 357–405.
36. Oran R. Young, "International Regimes: Problem of Concept Formations," *World Politics* 32 (April 1980): 331–56.
37. Ibid., p. 333.
38. Ibid.
39. Keohane and Nye, *Power and Interdependence,* p. 55. For another assessment of regimes, see Robert O. Keohane, *After Hegemony: Cooperation and Discord in the World Political Economy* (Princeton, NJ: Princeton University Press, 1984).
40. Susan Strange, "Care! Hic Dragones: A Critique of Regime Analysis," in *International Regimes,* ed. Stephen D. Krasner (Ithaca, NY: Cornell University Press, 1983), p. 345.

2 THE CREATION OF INTERGOVERNMENTAL ORGANIZATIONS (IGOs)

MOTIVATIONS TO FORM OR JOIN IGOs

What motivates states to establish IGOs? This question has not been discussed systematically in the comparative literature, although answers to it may well provide significant clues to the durability of, and prospective changes in, the role of IGOs.[1]

In Chapter 1 we pointed out that *the pursuit of particular interests by governments gave rise to the establishment of IGOs.* These interests are *the enhancement of a state's security* and, beyond that, the hoped-for *assurance that conflict does not become excessively destructive.* Another set of interests may be (1) *advancing the level of national economic development;* (2) *raising the economic and social well-being of a state's citizens;* (3) *managing economic interdependence;* and, in conjunction with national policy, (4) *participating in (and perhaps, in some cases, controlling) the exploration, marketing, and pricing of raw materials.* More recent motivations are for *human rights* and *humanitarian purposes.*

Another important interest pursued through the creation of IGOs may be the enhancement of the influence of states by the building of coalitions. This may be achieved through membership in security- or economic-oriented IGOs. A major set of interests also can be served by utilizing IGOs in the search for solutions to problems arising from the spread of *scientific knowledge and the accompanying technologies;* some examples are the spread of pollution of the global environment, nuclear proliferation, and extraordinary advances in worldwide transportation and communications.

While there are, indeed, a variety of motivations for the establishment of IGOs, under what conditions will a government resort to the instrument of an IGO to satisfy its interests? It is fair to assume that normally, a government will first seek national means to meet its security, economic, developmental, or scientific and technological needs. This is because if it does decide to become involved in setting up an IGO or joining an existing IGO for any purpose, its autonomy or freedom of action will be circumscribed to some degree, even if the management authority conferred on the IGO is very low. Moreover, the relations with other member states of the IGO impose differing and often unforeseeable restraints on the actions and behavior of all the participating governments. This is especially true for membership in alliances such as NATO and, in the post-Cold War period, multilateral peacekeeping, peacemaking, and peacebuilding activities such as those embarked on by ECOWAS in Liberia and by the United Nations against Iraq and in Somalia and Cambodia.

The governmental decision whether to organize multilaterally for the pursuit and satisfaction of particular interests depends to a large extent on a state's resources and capabilities. If these are perceived to be sufficient to ensure the successful implementation of appropriate domestic and foreign policies, then establishing or joining an IGO may not be desirable. If, on the other hand, the perception is of a deficiency in these areas, an IGO may well appear to offer the most likely path to assure the satisfaction of important national interests. In such a case, a state may be inclined to encourage the multilateral performance of the necessary tasks. In other words, calculations of national interests are central to understanding both the functions and structure of IGOs.

The primary—and fatal—weakness for most IGOs has not been the institutional arrangements but the historical political rivalries of the participating states. For example, the incentives for creating the CACM were offset de facto by the ebb and flow of externally as well as internally generated political hostilities, the most recent of which was the advent to power in Nicaragua of the Sandinista regime. The end of the Cold War brought the almost immediate demise of the Warsaw Treaty Organization (WTO), and shifts in the political loyalties of one or more participating states rendered the Central Treaty Organization (CENTO, or the Baghdad Pact) irrelevant.

PROPENSITY FOR INTERNATIONAL ORGANIZATION (A THEORETICAL MODEL)

The foregoing discussion of motivations forms the background for what John Ruggie calls a state's "propensity for international organization."[2] His premise is that every state is more or less willing to accept and, therefore, to engage to some extent in some form of international organizational or mutlilateral activity. He makes the useful distinction between institutionalized arrangements for joint and perhaps binding decision making (as reflected by various alliance systems and multilateral economic arrangements) and the informal coordination of states' unilateral behavior coupled with the systematic exchange of information (e.g., the annual economic summit meetings of the OECD's "Big Seven" industrial democracies, or various coalitions formed to deal with civil unrest or the possible—or actual, in the case of Yugoslavia—fragmentation of the state). In the latter case, discretionary national domestic policy formulation is retained, although foreign policy may be constrained somewhat, depending on the specific issue involved. The unilateral efforts are not always successful, however, as can be seen in the unsuccessful attempt by the United States at the 1982 Versailles economic summit to steer the other participating governments into a stronger anti-Soviet economic posture or its attempt during the 1992 meeting in Munich, which also proved unsuccessful, to move the Big Seven to the acceptance of the Uruguay Round of tariff reductions. In peacekeeping, the unsuccessful efforts of the United Nations and the EC to mediate an end to the warfare accompanying the breakup of the former Yugoslav federation reflect a hesitancy of the respective member states to move beyond economic and arms sanctions to outright intervention.

According to Ruggie, an assessment of a state's capability must include understanding the cause-and-effect relations that underlie national problems whose solutions may require IGO involvement. The lack or inadequacy of such knowledge could reduce a state's capabilities.[3] No better examples can be found than the Yugoslav situation or ethnic conflicts in Central Asia. The general loss of independence or the loss of control over a state's own activities resulting from the accumulation of collective constraints caused by the creation of (or participation in) IGOs is termed by Ruggie, "interdependence costs." It might be possible to view the UN attempts to implement its monitoring and surveillance resolutions against Iraq in the aftermath of the 1990–1991 Gulf War (partly through the IAEA) as "interdependence costs," which are borne, willingly or unwillingly, by member states. (We should note that our definition of interdependence, as put forth in Chapter 1, is more limited than that used by Ruggie.)[4]

Several propositions as formulated by Ruggie can provide insight into how governments assess whether to create or join an IGO:

1. The propensity for international organization is determined by the interplay between the need to become dependent on others for the performance of specific tasks and the general desire to keep such dependence to the minimum level necessary.

2. There exists an inverse relationship between the ratio of international to national task performance and the total level of national resources that a state possesses.[5] In other words, from the perspective of the state, the greater the resources it commands, the lower will be the number and scope of tasks it assigns to IGOs for performance, as more of its resources will be assigned to national task performance.

3. The propensity for international organization decreases over time, as national capabilities increase and become sufficient to perform a given task.[6] (This proposition is not actually relevant for the motivations that lead to the creation of an IGO, but it will be important for our discussion in later chapters regarding the durability, decline, or complete demise of these organizations.)
4. A process of encapsulation, built into the international performance of any given task, tends toward limiting further commitments to, or further increases in, the scope or capacity of the collective arrangements.[7]

It is obvious that the successful pursuit of important national interests in various policy sectors generates propensities toward creating or participating in intergovernmental, multilateral organizations if the national capabilities and resources are perceived as being insufficient to attain the desired goals through purely national policies and instruments.

When viewed in this way, it is no small wonder that the newer states and those that are most vulnerable politically and economically are generally the most supportive of IGOs. In the post-Cold War world, in which global economic competition among both large and small states within or between various regional or subregional groupings (some of which are discussed later in this chapter) can become more marked, IGO involvement has become almost a matter of national necessity. It was through the involvement of the UN Security Council that U.S. President George Bush was able to gain the support of his own citizenry for their involvement in Operation *Desert Shield* and later, Operation *Desert Storm*.

It is not surprising, however, that some developing states participating in economic cooperation IGOs tend to become quickly disillusioned when success proves slow to materialize. Protracted UN intervention in one or more member states, for whatever reason, can also result in diminished enthusiasm or expectations. This threatens to be the case, for example, in Cambodia, Angola, El Salvador, Somalia, and Afghanistan, to name some cases involving civil disorder. In the case of Iraq, the persistance of the Security Council to actively influence the internal affairs of Saddam Hussein's government might give way to an enhanced (or revived) concern for Iran's apparently renewed ambitions to obtain regional hegemony.

We must also keep in mind that a state's motivations underlying the creation of and participation in an IGO will continue to influence its propensity to continue participation in subsequent years. Trade-offs of advantages and costs among member states may strengthen the IGO. The buildup of national capabilities, either through participation in the IGO or for other reasons, may lead, however, to a declining interest in the IGO or, perhaps, to the complete withdrawal of a member state (although this final step rarely occurs). The motivations for the U.S. withdrawal from UNESCO are discussed as an illustrative case in Chapter 5. Hence, the interaction between purely national capabilities and the enhanced capabilities multilaterally through IGO participation is likely to exert a significant influence on an IGO's behavior internationally, and this is especially so in the post-Cold War world.

There is another theoretical dimension that may affect this propensity, especially in regard to military alliances: the public goods approach to the study of alliances.[8] The term *public goods,* which was coined by economists, refers to a good that exhibits properties of nonappropriability of benefits and indivisibility with respect to consumption opportunities. If it is a "pure" public good, the provider is completely unable to appropriate the benefits derived from the good, and one person or state's consumption of the good does not detract from another's consumption.

The classic case of a pure public good is common military defense among allies. A unit of defense is hypothesized to render full defense service to all citizens of the alliance member states regardless of the particular allied state in which they reside. It follows that all states of the alliance will benefit, irrespective of the size of the contribution they made to the common defense; and, indeed, a state might be a free rider in the alliance and contribute nothing, or might even receive the benefits without joining. In NATO, for example, Iceland has no armed forces to contribute to NATO's expenditures, while Spain benefited from NATO before it became a member in 1982.[9] The reactivation of the UN Security Council in the 1990s and its collaborative enforcement efforts with NATO and the WEU provided good, if limited, examples of the collective goods approach. The UN-sponsored Gulf War against Iraq might also be examined from this perspective: What elements of the public goods approach were reflected in the participation of Israel, Saudi Arabia, Egypt, Japan, Jordan, and Syria in the U.S.-led enterprise?

However, there is some doubt as to whether the totality of defense is a pure public good. Certainly, the hoped-for deterrence effects of nuclear defense or of the various early warning systems devised by the superpowers during the Cold War on behalf of themselves or their respective allies were such that no individual citizen, as such, could be excluded from their benefits and no individual's consumption of these presumed benefits necessarily would detract from another's consumption. For other forms of defense, however, characteristics of a pure public good may be lacking. For example, retaliation could be withheld or carried out in such a way as to benefit one ally more than another.

The public goods concept may also be applied to other issue areas, such as international pollution control efforts and large-scale climate modification. There is increasing collaboration involving INGOs interacting more extensively with their counterpart IGOs for humanitarian, disaster relief, environmental, or human rights purposes.

Whatever the particular ratio of pure to impure public goods in an alliance, for whatever reason, many states (especially smaller ones) may perceive that as a consequence of the applicability of the public goods concept, they may enjoy security or other, more economic and social advantages through their alliance membership, since such affiliation may lower their purely national defense or social expenditures. The effects of successful multilateral efforts with respect to these problems would benefit all states located in a particular region or provide worldwide benefits and, therefore, could either trigger or reinforce propensities of states for creating or joining appropriate IGOs.[10] The interest of the former Soviet bloc states—and of the members of the post-Soviet CIS—in affiliating with NATO can also be analyzed in this way.

Our next step will be to apply these basically theoretical considerations regarding the creation of IGOs to specific organizations in the world. As pointed out in the Introduction, three categories of IGOs will be set up: (1) the United Nations, including, in this chapter, its origins and objectives; (2) major regional IGOs composed of industrialized states—and here we will deal with the EC, NATO, and the OECD; and (3) major regional IGOs composed mostly of developing states, in which we will include LAFTA and its successors, the Organization of African Unity (OAU) and the Association of South East Asian States (ASEAN). Obviously, there are many other important regional IGOs, some of which we will discuss in the following chapters as we pursue our comparative analysis.

THE UN FAMILY

The United Nations Organization: History and Objectives

The basic motivation for the establishment of the United Nations, as well as its predecessor, the League of Nations, was to avoid the devastating loss of life and property caused by two world wars. The U.S. failure to join the League, which contributed to that organization's ineffectiveness in the maintenance of peace during the 1930s, was a prime stimulus for the United States to become a charter member of the United Nations.

The assumption was that if the goal of settling international disputes peacefully could be attained, the security of all states would be enhanced. Indeed, it had become obvious to U.S. President Franklin D. Roosevelt from the outset of World War II that even the most powerful state on earth might not be able to assure the security of its citizens and the integrity of its territory without the aid of some kind of international organization.[11] The need for such a peacekeeping IGO was inferentially recognized as early as 1941 in the famous Atlantic Charter, which was drafted by President Roosevelt and British Prime Minister Winston Churchill. This document aimed at the creation of a permanent IGO that would provide for the disarmament of aggressor states "pending the establishment of a wider and permanent system of general security."[12]

Following deliberations by the U.S. State Department's Advisory Committee on Post-War Foreign Policy and consultations between the president and congressional leaders, proposals were drafted for a permanent IGO for the maintenance of peace and security that became the basis of discussion during a conference at Dumbarton Oaks in Washington, D.C., in the late summer of 1944. While the United States and Britain had already agreed to seek the establishment of such an organization a year earlier, the Soviet Union, which was initially unsure about such a development, and the Republic of China added their informal consent in the fall of 1943.[13]

During the Dumbarton Oaks discussions, the question was raised as to whether economic and social matters should be included within the scope of the projected organization. Although the original position of the Soviet Union had been that the organization should be exclusively devoted to security matters and that it should not be concerned with the promotion of international cooperation regarding economic and social problems, the position of the United States and Britain finally prevailed. Nonetheless, the Soviet delegation did not display the same interest in the economic and social aspects of the new organization's work as in the political and security aspects.[14] Indeed, according to the Dumbarton Oaks agreements, the new IGO's primary function was the maintenance of international peace and security, although it was to seek also cooperation in the solution of international economic, social, and humanitarian problems.[15]

During the early 1940s, it was very difficult for the prospective member governments of the United Nations to foresee the economic configuration of the postwar period. The warring states, with the exception of the United States, were destroying each others' industries, and, as a consequence, the economic outlook in these areas was bleak. At that time, decolonization was seen by only a few as an inevitable process that would begin soon after the end of the war. As it turned out, the principles that were to be the foundation of the United Nations were to promote this process, especially the concept that was inherited from the League of Nations and embodied in the phrase "national self-government and political independence."

At the Yalta Conference in February 1945, another function was assigned to the prospective IGO: the establishment of a trusteeship system to replace the League of Nations system of mandates. This was perceived as a means, however imperfect, of improving the economic well-being of the populations of the colonial territories of the defeated states, and of leading eventually to self-government of these areas. This was viewed as an assumption by the United Nations of a serious responsibility.[16] However, by the end of the 1960s, most colonies had become independent states and, indeed, had become members of the organization.[17]

However, these newly independent states soon found themselves confronted with enormous economic, social, and political problems. Even though the United States emerged from World War II as the most powerful state economically, it had neither the resources nor the capabilities to deal with these issues alone. In contrast to the security-oriented genesis of the League of Nations, the member states of the United Nations were forced to seek multilateral means to deal with the various problems facing them.[18] Obviously, then, the motivations for the creation of the United Nations were multifarious. Indeed, it could be argued that the successful solution of economic and social problems in different areas of the world could make a major contribution to the assurance of peace.

Having acknowledged that powerful motivations existed worldwide for the establishment and enlargement of the United Nations, let us now briefly review the negotiating process involved in defining the obligations and rights of the member states, and the institutional framework and decision-making procedures that followed. These motivations were clearly reflected in the initial phases of the process. In paragraph 4 of the Declaration of Four Nations on General Security, which was signed in late 1943 by the foreign ministers of the Soviet Union, Britain, and the United States, as well as the ambassador of the Republic of China, the signatories declared that a general organization for the maintenance of international peace and security had to be based on "the principle of sovereign equality of all peace-loving states and open to membership by all such states, large and small."[19] The principle of the "sovereign equality" of all UN member states became a key provision of the UN Charter and is embodied in Article 2, paragraph 1. (See Appendix B for a complete copy of the Charter.)

This principle signifies that the usual powers of government are left to the UN member states and that the UN organs and institutions have only those functions and powers specifically conferred upon them. Hence, except for the explicitly stipulated powers of the Security Council (enforcement action such as the imposition of a boycott under Chapter VII of the Charter), no organ of the UN can obligate any member state to any substantial action in its relations with other states without its consent. Nor, according to Article 2, paragraph 7, can the UN intervene in any matter that is "essentially" within the domestic jurisdiction of a state. This provision reflected the special concerns of the American negotiators, and particularly, their congressional members, to make it clear that there would be no UN interference in U.S. domestic affairs.[20]

An exception to the principle of sovereign equality was introduced at the Yalta Conference. The emerging compromise was to create a privileged category of membership on the Security Council for five of the victorious states of World War II: Britain, France, the Republic of China, the United States and the U.S.S.R. We should note that the United States, Britain, and the Soviet Union were already in agreement before Yalta that some kind of veto should be given to the permanent members of the Council (that is, the "Great Powers") on decisions regarding nonprocedural (substantive) matters of peace and security. What was done at the Yalta Conference was to find an acceptable formula for the voting procedure, and this formula required that on substantive questions it was necessary that a majority of seven favorable votes (now nine) include the affirmative votes of the permanent members.[21] On procedural matters, nine votes are needed for a favorable decision and the veto does not apply. When efforts are made to settle a dispute by pacific means (Chapter VI of the Charter), a party to the dispute shall abstain from voting. The Soviet Union was initially opposed to this provision, but finally accepted it at Yalta.

The agreement on the voting procedure in the Security Council reflected the wartime perception of both the contemporary and the prospective postwar distribution of power. This power distribution accounts also for another exception to the principle of sovereign equality: the admission of two socialist republics (the Ukraine and Byelorussia) to full membership in the United Nations although neither of these republics was a sovereign state under international law because they were part of the Soviet Union and controlled by that government. The admission of these two so-called states was the result of various trade-offs between the Soviet Union, the United States, and Britain during the Yalta Conference.[22]

When, in 1945, the final draft of the Charter was negotiated in San Francisco, fifty states participated, and the smaller states were able to influence effectively the final shape of the General Assembly and the Economic and Social Council (ECOSOC), whose functions and powers were extended and clarified. In these efforts they were supported by the United States, which was especially sensitive to the interests of the Latin American delegations. (See Figure 2.1 for the complete structure of the United Nations.) The San Francisco Conference was a huge affair, attended by 282 delegates who were advised by more than 1,500 specialists and staff members.[23] It was not a peace conference to settle the global conflict and, unfortunately, the United Nations soon became itself a function of the failure of the major victorious powers to cooperate among themselves.

To return again to the relationship between maintaining the principle of sovereignty and the need to organize multilaterally, it is instructive to cite the comments of U.S. Senator Arthur Vandenberg regarding the issue of sovereignty, which he made during the U.S. Senate debate on the Charter: "These things [sovereignty] we toiled in San Francisco to preserve. We can effectively cooperate for peace without the loss of these things. To cooperate is not to lose our sovereignty."[24]

Obviously, in legal terms, the United States and the four other permanent members of the Security Council did not suffer any impairment of their sovereignty, but how much sovereignty did the other UN member states lose by accepting the obligation to permit the Security Council to act on their behalf and bind them by its decisions (Articles 24 and 25)? In terms of infringement of a state's national interests, the loss was most likely minor; if a government wanted to ignore or to disobey a decision of the Security Council in the event that its perceived vital interests were at stake, it could do so with impunity since the United Nations was not, in fact, given the means (police or armed forces) to compel compliance except in specific and unique circumstances. This changed dramatically during the Iraq-Kuwait crisis when the United States and other selected Western and Arab powers provided the necessary military muscle for the United Nations, an episode to which we will return in Chapter 5 in discussing post-Cold War interventions in "failed states," as well as "rogue states." Whether for better or for worse, the Security Council is now engaged in peacemaking and -building as well as in peacekeeping.

Nevertheless, Inis Claude's comment remains accurate: "The Charter left no room for doubt that San Francisco had launched a project for cooperation among independent states rather than for consolidation of the nations under a kind of super-sovereign."[25] This project for cooperation, however, is very extensive, consisting of a vast complex of international machinery, including an ever-expanding Secretariat and a Court of Justice carried over from the League. Its substantive scope is very broad, however, and its structure is characterized by decentralization and specialization. Its institutions and operations require skilled management to perform their assigned tasks (a subject to which we shall return in subsequent chapters).

The secretary-general can play a most significant role in the operation of the United Nations, and in some ways, his effectiveness is a kind of barometer for measuring propensity. He possesses four categories of powers: (1) express powers under Article 99; (2) implied powers under Article 99; (3) other political powers and functions under the UN Charter and under the Rules of Procedure and Resolutions of the General Assembly and the councils; and (4) mediatory, advisory and other powers. Although Article 7 of the Charter refers to the Secretariat and not to the secretary-general in naming the principal organs, Articles 97 and 101 underline that the Secretariat is composed of the secretary-general and a secretariat recruited by that person, who alone is responsible for the work of the Secretariat. Logically, therefore, the office of the secretary-general can be viewed as a "principal organ" within the meaning and scope of the Charter. We discuss this further in Chapter 3.

By creating this complex organizational framework, whose details are shown in Figure 2.1, the delegates to the San Francisco Conference attempted to meet the perceived needs of the participating states for international cooperation and for a (perhaps purposefully) somewhat ambiguous blueprint for global order, while at the same time satisfying national ambitions and interests. The smaller states accepted the principle of Great Power leadership because it was the only way they could enhance their own

Figure 2.1
The Structure of the United Nations

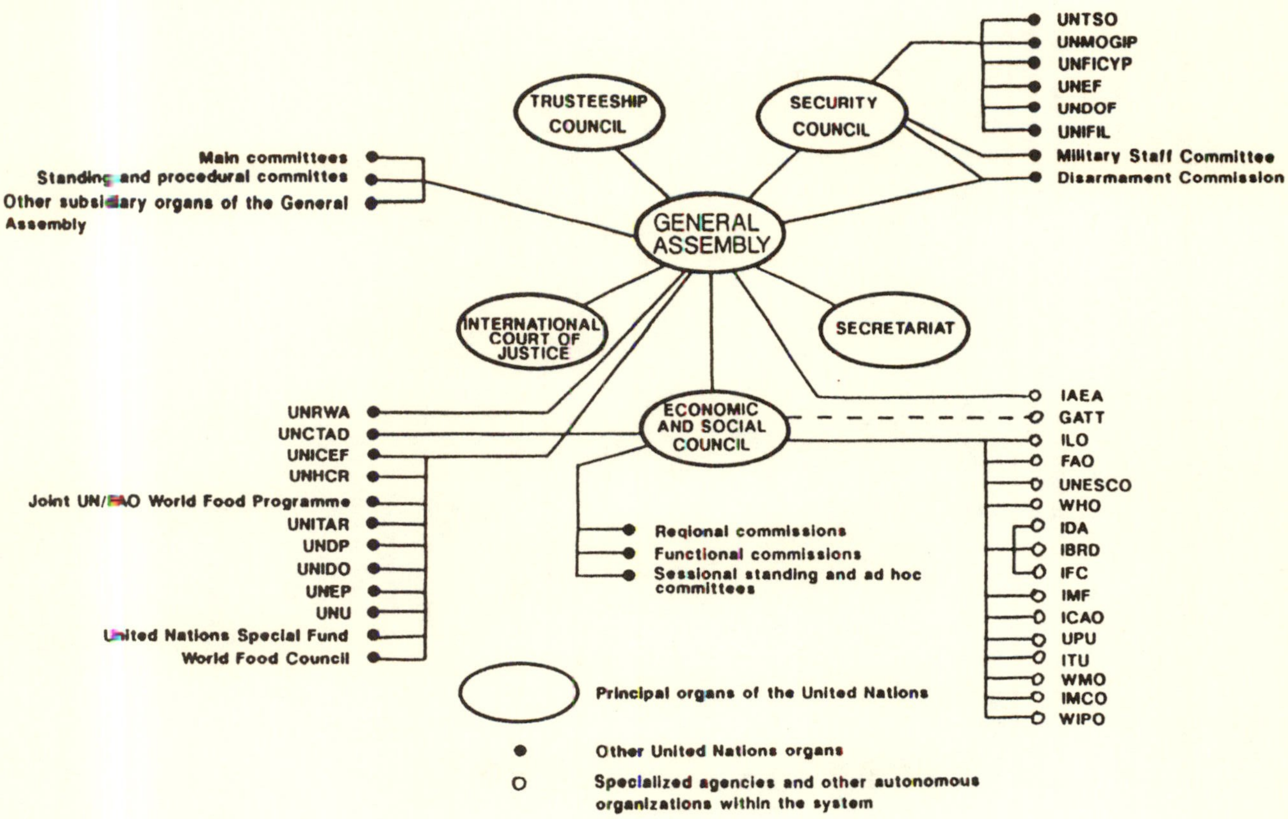

Source: UN Department of Information.

economic and security interests. Most likely, few participants in the San Francisco Conference realized that the unity of the Big Powers was to be broken before the end of the first decade of the life of the United Nations.

One of the most difficult tasks when negotiating the establishment of an IGO is the determination of the finances for operating the organization and how to distribute the burden of the cost to the member states. This was the case when the United Nations was founded in 1945, and it became more and more complicated as increasing numbers of newly independent but poor countries became members. The assessment for regular UN administration imposed on the United States in 1946 was nearly 40 percent (39.89%) of the total UN budget, while Brazil paid 1.94 percent. In the period 1983–1985, the United States was assessed 25 percent (the top figure), while a least developed country could not be charged more than the lowest rate, 0.01 percent. In 1992, some of the percentages were: Japan, 12.5; Russia, 6.3; Germany, 8.9; France, 6.0; Britain, 5.0; Italy, 4.3; United States, 25.0; and Brazil, 1.6.

In the early 1980s, the United States and other Western UN members became increasingly displeased with the steadily rising costs of the organization and its lack of efficiency in administration. In fact, several of the major contributors rebelled: the American, British, and Soviet ambassadors demanded that a ceiling be placed on the 1982–1983 budget. However, with the introduction of consensus voting on financial appropriations and the reduction of what seemed to be superfluous personnel, as well as with the United Nations playing what seemed to most Americans to be a more helpful role, U.S. Secretary of State James Baker said, in February 6, 1991, "We remain absolutely committed to full funding for U.S. assessed contributions . . . and to paying our prior year arrearages over the next four years."[26] This meant that it is the poor financial situation in the United States and not only displeasure with the United Nations that was, and is, the cause for payment delays. Indeed, other UN members have not paid all their dues to the organization, as can be seen from Figure 2.2, which compares assessments (regular budget and peacekeeping combined) with actual payments made from 1987 to 1991.

REGIONAL ORGANIZATIONS IN THE DEVELOPED COUNTRIES

The European Communities (EC)

The basic motivation for the creation of the three European Communities in the early 1950s was primarily economic, but political and certain technological considerations also played major roles. The capabilities and resources of the six charter members (France, West Germany, Italy, and the

Figure 2.2
Annual Assessments and Paid Contributions: Regular Budget and Peacekeeping Combined, 1987–1991

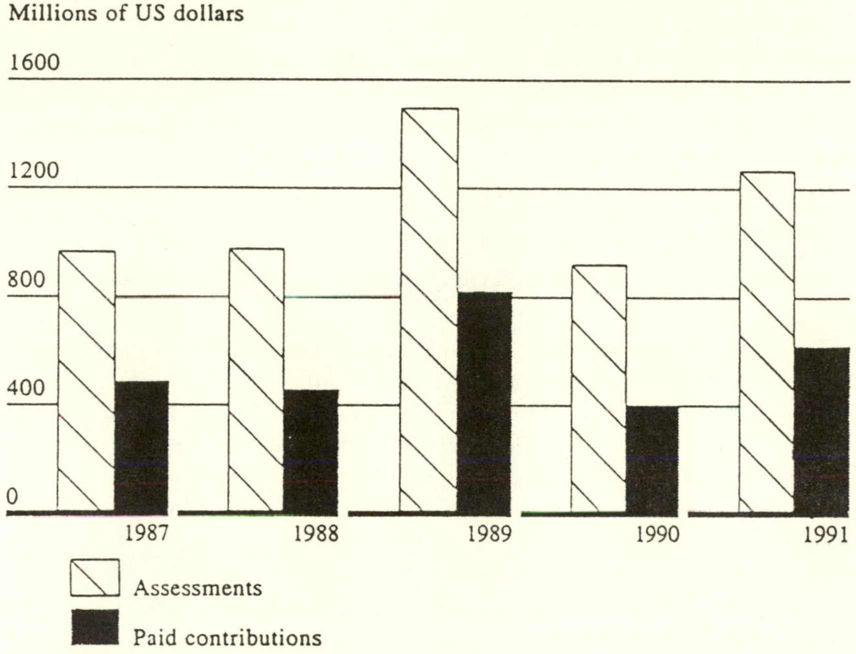

Source: UN Document A/47/1, September 11, 1992, p. 17.

Benelux states, consisting of Belgium, the Netherlands, and Luxembourg) were clearly at a low ebb at the end of World War II. This strengthened their desire to organize multilaterally in order to overcome national economic vulnerabilities and to pursue selected political goals. Moreover, the international political climate by 1950 favored efforts at regional economic integration.

The ground for the regional integration efforts was prepared by the European Union of Federalists, which was founded in December 1946. The Union, in turn, created national submovements in Austria, Belgium, France, Greece, Italy, Switzerland, and the Western zones of Germany. In Britain, a United Europe Movement was formed a year later to alleviate traditional Franco-German antagonism. Winston Churchill asserted in May 1947 that this problem could not be solved "except within the framework and against the background of a United Europe." In May 1949, as a result of various efforts toward European unity supported by many prestigious political leaders, the Council of Europe was created. Its Consultative Assembly held its first meeting in Strasbourg three months later. Paul-Henri

Spaak of Belgium, the first president of the Assembly, said: "I came to Strasbourg convinced of the necessity of a United States of Europe. I am leaving it with the certitude that union is possible."[27]

When French Foreign Minister Robert Schuman announced his now-famous plan for the creation of the European Coal and Steel Community (ECSC) in May 1950, he not only proposed an experiment in economic cooperation and integration; he also conceived this Community to be the beginning of the political unification of Western Europe. He stated that:

> [The pooling of coal and steel] would mean the immediate establishment of common bases of industrial production, which is the first step toward European Federation and will change the destiny of regions that have long been devoted to the production of war armaments of which they themselves have been the constant victims.[28]

This euphoric concept was shared by many governmental leaders in the prospective ECSC member states, but it is important to look in greater detail at the economic and political motivation of the two main powers involved in this integration experiment, West Germany and France. For West Germany, the direct economic benefits that might flow from a common market in the coal and steel sectors were not seen to be as persuasive as the indirect advantages. First, with the establishment of the ECSC, controls on the West German economy were lifted, especially those of the International Authority of the Ruhr which, under the direction of the French, had limited the resurgence of that vital industrial area.[29] Second, the Saar, which France had claimed as war reparations, would be removed from French administrative control and placed in the hands of the ECSC authorities; West Germany would have a degree of input concerning administration and also could entertain some hope for eventual repatriation. The ECSC also provided domestic benefits clearly in West Germany's interest, since it marked an end to export controls on that country's reviving steel industry and an end to tariff barriers against the export of West German coal: two major sources of badly needed foreign exchange.

The creation of the ECSC was also useful to West German foreign policy objectives. Through the ECSC, West Germany's presence as a minimally sovereign state within Europe was acknowledged, equipped as it was with the power to negotiate and conclude treaties with other states. Additionally, the ECSC gave West Germany the opportunity to participate within regional cooperative institutions as an equal with France and superior to other Western European states. Thus, two major goals of West German foreign policy were met.

For France, the direct economic benefits of the ECSC were also less important than certain political-security considerations. French foreign policy planners were cognizant of the fact that West Germany could not be kept for an extended period of time under the Tripartite American-British-

French allied occupation control that was set up following World War II. This seemed especially true in the heavy industry sector, where the Korean crisis that had erupted in June 1950 had increased sharply the demand for European steel. In fact, security was the motivation for the French decision to propose the so-called Schuman Plan, the genesis of which came from the foreign policy planning of Jean Monnet, Etienne Hirsch, Pierre Uri, and Paul Reuter. In April 1950, a memorandum had been submitted to French Prime Minister Georges Bidault which outlined the ECSC as a means of controlling West German industrial revitalization and of eliminating the possibility of renewed Franco-German hostilities on a long-range basis.[30] As Derek Bok noted, the ECSC presented France with the solution to a security dilemma:

> Without an expanding industry, and with the growing demand for steel production occasioned by the Korean War, France could not expect the controls upon German production to be continued indefinitely. At the same time, however, the French were fearful of an unbridled development of the Ruhr into a powerful arsenal which might once more become linked with the aggressive policies of a German government. Under these circumstances, the Schuman Plan was conceived by France as a compromise whereby she would give up a part of her sovereign power to secure a degree of international control over German coal and steel.[31]

The motivations of Italy and the Benelux countries in support of the ECSC were less complex. They perceived that the prospects for domestic economic rehabilitation were enhanced and that political advantages were to be gained on the national as well as the multinational level.

Britain was also invited to become a charter member of the ECSC, but it turned down the invitation, primarily on the grounds that membership would not be beneficial to either its economic or political interests. At that time, economically, and perhaps also politically, Britain's relations with the Commonwealth were regarded as holding the highest priority. In addition, Britain was apprehensive about the supranational powers that were to be conferred on the institutions of the ECSC.[32]

A comprehensive structure was created for the management and performance of the tasks assigned to the organization. The most important organ was the High Authority, which was conceived to be the major executive and administrative agency and to be endowed with supranational powers to issue binding decisions affecting coal and steel enterprises and individuals in the member states (Article 14, ECSC Treaty). Other major organs were the Council, consisting of ministers of the member states representing both national and multinational interests (Articles 26–30); an Assembly composed of delegates appointed by the parliaments of the member states and possessing only very limited powers (Articles 20–25); and a very powerful Court of Justice with extensive jurisdictional competences (Articles 31–45).

The voting procedures in the High Authority and the Council were based generally on majority rule but, in a number of cases, the treaty required unanimity of the Council. The High Authority was given limited taxing powers, but its decisions to impose financial obligations were enforceable only through the use of the legal procedures of the member states. National enterprises and member governments were given the right to appeal decisions or recommendations of the High Authority before the Court of Justice.

Talks on the treaty to create the European Economic Community (EEC), or Common Market, were opened in Messina, Italy, in 1956. Agreement was reached with impressive speed; the Treaty of Rome was signed in March 1957 and came into force on January 1, 1958. Despite the rapid pace of the negotiations, there were disparities of views among the six governments, and efforts especially by Jean Monnet, the first president of the ECSC High Authority, were necessary to overcome various obstacles. Concessions and counter-concessions had to be made, and crucial compromises had to be offered and accepted. The EEC Treaty itself became the basis for the Common Market, which became a reality ahead of the twelve-year schedule of the transition period. The treaty also suggested the necessary steps (e.g., the harmonization of national policies) that were required to reach the goals of economic and monetary union. Voting rules in the Council of Ministers were to be changed in 1966 on important matters from unanimity to qualified majority rule, although this stipulation has been largely ignored and modified by de facto consensus of the member governments. Finally, the treaty directed that there be eventual direct election of the Assembly, and this was finally implemented in 1979. In summary, then, the path to political integration had been opened, and this prospect was a strong encouragement for the supporters of European unification.[33]

On the other hand, the EEC Treaty contained a small retreat from supranationalism inasmuch as the issue of binding rules on the people living in the member states was more closely tied to joint action of the Commission (the independent executive body of the EEC) and the Council of Ministers. Under the ECSC Treaty, in this respect, the High Authority had greater freedom for independent action.

The treaty for the European Atomic Energy Community (EURATOM) was signed at the same time as the EEC treaty and went into effect also in January 1958. At the time of its establishment, EURATOM appeared to offer a significant instrument for political integration. Pooling the development of atomic energy resources seemed to be a logical step after the ECSC had created a common market in coal and steel. Moreover, although in the coal industry many long-standing vested interests had grown up in the private and public sectors, most European enthusiasts believed that in the field of atomic energy, fewer national interests existed that had to be accommodated. Hence, it was hoped that nuclear development for peaceful purposes could be accomplished more successfully on a regional than on a national basis, provided the appropriate resources for coordinated research could be made available. A joint agency for the supply of fissionable materials was to be established, and regional production targets for reactor projects were set. It was hoped that technological progress in the high-technology nuclear field could be made more rapidly and with less cost by pooling national resources and capabilities than by proceeding separately through the national frameworks alone. These hopes were not fulfilled, however, primarily because the member governments and national industrial groups wanted to retain control of the development of this key source of energy and national power. Consequently, national competitive pressures and other problems hampered the growth of EURATOM shortly after its establishment, and its contribution to regional integration has been minimal.

By the late 1950s, many Europeans felt that without Britain's membership in the Communities, there was no realistic prospect of creating a truly unified Western Europe. The U.S. government generally shared this view and made efforts during the establishment of both the ECSC and the later two Communities to bring Britain into the fold as a charter member. These efforts failed, however, because Britain continued to place its priority on relations with the Commonwealth countries and on an American "special relationship" for economic and political power reasons; moreover, in any case it was opposed to any impairment of its sovereignty. Nevertheless, it became interested in some kind of low-level economic integration. Hence, in the late 1950s, the British sponsored the European Free Trade Association (EFTA), which came into being in 1960 and included among its members Austria, Switzerland, Portugal, and the three Scandinavian states of Norway, Denmark, and Sweden.[34]

Then, to the surprise of many observers on both sides of the Atlantic, the British announced on July 31, 1961, that they now wanted to become a member of the EEC. The reasons for this change of heart were both political and economic. They felt that they were being increasingly affected by happenings on the Continent and that they had to take their place in any Western European movement toward greater integration. Also, they were concerned about their serious balance-of-payments deficits, which had been caused, in part, by a sharp drop of exports to the Commonwealth. Moreover, EFTA had turned out to be only a moderate success as an alternative trading group.

After long and difficult negotiations in 1961 and 1962, the prospects seemed good that an agreement could be reached for Britain to join the EEC. However, on January 14, 1963, French President Charles de Gaulle cast his famous veto on British entry. De Gaulle's professed reasons were his grave doubts about Britain's readiness for membership because its main orientation was insular and directed toward the other shore of the Atlantic, as well as to the Commonwealth. However, perhaps the most significant considerations for the veto were strategic and political. British membership was likely to threaten France's leadership in the EEC; in his view, Britain could constitute a Trojan horse for the United States: on the one hand, impeding Western Europe's emergence as a unified power under French leadership, and on the other, leading ultimately to an Atlantic Community under U.S. hegemony.[35] Consequently, it was not until January 1, 1973, that Britain could join the three Communities composing the EC. At that time, Ireland and Denmark also became members.[36]

The institutional frameworks hammered out in the negotiations for the EEC and EURATOM were similar to that of the ECSC except that the main executive and administrative organs in both constituent treaties were called Commissions. A Council of Ministers performed basically the same functions as did the ECSC Council but was given more power. The Council had the final word on all proposals submitted by the Commission. The intent of the two treaties was to draw a fine balance between the Council and Commission requiring the active participation of both bodies in the decision-making process. However, a shift of power toward the Council began in the mid-1960s and has continued slowly until today.

Several factors were responsible for this shift in power. Nationalism began to be revived not only in France, but in all the member states, rekindled principally, but not exclusively, by the actions and philosophies of Charles de Gaulle. There developed a slowly rising opposition to the progress of political integration on the part of basically nationalist-oriented bureaucracies of the member states. Finally, the French feared that a change of voting procedures in the Council from unanimity to a qualified majority for certain cases, scheduled to take effect in 1966 (Article 148 of the EEC Treaty), would be harmful to that country's vital interests. This resulted in an ambiguous and inconclusive compromise that weakened much of the pro-integrationist bias of the treaty. This compromise, known as the Luxembourg Compromise of 1966, strengthened the unanimity rule for a time but was partially reversed in the 1980s.

The Assembly and Court were part of the institutional framework of the EEC and EURATOM as well as of the ECSC, but the Assembly's name was later changed to the European Parliament. In 1967 the two Commissions (EEC and EURATOM) and the High Authority of the ECSC were merged into a unified Commission. The result was that four major organs—the Commission, the Council of Ministers, the European Parliament, and the Court—were now operating the three Communities, but each one was continuing to function under its own constituent treaty. The institutions as restructured in 1967 remain the same until now, although minor power shifts occurred among them when the Single European Act (SEA) became operational in 1987 (see Figure 2.3).

It appears that the economic calculations and aspirations that activated the EC member states to create the Common Market were confirmed and,

Figure 2.3
The Institutions of the European Communities, 1967–1992

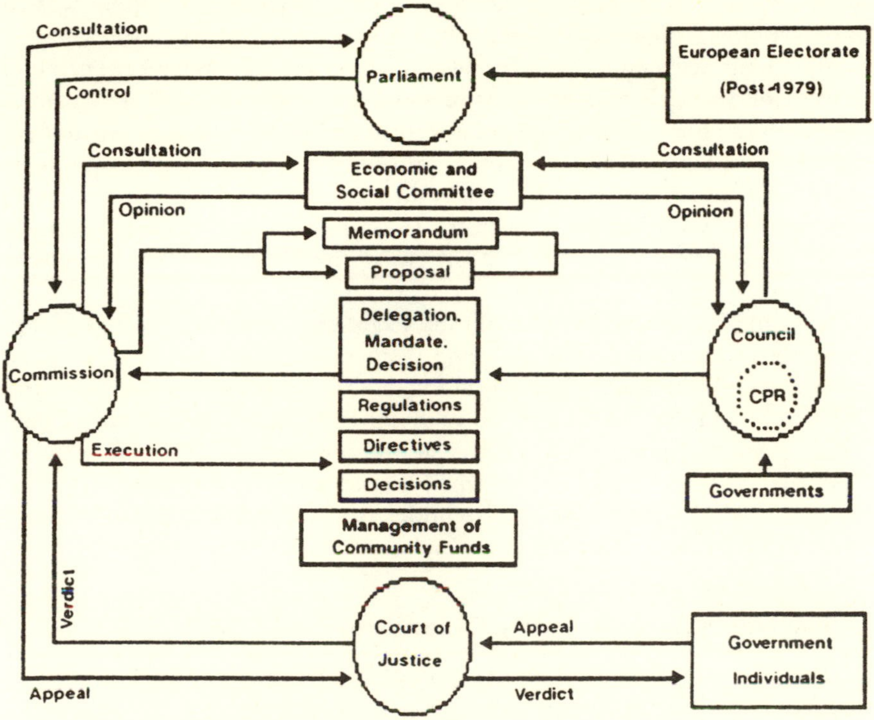

Source: European Communities Commission. *The Courrier: European Community-Africa-Caribbean-Pacific*, No. 48 (March-April 1978), p. 36.

largely, fulfilled by 1967. Within nine years from the beginning of the EEC, intra-Community trade had reached $24.5 billion, an increase of 326 percent over 1958. The standard of living in the EEC member states continued to rise dramatically, and their general economic posture attained impressive dimensions. Beginning in 1973, the EC membership was expanded: in 1973, Britain, Ireland, and Denmark were added; in 1981, Greece became a new member; and in 1986, Spain and Portugal made the EC a Group of 12. Despite the enlargement, however, enthusiasm about the Community began to falter in the 1970s and early 1980s, perhaps reflecting the states' hesitancy in their propensity. This was a period often characterized by what was called "Eurosclerosis" and "Europessimism," when some politicians and academics lost faith in European institutions.

A major change in this situation took place in 1986 when the EC heads of government approved the SEA and thereby launched a period of optimism and institutional momentum. Part of this new forward movement of the Community was contained in an EC Commission White Paper, which aimed to create, by the end of 1992, an area without internal frontiers in which the free movement of goods, persons, services, and capital was to be ensured. Considering that by 1991 the EC had become the world's largest trading bloc, with a population of 344.3 million and a gross national product (GNP) of $6,213.2 billion, the success of the Community is undeniable, although the final shape of the organization and possible new competences, which are subjects of many disputes among the member states, cannot be fully predicted at present. We will return to some of these issues later in this volume, when the Maastrecht treaty on Political and Economic Union is discussed. This is known as "deepening the obligations of the present membership of 12."

It should be pointed out that in June 1993, the terms for "widening" the membership to include the emerging decocracies of Eastern Europe were agreed upon. Six states—Poland, Hungary, the Czech Republic, Slovakia, Romania, and Bulgaria—were formally invited, although no target date was set, and the expectation was that admission could not take place before 2000. In contrast, Austria, Sweden, Finland and Norway are to join by January 1995. Negotiations are also under way for a partnership agreement with Russia, and Turkey has expressed strong interest in joining.

The North Atlantic Treaty Organization (NATO)

The basic motivation for the creation of NATO was clearly the enhancement of the security of individual charter members and the states that subsequently joined. The resources and capabilities of even the most powerful of the allies, the United States, were perceived as insufficient to forgo resorting to multilateral means to meet the threat of aggression in Europe by a militarily powerful Soviet Union.

The threat began with the attempt of a communist take-over by force in Greece in 1946; it increased with the communist coup and seizure of governmental power in Czechoslovakia in 1948; and it continued with heavy political pressure to establish pro-Soviet influence in Norway and Finland, efforts by indigenous communist parties to disrupt the economic reconstruction of Western Europe, and the blockade of Western road and rail access to Berlin in the fall of 1948.[37]

In Western Europe, the first organizational arrangements for the enhancement of security after the end of World War II were made by Britain and France when they signed the Dunkirk Treaty in March 1947. However, this treaty was directed primarily toward providing mutual aid in the event of a renewal of German aggression. It also aimed at economic cooperation and, therefore, adumbrated a longer-range goal to involve the Benelux countries and, perhaps later, other Western European states.

Consequently, in January 1948, alarmed by the expansion and consolidation of Soviet influence in Eastern Europe and the Balkans, the British government made a call for a "Western Union," which was followed up by preliminary negotiations with the Benelux countries and France. A treaty was signed in Brussels on March 17, 1948. This so-called Brussels Treaty made reference to Article 51 of the UN Charter, which authorized collective self-defense and stipulated that in the event of an armed attack on one of the signatories, the other parties to the treaty would come to the aid of the victim of aggression. Even though the treaty mentioned Germany as a potential aggressor, the Soviet Union was evidently the primary concern of the alliance partners.[38]

The principal policy organ of the Brussels Treaty Organization (BTO) was the Consultative Council, which was made up of the foreign ministers of the five member states. Between meetings, policy was determined by a permanent commission located in London with administrative matters handled by a Secretariat. A unified defense force was established in Fontainbleau, France, under British Field Marshal Lord Montgomery, but in fact, he had very few troops to command.[39] To the British government, it soon became clear that the BTO would not be sufficiently strong to deal with Soviet-inspired pressures, although Washington had promised to aid that organization in a way that was yet to be specified.[40] Ernest Bevin, the British foreign secretary, was particularly concerned about Norway becoming so intimidated by the Soviet Union that the collapse of the whole of Scandinavia would result. This would "in turn prejudice our chance of calling any halt to the relentless advance of Russia into Western Europe."[41] Bevin perceived two threats: a direct expansion militarily of the Soviet Union's sphere of influence to the Atlantic, and a political threat to undo all the efforts made (with U.S. approval) to build up a more broadly based Western Union. He, therefore, strongly recommended to the U.S. that a regional Atlantic pact be formed in which all states that would be adversely affected by a Soviet move to the Atlantic could participate. These were to include the United States, Britain, Canada, Ireland, Iceland, Norway, Denmark, Portugal, France, the Benelux countries, and Spain (when it had again a democratic form of government).[42] For the Mediterranean, he envisaged a separate system, with Italy playing a major role.

The U.S. response to the British proposal was given promptly by George C. Marshall, then U.S. secretary of state. He suggested that joint discussions on the establishment of an Atlantic security system be undertaken at once. These initial discussions began in Washington on March 22, 1948, and revealed a number of uncertainties in the British proposals regarding prospective membership and the geographic area to which the system was to apply. There seemed to be an increasing need to include Italy, Greece, and perhaps Turkey, but the acceptability of the Western zones of Germany as a member seemed at that time doubtful because of wartime enmities.[43]

Overall, the initial reaction of Marshall to the British proposal was somewhat negative. He considered U.S. participation in a military guarantee as impossible; U.S. aid would have to be confined to supplying material assistance to the members of a Western European security IGO. However, during the spring of 1948, the State Department, reacting to the Soviet coup in Czechoslovakia and the continued Soviet pressure on Norway, began to commit itself to the treaty. In April, the National Security Council approved a State Department recommendation that the president announce America's willingness to negotiate a collective defense agreement with the BTO members and Norway, Denmark, Sweden, Iceland, and Italy. Pending the conclusion of such an agreement, the United States would regard an armed attack against any signatory of the Brussels Treaty as an armed attack against itself.[44]

Since ratification of this proposed agreement would require Senate approval, and since the situation involved a Democratic president who needed consent from a Republican-controlled Senate, a bipartisan approach was essential. To this end, Senator Arthur Vandenberg, the Republican Chairman of the Senate Foreign Relations Committee, introduced a resolution which was adopted by the Senate by an overwhelming vote on June 11, 1948. The resolution advocated progressive development of regional and other collective arrangements for individual and collective self-defense in accordance with the UN Charter, and specifically referred to the right of collective self-defense under Article 51 of that document. It also approved American association with such arrangements "as are based on continuous and effective self-help and mutual aid, and as it affects national security."[45]

The Vandenberg Resolution opened the way for transatlantic negotiation of a treaty that included regular meetings with the Senate Foreign Relations Committee and its staff to discuss actual treaty language. These discussions were important because there were arguments over various specific provisions, particularly those with respect to the nature of the commitment, geographic coverage, duration, and which other governments should be invited to become members of the prospective security IGO.[46] The basic differences were due to the fact that the Western Europeans, especially the French, wanted as binding and as long a commitment as possible; while the Americans, although agreeing in principle, were constrained by what the administration believed Senator Vandenberg would accept.[47]

Disparities of views among the prospective alliance members about the substance of the treaty were not surprising in view of the large gap in the capabilities and resources of the individual states involved. France wanted to accept an Atlantic security pact only if unity of command of the armed forces of the allies would be achieved at once and American military personnel and supplies moved to France immediately. For Norway, the matter was urgent because the Soviet Union was pressuring them to sign a pact similar to the Soviet-Finnish agreement. Refusal to sign, it was feared, would trigger a Soviet attack on Norway and Sweden. Canada strongly advocated an effective treaty because of concern that, as a result of discussions in the Senate, the treaty might be watered down to the extent that it would not be much more than a Kellogg-Briand anti-war pact. On the other hand, Belgium was apprehensive about the provocative effect that any North Atlantic security arrangement might have on the Soviet Union. While the Belgians were anxious to obtain immediate help from the United States, they floated ideas about how "armed neutrality" of Western Europe would be preferable to a formal Atlantic relationship.[48]

It is not unreasonable to assume that the above-mentioned concerns of selected member states of the prospective alliance reflected their urgent need for bolstering their security through multilateral means. Obviously, the security of all the member states would be enhanced by the alliance, regardless of the size of the contributions they could or would make. In any case, agreement on the substance of the treaty was reached in April 1949.

The most controversial provision in the North Atlantic Treaty was the exact nature of the commitment to respond to armed attack on a treaty member state. The United States did not want to, and could not be obliged to, use its armed forces automatically to aid a victim of an attack because the U.S. Constitution stipulates that only Congress can declare war. After many negotiating sessions and consultations with the foreign ministries of the prospective members and the Senate Foreign Relations Committee, the crucial Article 5 of the Treaty was written as follows:

> The Parties agree that an armed attack against one or more of them in Europe or North America shall be considered an attack against them all, and consequently they agree that, if such an armed attack occurs, each of them in exercise of the right of individual or collective self-defence recognized by Article 51 of the Charter of the United Nations, will assist the Party or Parties so attacked by taking forthwith, individually and in concert with the other Parties, such action as it deems necessary, including the use of armed force, to restore and maintain the security of the North Atlantic area.
>
> Any such armed attack and all measures taken as a result thereof shall immediately be reported to the Security Council. Such measures shall be terminated when the Security Council has taken the measures necessary to restore and maintain international peace and security.[49]

In spite of the qualifying words, it was believed that Congress could be counted on to back the president with a declaration of war, particularly if the armed attack was not just an incident but a full-fledged initiation of extensive hostilities.

For the southern boundary of the territorial coverage of the treaty, the Tropic of the Cancer was adopted (Article 6). This avoided involving any part of Africa or of the Latin American states as areas where an armed attack would constitute a *causus belli*. However, consultation on threats or actual attack anywhere in the world was not restricted by the geographic parameters specified in the treaty. Indeed, consultation on possible threats is a major obligation of the member governments (Article 4). Although some European governments had insisted on a treaty duration of fifty years, the final agreement that was reached was limited to twenty years. It was doubtful that the Senate would have accepted a longer time span.

It should be noted that the treaty has an economic dimension. Article 2 emphasizes the elimination of conflict between the international economic policies of the member states and the encouragement of economic collaboration between "any or all of them." However, these provisions have been used only rarely; one example occurred when the NATO member states pledged contributions to an assistance program for Turkey, which faced serious economic difficulties in the late 1970s.

In terms of rights, the member governments were given the right to be consulted, which is the other side of the coin of being obligated to consult each other in case of threats to their individual or collective security.

It is noteworthy that the treaty negotiators did not spell out institutional and organizational details for the implementation of the agreement beyond stipulating the establishment of a North Atlantic Council and a Defence Committee, giving these organs the mandate to set up subsidiary bodies. (See Figure 2.4 for NATO civil and military structures.) No mention was made of voting procedures, but the basic rule developed in the Council was that no government could be forced to take action against its will, but conversely, no government could prevent other governments from taking such collective action as they agree to take.[50]

Finally, unanimous agreement is necessary to invite any state to accede to the treaty. However, only those states in a position to further the principles of the treaty and contribute to the security of the North Atlantic area may be invited (Article 10). This shows that the member states retained a maximum of flexibility for future decision making except for the obligations specified in Article 5 and for consultation. Thus, it can be inferred that the propensity was limited to achieving an increment of security by allying with the United States while retaining maximum national discretion as to how the collective relationship would be spelled out.

There is no doubt that NATO has been generally a very successful organization with a high level of task performance. It assured the security of Western Europe and contributed to the collapse of the Soviet Union and communism in general in Europe. Since the threat of an *organized* attack on Western Europe is now almost nonexistent, NATO needs a new rationale to remain a viable organization. With Washington anxious to retain NATO for its foreign policy purposes, attempt are being made to create closer relations with the former Warsaw Treaty members and the individual states of the Commonwealth of Independent States (CIS)—formerly the Soviet Union. Hence, NATO established a North Atlantic Cooperation Council (NACC) in 1991 that brings together NATO members on various occasions

Figure 2.4
NATO's Civil and Military Structures

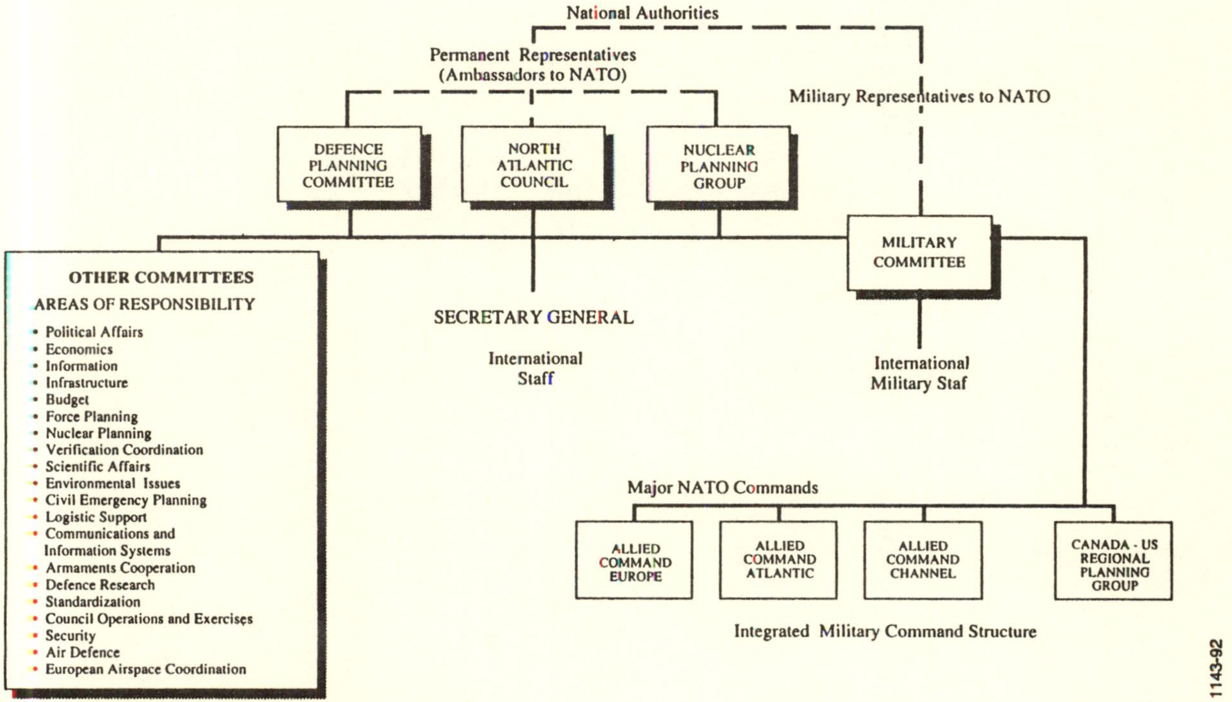

The North Atlantic Treaty was signed in Washington DC on 4 April 1949, by the Foreign Ministers of 12 nations : Belgium, Canada, Denmark, France, Iceland, Italy, Luxembourg, the Netherlands, Norway, Portugal, the United Kingdom and the United States. Greece and Turkey acceded to the Treaty in 1952, the Federal Republic of Germany in 1955, and Spain in 1982. The Treaty created an alliance for collective defence as defined in Article 51 of the United Nations Charter and led to the formation of NATO. The organisation thus links 16 independent nations in a voluntary security system in which roles, risks and responsibilities are shared.

Source: *NATO Handbook* (Brussels: NATO Information, 1992) p. 20.

for consultations. As discussed later in the text, NATO is also cooperating with other IGOs—notably the United Nations, CSCE, EC, and WEU—in post-Cold War peacekeeping and peacemaking efforts. This cooperation has been termed dealing with European-related affairs through "interlocking institutions," with only limited success so far.

In this respect, NATO has taken on several new roles and missions, serving as: (1) an instrument of crisis management in the context of the new international order; (2) the cornerstone of a security community encompassing both East and West; (3) an element of stability in Europe from which the new democracies in Central and Eastern Europe will also benefit; (4) an instrument to support the verification and implementation of arms control; and (5) a possible instrument to organize a missile defense in order to protect Europe from the dangers of the proliferation of missile technology.

The Organization for Economic Cooperation and Development (OECD)

The OECD was established by treaty in December 1960 and became operational in September 1961. It grew out of the Organization for European Economic Cooperation (OEEC), which was a tool for the administration of Marshall Plan aid and represented a cooperative effort to speed European recovery from the damages of World War II. By the end of 1960, many quantitative restrictions on trade within Europe had begun to disappear, currency convertibility was on the way, and the dollar gap had disappeared. The increased economic interdependence suggested the need for an organization in which North American states would participate on an equal footing with Europe; hence, the establishment of the OECD had three major purposes:

1. To help member countries promote economic growth, employment, and improved standards of living through policy coordination;
2. To help promote the sound and harmonious development of the world economy; and
3. To improve the lot of the developing countries, particularly the poorest.

The current OECD membership includes the twelve members of the EC and the United States, Canada, Australia, New Zealand, Japan, Austria, Finland, Iceland, Norway, Sweden, Switzerland, and Turkey. The Commission of the EC is a limited participant. The headquarters is in Paris, France.

The principal political organ of OECD is the Council, which convenes at the ministerial level at least once a year and in which all member states are represented. Generally, acts of the Council require unanimity, although different voting rules may be adopted in particular circumstances. Supervision of OECD activities is the responsibility of a limited participation Executive Committee made up of fourteen members elected annually by the Council, which normally meets once a week. The secretary-general, who chairs the regular Council meetings, is responsible for implementing Council and Executive Committee decisions.

Of considerable consequence with respect to OECD operations are two additional committees: the Economic Policy Committee and the Development Assistance Committee. The task of the first is to review economic activities in all member states, including the analysis of macroeconomic and structural policies and an examination of balance-of-payments problems. The second oversees the official resource transfers and has made a name for itself through continual encouragement of the member states to aid the economies of developing countries.

The propensity to organize multilaterally is relatively high because the services provided by the organization are very valuable for the member states and may not be available nationally, especially in the smaller states. With a highly skilled bureaucracy and a more than adequate task performance record, most member governments are satisfied with their OECD affiliation. The analyses generated by the organization, in part through the use of a highly sophisticated computerized model of the world economy, are widely respected for being free of political concerns that often skew forecasts issued by individual countries.

However, there has also been controversy among the OECD member states and the leadership. In 1987 the latter considered prevailing policies as insufficient to deal with the world's economic turmoil. While Japan was praised for recent policy changes, the United States was urged to speed up the pace of its budget deficit reduction and West Germany was criticized for inadequate stimulation of its economy. During the 1989 Council meeting, a degree of controversy developed over recent U.S. statements that Japan, India, and Brazil were "unfair traders" and hence, subject to possible penalties. Japan challenged the U.S. statement and asked for an OECD declaration criticizing Washington. The high cost of farm support evoked much discussion as well. During the annual Council meeting in 1990, the ministers gave the highest priority in the Uruguay Round of GATT to completing agreements on farm subsidies. As of this writing, the issue had not been settled.[51] France, in particular, has been reluctant to give ground. The annual "economic summits" of the group of seven are related to OECD.

REGIONALISM IN DEVELOPING COUNTRIES

The number of IGOs in developing countries, especially those dealing with economic cooperation, that have been established since 1960 is substantial, reflecting great propensity and interest initially in organizing multilaterally. Partially responsible for these developments were the studies of the UN Economic Commissions for Latin America (ECLA) and for Africa (ECA), as well as the increasing desire for "South-South Cooperation" stimulated by the developing countries and UNCTAD. However, not all the regional IGOs were successful; some, such as the East African Community (EAC), began with a great deal of promise but collapsed rather early. In Chapter 4 we seek to analyze the reasons for this and other breakdowns.

We will begin our discussion of the principles of IGO creation by examining three organizations that differ geographically and functionally. They are the Latin American Free Trade Association (LAFTA) and its successors; the Organization of African Unity (OAU), which is basically a political/security IGO; and the Association of Southeast Asian Nations (ASEAN), which began as a foreign-policy coordination IGO but has moved into the economic sphere.

The Latin American Free Trade Association (LAFTA)

Inspired by studies of the ECLA and emulating the initial successes of the three European Communities that were established in 1953 and 1957, the Latin American Free Trade Association became operational in 1961. The constituent document, the Treaty of Montevideo, was signed in February 1960 by Argentina, Brazil, Chile, Mexico, Paraguay, Peru, and Uruguay. Colombia and Ecuador joined in 1961, and Venezuela later became a member as well.

The hopes were high that LAFTA would become a viable experiment in regional economic integration. However, the dismantling of tariff barriers, a very complicated and cumbersome process under the constituent treaty, allowed nationalist and protectionist tendencies of the member governments to block real progress in creating a true free-trading area. Moreover, the same tendencies made it very difficult to implement an ingenious scheme for regionwide integrated industrialization through so-called complementary agreements (Articles 14–17). The agreements were designed to establish a program of sectoral integration through the liberalization of trade in the products of a particular industrial sector.[52] However, in spite of a promising start in the early 1960s, LAFTA has made little progress toward integration.

What, if any, has been the role of the institutions set up by the Treaty of Montevideo? The institutional framework of LAFTA was small, consisting mainly of the Conference of Contracting Parties and the Permanent Executive Committee, but the organization could have been useful to achieve the economic integration goals.

The Conference, a plenary body, normally met once a year. It was responsible for engaging in periodic tariff-cutting negotiations as required by treaty, but very little has been accomplished since the mid-1960s. It elected the secretary of the Permanent Executive Committee for a three-year term and approved its budget. The Executive Committee, also a plenary body, ran LAFTA's operations and supervised the implementation of the provisions of the Montevideo Treaty. It also convened the conferences, prepared work programs and budget estimates, and initiated studies of various kinds. It represented LAFTA in dealing with third states and other IGOs. A Secretariat provided administrative support to the Committee, and the Executive Secretary participated in Committee deliberations but did not have a vote. The bureaucracy of LAFTA consisted of about two hundred international civil servants, most of whom were technical experts who provided the staff for the various advisory and consultative committees. The budget hovered around $2 million.[53] The headquarters was in Montevideo, Uruguay, but LAFTA's very modest administration building cannot compare with the magnificent splendor and grandeur of the EC headquarters in Brussels.

As already intimated, LAFTA's level of task performance has been low. The original plan was to achieve a complete free-trade area by 1973, but by 1967 it was clear that this goal was unachievable. It was then decided to aim for a common market that would also incorporate Central America by 1980. This deadline passed without a successful outcome, however, and the prospects indeed seemed bleak that an all–Latin American common market would ever be realized, although new hopes were kindled in the 1990s. Exports among the member states had reached only 13 percent of total exports by 1978; only twenty-one complementary agreements to promote industrial integration had been signed by 1976, and they were concluded by subsidiaries of American multinational corporations located in different Latin American states. Most of the agreements involved the "Big Three" (Argentina, Brazil, and Mexico).[54]

Clearly, the management efficiency of the LAFTA Executive Committee and Secretariat was low and lacked the dynamic nature of the EC institutions. This is really not surprising because the Committee was not given powers of decision and action similar to those that had been conferred on the EC Council of Ministers, nor were the central institutions of LAFTA in a position to acquire powers over and above those conferred by the treaty.[55]

However, the real reasons for the poor task performance of the LAFTA lie elsewhere. One reason is the strong nationalistic and protectionist character of most Latin American governments. The second reason is succinctly spelled out by Yale Ferguson:

> A sore issue over the years has been one that has usually plagued integration experiments, the matter of an unequal sharing of benefits. Most benefits have plainly accrued to the three leading exporters of manufactured goods—Argentina, Brazil, and Mexico—and primarily to foreign multinationals operating in these and other countries.[56]

Latin American Integration Association (LAIA). In spite of LAFTA's inability to become a viable, economically integrated regional IGO, representatives of the member states met in Acapulco in June 1980 to draft a treaty for a new regional IGO called the Latin American Integration Association (LAIA). The treaty, which was signed in August of that year by the foreign ministers, aimed at the establishment, in a gradual and progressive manner, of a Latin American common market rather than a free-trade area. To avoid the mistakes of LAFTA, LAIA emphasized the differential treatment of member states, depending on the level of economic development. Existing tariff concessions, largely negotiated under the auspices of LAFTA, were to be renegotiated and, in some instances, suspended. New tariff negotiations were expected to include both reciprocal and preferential accords, but no deadlines were set.

The structure of this new IGO consisted of an annually convened Conference of Contracting Parties (composed of the same members as LAFTA), a Council of Foreign Ministers (LAIA's principal political body), and a Secretariat. Whether this new venture was nothing more than old wine poured into a new bottle was uncertain. Nevertheless, activities continue in LAIA, with resolutions approved in 1984 aimed at strengthening financial and monetary cooperation mechanisms, providing special aid measures for less developed members, and ending nontariff barriers. In 1987 the Council reaffirmed its "integrationist" will, announcing an agreement designed to yield a 40 percent increase in intraregional trade by 1991 and proposing the elimination of nontariff barriers.

Mercosur. Despite these new efforts, integration progress in Latin America generally remains slow. In 1986 Argentina and Brazil set up the beginning of a new economic integration system which was called *Mercosur* (Southern Common Market). In 1991 Paraguay and Uruguay joined and the Treaty of Ascension was signed. The four states planned a complete end to internal trade barriers by the end of 1994 as well as a 15 percent tariff on imports coming from outside the common market. *Mercosur*'s potential lies with the combined population of 190 million people (45% of Latin America), which in 1991 produced about $420 billion worth of goods and services.[57]

The institutions of *Mercosur* are a Common Market Council and a Common Market Group. The first is a political ruling and decision-making institution in which the Foreign and Economic Ministers coordinate economic measures for their respective countries and decide on common measures.

Economic difficulties may intervene with *Mercosur*'s ambitious schedule. One problem is the high inflation rate of the four member states, although this problem seems to have been overcome in Argentina. Another reason for concern is the high level of nationalism and economic egocentrism which has been a major reason for the difficulties encountered previously by

LAFTA and LAIA in attempting to implement their policies for economic cooperation and integration.

Other Economic Latin American IGOs. As far as Latin America is concerned, *Mercosur* is not the only economic cooperation scheme. Others are the Andean Common Market (ANCOM) with members primarily on the west and north coasts of the continent; the Central American Common Market (CACM), with an uncertain past and perhaps better future; and the Caribbean Community (CARICOM) which also hopes to establish a common market by 1994. We will return to these IGOs later.

The Organization of African Unity (OAU)

The motivational background for the creation of the Organization of African Unity (OAU) flows from two different concepts: (1) a desire to consolidate the postcolonial states within existing preindependence boundaries; and (2) a Pan-African movement to join together all such states or groupings of them for general or particular purposes. Whichever the orientation, there was agreement among the new African leaders that unity and solidarity would not only assure a common front to safeguard African interests; they also would give African states a more effective voice in world affairs, counter foreign influences in the solution of African problems, curb the danger of fragmentation among them, and enhance Africa's economic and social development.[58] The problems in South Africa were also a major concern.

Thus, the basic motivation for the establishment of the OAU was primarily political. This is confirmed in Article II of the OAU Charter, which was agreed upon at the Summit Conference of Independent African States in Addis Ababa in 1963. This article stresses the promotion of the unity and solidarity of the African states and the defense of their sovereignty, territorial integrity, and independence.

In order to achieve these objectives, the member states, which now number more than forty, committed themselves in the Charter to a number of obligations, while still retaining certain rights. There was, however, prior controversy about the extent of the commitment. For example, President Kwame Nkrumah of Ghana sought to set up a central political organization with powers to formulate a common policy in foreign affairs, defense, and economic matters. However, the majority of the Addis Ababa conference participants rejected this attempt at supranational Pan-Africanism and opted instead for the strict maintenance of the principle of sovereignty.[59] Indeed, the principles enumerated in Article III of the Charter include the sovereign equality of member states, noninterference in the internal affairs of these states, and respect for their sovereignty and integrity. On the other hand, the member governments pledged to settle all disputes among themselves by peaceful means (Article XIX) and affirmed a policy of nonalignment with regard to all blocs.

The supreme organ of the OAU is the Assembly of Heads of State and Government which meets at least once a year and can be convened in extraordinary session by a two-thirds majority of the member states. It can make only nonbinding recommendations, which require for their adoption a two-thirds majority vote.[60] Each member has one vote.

The executive machinery of the OAU consists of a Council of Ministers and a Secretariat. The Council, whose power has increased over the years, is composed of the foreign ministers of the member governments or other ministers when appropriate. It adopts resolutions by simple majority.[61] It prepares for the meetings of the Assembly, implements the latter's decisions, and coordinates inter-African cooperation (Articles XII–XV). The head of the Secretariat is called an administrative secretary-general, an indication that the member states were anxious to limit the powers of the office and to prevent any kind of enhancement of authority (Articles XVI–XVIII). Finally, a Commission of Mediation, Conciliation, and Arbitration was established, which was regarded as a principal organ. Consisting of twenty-one members elected by the Assembly for five-year terms, its mandate was dispute settlement. However, despite many disputes between the members, the services of the commission have been invoked rarely. Instead, ad hoc commissions and committees have been set up to address the underlying problems and to find acceptable solutions.[62] In 1977, the Commission was replaced with a ten-member Disputes Committee.

The fragile nature of most of the governments of the OAU member states tended to militate against a strong propensity to transfer too much authority to the OAU. Internal conflict as well as interstate conflict have been major preoccupations. In any event, the OAU has a mixed record in bringing about the settlement of the various—and all too frequent—disputes that have arisen. This is in spite of the use of ad hoc bodies and mandates by either the Council of Ministers or the Assembly to pressure the contending states to accept proposed solutions. While in the Algerian-Moroccan border dispute of 1963 the fighting and hostilities ceased and tensions were lessened, no permanent settlement was ever formalized. In other instances, such as the guerrilla fighting along the borders of Somalia with Kenya and Ethiopia, mediating efforts were only temporarily successful.[63]

Issues that have occupied the OAU include the Polisario involvement in the Western Sahara and the demand of Mauritius for the return of British-held Diego Garcia Island, which is located in the Indian Ocean. The Libyan intervention in Chad in 1980 prompted the OAU to establish a committee to investigate the crisis in this part of Africa. The OAU has attempted, through sending missions, to resolve the Liberian civil war and also has been concerned about the conflict in Somalia.

For the promotion of national independence and racial equality, the OAU in 1963 set up a Coordinating Committee whose tasks were to harmonize the assistance given by African states to all national liberation movements and to administer a special fund that was established for this purpose. The Committee provided monetary aid and political assistance to movements fighting against colonialism in Zimbabwe (formerly Rhodesia), as well as against South Africa's policy of apartheid. It also furnished military training and advice and distributed military equipment. While the efforts of the Committee in support of most liberation movements have been moderately effective, the successful struggle against South Africa could be carried out only through the comprehensive utilization of facilities offered by the United Nations. The Committee has sought to employ these means as much as possible, but ultimate results, of course, have depended on the success of the initiatives undertaken by various relevant UN bodies, as well as national governmental and nongovernmental individual and collective initiatives.[64] The end of the Soviet-American rivalry has also been a determining factor.

Intraregional conflicts have continued to divide the membership during the 1980s, although some progress was made toward their resolution. Because of difficulties in agreeing on a site for the annual assembly meetings, Addis Ababa in Ethiopia became the venue from 1983 to 1985. Little was accomplished during these assembly sessions except calls for a "new world economic order," creation of a special fund to aid African states affected by drought, rescheduling debt repayment (amounting to $170 billion), and advocating independence for Namibia.

During the 1989 summit in Addis Ababa, participants repeated an earlier call for an international conference on the external debt crisis and for modification of economic reforms required by the IMF and the World Bank. At the same time, member governments were in arrears by some $35 million in their annual dues, which created problems for continued operation of the organization. In the 1991 summit held in Nigeria, the first assembly outside Ethiopia since 1981, the participants passed an African Economic Community (AEC) treaty reflecting mounting concern that world affairs would "marginalize" Africa economically and reduce further Africa's already declining economic prospects. The Community is to be implemented by 2025 in six five-year phases.[65]

In sum and on balance, it appears that the OAU has only modestly strengthened the African states' political capabilities and resources, and therefore, propensity for continued OAU support remains mildly positive. However, in the final analysis, progress in economic development may prove to be much more important for the individual states than political actions by the OAU. However, what the future of the AEC will be is highly uncertain, and likely problems will be seen when we examine later two African regional IGOs: the East African Community and ECOWAS. Nonetheless, the OAU has provided some benefits, albeit at times only psychological, to all the member states, and the interdependence costs have been minimal.

The Association of Southeast Asian Nations (ASEAN)

ASEAN has developed into a regional IGO on the basis of political rather than economic motivations, as initially it did not aim at regional economic integration. Hence, ASEAN did not start out with a well-developed institutional framework; whatever modest institutions it has now have evolved gradually as needed.

When founded in 1967, it had as its primary goal to assure regional peace and stability. Its member states—Thailand, Malaysia, Indonesia, the Philippines, Singapore, and Brunei (since 1982)—called for "collective political defense" to protect individual as well as group interests.[66] They aimed at taking common positions when dealing with third states in order to strengthen their bargaining power. In the economic sphere, their objectives were to accelerate economic growth, social progress, and cultural development through "close and beneficial cooperation," but no plans existed at the time of ASEAN's formation to set up a free-trade zone or a customs union.[67] There was no intention by the member states to confer national government powers on a central body and, indeed, ASEAN operated without a secretariat until 1976.

However, the challenge of Vietnam put pressure on ASEAN member states to function as a cohesive group on a continuing basis. In addition, economic pressures from Japan reinforced the necessity for cohesion. As a consequence, a summit meeting of ASEAN member governments was held in February 1976 that resulted in a "Treaty of Amity and Cooperation in Southeast Asia," and some new institutions were also established. A Secretariat was set up in Jakarta, Indonesia, and a secretary-general was appointed. This post rotates every two years among nationals of the member states.

Prior to 1976, regular annual plenary meetings were attended only by the foreign ministers of the member states. Now, an ASEAN Economic Ministers Meetings has also become institutionalized as a formal structure for handling economic matters. Finally, a legal mechanism for the peaceful settlement of disputes among ASEAN members was created by the Treaty of Amity and Cooperation. A High Council is now available consisting of an ad hoc body of mediators who, however, do not possess any enforcement powers. Nonetheless, ASEAN member states are legally bound to seek the help of the High Council before turning to outside states to settle their disputes.[68]

In December 1987, ASEAN convened its first summit in a decade, during which the heads of state called for a reduction in tariff barriers between member states and a rejuvenation of regional economic projects. These objectives were to be carried out because of an increasingly hostile global trading environment and concern over growing Western protectionism. Another major development was an announcement by Japan offering the ASEAN countries $2 billion in low-interest loans and investments over a three-year period to finance private sector projects. This was followed by ASEAN's formation of an Asia-Pacific Economic Cooperation (APEC) Forum which includes the ASEAN members plus Australia, Canada, Japan, New Zealand, South Korea, and the United States. This was certainly an initiative toward regional economic cooperation, although the commitment of the members is uncertain and no formalized implementation has followed this announcement.

Within the Annual Meeting of Foreign Ministers, there is a Standing Committee that meets regularly between ministerial sessions and carries out executive functions. Working closely with the Secretariat, the Standing Committee has a large number of permanent and ad hoc committees dealing with various functional matters. A similar, though smaller, structure of committees also exists vis-à-vis the economic ministers. National ASEAN secretariats have been formed that are subordinate to the international Secretariat. This is a rather unusual institutional feature, perhaps either serving as a channel to the national governments for the ASEAN international Secretariat or as an oversight device by the latter to control the central organ.

It is too early to assess the task performance of the ASEAN institutions, which are clearly quite limited in scope and extent. However, the 1976 summit meeting adopted the so-called ASEAN Concord which is a blueprint for economic cooperation. The Concord includes preferential trade arrangements in basic commodities, joint investment in industrial projects, and trade promotion measures. There is also hope that, by the turn of the century, a free-trade area will be a reality. These goals and appropriate implementing measures present major challenges to the ASEAN institutions, all the more since the economies of the six member states are structurally more competitive than complementary. Nevertheless, the ASEAN Secretariat and the other institutions are functioning, and the Secretariat has begun to make a positive impact on the task of building economic cooperation leading gradually to economic integration. However, peace in Cambodia (Kampuchea) remains a major preoccupation of ASEAN's leadership and this includes strong opposition to Vietnam's presence in that area, although Vietnam is moving toward a market economy.

In 1993, responding to the economic and potential military dynamism of China, ASEAN foreign ministers proposed creating a Regional Security Forum that would include the U.S. and Japan, thus facilitating the retention of American power in the region. The overall purpose would be to head off conflicts as the region becomes increasingly important in the global economy. At the Asian Post-Ministerial Conference, a three-day session of 11 states that follows the annual ASEAN foreign ministers meeting, the notion of such a Forum along the lines of the ECSC in Europe was strongly endorsed by the U.S.

SCOPE AND STRUCTURE OF NEW IGOs

It is obvious that to translate the propensity of states for international organization into the establishment of a particular IGO requires bargaining-out the scope and structural dimensions of the new organization. This can be a complex and drawn-out process that can severely tax the endurance and creativity of the negotiators, who usually must operate under fairly strict directions from their governments. They must mesh their governments' nationalistic desire for maximum autonomy with the assurance that the prospective IGO can perform optimally and effectively the tasks for which it is being created.

One of the main questions to be settled in the bargaining process between the prospective member states is *the extent of the institutional framework and the degree of decision-making authority to be conferred upon the IGO.* Ideally, this authority should be commensurate with the performance of tasks expected of the IGO and involves the determination of such issues as the latitude of power to be granted to the IGO's executive head, or whether task management decisions by the regional institutions should be made by unanimity or by majority vote; perhaps either a qualified majority or weighted votes would be required. IGO task performance may also require the formulation of appropriate national policies and often national supervision over multilateral policy implementation, because these can be highly sensitive matters affecting the autonomy of the member states and, hence, are likely to produce interdependence costs. Will these costs exceed the benefits anticipated from the IGO or should the multilateral commitment be made more modest? Only the very best judgments of the political leaders of the governments involved and their negotiators can produce the necessary fine tuning of the IGO's scope and institutional structure to achieve a sound balance of benefits and costs.

Throughout this bargaining-out procedure, the prospective IGO member government must keep in mind the obligations (i.e., costs) that it is willing to assume and the rights it intends to exercise (i.e., benefits) as a consequence of membership. An important obligation beyond accepting a general limitation of its freedom of action in both foreign and, to a smaller degree, domestic affairs is the financial contribution to the IGO's operations. This includes expenditures for the construction and maintenance of physical facilities as well as salaries for necessary international civil servants. The size of the contribution usually depends on the economic prowess of the IGO member, including the size of its gross national product (GNP), or else it may be a reflection of the political benefits the state anticipates receiving. In a few cases IGOs have been given limited taxing power (as was done for the ECSC) or have been granted their own financial resources in the form of import duties collected by the member governments or by the allocation of a percentage of the value-added taxes of the member states. The EC now enjoys such revenue-raising resources. During the last few years, the United Nations also has attempted to generate its own resources through some kind of direct taxation of the member states; however, in the face of open hostility from the larger donors, the idea has withered on the vine.[69] Post-Cold War peacekeeping and -making activities have placed new pressures on financing of Security Council resolutions. The problems of financing were discussed earlier in this chapter and are referred to in Chapter 3.

Among the rights of IGO member states is that of participating in whatever decision-making process is stipulated in the underlying treaty or convention. This also includes, of course, the right of denial or consent on a particular issue. However, rights may not be equally distributed among IGO members; for example, the veto right in the UN Security Council is accorded in the Charter only to the five permanent members.[70] Weighting the votes of member states in such bodies as the EC Council of Ministers, where a qualified majority is required for a favorable decision, also affects an IGO member's power to deny consent on a particular matter.[71] The influence of the United States in allocation decisions of the IMF and in project decisions of the World Bank are well known.

Another important right of a member government is to deny or to delay accession to the IGO of new member states. The delay in the accession of Spain in NATO until after the Francisco Franco era and the French veto of British entry into the EC are examples.[72] The relatively prompt admission of the fifteen former republics of the Soviet Union into the IMF and the World Bank is another example. Whether to "broaden" the membership of the EC in face of post-Cold War pressures from new or newly autonomous states has become an important question for the IGO. The expansion of IGO membership could impair the task performance potential of the original organization, reduce the anticipated benefits for the charter members of the IGO, or increase materially the interdependence costs. The creation of "Associate" memberships, such as in the EC, or "Cooperation Partners," as in NATO, may be viewed as a way of avoiding these problems without rejecting entirely the interest of nonmember states in sharing in the presumed benefits of full membership. Generally, under international law, the consent of all member states is necessary before IGO membership can be enlarged. Nevertheless, an appropriate specific provision concerning new members (or withdrawal of members) in the treaty setting up a new IGO can avoid problems in the future.

As already pointed out, states participate in the creation of IGOs in anticipation of specific benefits. These may not always be made explicit in the constituent treaties, but there is at least an implied expectation in all the IGOs discussed in this chapter that the ratio of benefit to cost is not completely unreasonable. This is an issue that has surfaced in nearly all IGOs from the EC to the OAU and NATO. It can develop into a major problem in all IGOs, leading to serious disputes and, in some cases, to the complete disarray of the IGO. This is one reason that brought about the failure of the League of Nations. The discussion of the U.S. withdrawal from UNESCO in Chapter 5 provide a more contemporary example. The cost-benefit ratio should be very carefully considered when the contractual details of an IGO are negotiated by the prospective members or are renegotiated in the light of experience or the emergence of new conditions.

Finally, in negotiations to create a new IGO, there must be a carefully drawn division of functions between national and IGO institutions. This is a difficult task because national institutions have acquired over time a legitimizing power and authority that cannot be modified easily. Interest-group constituencies that have built up around national ministries or parliamentary bodies have buttressed the power of these institutions. These constituencies are often opposed to changes that might result in new (and competing) centers of influence. The discussion in Chapter 6 of the World Food Conference and its outcomes is an example of the influence of ministries of agriculture on an IGO and FAO. In most cases, loyalties have grown up around the national institutions, endowing them with symbolic as well as political legitimacy. Hence, it is clear that unless the national institutions are willing to accept a reduction in the scope and nature of their competences, or unless they can be persuaded over time to do so, the multilateral decision-making authority of the IGO institutions is likely to be rather limited, at least at the beginning; alternately, if there is an initial generous grant of power to the IGO, this grant can gradually be whittled down, although perhaps only temporarily, as has been the case in the United Nations in regard to the use of the veto in the Security Council, in LAFTA, and at times in the EC. Even though these circumstances may have been anticipated by the founders of an IGO, an initial conferral of broad decision-making competencies on the IGO institutions can suffer gradual erosion under the pressure of national political and bureaucratic forces. The incremental acquisition or diminution of decision-making authority is one criterion of whether an IGO possesses the political and administrative rigor to carry out its legal mandate.

SUMMARY AND CONCLUSIONS

Perhaps the greatest challenge to all IGOs is *the maintenance of their task performance*. Both domestic and external forces can sap the strength of the IGO institutions even after a certain level of performance has been achieved.

The conflicting forces caused by the states' propensity to buttress their national autonomy and enhance their national capabilities vis-à-vis the central management of capabilities and resources by the IGO institutions are a common theme of this chapter. It can be seen in the problems of the UN Security Council, the disparate views in and toward NATO, the bickering in the EC, and the weakness of the OAU. A plateau in IGO task performance and/or regional integration had been attained in all these examples, but any forward movement, especially if it hinted at supranationalism (as in the EC), has resulted in a decided weakening of national propensity. The turbulent history of efforts to maintain the Exchange Rate Mechanism (ERM) in the EC, as discussed in Chapter 7, is an example. In other words, interdependence costs have outstripped original motivations. The reasons for this phenomenon are discussed more fully in subsequent chapters. We can conclude so far that IGOs will, in the foreseeable future, remain vehicles through which nation-states conduct their affairs, but they are not likely to become decision-imposing entities on their member states. The paradox is that the political, economic, scientific, and technological aspects of the world we live in are, at the same time, creating, almost haphazardly, greater interdependence which, in turn, generates new or expanded expectations on, and demands for, IGOs.

Even though states may have a propensity for international organization, the force of nationalism and the desire of governments to attain short-term, immediate benefits rather than longer-term, more universal goals have impeded any thrust toward either global or regional political unification or economic integration. Nevertheless, the theoretical bases for the propensity of states to organize internationally, depending on the extent of or constraints on their national capabilities and resources and the concept of the collective good, provide useful comparative insights into the creation of IGOs. Indeed, the relevant variables explaining the genesis of IGOs can be extended beyond their creation and can help us to understand the evolution, stability, and even the possible dismantling of IGOs.

An additional factor, which is not always explicit, is the impact of extraregional external forces on the genesis of IGOs. Such forces indirectly affect the capabilities and resources of nation states and therefore must be taken into account by prospective member governments in their calculations as to the benefits for them of creating or joining an IGO. The effort at the unification of Eastern and Western Europe after World War II was encouraged by the external forces of both the United States and the Soviet Union, whose policies and influences, as indicated, were reflected in the way in which the EC, NATO, the Warsaw Pact, and COMECON were devised. The demise of the Cold War has, concomitantly, brought about a reassessment of IGO roles in both economic and security affairs in Europe. We discuss this phenomenon further in Chapters 5 and 6.

Moreover, the failures of the OAU can be attributed in part to the fact that states external to the region have intervened in various conflicts, and at times, sharp reversals of alliances have taken place as a result. Such external impact can result in a decline in IGO task performance which, in turn, will weaken its solidarity.

It is not yet clear that the African regional or sub-regional IGOs in the post-Cold War era can bring about successfully the resolution of conflicts exascerbated during the Cold War without the assistance of the United Nations. Angola, South Africa, and Liberia are cases in point. The political turmoil in Central America in the 1980s, which was caused in part by conflicting objectives of the U.S. and the Soviet Union has been responsible, to a large degree, for the decline of the Central American Common Market in recent years. As the political atmosphere improved with the demise of the Cold War the chances of revival for a regional organization there have also improved.

Finally, the creation of regional development banks whose memberships are not confined to the region provide examples of how the attraction and accumulation of adequate financial and technological resources, which require exra-regional involvement, can be crucial to the capacity of these IGOs to carry out their development missions.

NOTES

1. One exception is John Gerard Ruggie, "Collective Goods and Future International Collaboration," *American Political Science Review* 66 (September 1972): 874–93. For a thoughtful examination of the theoretical implications of the post-Cold War international system (if such may be seen as coming into existence), see Seyom Brown, *International Relations in a Changing Global System: Toward a Theory of the World Polity* (Boulder, CO: Westview Press, 1992).

2. Ruggie, "Collective Goods," pp. 877–82.

3. Ibid.

4. For a discussion of interdependence as viewed in the 1970s from the then Third World, see Guy F. Erb and Valeriana Kallab, eds., *Beyond Dependence: The Developing World Speaks Out* (Washington, DC: Overseas Development Council, 1975). For later views on this subject, see Hoyt Purvis, *Interdependence: An Introduction to International Relations* (New York: Harcourt Brace Jovanovich College Publishers, 1992); and Bruce Russett, Harvey Starr, and Richard Stoll, eds., *Choices in World Politics: Sovereignty and Interdependence* (New York: W. H. Freeman, 1989).

5. Erb and Kallab, *Beyond Dependence,* p. 882. This proposition is slightly paraphrased.

6. Ibid.

7. Ibid.

8. See Mancur Olson, *The Logic of Collective Action: Public Goods and the Theory of Groups* (Cambridge, MA: Harvard University Press, 1971), as quoted in Edward Mansfield, "The Concentration of Capabilities and International Trade," *International Organization* (Summer 1992): 731–63. See also Todd Sandler and John Cauley,

"On the Economic Theory of Alliances," *Journal of Conflict Resolution* 19 (1975): 330–48; and Joe Openheimer, "Some Reflections on Clubs and Alliances," *Journal of Conflict Resolution* 24 (September 1980): 349–57.

9. Various ways of looking at the member states' cost-benefit assessments of NATO are found in Steve Weber, "Shaping the Postwar Balance of Power: Multilateralism in NATO," *International Organization* (Summer 1992): 633–80; and in Robert L. Rothstein, *Alliances and Small Powers* (New York: Columbia University Press, 1968). For nonmilitary activities, see, for example, various issues of *Human Rights Quarterly*, published by Johns Hopkins University Press.

10. For a historical survey, see Alan James, *Peacekeeping in International Politics* (New York: St. Martin's Press, 1990).

11. For a thoughtful exposé of the dilemmas surrounding attempts to ensure nation-state security, see Charles Yost, *The Insecurity of Nations: International Relations in the Twentieth Century* (New York: Praeger, 1968). For a broader survey, see John Spanier, *Games Nations Play*, 8th ed. (Washington, DC: Congressional Quarterly Press, 1992).

12. Quoted in Leland M. Goodrich, *The United Nations* (New York: Thomas Y. Crowell, 1959), p. 21. See also Theodore A. Wilson, *The First Summit: Roosevelt and Churchill at Placentia Bay* (Boston: Houghton-Mifflin, 1969).

13. Goodrich, *The United Nations*, p. 22. A definitive work on the history of the negotiations leading to the creation of the United Nations is Ruth B. Russell, *A History of the United Nations Charter: The Role of the United States, 1940–1945* (Washington, DC: The Brookings Institution, 1958).

14. Goodrich, *The United Nations*, p. 23.

15. See Stephen S. Goodspeed, *The Nature and Function of International Organization*, 2nd ed: (New York: Oxford University Press, 1967), pp. 81–82.

16. Goodrich, *The United Nations*, p. 22.

17. For background, see David A. Kay, *The New Nations in the United Nations, 1960–1967* (New York: Columbia University Press, 1970).

18. For background see Robert S. Jordan, ed., *International Administration: Its Evolution and Contemporary Applications* (New York: Oxford University Press, 1971).

19. Goodspeed, *International Organization*, pp. 83. See also Article 1 of the UN Charter (Appendix B).

20. Goodspeed, *International Organization*, p. 30.

21. Article 27, par. 3. France and the People's Republic of China are also permanent members in addition to the United States, Britain, and Russia. The number of nonpermanent members was increased to ten from six in 1976. For a further discussion of the powers of the Security Council, see Davidson Nicol, ed., *The United Nations Security Council: Towards Greater Effectiveness* (New York: United Nations Institute for Training and Research, 1982). There is now a growing awareness that Japan and Germany should also be given permanent membership, if not the veto. Both Germany and Japan, with U.S. support, have indicated that they feel entitled to permanent membership. Britain and France have not as yet agreed.

22. See Goodspeed, *International Organization*, p. 83.

23. For details of the conference and discussion of selected issues, see ibid., pp. 85–102; and Russell, *United Nations Charter*.

24. *Congressional Record* 91, p. 6 (July 23, 1945): 7957.

25. Inis Claude, *Swords into Plowshares,* 3rd rev. ed. (New York: Random House, 1964), p. 64.

26. *Issues before the 46th General Assembly of the United Nations* (New York: University Press of America, 1991), p. 279.

27. Quoted in Richard Mayne, *The Community of Europe* (New York: Norton, 1963), p. 81. For background on why there was a propensity to form a regional IGO, see Lord Gladwyn, *The European Idea* (London: Weidenfeld and Nicolson, 1966).

28. Quoted in F. Roy Willis, *France, Germany and the New Europe, 1945–1967* (London: Oxford University Press, 1968), p. 80. For a comparative summary of attempts at regional political unification, see Amitai Etzioni, *Political Unification: A Comparative Study of Leaders and Forces* (New York: Holt, Rinehart and Winston, 1965).

29. For details, see Willis, *New Europe,* p. 105.

30. Richard Mayne, *The Recovery of Europe* (New York: Harper and Row, 1970), pp. 177–78.

31. Derek Bok, *The First Three Years of the Schuman Plan* (Princeton, NJ: Princeton University, Department of Economics and Sociology, International Finance Section, 1955), p. 3.

32. For background on the nature of the Commonwealth during this period, see W. B. Hamilton, Kenneth Robinson, and C.D.W. Goodwin, eds. *A Decade of the Commonwealth, 1955–1964* (Durham, NC: Duke University Press, 1966).

33. A survey of the early history of the European communities from the perspective of European union can be found in Susanne J. Bodenheimer, *Political Union: A Microcosm of European Politics, 1960–1966* (Leyden, Holland: A. W. Sijthoff, 1967).

34. For a description of the relationship of EFTA to other Western European IGOs in the early years, see J. Warren Nystrom and Peter Malof, *The Common Market: European Community in Action* (Princeton, NJ: Van Nostrand, 1962). See also Thomas Franck and Edward Weisband, eds., *A Free Trade Association* (New York: New York University Press, 1968). Most recently, EFTA and the EC have agreed to create a free trade area, thus drawing on the strength of each IGO in a complementary, rather than competitive, fashion.

35. For details, see Werner Feld, *The European Common Market and the World* (Englewood Cliffs, NJ: Prentice-Hall, 1967), pp. 71–76. For a review of the special position of France, see Simon Serfaty, *France, de Gaulle, and Europe: The Policy of the Fourth and Fifth Republics Toward the Continent* (Baltimore: Johns Hopkins University Press, 1968).

36. For a good overview of the status of Britain at this time, see David Calleo, *Britain's Future* (New York: Horizon Press, 1968).

37. For a detailed study of this period of postwar history, see Ernst H. Van der Beugel, *From Marshall Aid to Atlantic Partnership* (New York: Elsevier, 1966).

38. Eric Stein and Peter Hay, *Law and Institutions in the Atlantic Area* (Indianapolis, IN: Bobbs-Merrill, 1967), p. 1032. For a survey of the institutions of NATO as well as the conclusions of the North Atlantic Treaty, see Robert S. Jordan, *The NATO International Staff Secretariat, 1952–1957: A Study in International Administration* (London: Oxford University Press, 1967).

39. Stein and Hay, *Law and Institutions.*

40. See Theodore Achilles, "U.S. Role in Negotiations that Led to Atlantic

Alliance," *NATO Review* 27 (August 1979): 11–14. See also Lawrence S. Kaplan and Sidney R. Snider, eds., *Fingerprints on History: The NATO Memories of Theodore C. Achilles* (Kent, OH: Kent State University, 1992.)

41. Quoted in Alexander Rendel, "The Alliance's Anxious Birth," *NATO Review* 27 (June 1979): 15.

42. Ibid., p. 17.

43. For a full discussion of these problems, see ibid., pp. 17–20. See also Robert Strausz-Hupé et al., *Building the Atlantic World* (New York: Harper and Row, 1963).

44. Achilles, "U.S. Role."

45. Paragraph 3 of Senate Resolution 239, June 1948, *Congressional Record* 94, p. 7846.

46. Achilles, "U.S. Role," p. 14. See also Edwin H. Fedder, *NATO: The Dynamics of Alliance in the Postwar World* (New York: Dodd, Mead, 1973).

47. Achilles, "U.S. Role."

48. For details, see Endicott Reid, "The Miraculous Birth of the North Atlantic Alliance," *NATO Review* 20 (December 1980): 14–17.

49. Quoted in Theodore C. Achilles, "U.S. Role in Negotiations that Led to Atlantic Alliance: Part 2," *NATO Review* 27 (October 1979): 16–19.

50. *New York Times,* May 15, 1947. For a survey of how the treaty provisions were applied in the first 20 years, see Robert S. Jordan, *Political Leadership in NATO: A Study in Multinational Diplomacy* (Boulder, CO: Westview Press, 1979).

51. Arthur S. Banks et al., *The Political Handbook of the World* (Binghamton, NY: CSA Publications, 1990), pp. 824–25.

52. For details, see Sidney Dell, *A Latin American Common Market?* (London: Oxford University Press, 1966), pp. 125–34.

53. *The Yearbook of World Affairs* (Boulder, CO: Westview Press, 1979), p. 287.

54. Yale H. Ferguson, "Latin America," in *Comparative Regional Systems,* ed. Werner J. Feld and Gavin Boyd (New York: Pergamon Press, 1980), p. 342. Multinationals were attracted by the favorable investment climates in those states, especially Argentina and Brazil, and by the large internal markets these states offered.

55. For details, see Dell, *Common Market,* pp. 197–205.

56. Ferguson, "Latin America."

57. *Christian Science Monitor,* March 18, 1992, p. 11.

58. Rupert Emerson, "Pan-Africanism," in *Africa and World Order,* ed. Norman J. Padelford and R. Emerson (New York: Praeger, 1963), p. 7.

59. Berhanykun Andemicael, *The OAU and the UN* (New York: Africana, 1976), p. 11.

60. Ibid., p. 31; and Articles 8–11 of the UN Charter.

61. Andemicael, *The OAU,* pp. 32–33.

62. Ibid., pp. 36–39.

63. For a detailed analysis of the major disputes, see ibid., pp. 45–100.

64. For a very thorough analysis of the OAU-UN cooperation on this problem, see ibid., pp. 101–55.

65. Banks, *The Political Handbook of the World* (Binghamton, NY: CSA Publications, 1991), pp. 868–69.

66. Charles E. Morrison and Astri Suhrke, *Strategies of Survival: The Foreign Policy Dilemmas of Smaller Asian States* (New York: St. Martin's Press, 1978), p. 265.

67. Quoted by Termask Chalermpalanuapap, "A Novel Approach to Regional

Integration" (Paper presented at the 1982 Louisiana Political Science Association Meeting, New Orleans, March 12–13, 1982), p. 7.

68. Ibid., p. 17.

69. See, for example, Heinz M. Hauser, *A Financing System for Science and Technology for Development,* Science and Technology Working Papers no. 13 (New York: United Nations Institute for Training and Research, 1982); and Eleanor B. Steinberg and Joseph A. Yager, *New Means of Financing International Needs* (Washington, DC: The Brookings Institution, 1978).

70. For an examination of Security Council practices, see Sydney D. Bailey, *Voting in the Security Council* (Bloomington, IN: Indiana University Press, 1969).

71. See Article 148 of the EEC Treaty. A thorough discussion of the legal powers of the EC, its members, and their exercise can be found in A. W. Green, *Political Integration by Jurisprudence* (Leydon, Holland: A. W. Sijthoff, 1969).

72. For a thorough analysis of the earlier phase of Britain's relationship to the EC, see Miriam Camps, *Britain and the European Community, 1955–1963* (Princeton, NJ: Princeton University Press, 1964).

3 INSTITUTIONAL AND BUREAUCRATIC DEVELOPMENTS

It was pointed out in Chapter 2 that the establishment of an IGO requires the determination of the kind of structure the prospective organization is to have. The nature and shape of this institutional framework obviously must relate to the task performance and functions that the IGO is expected to carry out. However, as was also seen in Chapter 2, political desiderata may impose constraints on purely rational considerations that are used to set up an effective management model. These desiderata have an impact, not only on the organizational details of the IGO institutions, but also on the power conferred on them by the member states.

THE RANGE OF INSTITUTIONAL PATTERNS

A look at the many IGOs existing in the world today reveals a great variety of institutional frameworks. On the one hand, there are the very extensive and intricate frameworks of the United Nations and the EC, whose institutions are housed in skyscrapers and many other buildings in different cities and states. On the other hand, much smaller and less complicated IGOs also exist for political, economic, and technical purposes. Some of these were discussed in Chapter 2.

What are some of the basic factors that determine the extent and intricacy of an IGO's institutional framework? Perhaps the most important factor is *the scope and complexity of the tasks to be performed*. In some cases, these tasks are in several issue areas, as is the case with the United Nations whose concerns range from dispute settlement and conflict resolution to humanitarian and human rights concerns and economic and social development. In others, the tasks require the detailed management of various economic

Figure 3.1
Institutional Frameworks

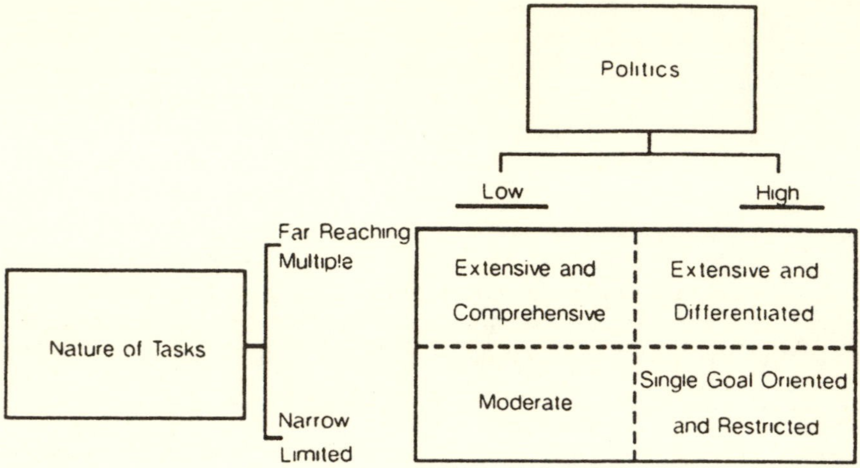

or functional sectors; the best example of this is the EC and its detailed operation of the Common Agricultural Policy (CAP), which was regenerated in the fall of 1992 within the context of world trade negotiations under GATT auspices.

Another influential factor is *the kind of politics involved in the IGO's operation:* low politics or high politics. The former term more often refers primarily to economic or social matters with accompanying technical problems, while the latter deals with strategic or defense issues and political matters that appear to affect significantly the national interest. Although the distinction between low and high politics has become blurred, in both cases, the more far-reaching and specific the tasks to be performed by an IGO, the more extensive and comprehensive will be the institutional framework; if the tasks to be carried out are relatively narrow, only a moderate framework is used. The matrix in Figure 3.1 provides a schematic picture. However, it should be noted that in actuality, IGO institutional frameworks do not always fit neatly into any schema. This is especially true when INGO activities play into IGO activities, which is increasingly the case. The United Nations is generally a high-politics IGO with multiple tasks (peacekeeping and concern for the global economy, humanitarian, and social matters). However, the United Nations also performs many tasks of a low-politics nature, primarily through its specialized and affiliated agencies. Moreover, many UN agencies today perform tasks that bridge the two distinctions, of which food relief (World Food Program or WFP), refugee resettlement (UN High Commissioner for Refugees or UNHCR), and nuclear arms control and inspection are examples. NATO's high-politics task has diminished inspection-relevance, although with the end of the Cold War, it is gradually redefining its role to be more of a peacekeeping organization in conjunction with both European and out-of-area conflicts. The EC is basically a multiple-low-politics IGO with some high-politics aspirations. An example is its attempt, along with the United Nations, to mediate a settlement to the ethnic warfare in the former Yugoslavia. If the Maastricht Treaty on Political and Economic Union were to be fully implemented, then the EC would clearly enter into the realm of geopolitics, at least potentially. The Universal Postal Union (UPU), which is a part of the United Nations, is a typical low-politics IGO with tasks limited to the postal service.

TASK PERFORMANCE

As discussed in Chapter 1, the fundamental mission of IGO institutions is *the management of cooperation* in various fields in order to carry out the tasks for which the IGO was created. This involves the search for compromises in conflictual situations whose origins may have been military, political, or economic. The conflicts also may have had ethnic origins. The mission also involves the coordination of the member states' national policies and activities in economic and security issue areas as far as necessary to assure the success of the IGO's assigned functions, under the powers conferred upon it.[1]

Depending on the issue area with which the IGO is concerned, the institutional framework must provide the appropriate means for its task performance (see Figure 3.1). This includes the necessary physical facilities for deliberation, consultation, and negotiations within and among institutions and between member state governments and institutions, as well as logistical support for its operations. For example, the sharply expanded responsibilities of the United Nations in peacemaking and peacekeeping require that new sources of funding be found. Secretary-General Boutros Boutros-Ghali has identified several possibilities for obtaining these funds. One could be a $50 million peacekeeping start-up fund; another could be a $1 billion peace endowment created from private and public donations; a third, which is doubtless not likely to be popular, could be charging interest on unpaid dues (the United States has been in arrears); while a fourth could be taxing such international activities as airline tickets or arms sales.

Another important instrumentality authorized for many IGOs is the *formulation and implementation of pertinent policies*. In some IGOs, such as the United Nations and the EC, several institutions or organs participate in policymaking. The implementation of these policies generally is carried out by member-state agencies, but also involves INGOs. Member governments opposed to the policies, therefore, are likely to forgo or frustrate implementing policies they oppose. However, in the EC, limited implementation is performed by the Commission in the agricultural and antitrust sectors, and both the IMF and the World Bank implement their own policies by granting or refusing loans according to predetermined implementation criteria. There have been, however, instances when the United States, as the largest donor, has influenced granting decisions for its foreign-policy considerations. Also, delicate issue areas of arms transfers and politically related "high-tech" purchases raise questions concerning the international control or monitoring capabilities of the United Nations. In the case of Iraq in regard to nuclear matters and the plight of the Kurds, or of Somalia in regard to food distribution, the UN Security Council has overridden questions of national sovereignty (i.e., interference in internal affairs) that often had prevented international action.

Policymaking and implementation by IGOs involve a series of decisions within the institutional framework. A taxonomy of IGO decisions and other factors of decision making in IGO institutions will be examined in Chapter 4.[2]

The instrumentalities for task performance vary from IGO to IGO. However, all IGOs *collect and disseminate information* on their issue areas. Dissemination can be to relevant institutional bureaucracies or organs or to the member states (usually through the governments, but sometimes also directly to the people). The higher the quality (in both form and substance) of the information disseminated, the more it can contribute to the success of deliberations, consultations, and possible negotiations within the institutional framework. The Bank for International Settlements (BIS) is a good example of an IGO that generates high-quality information with resulting success in task performance.

Regardless of whether IGOs themselves carry out the implementation of their policies or whether this task is handled by the member governments, IGOs often are called on to *monitor the implementation process.* In situations involving the possible use of force, this function is reflected in the mandate to investigate and report to the major political organ responsible for dispute settlement (such as the Security Council, the CSCE, or the regional peacekeeping body concerned). The recurrent stand-offs between Iraq and the United Nations over access of the UN teams for inspection purposes is an important example. This is, therefore, a very significant dimension of task performance, but one that may be difficult to achieve at times, as it may impinge on what member governments consider their national prerogatives, or it may be seen as interference in domestic affairs. The crisis in the former Yugoslav Federation is a case in point, in that it began as what Serbia (and Montenegro), at least, regarded as an internal matter. Then, after international recognition of the other seceding republics, Serbian attempts to rearrange through forceful means the ethnic configuration of the neighboring internationally-recognized republics drew the attention of the UN and European regional IGOs, as well as numerous INGOs.

For other IGO tasks, monitoring events and preparing reports for discussion and dissemination serve the function of supervision of policy implementation or "consciousness-raising" on both the international and national levels. The monitoring of the implementation of the resolutions (or plans of action) of various conferences, such as those concerning women, nuclear weapons, human rights, population movements, the environment, and food, are examples. Often review conferences are held to reexamine the issues. The Helsinki Accords, the implementation of which was the responsibility of the Conference on Security and Cooperation in Europe (CSCE), and the NPT Treaty, which involves the International Atomic Energy Agency (IAEA), provide for such reviews, as discussed in Chapter 7. The constant reexamination of the implementation of Security Council resolutions, such as those concerning the former Yugoslavia, Haiti, Israel, Somalia, and Iraq have resulted in new precedents being set which have widened the range of monitoring activities in member states. The increasing use of IGO and INGO personnel to monitor national elections, such as those held in Angola, El Salvador, Haiti and Cambodia, is another example. Regional IGOs also have played monitoring and inspection roles concerning such activities as elections, human rights abuses, arms transfers, refugees, and drug trafficking. Indeed, the scope and success of IGO policymaking and the successful supervision of the implementation process depend on the perceptions of the member governments as to how far IGO policies promote or hinder the attainment of national priority goals.

Less stringent (yet not unimportant, and often effective) institutional instrumentalities for task performance are *nonbinding recommendations and resolutions*. Obviously, they do not have to be heeded by any government objecting to them, but the repeated passage of recommendations, especially in a politically visible body such as the UN General Assembly, or a global ad hoc conference is bound to affect world opinion and influence the decision-making processes of member governments.

Finally, in some cases, IGO institutions are authorized to *render judgments* regarding obscure or ambiguous factual or legal situations. For example, the UN Security Council may have to issue a judgment as to whether the behavior of a state can be considered an act of aggression, or the EC Commission may need to make a determination as to whether the behavior of a company or corporation in the Common Market constitutes an infringement of the EEC antitrust provisions. Complaints to GATT concerning trade and tariff abuses can result in judgments noting offenders. The Security Council's attempts to inspect suspected Iraqi chemical, nuclear and ballistic missile testing installations is another example. The monitoring of elections, as mentioned earlier, can be considered yet another example. The authority to make such findings is a significant instrument in an IGO's performance of its various tasks.

IGOs WITH PLENARY GOVERNING BODIES

A large majority of IGOs have plenary bodies on which all member states are represented. Historically, these bodies were often known as *conferences,* and this designation continues to be used today, as exemplified by the General Conferences of the ILO and of UNESCO. Other names for plenary organs are congress (the Congress of Vienna, the UPU, and the World Meteorological Organization or WMO), assembly (the United Nations, the Council of Europe, and CSCE), parliament (the EC), and council (the conciliar tradition of Christianity as adapted to the modern state system, although this term can also refer to bodies with limited membership and executive functions).

The frequency of plenary body meetings varies with the kind of function for which the IGO was created. Some meet only once every five years (such as the UPU), while the European Parliament (EP) now meets monthly (except July and August) and the UN General Assembly meets at least once a year. Under the Nuclear Non-Proliferation Treaty (NPT), review conferences are held every five years. The General Assembly is formally in session from September through mid-December, although often it meets even longer, budget permitting, as reflected in its tendency to hold "resumed sessions" sometime in the following year. Some General Assembly "special" sessions can last up to a month.

Plenary bodies normally engage in deliberations on broad policy questions, make appropriate recommendations to member states, and give general directions to the IGO bureaucracies. However, in some cases, they become involved in IGO management or make proposals on more detailed issues. For example, the Plenipotentiary Conference of the ITU establishes the organization's budget for the forthcoming five years. The UN General Assembly, whether convened in general or in special session, often makes detailed recommendations on economic matters, such as the resolutions passed during the 1970s embracing the so-called New International Economic Order (NIEO).[3] The Consultative Assembly of the Council of Europe makes specific proposals on draft conventions of various kinds, and the UN Security Council has engaged in wide-ranging activities with what can be termed a policy-implementing as well as policymaking nature, involving, for example, Iraq, Somalia, and Cambodia. Incidentally, the United Nations had authorized twelve peacekeeping forces and observation missions from 1948 through 1988, and fourteen from 1989–1992. In many cases, the plenary bodies review and act on the work of standing committees whose membership is open to all members, or on responsibilities charged to the executive head, such as the secretary-general.

In the discussion that follows, the work of IGOs' plenary governing bodies is highlighted in order that their overall role can be understood. This role is one of transmitting political guidance and program instructions from governments to national, regional, or international bureaucracies. Our first category of IGOs to be discussed will be in the UN family, and here we will concentrate on the World Health Organization (WHO) and the International Civil Aviation Organization (ICAO). We will then consider regional bodies, including the Organization of American States (OAS) and the Central American Common Market (CACM). A more detailed, illustrative case is presented concerning the Economic Community of West African States (ECOWAS), especially in connection with its efforts to end the civil war in Liberia.

The World Health Organization (WHO)

The basic institutional structure of WHO consists of the World Health Assembly, the Executive Board, and the Secretariat.

The Assembly is composed of delegates representing member states, with each country having a chief delegate and up to three other delegates. They are chosen for their technical competence in the field of health, and preferably represent the national health administration of the member states. Each member country has one vote, regardless of the financial contributions made to the organization. The Assembly meets twice a year. Its main tasks are to approve the program and the proposed budget for the year and to make decisions on major questions of policy.

The Executive Board is made up of technical specialists in areas of health who are appointed by the Assembly. It meets at least twice a year to prepare the agenda for each session of the Assembly and to submit a general program for specific periods. Located in Geneva, Switzerland, meetings of the Assembly and Executive Board are normally open to the public.

The Secretariat, with a director-general as its technical and administrative head, provides the staff for WHO and is the real seat of power. It is important to keep in mind that the field staff serve in an entirely different capacity than the administrative staff and often work under extreme hardships in the field. Officials of WHO, as other international civil servants, are recruited not only for their efficiency and expertise, but also to keep the organization internationally representative. The staff, according to the WHO constitution, may not accept instruction from any authority external to WHO.

The operations of WHO are much more decentralized than those of other UN-related IGOs. The advantage has been to bring the organization into closer touch with the most immediate needs of the member states and has enabled WHO to begin to help each country in taking the appropriate steps toward developing effective public health services. To fully implement these objectives, WHO has set up six regional organizations, each headed by a regional director appointed by the Executive Board and aided by a regional staff and supporting committee. They are located in Washington, D.C. for the Americas, Brazzaville for Africa, Alexandria for the Eastern Mediterranean, New Delhi for South-East Asia, Copenhagen for Europe, and Manila for the Western Pacific. These widespread WHO structures have caused problems at times for other members of the UN family, such as the

Food and Agricultural Organization (FAO), that do not have sufficiently wide coverage to assure effective communications with the WHO regional offices.

The essence of WHO's work is the application of scientific knowledge and skilled manpower to the study of health problems and to the search for their solutions. The prevention and control of disease is a major activity, as witnessed by WHO's efforts to control the spread of AIDS. Tuberculosis and cholera are diseases that were once thought to be on the way to eradication but are making a comeback throughout the world, as both civil disorder and international travel proliferate. WHO cooperates in the achievement of this task with many other UN agencies, including the ILO, UNESCO, FAO, and the UN Development Program (UNDP). Indeed, a very large part of WHO's attention is devoted to problems of disease, where issues of health are intertwined with the general social and political environment, and cannot be solved by treating the medical aspects alone. Widespread hunger and malnutrition can be caused by both natural and man-made disasters. Whatever the policies adopted or actions taken by WHO, its ultimate organ to which to report is the ECOSOC.

The International Civil Aviation Organization (ICAO)

The ICAO also has a plenary organ for its policy and decision-making procedures, the Assembly, but its raison d'être flows primarily from technological reasons. Advances in technology and the necessity of border-crossing collaboration in order to enjoy the optimum benefits of this new technology have provided tasks for the ICAO. An obvious example is the advent of the jet aircraft (both supersonic and subsonic), with its tremendous increase in range, speed, and carrying capacity.

In a world of sovereign states, international collaboration is an imperative that was recognized as early as 1917 when the International Commission for Air Navigation was established by the Paris Convention, followed in 1929 by the creation of the Pan-American Convention for Air Navigation. An International Civil Aviation Conference, convened in the fall of 1944 and attended by representatives of fifty-two states, adopted an agreement for the establishment of the ICAO. This agreement reflects a compromise between the radical proposals of Australia and New Zealand, which called for complete international ownership of world airspace, and U.S. aspirations for maximum freedom of the air and unfettered competition. The agreement was ratified in 1947 by the necessary twenty-six states and, shortly thereafter, the ICAO became a Specialized Agency of the United Nations.

The tasks of the ICAO are to develop the principles and techniques of international air navigation and to foster the planning and development of international air transport. These tasks include as particular objectives: (1) to bring about the safe and orderly growth of international civil aviation throughout the world; (2) to encourage the development of appropriate airways, airports, and navigation facilities; (3) to assure safe, regular, efficient, and economic air transport; (4) to ensure respect for the rights of the member states and their fair opportunities to operate international airlines; and (5) to promote flight safety in international air navigation. Clearly, these tasks require the instrumentality of an IGO, although in the performance of these tasks, the ICAO is aided by an INGO, the International Air Transport Association (IATA), which can be, and is, influenced by the ICAO.[4]

In this connection, it should be pointed out that the world air-traffic market is far bigger than the sum of the bilateral air-traffic markets. Each state forms part of this world market. A state is not only an origin and a destination, but also a junction of international air service and international air traffic.[5]

The ICAO structural framework consists of a plenary Assembly in which every member state (164 as of 1991) is represented and a Council which (as of 1991) was composed of thirty-three members elected for three-year terms. Bridging the plenary and limited composition components of the ICAO is the Council, which is in permanent session and which deals with the day-to-day activities of the organization. The Council also elects between nine and eleven members of the Air Navigation Commission, who are chosen on the basis of their technical expertise in avionics. Another subsidiary organ is the Air Transport Committee, which has thirty members who must be representatives on the Council.[6] Two major issues recently addressed by the Council were the downing by the United States of Iran Airflight 655 in the Persian Gulf in July 1988 and the bombing of PanAm Flight 103 over Scotland in December of that year, in which 270 people died. The Soviet downing of the Korean Airlines Flight 007 was resolved when Russian President Boris Yeltsin, in a state visit to Korea in 1992, turned over the "black boxes" of the airliners to the Korean government and, for the first time, it was admitted that the plane had unintentionally strayed over (then) Soviet territory and had not been on a spy mission.

The ICAO Secretariat, another central body, is headed by the president of the Council, while the individual holding the title of secretary-general serves as deputy to the council president in charge of administrative matters. This means that the member governments are very much in control over the ICAO operations.[7]

The Organization of American States (OAS)

The aims of the OAS are detailed in the Charter signed in Bogotá, Colombia, in 1948 and amended in Buenos Aires, Argentina, in 1967. These aims make the OAS a very comprehensive IGO. They can be broken down into three categories:

1. Common action is authorized for the peace and security of the hemisphere, and disputes among member states are to be settled by pacific means (Article 4);
2. Common political, juridical, and economic problems are to be solved in the first instance through the facilities of the OAS; and
3. Cooperative action is to be taken to promote economic, social, and cultural development.

To assure proper task performance, the institutional framework of the OAS is quite extensive. The supreme organ, in which each member state has one vote, is the OAS General Assembly. Prior to 1970, this was called the OAS Inter-American Conference. While the Conference normally met only once every five years, the Assembly convenes annually. It decides general policy, determines the structure and functions of the OAS' organs, and has the authority to consider any matter relating to friendly relations among the member states (Article 33). Obviously, its terms of reference are very broad.

Another plenary body of the OAS is the permanent OAS Council, which meets very frequently and has executive functions. It operates at the ambassadorial level (through permanent representatives) and is the continuation of the former Governing Board. The Council's main tasks have been to supervise the Pan-American Union, which earlier had served as the international secretariat of the OAS; to coordinate the activities of specialized conferences and organizations; to promote collaboration with the United Nations and other IGOs; and to adopt the budget. In addition, it formulates the statutes of its subsidiary organs that are themselves plenary bodies: the Inter-American Economic and Social Council, the Inter-American Juridical Committee, and the Inter-American Council for Education, Science, and Culture. Finally, the OAS Council has the authority to create its own committees; for example, the OAS General Committee, the OAS Committee on Finance, and the OAS Permanent Committee on Inter-American Conferences.

In order to carry out the OAS peacekeeping function, the Meeting of Consultation of Ministers of Foreign Affairs plays a prominent role as a consulting organ. Its task is to consider problems of an urgent nature (Article 39) and to serve as the organ of consultation under the OAS Treaty. This body is also a plenary unit on which all member states are represented. It can be convened by a majority of the OAS Council at the request of any member government. However, a meeting is obligatory and must be convened without delay in the event of an armed attack against a member state or against the region as defined in the Rio Treaty (i.e., the Western Hemisphere). If the Meeting of Consultation of Ministers of Foreign Affairs is not obligatory, the Council may constitute itself as the provisional organ of consultation. This gives the Council considerable power and, in fact, it has often been able to settle disputes without summoning a meeting of foreign ministers. The instruments used by the Council are similar to those of the UN Security Council, including appointing investigating committees and receiving formal findings as to the responsibility of the parties involved.

The Pan-American Union was formerly the central and permanent bureaucratic organ of the OAS. This function is now carried out by the General Secretariat with a budget of more than $75 million. It is located in Washington, D.C., and is headed by a secretary-general who is elected by the Council. The secretary-general may participate in the work of any of the OAS organs but does not have the right to vote. The Secretariat consists of approximately 1,200 international civil servants who, in order to safeguard their independence, are under obligation not to seek or to receive outside instructions from the member states (which, in turn, are enjoined not to tempt them). Many of the civil servants are highly skilled specialists in the various fields of OAS endeavor.

Aiding in the task performance of the OAS are the aforementioned Inter-American Economic and Social Council and the Inter-American Council for Education, Science, and Culture. They supervise extensive programs, draft treaties, and initiate conferences under OAS Assembly guidance. Specialized organizations working with the OAS deal with problems of agriculture, child welfare, health, women's affairs, and Indian issues.

The membership of the OAS up to 1985 included the traditional South and Central American states plus the United States; Canada never expressed interest in becoming a member. In December 1985 a protocol amended the admission rules for the OAS, offering membership to all regional states that were members of the United Nations on December 10, 1985, and thus permitting the entrance to the OAS of Belize, Guyana, Bermuda, Guadaloupe, Martinique, and Montserrat. At the Twenty-First General Assembly, in June 1991, an interesting resolution was adopted to assure the maintenance of the democratic form of government which had by then been adopted by all OAS members (a "first" in OAS history). In the event of a coup against any of the governments, an emergency meeting of the General Assembly must be called within ten days to deal with the problem.[8]

The Central American Common Market (CACM)

Efforts to unite the states of Central America have a long history. After gaining independence from Spain in 1821, Guatemala, El Salvador, Nicaragua, Honduras, and Costa Rica formed a single political unit in 1824 called the Federation of Central America; its constitution was patterned after that of the United States.[9] This lasted until 1838, when it became apparent that it was impossible for the federal government to achieve full consolidation. Thereafter, the Federation was dissolved.[10]

Since then, several attempts have been made to link the five states again into a single political unit. For example, it appeared in the 1890s that a loose confederation—the Greater Republic of Central America—might succeed, but divergent politics in the individual states proved too strong and the attempt at creating a confederation ended in failure.[11]

Since all five Central American states have relatively small populations (only Guatemala has more than five million inhabitants) and since they form a compact geographic unit, a strong case could be made for multilateral economic cooperation, and this was indeed a strong motivation. Enhancing this motivation was the economic doctrine developed by the UN Economic Commission for Latin America (ECLA) which argued for regional economic integration. The central argument of ECLA was that the overall level of economic development could be raised only through forming a unified market, diversifying the Central American economies, encouraging industrialization, and changing the makeup of foreign trade.[12] Underlying these efforts, of course, was the history of the states' attempts at political unification during the nineteenth century and their low level of economic capabilities and resources.

To translate the ECLA blueprint and to satisfy Central American aspirations for closer collaboration, the CACM was created by the General Treaty of Central American Economic Integration, which was signed by Guatemala, El Salvador, Honduras, and Nicaragua in December 1960; Costa Rica acceded in July 1962. The treaty obliged the states to eliminate tariffs on intraregional trade and to establish a common external tariff. It provided for the establishment of the Central American Bank for Economic Integration and set up a special regime for industrialization to aid the integration process. Industries that qualified for this regime would enjoy privileged status within the five states, including free trade, special consideration with respect to the reduction of import duties on imported raw materials, and preferences on needed imports.[13]

The institutional structure agreed on in the General Treaty was limited. The highest organ, the Central American Economic Council, was composed of the respective economic ministers. Their task was to integrate the Central American economies and to coordinate the economic policies of the member states. Consensus appeared to be necessary for all Council decisions. The application and administration of the treaty were entrusted to an Executive Council consisting of representatives from each member government. Although it theoretically could adopt resolutions by majority vote, the Council (when ruling on a matter) had first to determine by unanimous vote whether the matter was to be decided by unanimity or by simple majority (Article XXI). A Secretariat, headquartered in Guatemala City, was headed by a secretary-general who was appointed by the Economic Council for a term of three years.

While it is apparent that the institutional voting procedures did not infringe on the autonomy of the member states, the regime for integrating industries imposed obligations that affected their freedom of action. New industries were to be distributed to all member states on as equal a basis as possible and, once a particular integrated industry was allocated to a specific state, a similar second plant could not be built in the same or another member state until all five member states had been assigned their particular industrial facilities. Hence, the Central American scheme insisted on direct and coordinated intervention in the distribution of industries in the region. This provoked considerable criticism as a restriction on the free operation of market forces. Moreover, once a plant in a particular industry was set up, its products enjoyed the benefits of free trade within the region. Member governments were enjoined from imposing any kind of trade barriers on the border-crossing movements of these products.[14]

The hopes of many Central Americans that the CACM could turn out to be a successful experiment in economic integration seemed to become realized in the 1960s. By mid-1966, almost all the tariffs on items in intra-CACM trade had been eliminated, and by 1969, a common external tariff protected 97.5 percent of the items imported into the region. Intraregional exports jumped from 8 percent of the member states' exports in 1960 to 27 percent in 1970. Equally important, the structure of intraregional trade changed during that period, with shipments of manufactured products increasing their share and foodstuffs and live animals decreasing as a percentage of exports. On the other hand, the regime for integrating industries yielded few results. Only Guatemala and Nicaragua experienced the establishment of such industries.[15] The likely reason was an unfavorable perception of prospective benefits by both entrepreneurs and governments; the latter also had a concern about rising interdependence costs.

By the early 1970s, a number of problems had arisen that had their roots in governmental and elite perceptions in some of the member states that benefits from the CACM were shared unequally and that the consequent disadvantages outweighed the advantages. Some governments attributed their balance-of-payment difficulties to the progress of trade liberalization. Others felt that the integration industries scheme did not work properly.

Finally, as the result of the so-called soccer war in 1969 between El Salvador and Honduras, trade between the two states ceased and some of the CACM institutions stopped functioning. The level of intraregional exports as a proportion of total exports declined.[16] Moreover, internal conflict in Nicaragua, El Salvador, and Guatemala had debilitating effects on the CACM. The capabilities and resources of the five Central American member states, which were strengthened initially during the 1960s, then weakened. National concerns with the unequal distribution of benefits among the members of the CACM, compounded by internal struggles for political power and external political-military intervention, caused cooperation through an IGO to appear as an exercise in futility. However, Honduras and El Salvador concluded a peace treaty in 1980 and regional economic ministers meeting in Managua in April of that year reaffirmed their basic support for the CACM. In the meantime, Nicaragua ended its civil war and the governments of all CACM states may now be considered to be in the "center-right" category.

Efforts that began in 1984 to "reactivate" the CACM have continued, and successful meetings were held with EC representatives to generate aid for that purpose. At their summit meeting in June 1990, the presidents of five CACM member states once again focused on regional economic integration, calling for the lowering of tariffs and other trade barriers and joint efforts to improve roads and other elements of the transportation sector. A follow-up summit in December of that year pledged to institute uniform customs tariffs by December 1992, which was an elusive goal although intrabloc trade in 1989 had reached 12 percent of total exports.[17]

The Economic Community of West African States (ECOWAS): An Illustrative Case

Since its establishment in 1958, the Economic Commission for Africa (ECA) has encouraged the formation of a West African regional economic community that would cut across the Franco-British linguistic barrier that was erected during colonial times. These efforts received a major boost in 1961, when Nnuamdi Azikiwe, then governor-general of the Federation of Nigeria, advocated the creation of a West African common market as a means of bringing about unity in the subregion.[18]

However, while the ECA and West African leaders such as Azikiwe were working toward integration, President Kwame Nkrumah of Ghana (the first British West African colony to gain independence) was disengaging from such British West African institutions as the West Africa Currency Board, the West African Produce Marketing Board, and the West African Airways.[19] These subregional institutions were among the few left behind by the British that could have served as foundations for post-independence cooperation. As the other British West African colonies gained their independence, they followed Ghana's unfortunate example, which led Azikiwe to observe that despite his much-espoused pan-Africanism, Nkrumah actually worked against his own ideology.[20]

In contrast, postcolonial French West Africa (excluding Sékou Touré's Guinea) remained under French leadership through a series of treaties of cooperation and the formation of such subregional organizations as the African and Malagacy Common Organization (OCAM) and the *Conseil de l'Entente*.[21] This solidarity among francophone states helped widen the gap that already existed between the English-speaking and the French-speaking states within the region.

The period from Ghana's independence in 1957 through the Nigerian civil war up to 1972 was marked by inaction, hesitation, and vacillation in regard to efforts leading toward integration. This was in spite of the institutional support from ECA, which organized periodic research conferences on economic integration.[22] However, soon after the conclusion of the civil war, the Nigerian Head of State, Yakubu Gowon, began to actively promote a regional common market. He believed that by creating the Economic Community of West African States (ECOWAS), the rift between anglophone and francophone states that had grown up as a result of the overt, and sometimes covert, support that Senegal and the Ivory Coast had given to the breakaway state of Biafra could be closed.[23] Gowon's diplomacy enabled Nigeria to win the cooperation of the other states in West Africa. The result was the negotiation of the Treaty of Lagos, which made ECOWAS the first economic and political grouping embracing all of the states of West Africa (including Liberia, which had never been under colonial rule).

The Treaty of Lagos. The principal policymaking organ of ECOWAS, as provided in Chapter II, Article 5, of the Treaty signed in 1975, was the Authority of Heads of States and Governments, known as "The Authority." It is composed of the heads of the sixteen member states and is responsible for setting the general policy of the Community, and for exercising control over the work of the Executive Secretary and the Secretariat.[24] The Authority meets at least once a year. The executive secretary, who is appointed by and is directly responsible to the Authority, serves a four-year term that can be renewed once. The official languages are French and English.

Article 6 of the Treaty provides for a Council of Ministers that is composed of two representatives from each member state. Meeting at least twice a year, the Council acts as an advisory body to the Authority but can also issue directives on its own to the subordinate institutions of the Community. These include the Tribunal, the External Auditors, the Defense Council (established by the 1981 Protocol on Mutual Defense Assistance), and other specialized commissions.[25]

Regarding defense matters, as a first step toward achieving stability in the region, the member states adopted a Non-Aggression Protocol in 1978. This was considered important because it was recognized that without an atmosphere free of fear of threats of attack, the chances for creating a common market would be slim.[26] In fact, this was the first purely political decision taken by ECOWAS. Articles 2–4 of the Protocol stipulated that member states shall refrain from committing, encouraging, or condoning any acts of hostility or aggression against the territorial integrity or political independence of other member states.[27] However, while the Protocol forbade the use of force as a means of settling disputes among the member states, it did not address the issue of external aggression: an issue that was vital to the security of the region as a whole.

The Protocol on Mutual Defense Assistance. At the summit meeting held in Lome, Togo, in 1980, the issue of concluding a defense agreement was raised.[28] A committee was created charged with merging two draft proposals put forward by Senegal and Togo. The final draft of the "Protocol on

Mutual Defense Assistance" was signed in May 1981 at a summit meeting held in Freetown, Sierra Leone.

The Protocol, otherwise known as the Defense Pact, became effective on October 23, 1987. Chapter II, Article 2, of the Pact stipulates: "Member states declare and accept that any armed threat or aggression directed against any member state shall constitute a threat or aggression against the Community."[29] Also, Article 3 specifies that "member states resolve to give mutual aid and assistance for defense against any armed threat or aggression." This provision means that if a member state becomes a victim of aggression by a nonmember, the other member states will *automatically* come to its aid.[30]

In the case of an intra-ECOWAS conflict or an internal conflict within a member state that is engineered or actively supported by sources external to the region and that is likely to endanger the peace and stability of the entire region, the Protocol in Article 4(b) stipulates that "the Authority shall decide on the situation in full collaboration with the Head of State and Government of the country concerned." As pointed out, however, the Defense Protocol prohibited military intervention by the Community if a conflict remained purely internal within the member state, thus excluding various forms of civil unrest that may or may not lead to civil war. Nonetheless, besides serving as a deterrent to potential outside intervention, the Protocol provided for a peacekeeping force if, in the judgment of the Community, the need for one should arise.

The benefits of such an arrangement for ECOWAS were obvious. It could help minimize the vulnerability of individual member states, and especially those that were very poor, through sharing in collective security. Thus, the member states could avoid a "permanent obsession with war and agression," thereby enjoying the peace of mind resulting from each state knowing that "it need not fear its neighbor which is ready to come to its aid in the event of any outside aggression."[31] Furthermore, to the extent that the member states refrained from unnecessary competition in arms acquisition, more of their resources could be diverted from defense to other, more productive uses.

This issue of excessive military expenditure is particularly significant because the efforts of leaders to retain their power (which is often obtained initially with barely legitimate means), would almost always take precedence over any considerations of the welfare needs of the peoples concerned. The politics of "regime survival" have often led governments to reward their supporters or to bribe them outright, or to engage in consumption-oriented policies at the expense of long-term economic development.[32]

Soon after the Defense Protocol had been ratified, Radio Nigeria pointed out its potential benefits:

> The significance of a defense protocol cannot be overemphasized, particularly at a time when almost every African country is becoming more and more vulnerable

to external aggression. It is a fact that there cannot be any meaningful development without peace and adequate security. In fact, both are necessary conditions for the welfare and prosperity of the citizens of any state, country, or region. And to the extent that this is the case for member countries of ECOWAS Union, such a pact is indispensable.[33]

In less than a decade, with the outbreak of civil war in Liberia, the Defense Protocol was to be put to the test.

The Liberian Civil War and Its Effect on ECOWAS. The first military operation attempted by ECOWAS was the Liberian peacekeeping operation, which was undertaken to bring to an end one of the most serious conflicts in West Africa since the Nigerian civil war. The problems in Liberia began in December 1989 when Charles Taylor, a minister in Samuel Doe's regime and the leader of the National Patriotic Front of Liberia (NPFL), launched a rebellion against Doe. This insurgence by a small band of dissidents then escalated into large-scale civil war, threatening to undermine the foundation of ECOWAS. There were several reports of border incursions along the Liberia–Sierra Leone and Liberia–Ivory Coast borders, arousing fear that the conflict would spread beyond Liberia. This danger prompted the U.S. embassy in Freetown to warn that "cross-border conflicts are a threat to regional stability and counter-productive."[34]

If the civil war was itself regrettable, its timing was also unfortunate because it coincided with dramatic changes taking place in Eastern Europe and in the Soviet Union that were of global concern. The crisis in the Persian Gulf was also unfolding from late 1990 through mid-1991. All this meant that the Liberian crisis came at a time when African countries were losing whatever leverage they may have had on the erstwhile Cold War superpowers, and thereby the marginalization of Africa in global politics was reaching a new high.[35] As one reporter put it: "Foreign powers with historic influence in West Africa—the U.S., France and Britain—appear to be too busy elsewhere in the world to worry about a region which has lost the limited strategic interest it held before the end of the cold war."[36]

As the global division between the two blocs dissipated, America's interest in Liberia, which historically was tied to the large military intelligence network based there, also dissipated. States that had been important in the Cold War context became not only less important, but dispensable. For example, when U.S. President George Bush expressed his concept of a "New World Order," most notably at the UN General Assembly in 1992, Africa was hardly mentioned.[37] In contrast, when Doe was at the height of his power, Liberia was the largest per capita recipient of American aid to sub-Saharan Africa.[38] An indication of the shift in the attitude of the United States is the fact that when the civil unrest reached dangerous proportions in the latter part of 1990, the 2,000 U.S. Marines sent to assist in removing

American citizens from Monrovia remained at sea rather than intervene to put a stop to the virtual massacre going on.

As a result, the leadership of ECOWAS had no choice but to conclude that the Liberian civil conflict was not only an essentially African problem, but a test of the political will and capacity of ECOWAS to manage the conflict according to the Defense Protocol. At an emergency meeting, the Authority authorized the creation of a peacekeeping force, called the Economic Community Monitoring Group (ECOMOG), to remedy the deteriorating situation. As a complement, a five-state mediating committee was formed to bring about a political solution to the conflict.[39]

The peacekeeping force consisted of 7,000 troops, of which about 75 percent were Nigerian, with the rest from Ghana, the Gambia, Sierra Leone, and Guinea. ECOMOG's mandate was to suppress tribal fighting, restore peace, organize a transitional government, and organize elections for a legitimate government.[40] As a leading newsmagazine put it: "If a five-nation African peacekeeping force can restore order to strife-torn Liberia, it will deserve the world's congratulations."[41]

Unfortunately, the decision to send the peacekeeping contingent led to a reopening of the anglophone-francophone rift in ECOWAS: only seven members of the sixteen-member Community attended, out of which only five states contributed troops. With the notable exception of Guinea, all the other contributing states were anglophone. This rift hindered ECOMOG's ability to achieve its mandate. For example, the recalcitrant Charles Taylor capitalized on the split to continue his war of attrition. He described ECOMOG as "a band of mercenaries" who had been brought in by Samuel Doe to continue his killing of the Liberian people.

Taylor accused Nigeria of being a party to the civil war because of Doe's friendship with President Ibrahim Babangida. Babangida was said to have offered Doe political asylum before he was killed by the Yormie Johnson faction. Taylor declared that Doe and ECOMOG are "our common enemy," and that he was declaring war on both.[42]

Nonetheless, in spite of these fissures, ECOMOG made significant progress when it imposed a shaky cease-fire on the country in November 1990, and some degree of calm was brought to Monrovia. This paved the way for the establishment of the ECOWAS-backed government of Amos Sawyerr.

On the diplomatic front, the ECOWAS mediating committee attempted many initiatives to find a political solution. Self-proclaimed parties and interest groups were invited to international conferences sponsored by ECOWAS to determine Liberia's future. At one such meeting, held in the Ivory Coast in February 1991, Taylor was persuaded to lay down his arms. Agreeing to work with the interim government of Sawyerr, he declared: "I think the Liberian people can be comfortable in knowing that there will be no more war in Liberia and no more problems about who will do what—Dr. Sawyerr and I are Liberians. We will work together to bring peace."[43]

This development was seen as a major achievement for ECOWAS. The United States praised the "statesmanlike intervention by African leaders to find a lasting solution to the crisis," adding that the government "welcome[d] and support[ed]" the peace conference. Sawyerr called the accord "a victory not only for Liberia, but also for Africa."[44]

This so-called February accord proved short-lived, despite Taylor's pledge to work for its success, when a new round of fighting broke out on the Liberian–Sierra Leone border between Taylor's troops and those of the United Liberation Movement for Democracy (ULIMO). Raleigh Seekie, spokesman for ULIMO, accused Taylor of stifling the ECOWAS efforts at finding a permanent solution to the war, adding that Taylor was deliberately "sabotaging peace efforts." According to Seekie: "Peace talks in our country's civil war have been held in five countries in West Africa with no solution only because Mr. Taylor said that he should rule Liberia through the guns."[45]

Taylor, on the other hand, accused the ECOMOG contingent of being biased and of taking sides, and insisted that it be replaced with a United Nations peacekeeping force. Alternatively, Taylor proposed that ECOMOG be broadened to include troops from Senegal, the Ivory Coast, and Guinea Bissau. He promised to disarm his guerrilla troops if his demand was met.

In response, a meeting of the ECOWAS mediating committee was convened on September 16, 1991, in the Ivorian city of Yamossoukro. This meeting was significant in two respects. First, all sixteen member states were, for the first time, invited to attend. Second, President Houphouet Boigney, who had been sympathetic to Taylor, switched his position on the eve of the meeting in regard to the question of revamping ECOMOG. He reportedly told Taylor that he would close his country's borders unless Taylor dropped his demand that ECOMOG be withdrawn. This was very significant because the Ivory Coast had served as Taylor's main conduit for military and other essential supplies.[46]

Faced with the prospect of losing his most valuable support as well as losing his main supply route, on September 18, Taylor informed the mediating committee that he would disarm his troops. The committee, on its part, agreed to meet his demand that the national representation of the peacekeeping force be broadened. The peace accord that was signed stipulated that all fighting factions would be disarmed, and that free and fair elections would be held within six months of November 1, 1991. However, then Taylor refused to permit ECOMOG to carry out any peacekeeping activity outside the environs of Monrovia, which meant that civilians were still not protected from the fighting forces, and the country could not be prepared for the proposed elections.[47] After renewed bloody fighting in 1992 and 1993, with atrocities being committed on civilians, the warring sides agreed, under UN auspices, in July 1993 to cooperate in finding a peaceful solution, even though previous attempts at cease-fires leading to a negotiated settlement and elections had failed. February 1994 was set for presidential and legislative elections. The real challenge, as revealed in the frustrating UN-supervised elections in Angola and Cambodia, is for the previously warring factions to accept the outcome.

Even though the Liberian OAU peacekeeping initiative was not a total success, given that 150,000 persons were killed over a period of 3½ years and 750,000 more fled the country out of a total population of 2.6 million, it did produce some positive developments for ECOWAS. Most significantly, it reflected an indigenous sense that the states of West Africa should together find solutions to conflicts in their region—thus transcending the anglophone-francophone colonial legacy. Furthermore, inter-IGO cooperation was reflected in the economic embargo mounted by ECOWAS, and in an arms embargo imposed by the UN Security Council. The experience of working together can strengthen the organization's capacity to move further in dealing with conflicts that can damage efforts at creating a common market.

The fact that ECOWAS was able to adapt itself functionally to assume new responsibilities, is reflective of what has been termed *spillover:*

> The process whereby members of an integration scheme—agreed on some collective goals for a variety of motives, but unequally satisfied with their attainment of these goals—attempt to resolve their dissatisfaction either by resorting to collaboration in another related sector (expanding the scope of the mutual commitment) or by intensifying their commitment to the original sector (increasing the level of the mutual commitment) or both.[48]

The ability of ECOWAS to adapt from its original purpose in order to achieve conditions to enhance that purpose reflects a response not only to a sharply altered global political-military environment, but also to a sense of shared "felt needs" that can enhance the members' sense of collective responsibility. In the meantime, the original purpose of ECOWAS—ultimate formation of a common market—has not been served well. Intracommunity trade remained relatively insignificant in comparison to the total world trade of the ECOWAS members, peaking at only 4.9 percent in 1988.[49] The success of the ECOWAS common market remains very much in doubt.

IGOs WITH LIMITED COMPOSITION GOVERNING BODIES

The executive functions of management in an IGO are often performed by a council or an executive board or committee with limited membership.

The members are usually elected by the plenary body (or organ) of the IGO, and it is not unusual for stiff competition to arise between different member states that want to be represented on these councils or boards, especially if they wield considerable power. The UN Security Council provides a prime example of such competition; in order to accommodate as many member states as possible for the ten two-year terms of the non-permanent members of the Council, the term has been split into two single-year terms.[50] There are also proposals to reform the membership of the Security Council. One such proposal suggests that permanent seats for the major less-industrialized states should be considered, along with seats for Japan and either Germany or the EC.

The size of the limited composition varies. ECOSOC, which is declining in importance at present, consists of fifty-four members; the ILO Governing Body has forty representatives; ICAO has thirty-three; UNESCO, twenty-four; and the Intergovernmental Maritime Organization (IMO) has sixteen. It is interesting to note that some constituent treaties contain guidelines for the selection of such council members. It is expected that the members should come from states with important interests in the subject matter for which the IGO was created. For example, Article 50(b) of the ICAO Treaty provides:

> In electing the members of the Council, the Assembly shall give adequate representation to (1) the States of chief importance in air transport; (2) the States not otherwise included which make the largest contribution to the provision of facilities for international civil air navigation; and (3) the States not otherwise included whose designation will insure that all the major geographical areas of the world are represented on the Council.

The IMO Convention in Article 17 states:

> (a) Six shall be Governments of the nations with the largest interest in providing international shipping services;
>
> (b) Six shall be Governments of other nations with the largest interest in international seaborne trade;
>
> (c) Two shall be elected by the Assembly from among the Governments of nations having a substantial interest in providing international shipping services, and
>
> (d) Two shall be elected by the Assembly from among the Governments of nations having a substantial interest in international seaborne trade.

Finally, it is important to point out that in regional organizations, councils as executive organs are usually composed of representatives of all member states. This is the case in the EC Council of Ministers, the NATO Council of Permanent Representatives, the Standing Committee of ASEAN, ECOWAS, and others. The reason has to do with the small number of member states normally found in regional organizations; it does not affect the power and influence of these organs, which depend on other factors.

In most cases, the organs of limited composition meet monthly or more frequently since they are engaged in the day-to-day operations of their IGO. Usually, they are authorized to set up subordinate committees (or working groups) concerned with various issue areas to help them in managing the IGO's task performance. In regional IGOs, these committees and other groups may not always have representation from all the states that compose the membership of the higher council. An example is NATO's Nuclear Planning Group (NPG), a seven-state suborgan that is ultimately responsible to the NATO Council.

Limited composition executive organs are particularly important and needed in IGOs dealing with economic matters such as trade and development. Good examples are the GATT and the United Nations Conference on Trade and Development (UNCTAD). Both are located in Geneva, where they cooperate in administering the International Trade Center.

The General Agreement on Tarriffs and Trade (GATT)

GATT is an IGO that in theory is universal, although not all states are members. From an initial membership in 1947 of twenty-three (mostly the Western industrial democracies), GATT has grown to well over one-hundred members, including Czechoslovakia (now the Czech Republic and Slovakia), Poland, Hungary, Romania, and units of the former Yugoslavia, and about seventy-five developing countries. In 1983, the Soviet Union applied for observer status, reflecting a sharp change in attitude toward GATT. This interest has been renewed by the Russian Federation and other states of the post-Soviet Confederation of Independent States.

Occasionally the question has been raised as to whether GATT can be considered an IGO since it consists mainly of a multilateral agreement embodying reciprocal rights and obligations designed to achieve certain objectives, followed up, and sometimes amended by, subsequent multilateral and bilateral agreements. Nonetheless, basic IGO principles and criteria seem to be useful for an evaluation of GATT's institutional framework and task performance. Put simply, "the original purpose of the GATT was to harmonize and moderate tariff schedules of the signatories by giving multilateral effects to bilateral negotiations."[51] Initially, this framework consisted of a Secretariat headed by a director-general and a meeting of the Contracting Parties to the agreement. These meetings usually take place at least once each year and last from two to three weeks.

GATT's supervisory functions over tariffs, nontariff trade barriers (NTBs), and the conduct of trade made it necessary as early as 1951 to set up an Intersessional Committee to deal with exceptional restrictive measures on international trade. The Committee was authorized to conduct voting between the sessions of the Contracting Parties by mail or telegram, thus making it possible for the parties to take joint action when they were not in session.[52]

In order to make GATT's work continuous and more effective, a governing body of limited composition, the Council of Representatives, was established in 1960. It replaced the Intersessional Committee and was endowed with more extensive powers. The Council consists of forty-nine representatives from those member governments that are willing to assume special responsibilities such as carrying out advisory work and recommending draft resolutions for mail or electronic approval by all the Contracting Parties.

Other bodies engaged in the performance of important tasks are the Committee on Trade in Industrial Products, the Committee on Trade and Development, and the Committee on Agriculture. These committees, in turn, have various subsidiary working parties and groups to study GATT-related problems caused by changes in tariffs and NTBs or by contraventions of the rules established for the conduct of international trade, and to offer suggestions for solutions.

The GATT Secretariat is has relatively few employees (about 200 civil servants), of whom about 50 percent are professionals and 50 percent are general service staff members.[53] The staff members appear to be very capable and dedicated, inasmuch as they have been able to cope successfully with the increasing complexities of international trade, 80 percent of which moves under the auspices of GATT. Thus, GATT's efficiency in its task performance must be evaluated as being high, especially when it is taken into account that all implementation of changes in the trade rules is ultimately in the hands of member governments. It should also be noted, however, that the erosion of GATT rules is not uncommon, in which case GATT performs a kind of monitoring function, as pointed out earlier in this chapter.

Since its inception in 1947, seven major trade negotiations under GATT auspices have taken place that have successfully reduced tariffs, and in some cases have eliminated duties completely. Efforts to dismantle nontariff trade barriers (NTBs) such as quantitative restrictions of imports, preferences by governments for the purchase of products, and many other ingenious devices of a protectionist nature, have been much less successful. However, the elimination of NTBs remains a high-priority GATT target.

In response to the demands of the developing states for more appropriate treatment of their exports, the GATT members have added a number of new clauses to the GATT General Agreement (Part IV) in order to promote the participation of developing states in international trade and promote the sustained growth of their export earnings. For this purpose, GATT also established, in cooperation with UNCTAD, an International Trade Center in Geneva.

Thus, over the years, some of the barriers to trade have been lowered or eliminated by GATT and its institutions, but other barriers are likely to tax severely GATT's ability to remain on top of the continual fluctuations in the global pattern of trade and economic competition. The trade tension that arose in the 1980s among Japan, the United States, and the EC states is a major case in point, as is the focus of ongoing negotiations which were launched in September 1986 with the so-called Uruguay Round. It was hoped that the completion of these negotiations, which for the first time included trade in services (banking, insurance, transportation, and others), would be a tremendous success. Developing countries generally objected to the inclusion of services as jeopardizing their own emerging service economies. However, as of the end of 1992, problems with agricultural subsidies, especially within the EC and between the EC and the United States, were delaying a successful conclusion of the Uruguay Round, although continuing efforts were being made to find a compromise solution.

GATT also got a boost at the so-called G-7 summit meeting held in July 1993 in Tokyo, when the U.S. and Japan agreed to search for ways to agree on a negotiating framework to deal with their trade disputes. In addition, the G-7 agreed to: eliminate tariffs unconditionally on pharmaceuticals, construction equipment, medical equipment, and beer, and conditionally on farm equipment, steel, distilled spirits, and furniture. They also agreed to work toward halving tariffs on glass, ceramics, textiles, and apparel, and to cut by at least one-third tariffs for scientific equipment, wood, paper, aluminum, and electronics.

The UN Conference on Trade and Development (UNCTAD)

Another IGO that is at least partially concerned with international trade, though primarily from the perspective of the developing countries, is the UN Conference on Trade and Development (UNCTAD), which was established as a permanent organ of the UN General Assembly by resolution 1995 on December 30, 1964. Since that time, UNCTAD has developed an impressive institutional framework; its budget exceeded $60 million in 1986–1987.[54] Joseph Nye has called UNCTAD the "poor nations' pressure group."[55]

The top layer of the institutional framework is a plenary body open to all UN member and nonmember states (for example, the Holy See and Switzerland are UNCTAD members). Called the Triennial Conference, it formulates basic policies and guidelines in the fields of primary commodities, trade in manufactured and semimanufactured goods, development financing, transfer of technology to developing countries, aid to the least developed and geographically disadvantaged countries, economic cooperation among developing countries regionally and otherwise, and problems of shipping and insurance.

The Conferences are huge affairs, lasting up to eight weeks and bringing together well over a thousand delegates from the member states. There is a full representation of developing countries (i.e., Group A, Afro-Asian states and former Yugoslavia; and Group C, Latin America), along with developed states with market economies (Group B) and former communist-bloc states (Group D).

The day-to-day business of UNCTAD is transacted through a number of organs of limited composition that operate below the Conference. The Trade and Development Board (TAB) is the permanent organ of the Conference; it meets at least once annually and more often if necessary. Composed of fifty-five member states elected by the Conference, the TAB assures continuity of activities between the Conferences. It initiates studies and reports, maintains links with intergovernmental bodies whose work is relevant to UNCTAD, and keeps close liaison with the five regional economic commissions of the United Nations and with other relevant regional organizations.

Subsidiary to the Board are several committees and other subordinate working groups, all of limited composition. The most important committees are the Committee on Commodities (120 members), the Committee on Manufactures (89 members), the Committee on Invisibles and Financing Related to Trade (94 members), and the Committee on Shipping (90 members). All members are elected by the Board, to which the committees report. Permanent committees exist also on the transfer of technology, tariff preferences, and economic cooperation among developing states.

UNCTAD is serviced by a full-time Secretariat functioning within the UN Secretariat and headed by the secretary-general of the Conference, who in turn is appointed by the secretary-general of the United Nations, with confirmation by the General Assembly. The location of the UNCTAD Secretariat is Geneva, which gives this organization a considerable degree of independence. The staff of UNCTAD consists of about 500 civil servants.[56]

One of UNCTAD's major aims was facilitating the creation of a New International Economic Order (NIEO) which would be designed primarily to assist the economies of the then Third World and to replace the existing free market system. This was to be achieved through a system of global negotiations in the early 1980s after UNCTAD conferences from 1964 to 1983 had made progress in attaining many goals of the NIEO. However, the worsening of the world economic situation in the early 1980s made some of these goals unrealistic, and the UNCTAD conferences in Belgrade in 1983 and Geneva in 1987 were unsuccessful. However, international economic cooperation continues with respect to developing countries, especially with the so-called least developed countries (LDCs) and, as former

Secretary-General Perez de Cuellar stated in 1990, "The last decade of this century is full of promise and hope" because of the end of the Cold War, although the disintegration of some states poses a threat.[57]

Other forms of conflict in the post-Cold War period, however, unfortunately have made the decade less than full of promise and hope. Indeed, UNCTAD VIII, held in Cartagena, Colombia, in 1991, was intended to concentrate on the improvement especially of the economic situation in Africa which was described "worse off today" than it was ten years ago. Secretary-General Boutros Boutros-Ghali commented in his 1992 Annual Report on the Work of the Organization: "In the present economic context, a greater appreciation of the linkages between trade, foreign investment, and the globalization of economic activities and corporate operations is critical."[58]

IGOs WITH ADJUDICATORY ORGANS

Only a few IGOs have adjudicatory organs. The United Nations has both the ICJ in the Hague and the Secretariat's Administrative Tribunal.[59] In terms of decisions rendered and complied with, the latter may have a better record, caused mainly by its considerable involvement in intra–United Nations matters.[60] In the EC, the Court of Justice is a very viable adjudicatory organ that has rendered more than three thousand judgments and opinions since its establishment in 1953. It includes a Court of First Instance, whose judgments can be appealed to the overall court. There also is the European Court of Human Rights, which is associated with the Council of Europe. The number of cases decided by this judicial body has remained small, though its decisions have had a significant impact throughout Europe. The institutional framework of the East African Community (EAC) had included a Court of Appeal, but with the demise of that organization, the Court has become inoperative if, indeed, it was ever used. Another court established in Africa is part of the ECOWAS structure discussed earlier. There is also the Inter-American Court of Human Rights, which has been active. Finally, there is growing sentiment in the United Nations in favor of creating a "war crimes" tribunal to address alleged atrocities—especially crimes against defenseless Bosnian Muslim women and children by Serbian militias and their leaders—in the warfare in the Balkans in 1992–1993. It is interesting to note that the Convention on the Law-of-the-Sea envisaged the creation of an International Tribunal connected with the regime of the Enterprise that would be charged with the deep-seabed mining of the oceans.[61] This suggests that as the number of IGOs and the scope of their activities expands further, there may very likely be additional adjudicative organs created.

IGO ADMINISTRATION

As already noted, virtually all contemporary IGOs have a secretariat as the basic administrative organ, although the name for this organ may vary. For example, in some IGOs the name "bureau" is used: a case in point is the UPU, while in the EC, it is the Commission that is in charge of administration.

The executive head of an IGO may be called the "secretary-general," as in the case of the United Nations, or "president," which is the title of the head of the EC Commission. "Director-general" is another title for a chief administrator, and this is used for the chief of the Secretariat of GATT and throughout the United Nations.[62] It is important to note that often these chief administrative officers also have important initiatory, as well as responsive, executive functions that flow either from provisions in the constituent treaties (e.g., Article 99 of the UN Charter) or from the development of continuing practices, such as those that have occurred in the case of GATT's director-general.

Characteristics of an International Civil Service

The traditional concept of a truly international civil service is that it must serve the interests of the organization as a whole.[63] This concept can be said to consist of four basic principles. The first, and probably the most crucial, principle is that of *loyalty:* the employees of an IGO must shed their national loyalties to some extent and consider only the interests of the IGO that employs them in carrying out their professional responsibilities. A corollary to this first principle is that international civil servants, while in international employment, should not receive instructions of any kind from their own governments or attempt to represent the interests of their national governments in any manner.

The second principle is that of *impartiality*. International civil servants are to be administrators, not politicians. It is their function to implement conscientiously decisions that were reached elsewhere and to avoid, if at all possible, involvement in the controversy that often surrounds IGO decision making. International civil servants should be politicians in the sense that they willingly implement whatever policy decisions are reached by the governing political bodies or organs (i.e., those composed of representatives of the member states). This principle is more easily practiced by nationals from the industrial democracies, where the state is circumscribed in its capacity to control a person's career or to intrude in matters of human rights or fundamental freedoms.

A third principle is that of *independence*. Independence, in the sense of international secretariats being independent of political pressure from any national government or group of member states, is implied by the first principle discussed above. However, the principle of independence of the international civil service has a very important organizational dimension as well. It has been suggested that for any international secretariat to maintain its independence, it must be composed of career civil servants who enjoy a considerable degree of job security. Hence, career or indefinite contracts should be given to international civil servants so that they can feel confident that if they promote the best interests of the organization, they will be free from retribution or removal from office for political reasons. The expectation is that a predominantly career civil service would thus facilitate the creation of an international identity or esprit de corps. In contrast, individuals who are seconded (on leave of absence from their national governments) to an IGO on a fixed-term contract might find it difficult not to retain their national political self-consciousness. Therefore (so the argument goes), they would not develop the same type of nonnational attitudes and behavior patterns as individuals who are not concerned that their official actions might influence their subsequent national career fortunes or living conditions.

The fourth and final principle relates to *recruitment practices*. Those persons who still adhere to the traditional concept of an international civil service maintain that individuals should be recruited primarily on the basis of merit: "primarily," because it is recognized that a certain amount of geographical representation (or distribution) is also a prerequisite. The rationale for geographic representation is that IGOs basically reflect a common effort of the member states and that nationals of all states should participate as civil servants in this effort. Consequently, because of decolonization and the rapid increase in new states, a form of international affirmative action has been practiced in the United Nations and many other IGOs, whereby the newer member states have claimed that geographical distribution should be equal to (or even take priority over) merit and objective criteria of personal competence. States that have been the major financial contributors in such affected IGOs—and that obviously have something to lose in terms of the numbers (and rank) of their nationals in the various secretariats—have protested this preoccupation with geographical representation. However, no effective barrier to this trend has been erected, although UN reforms in the budgetary process in the 1980s and also in 1992, as initiated by Secretary-General Boutros Boutros-Ghali, have helped to restore more internal political and administrative stability, although the drastically increased responsibilities placed on the Secretariat in the post-Cold War period have set back some reforms. What impact is achieved in terms of maintaining the integrity of the international civil service remains to be seen.

The UN Civil Service. The United Nations is the largest employer of an international civil service. As of June 1992, the United Nations had a grand total of 31,127 persons: 13,883 (44.6%) in the UN Secretariat; 1,106 (7.1%) in the UNHCR; 8,708 (28.0%) in the UNDP; and 722 (2.3%) in other areas (see Table 3.1). However, in the 1990s there have been sharp cutbacks. The insistence of the developing states that more of their nationals be recruited led to the weakening in the UN bureaucracy during the 1970s and 1980s of the principles of impartiality and complete independence and has directly affected task performance. This should not be surprising in an organization that not only is highly political but also has a staff that is both multinational and multicultural. A similar situation existed, incidentally, in the League of Nations. In 1991, Secretary-General Boutros Boutros-Ghali instituted a reform of the higher levels of the administration, eliminating many posts at the levels of under secretary-general and assistant secretary-general, but also consolidating and eliminating many functions.[64]

Another factor contributing to this trend is increased organizational concern with economic and social activities within the context of development which, in itself, has become a highly sensitive political issue. As a consequence, greater emphasis has been placed on the recruitment of technical staff over the recruitment of generalists and on the use of short-term staff and outside experts, all of which tends to undermine the concept of a traditional career international civil service.

This trend is also reflected in lobbying efforts by UN civil servants seeking to persuade delegations of particular member states to take certain actions. A former chairman of the Fifth Committee, dealing with UN administrative and budgetary matters, strongly criticized such activities when he stated, somewhat self-righteously:

> No member of the Secretariat should be allowed in a conference room, unless officially authorized to be there by virtue of his functions. . . . That matter should be brought to the personal attention of the Secretary-General. It was particularly annoying and unacceptable to see self-styled emissaries of international civil servants preaching what they considered to be right while problems involving the material interests of the staff were being discussed.[65]

As mentioned, budgetary pressures caused by poor global economic conditions in the 1980s and early 1990s led to staff reductions and freezes in recruitment and, when appointments were made, often only fixed-term contracts were given. For example, former Secretary-General Javier Perez de Cuellar moved promptly to implement some of the most controversial resolutions adopted by the General Assembly in December 1986, including implementing a 15 percent staff cut over three years and a 25 percent cut in top posts, from fifty-seven to forty-three. Furthermore, a hiring freeze begun in 1986 left the organization with a 13 percent job vacancy rate. To reduce the budget of $841 million by $83 million, there were heavy cuts in overtime and travel, restrictions on meetings and documentation, deferment of a 4.3 percent cost-of-living increase, and mandatory retirement at age sixty.

All this affected morale and brought about an increasingly strident tone

Table 3.1
Staff of the UN Secretariat and of the Secretariats of Other UN Organs by Category and Source of Funds as of 30 June 1992

	Regular Budget			
Organiation	Professional and above	Project personnel	General Service and others	Total
United Nations Secretariat	3,287	57	5,740	9,084
UNDP	-	-	-	-
UNHCR	71	21	166	258
UNICEF	-	-	-	-
UNITAR	-	-	-	-
UNRWA e/	82	-	10	92
ITC f/	-	-	-	-
ICSC	19	-	25	44
ICJ	17	-	27	44
UNU	-	-	-	-
Total	3,476	78	5,968	9,522

Extrabudgetary Sources				
Professional and above	Project personnel	General Service and others	Total	Grand Total
658	864	3,277	4,799	13,883
837 a/	995 b/	6,876 c/	8,708	8,708
490	275	1,183	1,948	2,206
1,267 d/	663	3,678	5,608	5,608
12	-	11	23	23
61	-	-	61	153
66	84	199	349	349
-	-	-	-	44
-	-	-	-	44
24	14	71	109	109
3,415	2,895	15,295	21,605	31,127

a/ Includes only UNDP core budget.

b/ Includes all UNDP other funds.

c/ Includes national officers, Field Service level.

d/ Includes national officers.

e/ UNRWA has also 18,969 area personnel (37.0 percent women).

f/ A number of posts in the International Trade Centere (ITC) are financed jointly by the UN from the regular budget and by the General Agreement on Tariffs and Trade (GATT).

Source: UN Document 47/416 (1992), p. 4.

in talks between the representatives of the UN civil servants, the staff union comprised of the Federation of International Civil Servants Associations (FICSA) and the Coordinating Committee for Independent Staff Unions and Associations of the UN System (CCISUA), with the UN assistant secretary-general for personnel services. Complaints continue to be voiced by the unions about poor working conditions. To put pressure on the UN administration, staff strikes have been called in Geneva and New York, although they are strongly condemned by almost all member governments and by the secretary-general.

It is interesting to note that the UN civil servants' discontent is caused partly by the erosion of the application of the aforementioned principles and the activism by the staff unions. They justify their activism in part by their desire to conserve something close to the traditional concept of the international civil service. The president of the Staff Committee, acting for the staff union of the United Nations in New York, has stated what he considers are the conditions required to rescue the international civil service from demoralization:

1. A new dynamic and more progressive leadership based on . . . personal qualities of integrity, courage, and competence; . . .
2. A positive, open personnel policy based on merit which seeks out the best qualified of all countries without regard to political connections and which ensures a rational system of career development free from political interference;
3. A revitalized sense of accountability to the world public which provides the financial support for our work;
4. A unified international service which puts an end to dubious "class" distinctions and recognizes that members, no matter where or in what capacity they serve are entitled to equal standards of dignity and treatment;
5. A renewed commitment to and respect for staff participation in decisions affecting the conditions of service and management of the various organizations as a means to maintain the active interest and involvement of the staff in the purpose of international service.[66]

This statement in itself may not reflect widespread staff consensus, but it is important in that it is illustrative of the effort by staff members to articulate broad principles as well as specific claims.

Secretary-General Boutros Boutros-Ghali, in his first Annual Report, directed attention to the sharp increase in UN staff activities in the post-Cold War period:

Since I assumed office I have been repeatedly impressed by the dedication and versatility of the United Nations staff. In the course of less than a year they have responded to many hitherto unfamiliar tasks. Many have assumed new or additional functions or volunteered for mission service at short notice, often in hardship and

> dangerous situations—frequently compelled to leave their families behind for extended periods. They have done so willingly, in the interests of building a new society, ensuring the fairness of an electoral process or facilitating the delivery of humanitarian assistance. At headquarters, staff members are responding on a 24-hour basis to the constant requirements of complex operations in many time zones, servicing double or triple the number of meetings, and producing increasing volumes of documentation with shorter and shorter deadlines. They are being called upon to undertake research and provide policy options in a rapidly changing world where long-established modes of thinking and acting are constantly questioned or redefined. Others are managing, in a situation of financial uncertainty, complex operations involving tens of thousands of military and civilian personnel in the field.[67]

The International Civil Service Commission, which is composed of individuals who, acting in their private capacities, are to be competent and experienced in personnel management (no two of whom can be nationals of the same state), continues to make a serious effort to deal with questions of recruitment, career development, and the career concept. However, whether the effort can be translated into useful results in the foreseeable future is far from certain because the Commission has become part of the politics that permeate the issues and principles of a genuine international civil service.[68]

There are, of course, proposals that have originated from outside the UN institutional framework for upgrading the whole complex of the UN civil service through the formulation of career development programs. One of these proposals, aiming at a program that differentiates between the capabilities and needs of the highly specialized technical organizations such as FAO, UNESCO, IFAD, and WHO, and more diversified organizations such as the UN Secretariat, ILO, UNDP, and others, has been developed by Norman A. Graham and Robert S. Jordan.[69] However, whether their detailed suggestions for recruitment, appointment policy, career management, training, and motion/mobility opportunities will find acceptance during the turbulent phase through which the UN civil service is passing is unlikely. It seems that as long as member governments tend to look at recruitment and promotion first from their own national viewpoints rather than from the organization's overall perspective, the bureaucracy (whether management or labor) will tend to push its particular interests first. Nonetheless, some progress has been made in "unencumbering" high-level positions that previously had been kept as the privileged reserve of particular states and working more vigorously to open wider opportunities for women to serve in positions of increasing responsibility. Since there is no unified system of governance of the United Nations as a whole, there would appear to be little prospect of the emergence in the foreseeable future of a unified career concept or what has become known as a Common System.

The question may be asked whether a socialization process operating among UN civil servants might produce attitudes more supportive of UN principles and goals, thereby strengthening their commitment to the ideal of an effective international civil service as outlined in Article 101, paragraph 3, of the UN Charter.[70] A number of studies have been undertaken to test the learning process that national participants (mostly delegates in various UN bodies and specialized agencies) might be undergoing and to determine what cognitive, affective, and evaluative changes in their attitudes may have occurred.[71] However, similar research on UN civil servants appears to be lacking. The results of these studies have been far from uniform and they suggest multidimensional effects of the experiences on the attitudes of the participants. A positive socialization process and the degree of its intensity are likely to depend on the nationality of the participants, which would include the extent that domestic bureaucratic principles interfere with those of the United Nations, the commitment to foreign aid and development in general, and his or her view on the principle that sovereignty is transferable.[72]

Another factor that might influence not only the morale of UN civil servants but also their commitment and interest in assuring that the principles of Art. 101, par. 3, are fully maintained, could be the esteem in which they are held by their national colleagues and working partners and the quality of their relations with national officials. The higher the national officials value the competence and skills of the UN bureaucracy and the more harmonious the interbureaucratic relationships, the greater may be the incentive of the latter to justify fully this evaluation. This, in turn, could engender a stronger desire to meet the requirements of a dedicated international civil service. Again, no relevant attitude surveys on these aspects of the UN bureaucracy appear to have been made and, therefore, no definitive propositions can be advanced.

Many member governments are often still very critical of efforts at eliminating or terminating what other states might regard as unnecessary or ineffective programs. As of September 1992, only fifty-two member states had paid in full their dues to the regular budget. Unpaid assessed contributions totaled $908.5 million, while unpaid contributions toward peacekeeping operations stood at $844.4 million. This was in spite of the fact that some of the recent major peacemaking operations, such as those mounted in Kuwait and Somalia, were heavily financed by some of the major donor states that did not provide troops.

In this respect, Secretary-General Boutros-Ghali has set in motion a review of the work of the Administrative Committee on Coordination as well as the Economic and Social Council. He explained why this is important:

> One reason why the problem of coordination has appeared intractable is the fact that the structure was devised in 1946 at San Francisco on the basis of a deliberate decision to organize international cooperation through the combined action of the

United Nations, on the one hand, and a number of autonomously functioning specialized agencies, on the other. Functional autonomy is explicitly and implicitly recognized in the agreements concluded from that time onwards between the United Nations and the existing or future specialized agencies. The system we are operating with has remained virtually unchanged over the last 46 years.[73]

The EC Civil Service. The civil service of the EC—the ECSC, EEC, and EURATOM—suffers from many of the same problems as the UN bureaucracy. Since 1958 when the EEC and EURATOM were established, the Eurocracy (as the Communities' civil service is often called) has grown steadily. Indeed, the size of the Commission staff alone rose from 1,108 in 1958 to nearly 8,000 in 1976, and has expanded further since then, numbering over 13,000 on January 1, 1992. Of these, 10,000 are engaged in policy and executive tasks and 2,700 in translation work flowing from the Community's nine working languages. However, the staff of the Commission is only part of the total Eurocracy; over 2,000 civil servants serve in the Council of Ministers, and still others serve in the European Parliament and the Economic and Social Council. A number of Eurocrats also serve in scientific research. The total of this impressive international bureaucracy, therefore, exceeds 20,000. However, this represents only about 0.005 percent of the 1990 population of the twelve member states, which totals 345 million. Not surprisingly, this is a much smaller percentage than the national bureaucracies of the EC member states. After all, the Eurocracy deals only with a very limited range of functions and not with all the aspects and levels of administration of the national civil services.

The civil service of the EC is divided into four basic categories: A, B, C, and D. The officials in category A constitute the administrative elite, and they, in turn, are divided into seven groups (A1-A7). The highest positions of leadership, the directors-general and their deputies, are assigned to the A-1 group. Directors are normally A-2s, and a division chief usually holds the rank of A-3. Below them are various classes of senior administrators.

While, as has been seen, ideally an international civil service should recruit individuals untainted by continuing ties to their national administrations in order to ensure their complete independence and full commitment to the goals of the organization, the need at the inception of the three Communities for immediate administrative competence and political considerations produced a different situation. In order to assure the proper development of the Communities during their fledgling years, they resorted to widespread secondment from the national bureaucracies of their member states to provide much of the initial staffing in the A category of the Eurocracy. It was felt that seconded national administrators already knew their way through the corridors of national power and politics and, therefore, could ease very markedly the burden of the neophyte organization. A seconded official, by definition, is expected to return to his national service; however, some have made a career of the Eurocracy while others, after an initial attempt to pursue such a career, have changed their minds and returned to their capitals.[74]

It is difficult to determine exactly how many national officials were tempted by the integration adventure to move to Luxembourg (ECSC) or to Brussels, and it is even more difficult to find out how many have returned to their national services after their allotted time expired. Clearly, however, a large number of Eurocrats came initially from the national civil services. In his pilot study on the EEC, Leon N. Lindberg notes that, of the Commission bureaucracy in 1961:

> Approximately 50 percent . . . has been drawn from the administrative services of the Member States. This figure however, rises to 75 percent for the major administrative posts (category A), and if we take only the major policymaking posts (Categories A-1 and A-2), 57 of which are authorized in the 1961 budget, we find that all are drawn from the national administrations.[75]

More recent data confirms the pattern that the higher the officials are placed within the A category, the greater the likelihood that they had been employed by their national governments. Of the A-3 officials, 46 percent had prior experience in public service, while only 28.6 percent of the A-4 through A-7 civil servants seem to have had such service.[76]

As with all major international civil services, in their recruitment and selection, the EC has attempted to reconcile the principles of maintaining the highest professional competence with equitable geographic distribution. Up to the accession of Greece in January 1981, each of the four largest member states (Britain, France, West Germany, and Italy) were allocated an 18 percent quota, while the remaining 28 percent was given to the five other members: 9 percent each to Belgium and the Netherlands, 5 percent each to Denmark and Ireland, and 2 percent to Luxembourg. A slight modification took place with the expansion to twelve of the EC membership.

The implications of the quota system are far-reaching. In staff changes, nationality is likely to become overemphasized, with insufficient attention paid to administrative competence and quality. Every member government seeks to retain the balance it has in the different directorates-general: the basic organizational units of the Commission, of which there are now twenty-three. Promotions are difficult because, for the positions of director-general, deputy director-general, and division chiefs, the member governments may insist on appointing their preferred choices. Hence, less-qualified persons may be appointed or promoted; as a consequence, overall morale may suffer severely. The promotion situation is compounded by the need for bargaining between the superior of an official who is being considered for advancement and the unions representing all EC civil servants. The unions are often reluctant to make competence and merit the decisive criteria for promotion; rather, they prefer promotions to be based on age and seniority. At the same time, it may become very difficult to remove an official even if he or she is clearly incompetent, because it could unbalance the geographic quota system unless the superior can find a qualified substitute of the same nationality and the unions do not oppose the dismissal.

When the Communities were first established in the 1950s, the greatest appeal for many of the job applicants was not high pay but the opportunity to participate in an exciting experiment, namely, the creation of a United States of Europe. Today, the spirit of a united Europe as a motivation for service in the EC has receded, if not entirely vanished, although movement to a European union may revive this motivation. Meanwhile, the financial emoluments for the Eurocrats have become extremely attractive, and this attractiveness has been further strengthened by various tax advantages that, although not as favorable in 1992 as they were in the early 1960s, still are the envy of the national bureaucracies.

Indeed, the salaries of the Eurocrats are very high by any standard. In the middle and junior grades they are paid two to three times as much as they would receive if they were employed by their national governments. For example, an EC chauffeur has a take-home pay equal to the salary of a minister in the Belgian government. On higher levels, Eurocrats earn roughly twice the salary of comparable civil servants in the EC member states (often exceeding $100,000). In addition, EC civil servants benefit from special privileges. For example, they can buy subsidized liquor in the Commission's own supermarket and they receive discounts on gasoline purchases. They can also send their children to special free European schools.[77]

The high salaries of the Eurocracy and the various privileges granted them have displeased those national civil servants whose salaries are substantially lower. At the same time, elite survey research has indicated that national civil servants in the member states do not have the highest esteem for the working habits and qualifications of their colleagues in the EC.[78] However, these perceptions of the national officials interviewed may have been colored by concerns that the EC institutions might expand their powers at the expense of national prerogatives and by understandable envy of the Eurocrats' much higher salaries and other benefits. Indeed, this envy, which exists in all member states, has induced the Council of Ministers to seek a gradual harmonization between the salaries of EC and member government bureaucracies.

For the Eurocrats, the Council decision conjured up vistas of net losses in their incomes and the possibility of the nationalization of the EC's civil service. Hence, a rash of protest strikes by the Eurocracy broke out in the winter and spring of 1981, on several occasions bringing most EC activities to a complete standstill.[79] A compromise between the Council (representing governments) and the Commission, which had opposed the Council's suggestions, settled the dispute.

There was much hope in the 1950s and 1960s that national officials who went to work for the EC would adopt more intensive European values and that, through this socialization process, these values would spread among the national bureaucracies. While this process seemed to work successfully at the beginning, counterorganizational socialization forces exerted by the national bureaucracies and adverse attitudes of national civil servants toward the possible transfer of power to the EC institutions seem to have carried the day. Although a continually increasing number of national officials (well above 12,000) are called to serve in Commission study and working groups every year, during the second half of the 1970s and early 1980s the EC institutions were losing political ground vis-à-vis the national governments.

There is little doubt that Western Europe was witnessing a trend toward the renationalization of policy and, perhaps, EC institutional authority, despite some rhetoric to the contrary by some of the leaders of the member governments. The onslaught on EC salaries may be part of this trend, ultimately aiming to abolish the Eurocracy's status as a truly international civil service. The Eurocracy has become vulnerable to this attack and the Commission's personnel management of the top levels in the directorates-general may have been a contributory cause. This, in turn, was prompted by the national governments: they prefer a pliable Commission that shows little interest in abandoning the principle of national allocation of senior posts.

This situation seems to have been reversed when Jacques Delors became Commission president and instilled a new spirit of European support through the "1992" program, the vista of European political union, and the Economic and Monetary Union proposal. All this led to a new infusion of European enthusiasm which strengthened the flagging spirits of the Eurocracy. However, with the recent revival of ancient European ethnic hatreds and nationalistic fears, a "United Europe" still seems out of reach.

THE PLACE OF BUREAUCRACIES IN IGOs

Bureaucracies are commonly considered to be a phenomenon of the rise of the modern industrial state. This does not mean that there were not cadres of officials who were concerned primarily with transacting the public's business before the industrial revolution. What makes modern states different is both the scale of their activities and the pervasiveness of their bureaucracies into all aspects of daily living of the citizenry. As one observer put it: "[Both] liberals and . . . conservatives strongly objected to the bureaucracy and depicted it as a colossus which would engulf the various areas of life and cancel the traditional liberties of the people and which would engender a mechanized and oppressive civilization, choking the individual and regimenting his every activity."[80] The nineteenth-century expectation that the role of public administration at the national level was to help solve society's ills gave way, by the third quarter of the twentieth century, to the belief that bureaucracy should be controlled. Ironically, this change in attitude occurred during the same period when greater confidence was being expressed about the desirability of creating more bureaucracies at the international level. For example, Jean Monnet, the Frenchman who became known as the foremost advocate of European unification, had succeeded by the early 1950s in convincing the major European industrial democracies that the creation of the bureaucracies of the EC would be for the mutual benefit of all participating member states.[81] The growth of the civil service in such regional functional IGOs was paralleled by the proliferation of the international bureaucracies of the United Nations and its specialized and affiliated agencies. Unfortunately, complaints of politicization and preoccupation with geographic distribution (both of which were alluded to earlier with respect to the United Nations and other IGOs) have also been heard concerning the bureaucracies of the EC. Consequently, rather than increasing in prestige and in attracting the confidence of the member states as their functions have expanded, they have diminished in prestige.[82] Thus, by the 1980s, the bureaucracies of regional IGOs, derived as they are from the same tradition as the United Nations and its various affiliated agencies' bureaucracies, have been subjected to similar criticism and suffer increasingly from low esteem.

Is this decline justified? If the conception of the proper role of international bureaucracies is to reflect the bureaucratic behavior of national bureaucracies, then, as regards Europe, both the Western European industrial democracies and the former Eastern European socialist (or people's) so-called democracies may have approved the decline. However, when the governments of the newer member states of the United Nations—and the developing states generally, as represented by the Group of 77—are taken into account, then a sense of alarm can be detected. They are keenly aware that their national bureaucracies (most often the legacies of colonial rule) are either so fragile or so inexperienced that simply to leave them to their own administrative and bureaucratic devices would be to assign these states to a condition of permanent inferiority in the international political scheme. Quite naturally, the governments of these states are unwilling to see this happen; so, from the 1960s onward, and with accelerating pressure, the developing states have been pressing for the creation of more international bureaucracies that are committed to promoting actively their interests and serving their urgent national needs.

ORGANIZATIONAL IDEOLOGY

In every IGO, as indeed in every organization, some kind of organizational ideology develops that impinges on the effectiveness of the IGO's task performance. A basic concern of employees in any organization is the latter's continuity and, hopefully, its expansion. If an organization expands its functions, the prospects are good for promotion, greater personal prestige, higher salaries, and other rewards and, of course, these are major personal objectives of those working for the organization. However, the organizational growth of most IGOs is not assured and, in fact, the member states may have little interest in an IGO's further growth. Both the former Soviet Union and the United States, for example, opposed the growth of the UN bureaucracy at various times.

Since the civil servants of an IGO are also nationals drawn from the member states, this situation exposes officials to conflicting loyalties and pressures. The result could well be a decline in the quality of task performance that could compound already existing dissatisfaction with the manner in which the normal functions of the IGO are carried out. This can create serious dilemmas for the executive leadership which would like to see maintained a firm commitment of its staff to a strong organizational ideology in order to ensure a high quality performance of the assigned tasks. On the other hand, trying to accommodate the national policy goals of the member states may result in a negative reaction of the bureaucracy and poor performance of the IGO's functions and tasks.

Management Efficiency

Management efficiency in the task performance of an IGO is considered high if its institutions have a good record in attaining desired outcomes. This, in turn, requires superior knowledge of cause-and-effect relationships and of political, social, and economic environmental elements in the issue areas in which a particular IGO is involved. The more limited this knowledge, the greater are the difficulties for goal achievements.[83] Task performance is also likely to be improved, or at least not likely to be impaired, if the relevant institutions can adjust themselves to constraints and contingencies not controlled by the IGO itself.

An important element in achieving good task performance is the leadership quality of the executive head. According to Robert W. Cox, the executive head plays a big role in converting an IGO that was conceived as a framework for multilateral diplomacy into one that is an autonomous actor in the international system.[84] However, there are also significant constraints on the executive's leadership ability to bring about full management efficiency. These include bureaucratic immobility, increasing client control benefiting from intrabureaucratic tradeoffs of benefits, and the patterns of conflict and national power alignments that make it difficult to mobilize uncommitted supporters for particular IGOs.

The greatest thing any executive head can do to improve task performance efficiency is to alter the policies of the member states into greater conformity with the decisions and interests of the IGO. In order to do this, the head must have: "(1) access to domestic groups having influence, (2) adequate intelligence concerning their goals and perceptions, and (3) ability to manipulate international action so that these groups can perceive an identity of interest" with the IGO.[85] Such a strategy is likely to work best in a pluralistic national political system, and most states do not fall into this category. However, even in pluralistic politics, this is a difficult undertaking, except perhaps in small states. Few presidents of the EC Commission have been successful in persuading the larger EC member states of this identity of interests, and even the dynamic Jacques Delors has had his problems with this task, as some of the opposition to the ratification of the Maastricht Agreements on political and economic union has shown. Nor has the UN secretary-general been able to do this for many years as far as the United States and other major powers were concerned. It is only the extraordinary changes in the international arena in the late 1980s and early 1990s that produced policy harmony between Washington and other powers in the UN executive leadership. Clearly, as we will also see in the next two chapters, the coincidence of IGO member state interests fluctuates according to the political environment of the larger world in which both rest.

The secretary-general has ample opportunity to function as a mediator or adviser and is expected, in fact, to perform this function, keeping the major political organs—and relevant member states—informed along the way. The problem is not that there are too few opportunities for this kind of activity but, rather, that the secretary-general is called on only too often under the most unpromising circumstances. As Kurt Waldheim put it:

> A day seldom passes without approaches to the Secretary-General from one of the Member Governments for assistance in solving problems which have defied solution by other means. Even if the Secretary-General, as often happens, cannot succeed where others have failed, the fact that Governments can, in certain situations of crisis, place their worries before him and discuss them in full confidence can in itself be helpful to Governments.[86]

By 1956, then-Secretary General Dag Hammarskjöld had taken the power of the office to its highest point up to that time when the General Assembly overwhelmingly approved his plan for a UN Emergency Force (UNEF) to resolve the Suez crisis. His handling of the crisis in such a fashion was important because it marked the first use of what Hammarskjöld came to term "preventive diplomacy," namely, using the United Nations to intervene in order to forestall or to preclude intervention by the major world powers, and in particular, the two superpowers. Perhaps more important in practical political terms, the secretary-general had delegated to himself discretionary power to organize and administer an international military force. He became a commander-in-chief of his own army: a role for which

Sir Eric Drummond, the first secretary-general of the League of Nations, would never have hoped, or for that matter, wanted.[87]

The growth of the responsibilities placed on both the secretary-general and the Secretariat since Dag Hammarskjöld's death has been remarkable. A virtual doubling of the membership has not only shifted the political balance of the organization, it has altered fundamentally the nature of the political dialogue because of the emergence during the Cold War of the Third World (or Group of 77) as an influential force in the politics of the United Nations. Even though, to many observers, the Third World pursuit of the New International Economic Order (NIEO) appeared at the outset of the 1970s to have burst with dramatic suddenness onto the international agenda, it was, in fact, ignited by a slow fuse that had been burning since the Hammarskjöld era.

With the end of the Cold War, the fusing of concepts of the proper use of military power to intervene in the affairs of another state with traditionally nonmilitary concerns related more to issues of human rights and humanitarian assistance, as well as overall economic and social development, has taken center stage in world politics. Put another way, the resources of the only remaining superpower—the United States—are now being placed at the disposal of the Security Council, although not without significant shifting and hauling as mandates are written, rewritten, or ignored. This is discussed further in Chapter 6.

Organizational Structure of Institutions

Another factor affecting the efficiency of IGO task performance by civil servants is the organizational structure of institutions. Edouard Poullet and Gerard Deprez, who have made a careful study of the EC Commission's administrative efficiency, stress that "the multiplication and differentiations of principal administrative units (especially directorates-general and directorates) have contributed to the compartmentalization of policies and made the means for the coordination needed more numerous and expensive."[88] They conclude that the organizational pattern that has gradually developed has been imposed on the Commission by events and external pressure. They believe, however, that it represents, in effect, nothing other than the perpetuation of a simple hierarchical model which was well suited to a small organization but poorly suited to a large organization operating within a very complex system, which is what the EC now represents.[89]

The consequence of the resulting organizational pattern of the Commission was the breakdown of the organization internally into separate subsystems, each acting for its own account, defending its own interests, having recourse to its own policies, and coexisting rather than interacting with the others.[90] Efforts at restructuring the United Nations have also met with only limited success although, as mentioned earlier, managerial and budgetary reforms have been pressed on the secretary-general.

This raises the question of rationalization; that is, the process of attempting to remove duplication of activities between and among units, which is a perennial problem, not only in IGO institutions, but for public administration in general.

The expansion of the EC Commission's organization reflects the enlargement of the membership of the Communities since 1973 as well as an increasing work load as the result of new tasks that need to be performed by the EC's international civil service.[91] Examples are the ever-increasing functions that had to be performed to meet the needs of the Common Agricultural Policy (CAP) or the establishment of the European Regional Development Fund in the early 1970s. Does this development of the Commission's organizational structure suggest a confirmation of Mitrany's proposition that "form follows function"?[92] Alternately, are other forces at work that generate, not only the expansion of institutions, but also their proliferation?

Clearly, the neofunctionalist argument of spillover is attractive. If an IGO institution does not have the capability to carry out satisfactorily its assigned tasks, thus jeopardizing the goals pursued by those states that establish the IGO, institutions are automatically expanded or new institutions are created to perform the tasks in order to attain the original goals.[93] This is what happened in the United Nations in the 1970s. It may not only be functionalist logic that was the incentive for institutional expansion but also simply the desire for growth, a normal organizational goal.[94]

In this respect, the leadership role of the executive head may be crucial.[95] Institutional clientele and bureaucracy are apt to be strong supporters of institutional growth, and the former may provide the needed political interference on the national level to assist institutional expansion. Indeed, this clientele may also assist in bringing about a proliferation of institutions. For the bureaucracy of an IGO, institutional expansion or proliferation may offer a greater specialization of expertise which, in turn, is likely to result in promotions and salary increases.

The efficiency of the management of task performance in IGO institutions may also be improved by innovations in the processes used to achieve the various tasks. "Form follows function" might also apply in this respect. However, whether this motto provides many answers is doubtful, because innovation analysis is highly complex. Innovation may flow from various sources, including intellectual vision, disillusionment with existing institutions and procedures, and new or renewed substantive needs. Civil servants may undergo learning processes in their institutional positions that might trigger innovation. Also, crisis conditions (institutional survival) may stimulate innovative proposals and so will expectations of major rewards.[96]

Certainly the sharp growth of UN peacemaking and peacekeeping activities can be attributed to the pressure of world opinion—buttressed or shaped by media depictions—on both the United Nations and its major members, to attempt mediation, as in the case of the ethnic fighting in the former Yugoslavia, in Angola, and perhaps soon in Zaire, or the clan fighting in Somalia. Also, in the post-Cold War period, there appear to be elements of an ideological motive for the task expansion of IGOs, that is, to encourage or sustain some form of political consent as the most widely accepted means of legitimizing, for example, the successor states of the former Soviet Union, as well as attempting to effect a transition to peace in Cambodia and Angola by means of supervised elections, or to restore a deposed elected president, as in Haiti.

How far innovation stems from the operation of functionalist logic is difficult to judge, for functionalists have assumed that everybody (whether governments or peoples) will value the fruits of international cooperation in specific functional areas and that most participants will find the process in itself rewarding. However, basing innovation on expectations of concrete rewards seems to be more in line with realistic thought.[97]

An example, perhaps, of confusing calculations of costs versus benefits, in the post-Cold War period, is the sharply increased responsibilities of UNHCR in coping with the rising tide of refugees—dislocated because of either civil war or economic deprivation—at the same time that receiving states are closing their borders. The result has been severe financial strains on UNHCR's budget, even though the major donor states are also the reluctant receiving states. The agency's costs doubled in 1900–1992 from $544 million to $1.1 billion, and continue to rise. The number of refugees has increased from 10.3 million in 1982 to 18.9 million in 1992.[98]

SUMMARY AND CONCLUSIONS

It is quite clear from the foregoing discussion that even though the numbers of IGOs—and their consequent bureaucracies—have increased, their prestige and overall effectiveness may not have increased commensurately. It is apparent that the level of task performance was generally high at the inception of those IGOs: to which the idealism of the initial UN and EC civil servants bears testimony. However, as the various bureaucracies gained more responsibilities and became more formalized administratively, the governments of the member states began to resist either the growth of the budgets or the distribution of the benefits, which has resulted in increased acrimony by the member states composing the governing bodies. No better example of this observation can be seen than the difficulties in the EC in 1992 and 1993 over whether to implement the so-called Maastrich Agreement which will move the EC a significant step closer to financial and monetary union. On a positive note, however, is the expansion of United

Nations tasks to deal with problems of civil unrest (as in Somalia and El Salvador), as well as with military interventions by one state into another (i.e., Kuwait, Bosnia-Herzegovena, and Cambodia).

So far, the notion that sustained interaction among international civil servants (preferably those committed to the career concept) would lead to a greater institutional socialization which, in turn, would break down nationalistic sentiment among the member states has not been fulfilled. However, the intermingling of regional IGO personnel with UN personnel and, increasingly, with NGO volunteers and staff in attempting to resolve post-Cold War problems has the promise of creating a climate or habit of "working together" that may have a spillover effect. The precedents being set by the United Nations—including dealing with the Iraq invasion of Kuwait and its aftermath, monitoring Iraqi compliance with various Security Council resolutions, attempting to facilitate the transition to democratic governments in Angola, Cambodia, and El Salvador, and rescuing the abused populations in such places as Afghanistan, Bosnia, and Somalia—provides experience in multilateralism that can reinforce the inclination of the world community toward international organization.

Even though the dispute settlement functions of the UN secretary-general have at times not given this office the prestige that is required for the incumbent to carry out his mandate, Javier Perez de Cuellor's prestige increased as he was continually asked to provide his good offices in dispute settlement activities. The trend is uneven in regard to his successor, Boutros Boutros-Ghali. In fact, although at times the secretary-general has been criticized (perhaps unfairly) for appearing willing to compromise the integrity of the civil service in order not to antagonize the member governments, lately the secretary-general has been criticizing the member states for not providing the financial means to create and maintain the best possible international civil service and adequate peacekeeping/peacemaking forces to deal with the challenges of the emerging, post-Cold War new international order. This is discussed further in Chapter 5.

The quality of the executive leadership of the United Nations, and of all IGOs, therefore, is an essential feature of the ability of the organization to adapt to the political, economic, and social environments in which they must exist. This adaptation is essential if IGOs are to fulfill their very important, indeed vital, functions.

NOTES

1. In this connection, see James M. McCormick, "Intergovernmental Organizations and Cooperation among Nations," *International Studies Quarterly* 24 (March 1980):75–95.

2. See also Johan Kaufmann, *United Nations Decision Making* (Rockville, MD: Sijthoff and Noordhoff, 1980).

3. See M. J. Peterson, *The General Assembly in World Politics* (Boston: Unwin and Hyman, 1990).

4. Robert L. McLaren, *Civil Servants and Public Policy* (Waterloo, Ont., Canada: Wilfrid Laurier University Press, 1980), pp. 52–53.

5. H. A. Wassenbergh, *Aspects of Air Law and Civil Air Policy in the Seventies* (The Hague: Martinus Nijhoff, 1970), p. 32.

6. McLaren, *Civil Servants,* p. 53.

7. Ibid., p. 54. For additional details, see Young W. Kihl, *Conflict Issues and International Civil Aviation Decisions* (Denver, CO: University of Denver, 1971), pp. 2–9.

8. Arthur S. Banks et al. *Political Handbook of the World* (Binghamton, NY: CSA Publications, 1991), pp. 870–71. See also Thomas M. Franck, "The Emerging Right to Democratic Governance," *The American Journal of International Law* 86 (January 1992):46–91.

9. For background, see Thomas L. Karnes, *The Failure of Union* (Chapel Hill: University of North Carolina Press, 1961), pp. 30–68.

10. Ibid., pp. 84–86.

11. Ibid., pp. 164–74.

12. James D. Cochrane, *The Politics of Regional Integration: The Central American Case* (New Orleans: Tulane University, Tulane Studies in Political Science, 1969), pp. 37–46.

13. For details, see ibid., pp. 68–84.

14. For a more detailed analysis of this problem and experiences in other regions, see Sidney Dell, *A Latin American Common Market* (London: Oxford University Press, 1966), pp. 53–57.

15. Harold K. Jacobson and Dusan Sidjanski, "Regional Pattern of Economic Cooperation," in Werner J. Feld and Gavin Boyd, eds., *Comparative Regional Systems,* (New York: Pergamon Press, 1980), p. 82.

16. For a comprehensive analysis of the CACM problem, see Royce Q. Shaw, *Central America: Regional Integration and National Development* (Boulder, CO: Westview Press, 1978), pp. 84–214.

17. Arthur S. Banks, ed., *Political Handbook of the World,* (Binghamton, N.Y.: CSA Publications, 1991), p. 815; and *Christian Science Monitor,* March 18, 1992, p. 11.

18. Bingu W. T. Muntarika, *Toward Multinational Economic Cooperation in Africa* (New York: Praeger, 1972), p. 12.

19. UNESCO, *Statistical Yearbook 1969* (Paris: UNESCO, 1970), p. 69.

20. See John P. Renninger, *Multinational Cooperation for Development in West Africa* (New York: Pergamon Press, 1979). Other subregional institutions that were dismantled as a result of Nkrumah's initiatives were the West African Frontier Force, the West African Institute for Social and Economic Research, and the West African Cocoa Research Institute.

21. R. I. Onwuka, *Development and Integration in West Africa: The Case of ECOWAS* (Ife, Nigeria: Ife University Press, 1982), p. 7.

22. Ibid.

23. For example, the Ivory Coast had accorded de jure recognition to Biafra, which obviously did not please Nigeria.

24. The member states are Benin, Burkino Foso, Cape Verde Islands, Ivory

Coast, Gambia, Ghana, Guinea, Guinea-Bissau, Liberia, Mali, Mauritania, Niger, Nigeria, Senegal, Sierra Leone, and Togo.

25. Chapter 2, Article 4 of the Treaty lists the main organs, institutions, and specialized commissions.

26. The actual language was: "an atmosphere of peace and harmonious understanding."

27. Reference was made to Articles 2 and 3, respectively, of the Charters of the United Nations and the OAU. See J. E. Okolo, "Integration and Cooperative Regionalism," *International Organization* 39 (Winter 1985):121.

28. Ibid., p. 127.

29. ECOWAS, *Official Journal* 3 (1981):9. This is an "all-for-one-and-one-for-all" definition of collective security.

30. The Protocol excluded armed conflict between member states because, as pointed out earlier, such conflict already came under the provisions of the 1978 Non-Aggression Protocol.

31. ECOWAS, *Protocol on Mutual Defense Assistance,* 1981, p. 140.

32. These activities, which are not unusual in other parts of the world, could exacerbate the problem of scarcity of resources within the region as a whole. See Robert Rothstein, *The Weak in the World of the Strong* (New York: Free Press, 1972), esp. ch. 6.

33. *Africa Research Bulletin,* July 15, 1991, p. 6072.

34. *Arab News,* September 12, 1991.

35. M. Musoke, "Reform Must Come from Within," *World Press Review,* August 1991, p. 11.

36. Nicholas Koch, *Arab News,* September 12, 1991, p. 12.

37. Musoke, "Reform."

38. At one point, to help the Doe government overcome its ineptitude, the United States sent a team of 17 budgetary and financial experts to help. One year and more than $500 million later, the team gave up, thus jeopardizing American aid. See *Africa Report,* November–December 1990, p. 16.

39. The mandate was initially considered by some to be legally questionable because it was an initiative of ECOWAS under its own Defense Protocol rather than of the OAU or the United Nations. However, this mandate was subsequently approved by the OAU. The important point is that this was the first time that such a multinational peacekeeping effort had been attempted in Africa.

40. *Economist* (London), August 18, 1990, p. 37.

41. *Economist* (London), April 16, 1991, p. 43.

42. *Newswatch,* September 17, 1990, p. 31.

43. *Arab News,* September 10, 1991, p. 4.

44. *Arab News,* September 18, 1991, p. 4.

45. *Africa Report,* November–December 1991, p. 20.

46. Perhaps the change was related to the fact that then Vice President Dan Quayle had visited the Ivory Coast and had expressed strong support for ECOMOG on behalf of the United States.

47. *Africa Report,* November–December 1991, p. 7.

48. Philippe C. Schmitter, "A Revised Theory of Regional Integration," *International Organization* 24 (Autumn 1970):840.

49. UNCTAD, *Handbook of International Trade and Development Statistics* (Geneva:

UNCTAD, 1990). See also Julius E. Okolo, "The Development and Structure of ECOWAS," in *West African Regional Cooperation and Development,* ed. J. Okolo and F. Wright (Boulder: Westview Press, 1990), p. 44. This illustrative case was adapted, with permission, from the unpublished M.A. thesis by Joseph Tobore Okrakene, "Economic Community of West African States (ECOWAS): Its Political and Economic Dimensions" (University of New Orleans).

50. For an elaboration on the powers and functions of the Security Council, see Davidson Nicol, ed., *The United Nations Security Council: Towards Greater Effectiveness* (New York: United Nations Institute for Training and Research, 1982). See also N. D. White, *The United Nations and the Maintenance of International Peace and Security* (New York: St. Martin's Press, 1990).

51. This is quoted from a review by Peter D. Ehrenhaft of the book *Restructuring the GATT System,* by John H. Jackson (New York: Council on Foreign Relations Press, 1990), which appeared in *The American Journal of International Law* 86 (January 1992):232.

52. Robert Cox and Harold K. Jacobson, eds., *The Anatomy of Influence* (New Haven, CT: Yale University Press, 1973), p. 30.

53. Ibid., p. 303.

54. *The Yearbook of World Affairs* (Boulder, Colo.: Westview Press, 1986). See also Jack A. Finlayson and Mark W. Zacher, "The GATT and the Regulation of Trade Barriers: Regime Dynamics and Functions," *International Organization* 35 (Autumn 1981):561–602.

55. Joseph S. Nye, "UNCTAD: Poor Nations' Pressure Group" in Cox and Jacobson, *Anatomy of Influence,* pp. 334–70.

56. See also ibid., pp. 335–38.

57. Quoted in the report by Johan Kaufmann and Nico Schrijven, "Changing Global Needs: Expanding Roles for the United Nations System" (Academic Council of the United Nations System, Third Annual Conference, June 21–23, 1990), p. 30. See also pp. 29–33.

58. Banks, *Political Handbook of the World,* p. 902; and UN General Assembly, Doc. A/47/1 (September 11, 1992), p. 21.

59. See, for example, Keith Highet, "The Peace Palace Heats Up: The World Court in Business Again," *American Journal of International Law* 85 (October 1991):646–54.

60. See C. Amerasinghe, *Documents on International Administrative Tribunals* (Oxford: Clarendon Press, 1989); and Richard Lillich, ed., *Fact-Finding before International Tribunals* (Ardsley-on-Hudson, N.Y.: Transnational Publishers, 1992).

61. For a general reference that elaborates on this point, see Alfred H. A. Soons, ed., *Implementation of the Law of the Sea Convention through International Institutions* (Honolulu: Law of the Sea Institute). Concerning human rights, see Theodor Meron, *Human Rights and Humanitarian Norms as Customary Law* (Oxford: Clarendon Press, 1989).

62. For a summary discussion of the origins of the office of secretary-general, see Robert S. Jordan, "The Influence of the British Secretariat Tradition on the Formation of the League of Nations," in *International Administration: Its Evolution and Contemporary Applications,* ed. Robert S. Jordan (New York: Oxford University Press, 1971). See also Robert S. Jordan, ed., *Dag Hammarskjöld Revisited: The U.N.*

Secretary-General as a Force in World Politics (Durham, NC: Carolina Academic Press, 1983).

63. Portions of this section are derived from chapter 1 of Norman A. Graham and Robert S. Jordan, *The International Civil Service: Changing Role and Concepts* (New York: Pergamon Press, for the UN Institute for Training and Research, 1980). See also Theodor Meron, *The United Nations Secretariat: The Rules and the Practice* (Lexington, MA: Lexington Books, 1977). For background, see Robert S. Jordan, "What Has Happened to Our International Civil Service? The Case of the United Nations," *Public Administration Review* 41 (March/April 1981), pp. 236–45. See also David Pitt and Thomas George Weiss, eds., *The Nature of United Nations Bureaucracies* (London: Croon Helm, 1987).

64. UN General Assembly, Doc. A/47/416 (October 7, 1992), p. 15.

65. UN General Assembly, Doc. A/C.5/34/SR88, (January 4, 1980).

66. Jordan, "Our International Civil Service," p. 239. See also "Envoys Say U.N. Has Made Changes Washington Demanded," *New York Times,* May 19, 1987, p. A-33.

67. *Report of the Secretary-General on the Work of the Organization,* UN General Assembly, Doc. A/47/1 (September 11, 1992), p. 10.

68. See Robert S. Jordan, " 'Truly' International Bureaucracies: Real or Imagined?" in *Politics in the United Nations,* ed. Lawrence Finkelstein (Durham, NC: Duke University Press, 1988).

69. Graham and Jordan, *International Civil Service,* 148–67.

70. "The paramount consideration in the employment of the staff and in the determination of the conditions of service shall be the necessity of securing the highest standards of efficiency, competence, and integrity. Due regard shall be paid to the importance of recruiting the staff on as wide a geographic basis as possible (Article 101, UN Charter)." See also Yves Beigbeder, *Threats to the International Civil Service* (London: Pinter Publishers, 1988); and also Theodor Meron, *Status and Independence of the International Civil Servant* (Leydon, Holland: Sijthoff and Noordhoff, 1981).

71. See Robert E. Riggs, "The FAO and USDA," *Western Political Quarterly* 33 (September 1980):314–29; and the detailed literature listed there, as well as Riggs, "The Bank, the IMF, and WHO," *Journal of Conflict Resolution* 24 (June 1980):329–57.

72. Riggs, "FAO and USDA," pp. 317–18.

73. UN General Assembly, *Report of the Secretary-General on the Work of the Organization,* Doc. A/47/1 (September 11, 1992), p. 9.

74. For details, see Lawrence Scheinman and Werner Feld, "The European Economic Community and National Civil Servants of the Member States," *International Organization* 26 (Winter 1972):121–35. See also Robert Keohane and Stanley Hoffman, eds., *The New European Community: Decision-Making and Institutional Change* (Boulder, CO: Westview Press, 1991).

75. Leon N. Lindberg, *The Political Dynamics of European Economic Integration* (Stanford, CA: Stanford University Press, 1963), p. 55.

76. For a detailed discussion of this problem, see Hans J. Michelmann, *Organizational Effectiveness in a Multinational Bureaucracy* (Westmead, UK: Saxon House, Teakfeld Ltd., 1978), pp. 23–38.

77. *Guardian* (Manchester, UK), January 24, 1981, p. 19.

78. See Werner J. Feld and John K. Wildgen, *Domestic Political Realities and European Unification* (Boulder, CO: Westview Press, 1976), p. 126.

79. *Europe* (March–April 1981), p. 45.

80. S. N. Eisenstadt, *Essays on Comparative Institutions* (New York: Wiley, 1965), p. 180; see also Paul Reuter, *International Institutions* (London: Allen and Unwin, 1958).

81. C. Grove Haines, ed., *European Integration* (Baltimore, MD: Johns Hopkins University Press, 1957).

82. See Werner J. Feld, "The European Community's Civil Service: Bureaucracy in Crisis" (Unpublished paper delivered at the annual convention of the Southern Political Science Association, Memphis, TN, November 5–7, 1981).

83. See James D. Thompson, *Organizations in Action* (New York: McGraw-Hill, 1967, pp. 14–24, 159–60.

84. Robert W. Cox, "The Executive Head: An Essay on Leadership in International Organization," *International Organization* 23 (Spring 1969):205–30.

85. Ibid., p. 230.

86. Kurt Waldeim, *Building the Future Order,* ed. Robert L. Schiffer (New York: Free Press, 1980), p. xxii.

87. For a survey of the evolution of all aspects of international administration, see Jordan, *International Administration.* For a discussion of Dag Hammarskjöld, see Jordan, *Dag Hammarskjöld Revisited.*

88. Christoph Sasse, Edouard Poullet, David Coombes, and Gerard Deprez, *Decision Making in the European Community* (New York: Praeger, 1977), p. 176.

89. Ibid., p. 178.

90. Ibid., p. 157. See also Michelmann, *Organizational Effectiveness.*

91. See, for example, Lawrence Scheinman, "Economic Regionalism and International Administration: The European Communities' Experience," in Jordan, *International Administration.*

92. David Mitrany, "The Prospect of Integration: Federal or Functional?" in *Functionalism,* ed. A.J.R. Groom and Paul Taylor, (New York: Crane, Russak, 1975), pp. 71–72.

93. See Philippe C. Schmitter, "Three Neo-Functional Hypotheses about International Integration," *International Organization* 23 (Winter 1969):162–64.

94. See Norman F. Dufty, "Organization Growth and Goal Structure: The Case of the IGO," *International Organization* 26 (Summer 1972):479–98.

95. See Cox, "The Executive Head: An Essay on Leadership in International Organizations," *International Organizations* 23 (Spring 1969):213–26.

96. See some of the comments made by Henry Nau in "From Integration to Interdependence: Gains, Losses, and Continuing Gaps," *International Organization* 33 (Winter 1979):119–47. See also R. G. Havelock, *Planning for Innovation through Dissemination and Utilization of Knowledge* (Ann Arbor, MI: University of Michigan, Institute for Social Research, 1973); and James Q. Wilson, "Innovation in Organization: Notes Toward a Theory" in *Approaches to Organizational Design,* ed. James D. Thompson (Pittsburgh, PA: University of Pittsburgh Press, 1963), pp. 194–218.

97. See Riggs, "The Bank, the IMF," and his "FAO and USDA."

98. Paul Lewis, "U.N. Refugee Official Seeks Pledges from Donors," *The New York Times,* June 20, 1993, p. 3.

4 DECISION-MAKING PROCESSES AND POLICYMAKING SCOPE

The creation of IGO institutions and the employment of civil servants in these institutions have as their major purpose accomplishing the tasks for which the IGOs were created. The attainment of this goal requires national and multinational decision making to form the basis of IGO policies and implementing actions. For a comparative analysis and evaluation of IGO decision- and policymaking processes, we will examine in the following pages the voting systems used in IGOs; the scope and level of decisions authorized in the constituent treaties, including a taxonomy of decisions; changes in the locus of decision making and their implications; special strategies used in IGO decision making, such as package deals and bloc voting; and the implementation and evaluation of decisions.

In most cases, the IGO decision-making process consists of many activities and actions prior to actually reaching a particular decision. Other activities and measures follow in order to implement that decision. Hence, David Easton's input-output model can serve as useful background for understanding the political environment that is likely to surround IGO decision making.[1] Easton suggests that, just as in national decision making, it is reasonable to expect a variety of efforts by interested parties to influence the shape of the decisions that are eventually made in IGO institutions. These efforts may consist of logrolling, corridor deals, and the many other activities normally associated with inputs into political decisions.

VOTING SYSTEMS

Majority Rule

There is a clear historical trend away from the rule of unanimity to majority rule in decisions made within IGOs. In the course of drafting the

Covenant of the League of Nations, Lord Robert Cecil declared that "all international decisions must, by the nature of things, be unanimous."[2] Therefore, it is not surprising that in the Covenant, the unanimity rule was generally preserved, although some explicit exceptions were made in which majority voting sufficed. These exceptions included procedural questions, the admission of new members, and other instances in Assembly voting—and even, in a few situations, in Council decisions.[3] In the United Nations, the majority vote has become the rule in most bodies except the Security Council, but it has come under increasing challenge in recent years as the major donor states (which are in the minority numerically) have argued for more voting influence. In the post-Cold War period, the Security Council has emphasized "consensus" to describe decision making in peacemaking and peacekeeping. In the General Assembly, the basic rule remains that a simple majority is sufficient unless the decision to be made deals with an important question (Article 18).

Majority rule also prevails in the specialized agencies of the United Nations. In fact, because of the technical nature of their task performance, public unions—some of which were the predecessors of these agencies, like the Universal Postal Union, which was formed in 1894—employed majority rule much earlier than other IGOs.[4] On the other hand, unanimity (or rather, the absence of a negative vote) remains the basic rule in the Committee of Ministers in the Council of Europe, the Council of the OECD, the Council of the Arab League, and the NATO Council. In the Council of Ministers of the EC, a trend to increased qualified majority voting has become visible in the Single European Act of 1987 and the Maastricht Agreement on European Union, which was signed in February 1992. It was ratified by all member states at the end of 1993. Denmark and Britain in particular, had strong formal reservations that were included in their ratifying documents. Denmark, only on the second try, through a national referendum voted in favor; Britain did likewise only after the Conservative Prime Minister John Major made the issue a vote of confidence in his government, thus provoking a parliamentary political crisis.

The use of "side agreements" to deal with migratory labor and environmental concerns, in the protracted negotiating and ratifying process of the North American Free Trade Agreement (NAFTA) between Canada, the U.S. and Mexico, is an example of an attempt to adjust an agreed-upon draft treaty signed by the proper executives, to allow for legislative alterations that avoided reopening the negotiations themselves.

At times there are differences in the voting system depending on whether procedural or substantive issues are involved. In the latter case, the majority requirements are often a two-thirds vote rather than a simple majority. There are also instances when continuing practices may change voting systems and this change, in turn, develops into customary law. Examples will be provided later in this chapter.

Variations in the Equality of Voting Power

If one were to follow strictly the principle of cosovereign equality, each member state of an IGO should have the same voting power. However, in the real world of unequal power distribution, and considering the concern of the larger states especially to retain as much of their political freedom of action as possible, some means have had to be found to deviate from this principle. One way has been to allow a state extra representation through assigning sovereign status to territorial units within a state. This was the reason for admitting Byelorussia and Ukraine to full status as member states in the United Nations when they were still part of the U.S.S.R.

Another means of breaking the principle of one state, one vote is weighting the votes of IGO members. This has been defined as a system that assigns to members of IGOs votes proportioned on the basis of predetermined relevant criteria.[5] Such criteria may be the financial contributions of member states to the IGO, as is done in the World Bank, the International Monetary Fund (IMF), and the International Development Association (IDA); or they may be the size and economic power of the member states, as exemplified in the voting arrangements of the Council of Ministers of the EC. Under the latter arrangement, the four largest members (France, Germany, Italy, and Britain) have ten votes each; Spain has eight; Belgium, Greece, the Netherlands, and Portugal have five each; Denmark and Ireland have three each; and Luxembourg has two.[6]

Other systems of weighting have been proposed. For example, the suggestion has been made to base the voting system in the UN General Assembly on population figures.[7] However, while an interesting suggestion, this was politically unacceptable. Finally, the one state, one vote principle is circumvented when some member states are given a veto power over decisions. The obvious case is the UN Security Council, where the five permanent members (the United States, Russia, China, Britain, and France) can veto any substantive Council decision. Consideration is now being given to expand the permanent membership to include Germany and Japan, plus possibly several states drawn from the Group of 77 such as India or Brazil. The U.S. has formally called for such expansion, which has been opposed by Britain and France.

In summarizing our discussion of voting systems, it appears that the more technical (or, perhaps, low-politics) the issues areas in which an IGO is concerned, the greater the chances that simple majorities are employed for arriving at decisions. Where the issues are very general, such as those that composed the NIEO debate in the United Nations in the 1970s and discussions of the "new international order" of the 1990s, reliance on consensus decision making has helped to paper over real and specific differences that have hampered, or may hamper, effective implementation. Conversely, the more that security or economic high politics are involved in particular decision making within IGOs, such as in NATO or the Western European Union (WEU) or in the ratification of the Maastricht Treaty on European Union, the greater the tendency to insist on unanimity. In this way, it is perceived that vital interests of member states will not be adversely affected.

THE SCOPE AND LEVEL OF DECISIONS

The term *decision* in this discussion covers all types of action taken by vote, whether framed as a resolution, directive, or recommendation, or otherwise described. Most decisions are not automatically binding on the member states of an IGO; indeed, the majority may be nonbinding and often programmatic, especially as far as those in the UN family are concerned.

Decisions may be rendered at different levels of an IGO's activities. Usually, decisions at lower levels (for example, in committees) will become building blocks for the decisions at the top levels. The international political significance of an IGO's decisions depends in large part on the level where they have been made, although in some cases—such as the large body of antiapartheid resolutions passed in the UN organs—the higher political level may not result in a significant change in national policies for many years. On the other hand, a resolution by the ECOSOC on some development issue may gain considerably in importance if it is endorsed by an appropriate resolution in the General Assembly. In the EC, a decision of the EP (European Parliament) will have saliency only if the EC Council of Ministers adopts it and gives it political and legal support.

The circle of decision makers in IGOs consists of more than IGO civil servants. While these individuals (especially those in high or top executive positions) play the main roles in decisions made in the secretariats of the organs they serve or in the plenary bodies and councils of the organization, it is the representatives of the member governments who, as the appointed delegates of their governments, have the prime responsibility in the decision-making process. In some cases, these individuals (who may be national civil servants, legislators, or ad hoc appointees) may also participate in preliminary decisions, either in IGO committees, their diplomatic missions at the seat of the IGO, or committees composed of mission staffs, such as the Committee of Permanent Representatives serving the EC or the Council of Permanent Representatives (CPR) of NATO. In some instances, a government may use representatives of interested groups or commercial enterprises as participants at various levels in the IGO decision-making process. This method is often employed by the U.S. and offers splendid opportunities to interest groups and enterprises to directly influence the IGO decision-making process. The ILO is the most obvious case in point.

In many IGO decisions, the economic and political stakes are high and, therefore, the utilization of appropriate strategies may be crucial. This may require launching particular initiatives by some participants in the decision-making process, expressing support for these initiatives by others, or seeking to defeat them by still others. Some may serve as power brokers or consensus builders, depending on the particular interests pursued by governments and private groups.[8] Finally, some may prefer to express disapproval by withholding funds or even withdrawing from the organization, as in the U.S. action toward UNESCO, as discussed in the illustrative case in Chapter 5.

A TAXONOMY OF DECISIONS

Robert Cox and Harold Jacobson have developed a taxonomy of seven categories of decisions that we have found useful for the comparative analysis of IGOs.

Programmatic decisions refer to the strategic allocation of the IGO's resources among different types and fields of activity. Such decisions are frequently made in the framework of the budget and are inherently related to the effective task performances of the organization.

Rule-creating decisions produce the rules within the substantive scope of the IGO and also relate to task performance. They include binding norms on governments and individuals if such decisions are authorized in the constituent treaties, as is the case with the ECSC and EEC. They may also include directives to governments where authorized. In addition, they may take the form of agreements; for example, GATT's activity in the conclusion of tariff accords and codes on nontariff barriers or labor conventions by the ILO.

Operational decisions refer to the utilization of resources for task performance and the IGO's provision of services in accordance with established programs and policies. Operational decisions are often made between national civil servants of the member states and international bureaus, and these may suffer from pressures by various clienteles who seek to promote their own objectives.

Rule-supervisory decisions deal with the application of approved rules and supervision over the proper implementation of approved programs. One example is the implementation of the safeguard provisions of the International Atomic Energy Agency (IAEA). Supervision may be carried out by national and international civil servants acting singly or jointly, or by private specialists. Where realistic enforcement is possible, supervision can be crucial for proper task performance.

Representational decisions are concerned with membership issues in the IGO and representation in international bodies, and deal with questions such as, who is to be admitted to membership and who should be expelled if the possibility of expulsion is stipulated in the constituent treaty. Other issues include the validity of credentials and the determination of representation on executive organs and committees.

Boundary decisions refer to an IGO's relations with other universal and regional IGOs regarding their respective scope and competence, cooperation among the different units, and various kinds of interaction.

Symbolic decisions are primarily tests of "the acceptability of goals and ideologies intensely espoused by one group of actors or [of] the legitimacy of long-accepted norms of dominant elites."[9] These decisions have no practical consequences in the form of actions that flow directly from them, but they may provide a sensitive measure of changes in the internal distribution of influence.

CHANGES IN THE LOCUS OF DECISION-MAKING

The preceding discussion has indicated that national governments participate in IGO decision making in various ways. This raises the question of where the primary locus of the decision-making process lies in particular issue areas. It also raises the question of the extent of integration in an IGO which, as pointed out in Chapter 1, can range from a very loose and limited organization with very restricted decision-making authority to one that is tightly organized, possesses an extensive institutional framework, and is endowed with supranational powers. These powers permit IGO institutions to make decisions that are directly binding on the member states without specific action by the governments or legislatures.

If IGOs have such powers, it implies that slices of sovereignty have been transferred from the member governments to the IGO. Functionalist theory claims that this transfer occurred as the result of functional border-crossing cooperation which satisfied the needs of the people in the collaborating states. The neofunctionalists might contend that this process is the consequence of sector and institutional spillovers and of appropriate strategies employed by IGO technocrats. Still others argue that the degree of integration progress depends on the foreign policy goals of the member states intertwined with the need to meet domestic political demands by various constituencies.[10] All these points have been used in the national debates in the EC over ratification of the Maastricht Treaty. As mentioned earlier, not only Denmark and Britain—the most outspoken critics of the Treaty—had reservations of one kind or another, especially over issues such as a common currency, common defense forces, common taxation policies, and the proposed social policy. Already, in response to meeting the January 1993 goal of achieving a truly single market (i.e., from customs union to common market), national laws have had to be adjusted which clearly will have the effect of shifting the locus of decision-making in key sectors of national life from national parliaments or executives to the EC decision-making institutions. (This is discussed further in Chapter 5.)

Regardless of the theory favored, Leon N. Lindberg and Stuart A. Scheingold have developed a useful scale of the locus of decision making in their study of the EC that can have application to other IGOs.[11] They explored movement from a situation in which individual national governments make

Table 4.1
A Scale of the Locus of Decision Making

Low Integration

1. All policy decisions by national processes
2. Only the beginnings of Community decision processes
3. Policy decisions in both but national activity predominates
4. Policy decisions in both but Community activity predominates
5. All policy decisions by joint Community processes

High Integration

Source: Leon N. Lindberg and Stuart A. Scheingold, *Europe's Would-Be Polity* (Englewood Cliffs, NJ: Prentice-Hall, 1970), p. 69.

all fundamental policy choices by means of a purely internal process of decision making or make them in nonnational settings such as NATO, to a terminal situation where all these choices are subject to joint decision making within an IGO. To show various points on the integrative continuum, they prepared an illustrative table that we have reproduced in this volume. Table 4.1 suggests different loci of decision making on this continuum or, in other words, different levels on which decisions are made. We should note that a higher level of decision making does not automatically broaden the scope of decisions authorized for an IGO, although upward movement of this scope may occur in individual cases and, conceivably, continuing practice may bring about such a result. This has happened in the EC, as demonstrated by Lindberg and Scheingold, where it has continued into the 1990s.[12]

The trend of movement in the locus of decisions in an IGO may also go in the opposite direction, resulting in a gradual "renationalization" of the IGO decision-making process. Such a trend has been observed more in regional IGOs embracing developing countries than in IGOs in Europe. However, it has also happened in UN units. For example, we find that the UN agency established after the 1972 Stockholm Conference on the Human Environment to create a global program—the UN Environment Program (UNEP)—has been losing the support of its participating member states. The successor 1992 Conference on the Environment and Development (UNCED) endured the foot-dragging (if not, in some issues, the outright opposition of the United States, as discussed in the illustrative case in Chapter 6) for fear that the option to "rationalize" might be lost. Preoccupation with failing economies, shortages, and global competition has at times taken precedence over supporting environmental concerns.[13] The projects of the UN Development Program (UNDP) need host government involvement. The enforcement of human rights and other "rights-related" IGO decisions has encountered strong opposition at the national level, although the record of successes and failures of IGO attempts has been misled.

The UN Family

In our examination of specific decision-making activities and procedures in the UN family, we will begin with a discussion of conference strategy, followed by special decision-making tactics, UN bloc voting, and voting practices in the Security Council, the IMF, and the International Labour Organization (ILO).

Conference Strategies. The use of ad hoc global conferences as a means to obtain favorable decisions has been perceived, especially by the developing countries, as a valuable strategy for the attainment of goals that cannot be realized through well-meaning, nonbinding resolutions passed by the UN General Assembly or other UN bodies. In other words, conferences on specific important issues may reflect more concretely the interests and power of certain groups of states vis-à-vis the advanced industrial states than would be possible in other forums as a means to achieve important results. They also are a reflection of Cox and Jacobson's taxonomy regarding IGO decisions.

Johan Kaufmann, in discussing UN decision making, stresses the role of global conferences in the past two decades which, mostly under UN auspices, are increasingly being used to deal with certain worldwide issues that do not lend themselves to handling by a single agenda (boundary decisions).[14] The consequence of this development is that the governments, INGOs and IGOs composing the international political community are much more aware of the importance and complexity of economic issues. Even though the world is still very much fragmented politically into competing/cooperating states, it has grown increasingly interdependent economically. This interdependence requires multilateral methods to be employed in avoiding or resolving disputes (rule-creating decisions). Closely related to this multilateralism is the use of groups of states to participate in such negotiations (representational decisions). These groups can perform the following conference functions: exchange information on all or part of the agenda of a conference, either in advance or during the conference; develop common general positions on important agenda items without definite voting commitment; develop common positions on certain agenda items or initiatives with agreement on how to vote; agree on candidates to be put forward by the group or on a common vote for candidates outside the group; agree on a common spokesperson and on the contents of the statement to be delivered; and undertake joint action for or against a proposal.[15]

During the past twenty years, the two-week-long, single-agenda-item global conferences sponsored by the United Nations to deal with critical economic and social problems of a developmental nature have become so much a part of the United Nations that they might be seen collectively as a separate, powerful strand in the growing web of dialogue dealing with North-South issues. In fact, in the opinion of some qualified governmental observers, these conferences should be recognized by development experts as representing a new and innovative technique for achieving policy change at the national level.[16]

Not only have these global conferences sponsored a host of new institutions, new funds, and new mechanisms for action at both the national and international levels (programmatic decisions), they have also been responsible for generating two new developmental ideas: putting much greater emphasis on the provision of basic human needs to the poorer states and calling for greater self-reliance on the part of the developing countries by advocating technical, banking, and other forms of cooperation among them (operational decisions). They also are viewed as norm-producing. Currently, these ideas are having a major impact on the thinking of development planners in many parts of the world (symbolic decisions).

The first in this series of conferences was the 1972 global meeting on the environment at Stockholm. Three years in the planning, it grew out of the West's concern about runaway industrial growth and focused particularly on the impact of this growth on the total human environment, including air and water pollution. It did not attract high-level attention from the developing states until shortly before the conference opened, when concern began to spread that environmental cleanup costs in the industrial West could be passed on to the developing countries via higher prices, and thereby could slow the development process of these countries. There was also a concern that any obligation to observe environmental standards would slow the industrialization of developing states (the "right to pollute" argument).

A plan of action was adopted at Stockholm laying out recommendations for national, regional, and international action. It also called for the creation of a new UN agency, the UN Environment Program (UNEP), a secretariat to staff the agency, a special voluntary fund for technical assistance projects, an intergovernmental council to supervise the new agency, and a new body in the UN Secretariat to coordinate the work of the existing UN agencies that were already working on various aspects of the environmental problems. Stockholm was one of the most successful conferences in this series. In addition to developing such innovative programs as an international treaty that has as its goal a pollution-free Mediterranean and that has been signed by every state bordering the sea except Albania, UNEP has stimulated the creation of intergovernmental mechanisms for the coordination of national environmental programs in more than one hundred states around the world.

The second single-agenda-item conference concerned population and took place at Bucharest in August 1974. It, too, was three years in the making. The draft plan of action was carefully put together by a small intergovernmental preparatory committee made up of national population and demographic experts who, it turned out, were generally out of touch with their political mentors. The conference declaration and plan of action were finally adopted by consensus, but only after over one hundred votes on specific language changes had been taken at the committee level. In the reshaping of the plan of action, the politicians on the delegations of the developing states placed the population issue in the context of the New International Economic Order (NIEO), which had been proclaimed a few months earlier at the Sixth Special Session of the UN General Assembly. They forced a broadening of the population experts' narrow focus on family planning objectives and emphasized instead the general developmental aspects of the population problem. This world conference demonstrated the significance of timing and the linkage of specific global concerns outside the trade and aid field with the North-South dialogue of the 1970s.

No new institutions or funds were established, but the existing UN Fund for Population Activities (UNFPA) was strengthened and a great deal of high-level political attention was focused on this major developmental issue. Therefore, Bucharest should be viewed as a success since many persons had not believed it was possible even to convene a world meeting on the subject of population. In 1984 in Mexico City there was a follow-up International Conference on Population at which was adopted a "Declaration on Population and Development," in part to hasten implementation of the 1974 World Population Plan of Action.

The third conference in this series was on food and took place in Rome in November 1974. It was organized in a remarkably short time. In early September 1973, the heads of state of the nonaligned states, responding to a proposal made by their host, President Houari Boumedienne of Algeria, urged the holding of a joint FAO-UNCTAD conference to discuss "the serious food crises confronting vast areas and populations of the world." The United States picked up on this idea at the General Assembly a few weeks later and called for a UN World Food Conference.[17]

In December 1973, the General Assembly agreed to host the conference in Rome the following November. Considering the short time involved in planning for such a complicated gathering, this was a remarkably successful meeting. It was one of the few times that the nonaligned states and the U.S. were in full agreement on the urgent need for substantial action on a given subject, and so the usual UN political issues, and even the NIEO, failed to hamper the conference outcome. The conference plan of action was adopted by consensus and was seen by almost everyone as a positive step forward in the North-South dialogue. It focused national and global attention on the food problem and stimulated governments to take positive action toward solving those problems. Two new UN agencies were established by the conference, over the objection of the FAO, which is the primary UN body to deal with food matters. The World Food Council (WFC) was designed to establish global food policies, and the International Fund for Agricultural Development (IFAD) was designed to serve as a financial source for agricultural projects in the developing countries. This is discussed further in Chapter 5.

These three conferences were followed by global meetings dealing with women and development (Mexico City, 1975), basic human needs (Geneva, 1976), human settlements (Vancouver, 1976), water (Mar del Plata, 1977), deserts (Nairobi, 1977), technical cooperation among developing countries (TCDC) (Buenos Aires, 1978), rural development (Rome, 1979), science and technology for development (Vienna, 1979), women (Copenhagen, 1980), new and renewable energy (Nairobi, 1981), problems of the least developed countries (Paris, 1981), and the World Assembly on Aging (Vienna, 1982). The 1992 UN Conference on Environment and Development (UNCED) is discussed in Chapter 6. A 1993 conference on human rights was held in Vienna, but aroused more debate over varying conceptions of human rights (economic and social or political) than concrete implementable decisions. A proposal to create a UN High Commisioner for Human Rights, for example, was shelved.

These global conferences have a number of elements in common:

1. Their convening was blessed by a unanimous resolution of the General Assembly, which was primarily a programmatic decision fraught with symbolic overtones;
2. The documentation for conference consideration was prepared by existing or newly created units within the UN family of agencies;
3. The conferences were of two weeks' duration;
4. Parallel meetings of interested nongovernmental organizations were simultaneously held in the same city;
5. The conferences often generated a new UN entity or UN fund designed to focus more attention on the subject as part of the postconference follow-up;
6. The conference plan of action was usually adopted by consensus;
7. The recommendations were approved by the subsequent General Assembly; and
8. All the recommendations were designed to change attitudes, stimulate political will, and raise the level of national and global interest in the subject.

Clearly, some of these conferences were more effective and had a greater impact on the world scene than others, but they all succeeded in focusing governmental attention on often neglected or emerging problems. Frequently, there were intrusions of political issues that clearly had no place in such conferences, but by and large, these were dealt with and were widely perceived as diversions from the purposes for which the conferences had been called. When a global conference is carefully planned and orchestrated, it is well worth the effort because it can highlight the complexity of problems surrounding a particular development or global issue.

The eight strands described in this overview on conference strategy each made up an important aspect of the North-South dialogue of the 1970s, and each had its strengths and weaknesses. The developing states will continue to work for a world economic system that will be more to their advantage and for commitments from individual donor governments that will advance the South's goal of a more favorable distribution of the world's resources and income. The industrialized states, although reluctantly, in general continue the dialogue in their own enlightened self-interest.[18]

The "Report of the Group of High-Level Intergovernmental Experts to Review the Efficiency of the Administrative and Financial Functioning of the United Nations" recommended to the Forty-First Session of the General Assembly (1986) that no more than five special conferences should take place in a given year in order to reduce their proliferation and, hence, reduce budgetary pressures. Nonetheless, conferences as strategies for favorable decisions to be taken ultimately in plenary bodies seem to be characteristic of the UN family of IGOs and became especially prominent on economic issues within the North-South dialogue in the 1970s. As mentioned, in 1992, UNCED, a major UN Conference, was held in Rio de Janeiro, and another World Population Conference is planned for 1994. These conference strategies have little utility in other IGOs, whose memberships are much smaller and rarely as polarized as in the United Nations. In both large and small IGOs, other strategies for favorable decisions are employed, including package deals and intergovernmental and interbureaucratic lobbying and trade-offs.

Special Decision-Making Tactics. Special tactics in IGO decision making are employed by the IGO leadership, international civil servants, and member governments. They are designed to attain important goals in which these actors are particularly interested. These tactics may include the utilization of conferences, first to prepare and then to vote on relevant issues; the use of special sessions in various deliberative IGO bodies; the repeated introduction and passage of the same pertinent resolution, first in subsidiary bodies and later in such top-level plenary bodies as the General Assembly; proposals by IGO executives for package deals in stalemated negotiations; and the formation of voting blocs by states with common or converging interests.

Since the emergence of the developing countries as a major bargaining force in the international political process, there has been a tendency to view conference diplomacy as a primary strategy to achieve the goals of the Group of 77. Challenges to the global status quo have been expressed multilaterally through IGOs as well as through other forms of coalitions. Single-issue, or ad hoc, conferences have received a great deal of attention in this regard.

They have been utilized (mostly, but not always, under the sponsorship of the United Nations), to give expression to the desires of the developing countries for a change in international economic relationships or to enhance their development processes. Their value has been summarized as follows:

> If one views global, ad hoc conferences as vehicles for the interaction of public and private, national and international bureaucracies, an appropriate question to ask is, "What would have happened without the conference?" Our answer lies in investigating the two important functions of these conferences: 1. *to give publicity to an issue-area and to change the dominant attitudes surrounding the definition of the issue-area;* 2. *to initiate actions designed to alleviate the problem by an agreement on how to strengthen the existing institutions or an agreement on new and more appropriate institutional machinery* (italics added).[19]

A second tactic in conference decision making is the use of special sessions of the General Assembly to take up important issues outside its normal program of work or traditional Charter responsibilities. The special sessions on disarmament, held in 1978 and 1982, could be considered in this category, as well as the sixth (1974) and seventh (1975) special sessions dealing with NIEO issues, and even possibly the UN General Assembly's Committee of the Whole, which was charged in 1980 with reconciling the issues that comprise the so-called North-South dialogue, but which had to report in 1980 to another special session its inability to do so.[20] In 1986, for the first time, a session of the General Assembly was convened to consider the economic and social needs of a particular region, in this case Africa.

Probably the apex of the use of the General Assembly as a special-issue negotiating forum was the eleventh special session, which was held in August 1981, presumably to launch global negotiations that previously had not succeeded in other forums. The reason for the failure of this session, therefore, can be traced to the general inability of intergovernmental conferences—whether ad hoc, specialized agency—sponsored, or General Assembly special sessions—to resolve issues of immense complexity that address the vital interests of major participating states.

A third tactic in promoting particular goals through appropriate decisions is the practice in the United Nations of making use of a subsidiary body or specialized agency to serve as the convener of a conference and to provide the secretariat. This was done, for example, for the World Employment Conference of 1976, for which the ILO was the convener, and for the World Conference on Agrarian Reform and Rural Development (WCARRD) of 1979, for which the FAO convened. Another example is the 1987 Safe Motherhood Conference, which was cosponsored by the World Bank, WHO, and UNFPA.

The resolutions introduced and approved by basically sympathetic delegates to these conferences and subsidiary bodies are usually then moved to higher bodies for further approval and ultimately are presented to the General Assembly for consideration. Given the substantial majority of developing countries in the Assembly, it is not surprising that these resolutions are adopted in that body, receiving thereby the highest legitimacy within the UN framework. In 1986, the Conference on the Law of Treaties between States and International Organizations or Between International Organizations adopted a convention delineating how IGOs should conclude, adopt, enforce, and observe treaties.

A final step in the use of General Assembly resolutions is the movement toward global negotiations in the Assembly. The hopes (so far unrealized) of the developing states that compose the Group of 77 have been that, through such negotiations, their economic and political objectives would find acceptance by the industrialized states, perhaps with the help of a sympathetic global public opinion. So far, this has been largely unrealized. The stalemate over the Uruguay Round of GATT contains elements of both North-South and North-North contention, played out in another conference forum that many developing states distrust.

While the focus here has been on the United Nations, the three strategies conceivably can also be employed in regional IGOs if they have a hierarchical structure, as has the UN family of IGOs. However, success depends also on the distribution of decision-making powers to subsidiary organs and on the fervor with which conflicting interests are pursued. Hence, a regional IGO such as the OAS might be suitable for the employment of these strategies. An additional factor is the interaction of the IMF, regional development banks, and private banks (or banking consortia) in attempting to deal with the debt problems of developing countries.

"Package Deals." When negotiations on an important issue are stalled in an IGO and votes on that issue either cannot be scheduled or are likely to be inconclusive, package deals can be, and have been, used successfully by the executive heads of IGOs or the conference chairs or presidents, to break the stalemate and achieve an acceptable outcome to the negotiations. A reason for such success is the comprehensive knowledge possessed by IGO executives regarding all elements of an issue, which enables them and their colleagues to prepare a solution with an acceptable distribution of gains and concessions for all parties. Such package deals have become a stock-in-trade of the EC Commission over the years and have been employed successfully on several occasions by the director-general of GATT.[21] However, these IGOs may be only the best examples; the making of package deals may be found in other IGOs as well, such as arms reduction negotiations between the United States and the former U.S.S.R. involving NATO and the defunct WTO, and in UNCTAD in the negotiations of commodity agreements.

Somewhat similar to proposals of a package deal is the utilization of a chairman's text to galvanize consensus and movement on outstanding issues, mostly in working groups set up by UN bodies and specialized agencies. The chairman of such a group will formulate a proposed text for an international convention, such as an accord on the code of conduct for transnational corporations. This tool, which may contain agreed and nonagreed portions of articles and clauses of the prospective convention, can serve as a stimulus for further negotiations by the parties involved and has been effective in reaching final consensus on contested parts of the convention. An example of an attempt that failed is the use of a package deal approach to the Convention on the Law-of-the-Sea.[22] Instead, the United States and other states registered their exceptions to parts of the overall treaty and, although not moving the treaty to ratification, agreed to observe acceptable parts de facto, even if not de jure. A similar procedure has been used in regard to strategic arms reduction, both before and after the demise of the U.S.S.R.

Caucusing Groups and Voting Blocs. Although the term *voting bloc* is frequently used in the literature when voting in the General Assembly or in other plenary bodies is discussed, the term *caucusing group* might be more appropriate because continuous solid bloc voting is rare. A bloc may be defined as a group of states that meets regularly in caucus, has some degree of formal organization, and is concerned with substantive issues and related procedural matters that may come to a vote in plenary IGO organs.[23] These groupings include the developing states (the Group of 77), which may be broken down further into the Afro-Asian, Latin American, and other developing countries. Another group is made up of the EC states, sometimes voting with other Western states such as the United States, Canada, Japan, Australia, or New Zealand, and, of course, another bloc was composed of the Soviet Union and the so-called People's Democracies (but not the People's Republic of China). Any reform of the voting provisions of the Security Council will still have to take account of regional representation and the veto.

Group cohesion in voting depends on the issues and caucus leadership. Anticolonialism and the NIEO had been powerful stimulants to coalesce developing states, but with the end of the Cold War, other cohering motives are emerging. An example could be efforts to control drug trafficking regionally. Although there have been the suggestions to create "drug-free" regions similar to proposals to create "nuclear-weapons-free" (NWFZ) regions (as, for example, for the Antarctic), the actual level of common interests and patterns of cooperation have not yet been achieved.

In July 1993, a precedent in bloc politics was made in the Security Council when the non-permanent—mostly non-Western—members expressed their united opposition to the policy of the permanent members not to free the Muslim-led government of Bosnia-Herzegovina from the arms embargo applied to all combatants in the warfare that erupted in the former province with the collapse of Yugoslavia. This event could be viewed as an attempt by non-Western, non-Christian elements of the international community to express their view that UN peacemaking had become too selective, and in particular that the selection was being made primarily by the Western Powers with the acquiescence of China and Russia.

Lastly, caucus leadership is closely related to persuasive skill, careful presentation of issues and possible outcomes, and, in some cases, the charisma of the caucus leader.

It is interesting to note that during the Cold War, the United States and the Soviet Union voted more often against the majority in the General Assembly than did most UN members. The voting analyses presented later in this chapter offer detailed insights into the intricacies of bloc voting and possible motivations for states joining different caucuses on various issues.[24]

While it is important in both theoretical and practical terms to understand the political and economic implications of voting patterns in IGO plenary organs, as well as to comprehend the reasons for these patterns, it would be even more valuable if one could predict future voting outcomes in IGO institutions. Jack E. Vincent, whose statistical inquiries will be discussed later in this chapter and who considers economic development to be one of the most important predictors of voting behavior, believes that economically underdeveloped states are more apt to want to expand the work of IGOs because it offers prospects of substantial improvements of their capabilities. Other important predictors, according to Vincent, are democracy as the political system used in particular states and the nature of the relations with the United States.[25]

There are a number of studies in the literature that have dealt with the definition and identification of voting blocs or caucusing groups within IGOs as well as some empirical studies on the measurement of such blocs' degree of cohesive behavior/level of voting agreement. The UN General Assembly, however, has received most of the attention. Studies have offered some predictor variables of voting behavior within the United Nations. A good review of the earlier work has been presented by Arend Lijphart.[26]

As Lijphart writes, one of the major weaknesses of the early analyses of bloc politics in the General Assembly was "the lack of a satisfactory identification of blocs" because most provided a list of blocs or groups "without attempting to distinguish between different types." In addition, these studies were quite deficient in their avoidance of precise empirical measurement. Notwithstanding these weaknesses, however, there were stands of common agreement across the various descriptions: the Afro-Asian, Arab, Latin American, Soviet, and West European–North American states, as well as the Commonwealth, and NATO, were all identified as blocs or groups.

As mentioned above, however, most of these analyses did not provide very precise definitions, nor did they distinguish between the different groups in the General Assembly. These defects are addressed by Thomas Hovet, Jr., who identified different types of blocs and groups.[27] He employs explicit terms when defining each type: caucusing blocs, caucusing groups, geographical distribution groups, regional organizational groups, common interest groups, and temporary groups. Hovet named nine caucusing groups: the Afro-Asian, Arab, African, Benelux, Commonwealth, Latin American, Scandinavian, Soviet, and Western European. Some members of the United Nations (the United States, China, Israel, and South Africa) were not located in any caucusing group and, conversely, some members were placed in more than one group.

Lijphart has examined bloc voting in the General Assembly (forty-four roll calls on colonial issues from 1956 through 1958). He employed an adaptation of the Rice-Beyle Index of Voting Agreement. The underlying principle of this method, as Lijphart explains, is that, instead of first "postulating the existence of certain blocs and then measuring their cohesiveness, it performs both tasks—identification of blocs and measurement of their cohesion—simultaneously on the basis of the voting records." The Rice-Beyle method compares the vote of every single member to the vote of every other member and a bloc is defined as a group of members "between all possible pairs of whom the voting agreement is equal to or greater than an assigned minimum figure."[28]

By the use of this method, Lijphart discovered several voting blocs located at different levels on the 0–100 voting agreement index. The bloc composed of the Soviet Union, its two Union Republics, and its East European satellites (but not Poland) was at the 100 level; at the 95.5 level were Iraq, Saudi Arabia, Jordan, and Libya—all members of the Arab caucusing group; Ceylon (Sri Lanka), India, and Nepal were at 90; Australia, Canada, New Zealand, and Britain were also at 90; and there were two large voting blocs at the 75 level: a twenty-nine-member Asian-African-Soviet bloc and an eighteen-member Western bloc.

Some analyses of voting behavior and bloc cohesiveness have employed quite sophisticated methodological approaches. Hayward R. Alker, Jr., employed the form of factor analysis termed *R-analysis* to the Sixteenth Session of the UN General Assembly (1961–1962).[29] Seventy votes were examined, which included all distinct, nonunanimous, nonprocedural, plenary roll calls as well as twenty-six of the most important committee votes. Alker's findings can be summarized as follows: six major factors were identified and eight main groupings emerged. The main blocs or groups were characterized as the Old Europeans, Latin caucus, Soviet bloc, Arab caucus, Casablanca group, Brazzaville group (mostly former French colonies), Africans, and Asians. Yugoslavia, Israel, and the Republic of China (Taiwan) were not listed within any group. The factors of conflict identified by Alker were East versus West, North versus South, self-determination, Cold War, Muslim questions, and UN supranationalism.

Bruce Russett employed the form of factor analysis termed *Q-analysis* to the Eighteenth Session and examined all plenary and committee roll calls except those seen as virtually unanimous (more than 90 percent on any one side).[30] A total of sixty-six votes were analyzed by Russett. His analysis found six factors, but with Q-analysis, the factors are defined as the country groupings or blocs. These six were the Western community, Brazzaville Africans, Afro-Asians, communist bloc, conservative Arabs, and Iberia.

While most of the studies cited above dealt with the identification of blocs or groups, the measurement of such groups' degree of cohesion, and the dimensions of conflict within the United Nations, a series of studies by Jack E. Vincent correlated national attributes of member states with their voting record in order to predict future voting outcomes.[31] The techniques employed by Vincent included survey data, correlation techniques, factor analysis, and canonical correlation.[32] In one study, Vincent identified the roll-call content areas as "votes East," "votes South," "votes East in Cold War," "self-determination," "supranationalism," "pro-Arab," and "against UN intervention." The voting groups were identified as Western Community, Brazzaville Africans, Afro-Asians, communist bloc, conservative Arabs, and Iberia. Table 4.2 presents a summary of Vincent's findings.

Vincent writes that, although his studies include a number of variables other than just the economic variable, "It can be seen that, compared to other predictors, economic development measures have emerged again and again as primarily important. Further, concerning the UN system, high development tends to predict negativism . . . whether one is dealing with attitudes toward specific organs, procedures, or voting behavior."[33] His findings tend to corroborate the general view that IGO member states with greater capabilities tend to have more negative attitudes toward the IGO (at least within the UN system). This is a very pessimistic finding in light of the fact that the more economically developed countries are—and will continue to be—the main source of financial support of the United Nations.

The Security Council: Voting Practices and Decision Strategies. One of the perennial complaints about the Security Council has been the veto. However, it is important to note that the veto has been somewhat softened by practices that have evolved over time; some of these practices—such as distinguishing between procedural and non-procedural questions—have taken on a legal character while others are viewed as informal precedents, or perhaps, customs.

Article 27, paragraph 3, of the Charter, which established the veto of the five permanent members, states that for a favorable vote on substantive matters before the Council, "the concurring votes of the permanent members" must be included. It does not stipulate all the members. Hence, very early in the history of the Security Council, the usage developed that abstention of permanent members from the vote on a substantive matter should not constitute a veto.[34] This usage has given permanent Council members greater latitude in the expression of their views and the imple-

Table 4.2
Summary of Findings on Predictor Variables

Year	Subject	Findings
1961-62	UN caucusing groups	Average per capita GNP of the members of caucusing groups predicts attitudes held by delegate members in groups.
1965-66	UN delegate attitudes toward organs	Economic development predicts negative attitudes.
1967-68	Relationship of voting and attitudes	Western voting states have negative attitudes. Afro-Asian, African, and communist voting states have positive attitudes.
1968	UN delegate attitudes toward organs	Economic development receives largest weight in canonical correlation between attitudes and predictors, predicting negative attitudes.
1969	Regional groups	Economic development discriminates four regional groups better than any other predictor, followed by democracy and U.S. relations.
1971	UN delegate attitudes toward the IR system	Economic development predicts negative attitudes while democracy and U.S. relations predict positive attitudes.

Source: Jack E Vincent, "An Application of Attribute Theory to General Assembly Voting and Some Implications," *International Organization* 26 (Summer 1972): 576, Table 7, "Summary of Studies."

mentation of their foreign policies. At the same time, it has significantly reduced the negative impact of the veto on the working of the Council.

The Security Council adopted a similar practice with respect to the physical absence of a permanent member. Absence, therefore, does not have the effect of a veto. The best-known case for this interpretation of Article 27 was the Korean crisis of June 1950, although earlier precedents existed.[35] The Soviet Union representatives had absented themselves from Security Council proceedings from January to August 1950 in protest against occupation of the Chinese seat by a representative of the Republic of China, the nationalist government on Formosa (Taiwan). The absence of the Soviet representative during the deliberations on the North Korean aggression on South Korea made it possible for the Council to pass important resolutions including, for the first time in the history of the United Nations, the recommendations of enforcement measures.[36] The Soviet Union denied the legality of these resolutions, but it has not consistently opposed the thesis that "the absence of a permanent member should be construed as acquiescent abstention rather than veto in absentia."[37]

The Uniting for Peace Resolution, which was passed by the General Assembly in November 1950, also undermined the power of the veto in the Security Council. It authorized the General Assembly to confer on the secretary-general the authority to take a number of measures when the Security Council is unable to act as the result of a veto being cast. The measures range from the establishment of peace observation commissions to the recruitment and dispatch of military contingents as peacekeeping forces.

It is interesting to note that over time, the United States and the Western permanent members of the Security Council have changed their view about the undesirability of the veto. Being outvoted in the General Assembly by the coalition formed by the Soviet Union and the developing countries from the 1960s through the 1980s, these states now see a virtue in the veto that offers them opportunities to counter these majorities, at least in those peace-related cases that are brought before the Security Council. The contemporary usefulness of the veto and subsequent innovations are illustrated by the fact that Britain used the veto in its 1982 Falkland Islands dispute with Argentina, while the Uniting for Peace Resolution was used in 1981 to overcome a Soviet veto of what it considered a hostile resolution in the Security Council concerning the Soviet military presence in Afghanistan.

Toward the end of the 1980s, the United States changed its generally cool and critical attitude toward the United Nations which had been the hallmark of the first Ronald Reagan administration. This was done mainly because Washington felt that the United Nations, and especially the Security Council, could be a desirable instrument for the achievement of American foreign policy goals. This attitude was helped by the fact that, due to Washington's complaints, the administrative efficiency of the UN Secre-

Figure 4.1
Security Council: Number of Official Meetings, Resolutions, and Presidential Statements, 1987–1992

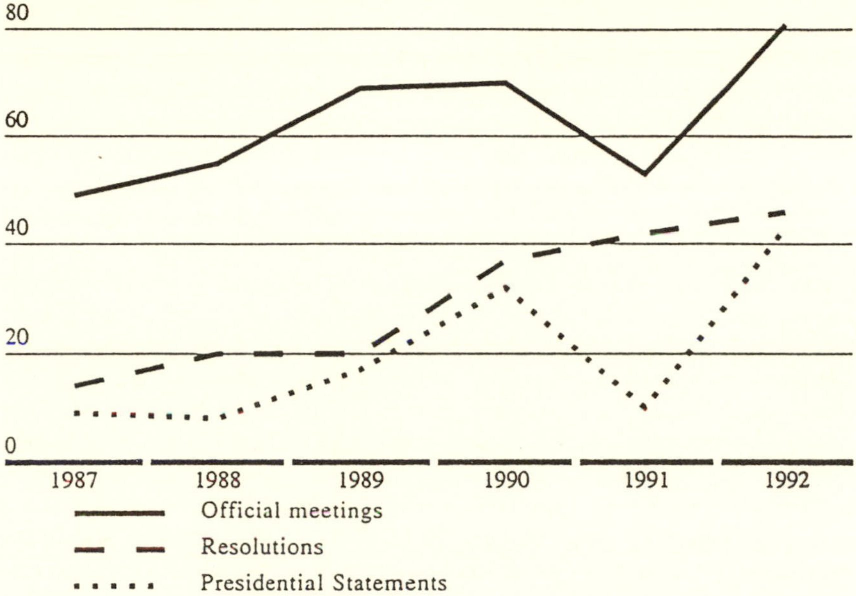

Notes: 1990 includes one resumed meeting; 1991 includes six closed sessions of the same meeting, in addition to an open session of the meeting; 1992 includes one resumed meeting.

Source: United Nations, *Report of the Secretary-General on the Work of the Organization* (GA Doc. A/47/1, September 11, 1992).

tariat had improved. The Security Council now plays a much more active role in international developments, and especially conflict resolution, than ever before. See Figure 4.1 for a graphic illustration of the rate of Security Council decision-making. Aside from the veto, today the Council usually votes by consensus.

While some observers asserted initially that the United Nations acted either as a face-saving instrument or a cover for cooperation, the major powers of the world now have acknowledged the value of UN involvement in post-Cold War peacekeeping and peacemaking and for achieving their own foreign policy objectives. An obvious example is the invasion of Kuwait by Iraq in August 1990, which led to a number of Security Council resolutions that, inter alia, condemned Iraqi aggression, called on Baghdad to withdraw, imposed economic sanctions, and authorized the use of force if necessary. Thus was made possible the war known as Operation Desert Storm, which was conducted by a coalition of Western and Middle Eastern armed forces under the leadership of the United States. Japan and other nonparticipating states contributed financial aid. The implementation of the Security Council Resolutions ending the war (most notably Resolution 687) and imposing a full military settlement on Iraq continues to be carried out by multinational inspection teams, some under the auspices of IAEA. In addition, the United States has imposed "no-fly" zones over both northern and southern Iraq to protect threatened minorities with UN approval. The UN economic sanctions have also been enforced. Persistant non-compliance with all aspects of the conditions of settlement—in particular concerns about Iraq's rebuilding its nuclear, chemical, and missile warfare capacity—has resulted in periodic crises with the United Nations.

The Yugoslav crisis also reached the Security Council in 1991. Initial attempts by the EC Foreign Ministers to settle the dispute between Serbians, Croats, and Muslim inhabitants of Bosnia-Herzegovina were unsuccessful; consequently, the Council was asked to furnish more than 10,000 peacekeeping forces. However, as no enduring cease-fire could be ensured in the area and as fighting has continued, the UN peacekeepers have had difficulty making progress in their assigned mission. Furthermore, there is debate as to whether the UN presence has actually achieved its purpose. The arms embargo largely failed to restrain Serbia, even though naval units from NATO, WEU, and the United States were authorized in November 1992 to stop and inspect ships. By late December, NATO offered to send a multinational force of about 8,000 troops under UN auspices to assist in securing roads and airfields to relieve, in particular, the Serbian seige of Sarajevo in Bosnia. NATO aircraft also supported UN observers. In Croatia, although UN Protection Forces (UNPROFOR) protected Serb-controlled areas in "Sector West," both Serbs and Croats used the winter of 1992–1993 to rearm and prepare for further warfare over territory with the arrival of spring. By the Fall of 1993, the two countries were close to partitioning Bosnia-Herzegovina after the United States and other Western powers could not agree on using force to end the fighting. Additionally, the refugee problems created from the Yugoslav warfare have overextended such UN agencies as UNHCR, as Slovenia and Croatia have closed their borders to the flow of refugees from Bosnia-Herzegovina. This is discussed further in Chapter 5.

The United Nations was also called on to help the emaciated and distraught people of Somalia, who were suffering from advanced starvation. Despite a sudden and growing world concern for Somalia—nineteen months after its agony of starvation and anarchy began, supplies from UNICEF, WHO, and other relief agencies, both public and private, were insufficient, in large part because distribution was being impeded by warring militias. The Security Council agreed to send 500 armed Pakistani troops to guard the distribution of supplies sent to Somalia, but this proved inadequate. Subsequently, a force led by the United States was sent to bring about effective aid distribution pending a transfer of authority to the UN. Other national contributions brought the total figure to over 50,000 troops. The withdrawal of U.S. troops began in February 1993, and the handing-over to the UN took place in May. Unfortunately, fighting between UN forces and clan warlords, especially in Mogadishu, not only continued but increased, prompting a reintroduction of American forces, primarily helicopter gunships and marines. In September and October 1993, the United States declared its intention to withdraw again by March 1994 after failing to assert military control over southern Mogadishu because of aggressive clan opposition. This inability of the UN forces to achieve stability threatens the humanitarian aid goals of both the UN and INGOs, as well as the political cohesiveness of the UN.

The ethnic warfare in the former Yugoslavia and in Somalia are just the most visible manifestations of the fact that the post-Cold War "new international order" is not likely to be very orderly. In fact, the level of human displacement and suffering will likely exceed that of the Cold War period. Angola, Afghanistan, Sudan, Mozambique, Liberia, Cambodia, and the former Soviet Central Asian republics all appear as good examples as the world approaches a new century.[38]

The International Monetary Fund (IMF). Another example of weighted voting in an IGO, although one that is quite different from the Security Council, is found in the IMF. To understand this system requires a brief discussion of the IMF's history, structure, and functions.

The IMF is one of two key IGOs that emerged from the Bretton Woods Conference in New Hampshire in July 1944; the other IGO was the International Bank for Reconstruction and Development (IBRD), which became known as the World Bank Group. The basic purposes for the creation of the IMF were to safeguard international financial and monetary stability and provide financial backing for revival and expansion of international trade.

Although initially the product mostly of Anglo-American discussions, the Articles of Agreement of the Fund (its basic constituent treaty) were ratified by 28 states before the end of 1945, and formal IMF operations began March 1, 1947. By the early 1990s more than 155 states were members of the Fund, including many formerly communist countries such as Russia and the Peoples Republic of China.

The two bodies in the Fund that are formally responsible for making decisions are the Board of Governors and the Executive Board. The Board of Governors meets once a year and is composed of one representative from each member state (usually the minister of finance or economics). It constitutes the deliberative organ of the IMF. However, while each member state is represented, the voting is not equal, as it is based on a system of quotas. The size of the quotas of individual member states depends on their contributions to the Fund which, in turn, determines its borrowing rights as well as its voting power. The largest contributor currently is the United

States, which has 19.11 percent of the voting power; the smallest contributors have considerably less than 1 percent each. Over the years, the quotas have undergone changes, and the EC's quota now exceeds 15 percent. A sharp increase in the U.S. contribution (along with that of other states) of nearly 50 percent was authorized in 1983 by the IMF's policymaking Interim Committee to help avoid bankruptcies in the developing countries.

This change was important because the Articles of Agreement require not only qualified majorities of weighted votes on important issues, but also a minimum number of member states for the approval of proposed resolutions in particular cases. For example, any general revisions of quotas in the Fund must be approved by a four-fifths majority of the total voting power. Any changes in the Articles of Agreement have to have the concurrence of three-fifths of the members having four-fifths of the votes. Such a change was made to increase the minimum total votes from four-fifths to 85 percent in 1968.[39] As a consequence, the United States and the EC were placed in the position of being able to veto important decisions. It should be noted that, on less important issues, a simple majority of the voting rights of the member states is sufficient.[40] Between the annual sessions of the governors, votes can be taken by mail or other means.

The Board of Governors has delegated many of its powers to the Executive Board but has retained its authority over the admission of new members, quota changes, and the election of Executive Board members. The latter body is, in effect, in permanent session in Washington. It consists of a total of twenty-two directors, five of whom are appointed while the others are elected. The appointed directors are nominated by, and represent, the five states with the largest quotas in the Fund, namely, the United States, Britain, West Germany, France, and Japan. The elected directors are nominated by and act for groups of member states. The chairman of the Executive Board is the Fund's managing director, who is assisted by approximately 1,400 staff members.

In 1974, a twenty-two-member Interim Committee of the International Monetary System was established to advise the Board of Governors regarding the management and adaptation of this system. This body also makes recommendations to the Board on how to deal with sudden disturbances that threaten the system. The Committee has now been transformed into the IMF Council, which concerns itself with global liquidity and monetary adjustment problems.

The IMF's central function is to assist members in meeting short-term, balance-of-payments difficulties by permitting them to draw temporarily upon the Fund's reserves. An instrument in carrying out this function was the creation in 1968 of new international reserves through the establishment of special drawing rights (SDRs) over and above the drawing rights already available to Fund members. Since then, the quotas for drawing rights have been increased substantially; by 33 percent in 1976 and 1978, and a further

50 percent in 1980.[41] At present, the total of SDRs is 135 billion (nearly $180 billion).

A second major IMF responsibility is supervision of the operation of the international exchange-rate system in order to maintain stability among the world currencies and prevent competitive revaluations and devaluations. A second amendment to the Articles of Agreement, which entered into force in 1978, legalized the system of floating exchange arrangements and ended the existing system of par values based on gold.

Finally, a most essential function of the IMF is assistance to developing states. For this task it conducts a program of technical assistance—largely in the field of banking and fiscal problems, both through its own staff and outside experts, as well as through a training program organized by the IMF Institute in Washington. Standby credits are granted to developing states, but only if certain conditions are met, such as the reduction of imports, the devaluation of currencies, and the tightening of domestic money supplies. A number of states have protested the imposition of what is called the IMF's standard package (or conditionality) for the provision of loans and have called for a reform of the Fund's procedures.[42] However, it is doubtful whether the IMF will accede to these demands, and if changes occur at all, they will come very slowly considering the current distribution of weighted votes.

This also shows the tremendous importance of weighted votes for the Western industralized states which are the strongest financial contributors to the IMF. On the other hand, the developing states also benefit from this arrangement because, without the protection of the influence that the Western states enjoy through the voting system, the resources of the IMF in all likelihood would be much smaller. This is one important reason why all recent U.S. presidents, regardless of party affiliation, have resisted congressional efforts to limit U.S. contributions to international financial agencies.

The International Labour Organization (ILO): Unusual Decision-Making. The ILO is set apart from other IGOs because, although its members are nation-states, their representatives in the major organs of the ILO are not only government officials, but also individuals representing the views of employers and workers.

The ILO is one of the oldest IGOs; it was established in April 1919 as an autonomous organization associated with the League of Nations. In 1946 it became associated with the United Nations as a specialized agency.

Major goals of the ILO include full employment, raising the standard of living, the assurance of proper earnings and working conditions, the provision of adequate training facilities, effective recognition of the right of collective bargaining, and appropriate social security measures.[43]

The General Conference is the top-level plenary organ of the ILO. Each member state is represented by two government delegates, an employers' delegate and a workers' delegate. In the choice of these delegates, the member governments are obligated to consult "with the industrial organizations, if such organizations exist, as the case may be, in their respective countries."[44] Each delegate has one vote.

Most of the decisions of the Conference deal with setting standards for the improvement of working conditions and require a two-thirds vote for adoption. The decisions are in the form of draft conventions and recommendations and fall into the category of rule-creating decisions. Although they are not binding on the member states, they are expected to be ratified by the approximately 130 member governments for incorporation into their national law. However, while France and Belgium, for example, have ratified more than seventy of these international instruments, the United States, a member of the ILO since 1934, has ratified only seven.

Below the Conference is a body of limited membership, the Governing Body, whose composition also follows the tripartite pattern. It consists of twenty-four government officials: twelve employers' and twelve workers' representatives. Ten of the government representatives are required to be from the state of "chief industrial importance" and the employers' and workers' representatives are to be "elected respectively by the employers' delegates and workers' delegates to the Conference.[45] The functions of the Governing Body include the selection of the director-general of the International Labour Office (the Secretariat of the ILO) and the supervision of this organ and the many subsidiary committees and commissions of the ILO.

On November 5, 1975, then U.S. Secretary of State Henry Kissinger notified the ILO of the U.S. intention to withdraw its membership, setting out "four matters of fundamental concern" which were the main—but not the only—reasons for leaving the Organization: (1) the erosion of tripartite representation, (2) selective concern for human rights, (3) disregard of due process, and (4) increasing politicization of the organization.[46] At least four other concerns were apparently in the minds of government, labor, and management representatives (the tripartite character of the ILO): (5) declining ILO interest in the development of technical standards through conventions and recommendations, (6) excessive use of flexibility devices that permit developing countries and others to avoid the full obligation of conventions, (7) lack of connection between ILO technical cooperation programs and the supervision and enforcement of labor standards, and (8) misdirection or inappropriateness of International Labour Office research and publications. Despite a two-year effort by both the United States and the ILO to change the things Washington did not like, the United States decided on November 5, 1977, to allow its withdrawal to take effect. Thus, on that date, it ceased to be a member of the ILO.

This step was significant because actual withdrawal from the United Nations or one of its specialized agencies or activities weakens the notion of universality or equality of membership that is one of the cornerstones of the present political configuration of world politics. It also signified, in a more fundamental sense, that one of the major supporters of IGOs—the United States—was becoming disenchanted with the benefits that such support presumably could bring. Without the political and financial sustenance of the United States, many IGOs would be hard-pressed to continue the range and variety of their programs.

Following the withdrawal, U.S. President Jimmy Carter established a cabinet-level committee to monitor developments and advise him on ILO matters. Reflecting the ILO's tripartite structure, the AFL-CIO, the U.S. Council of the International Chamber of Commerce, and U.S. government representatives were given an equal voice on the committee.

An underlying condition that set the stage for this development was the fact that the initial dominance in the ILO of industrial states with market economies had given way to a more varied membership, with important parts being played by the centrally planned economies of Eastern Europe, many newly independent states, and the developing countries.[47] In fact, Secretary Kissinger had asserted that the United States could not accept a growing tendency for workers' and employers' groups to fall under the domination of governments.

Specifically, in 1970 the new ILO Director-General Wilfred Jenks of Britain appointed a Soviet assistant director-general as one of his first official acts. The hostile reaction of the AFL-CIO, which has a very strong anticommunist tradition, led the U.S. Congress to suspend temporarily the payment of the U.S. contribution to the ILO. In addition, in 1975, the ILO granted observer status to the Palestine Liberation Organization (PLO), and this created widespread resentment in the United States.

Nonetheless, there was great uneasiness among some informed sectors of the American public that, by withdrawing from the ILO, the United States would be sacrificing the necessary political leverage needed to bring about the reforms or other changes that it desired. In other words, working from within would be better than simply walking away. Furthermore, examples could be found in which the system of tripartite voting had indeed benefited U.S. interests, even though one of the major U.S. complaints was that the ILO reports and complaint procedures were biased against the Western industrial states, with the socialist states of the former Soviet bloc in particular being given less intensive scrutiny, even to the point of the ILO simply ignoring blatant violations of workers' rights. The report of the private, nonpartisan Commission to Study the Organization of Peace put this question of politicization in the following way:

> Since ILO voting rights extend beyond governments, empowering non-government delegates to vote on issues normally reserved to governments, the ILO should be even more careful than the other Specialized Agencies to avoid involvement in issues of international politics unrelated to ILO's substantive work. Assuming that a par-

ticular political issue is extraneous or tangential to the central core of ILO's mandate, there is even less reason for workers' or employers' delegates to become involved than there is for governments to seek to raise such issues in an ILO forum. When such issues are raised, however, in some circumstances workers' and employers' delegates may be able to exercise greater freedom of action than governments. In such a case, tripartism, fortified by the new secret ballot rule, can help to insulate the ILO from excessive political use.[48]

As an example, in the 1978 General Conference, a Syrian resolution condemning Israel received the support of a bare majority of the governments represented at the Conference (63 out of 125 states), but failed to win adoption because a number of employers' and workers' delegates failed to vote with their governments in favor of the resolution. From the U.S. viewpoint, the Syrian resolution would not have been proper for General Conference adoption; however, as it happened, its defeat would not have occurred were it not for the independent vote exercised by workers' and employers' delegates.[49] The resolution had sought to extend a 1974 resolution that had condemned Israel without any investigation of the facts. Consequently, a new mechanism to eliminate resolutions representing such violations of due process was negotiated by Western and developing governments, thus making the fact-finding aspect of the ILO's functions more balanced.

Another reform was to strengthen the tripartite decision-making system itself. For example, as mentioned above, a new secret ballot procedure for the General Conference was instituted over the strong resistance of the Soviet Union. By instituting a secret ballot, the employers' and workers' representatives are encouraged to vote their consciences without fear of governmental recrimination.

Furthermore, the ILO began applying its human rights machinery to Eastern Europe. In November 1978, the ILO Governing Body censured Czechoslovakia for illegally firing dissidents from their jobs, an action exemplifying rule-supervisory decisions. By 1980 it was examining worker complaints against the Soviet Union and Poland for violating trade union rights. By following the ILO procedures for handling complaints of workers against their governments, what would otherwise have been a domestic quarrel between a government and its employers' or workers' organizations becomes internationalized, thus bringing to bear the weight of international public opinion. Without a doubt, the strong backing of the Western trade unions in support of the Polish Solidarity trade union gave the indigenous movement increased international significance.[50] With the collapse of the Soviet Union and its control over Eastern Europe, the ILO has sought to assist East European unions in learning how to function effectively in a market economy.

In 1980 the stage was set for the U.S. return to the ILO when the cabinet-level committee recommended such action to President Carter in February 1980.[51] The rationale that proved persuasive was that, although withdrawal may have promoted reforms, continuing to remain outside the ILO would not have yielded additional benefits to the United States. Those ILO members who worked to achieve the gains that were made would have felt disillusioned if the United States had failed to return. Also, the U.S. lead in human rights issues would have been sorely missed, even though the rest of the Western group of members had become more cohesive and effective on this issue. Specific reasons for rejoining were:

1. The opportunity to participate in and influence the formation of international labor standards, which directly affect labor codes in developing countries;
2. A chance to participate in and influence voluntary agreements, such as codes of conduct for multinational enterprises, the ILO version of which is regarded by U.S. labor and business as the most constructive yet developed;
3. A framework in which the U.S. labor movement and business community can be in contact with their counterpart organizations throughout the world;
4. Influence over ILO execution of UN Development Program (UNDP) projects;
5. Participation in the UN system's most effective mechanism for promoting the human rights of workers; and
6. Participation in the ILO's studies of development, which pioneered the basic human needs approach to development and directly influenced World Bank and U.S. Agency for International Development (AID) programs.

This experience of withdrawal rested on such a unique organizational structure and political circumstances that it is difficult to draw the conclusion that the interests of the United States were better served by taking this unusual step. Attempts by the United States to withhold funds from international organizations in order to exert political pressure on decisions are becoming more common, with such resolutions increasingly showing up in the agenda of both houses of the U.S. Congress. Usually the White House opposes such resolutions because to allow the Congress to make such determinations leaves open too many opportunities for a consistent U.S. policy toward the IGO at issue to become a casualty of domestic politics—especially in an election year. Nonetheless, such congressional pressure on the White House has at times served to help the government in its negotiations with other governments in trying to bring about reforms in those IGOs in which the United States is a member. (See, for example, the illustrative case discussing the U.S. confrontation with UNESCO in Chapter 5.)

Following up further its general desire to push for improvements in UN activities, in 1986 the United States reduced by over half its annual assessed UN contribution, thus creating a major crisis that added urgency to the work of the so-called "Group of High Level Experts to Review the Efficiency of the Administrative and Financial Functioning of the U.N." One of the recommendations of the Group was for the United Nations to adopt a two-year program budget and a six-year medium-term plan. Another international panel recommended that the UN budget should be approved by general agreement rather than by majority vote, thus allowing any country to veto it. This reform would give more influence in decision making to the larger donor states, and especially the United States. In any case, as the ILO episode reveals, the locus of decisions can be defined, not only in its institutional sense, but also in a programmatic sense.

Regional Organizations

The European Communities: The Role of the Council of Ministers. Examples of weighted voting, as well as of continuing practices developing into something akin to customary law, can be found in the EC. As mentioned in the introduction to this chapter, the Council of Ministers uses a weighted voting system where the votes of the larger states have a weight of ten, while the vote of the smallest, Luxembourg, has only a weight of two (with the remainder of the member states having weights in between these two values). However, this voting arrangement is only part of a complicated decision-making process outlined in the constituent treaties, a process that has become much more complex through practices that have developed during the last thirty years. In 1987, the adoption of the Single European Act (SEA) has further changed the process, assuring more qualified majority voting and a somewhat greater influence of the European Parliament.

According to the ingenious arrangement devised by the treaty framers, it is the Commission that is to act as the driving force of the decision-making apparatus. The Commission is the initiator of proposals upon which the Council is called to act. As the Common Market moved through the three stages of the transitional period from 1958 to 1970, the Council was authorized increasingly to make its decisions with a qualified majority.[52] However, it cannot amend a Commission proposal except by unanimous vote. In the majority of cases, the Council is not able to make a decision unless a Commission proposal has been offered, and it does not have a legal tool to force the Commission to submit a specific proposal. On the other hand, the Commission can modify, substitute, or withdraw its proposal at any point up to the last moment prior to the Council's decision unless the timetables of the treaties preclude such withdrawal. Thus, the treaties have drawn a careful balance of power between the two organs, which forces them to cooperate in governing the affairs of the EC. However, in practice (as will be pointed out), there is considerable imbalance, weighing heavily in favor of the Council.

A third organ, the Committee of Permanent Representatives (CPR or COREPER, following the French title), has the duty of preparing the sessions and decisions of the Council (which usually meets only a few days each month) and of carrying out any tasks assigned to it by the Council. In addition, the staff of the CPR is frequently consulted informally by the Commission before it submits a formal proposal to the Council. In order to accomplish these missions, the CPR, which is composed of the ambassadors from the member states and their staffs, totaling more than four hundred civil servants, has established a number of working groups, subcommittees, and special ad hoc committees patterned after the administrative structure of the Commission.[53]

Clearly, the CPR, as the assistant of the Council, has increased in importance and influence over the years and has contributed materially to the shift in the balance of power from the Commission to the Council. Prior to submitting a proposal to the Council, the Commission engages in preliminary and informal consultations with staff members of the CPR in order to gain more knowledge about the views of the member governments. Information is sought through meetings with national officials who possess expert knowledge of the matter under consideration, as well as through formal meetings and informal contacts with national and European-level interest-group associations.

The power of the Commission, and indeed, the entire integration process of the EC, sustained damage in 1965 when France blocked the implementation of the EEC Treaty's provisions for decision making by qualified majority in the Council. Using as a pretext certain problems in the financing of the Common Agricultural Policy (CAP), the French government started, in July 1965, to boycott all EC proceedings, an action that became known as the "policy of the empty chair." The basic rationale for this policy was de Gaulle's opposition to strengthening in any way the political powers of the Community's central institutions.

When, in January 1966, the Luxembourg Conference of the EC foreign ministers settled the crisis provoked by the French boycott, it was on the basis of allowing any member state a veto on matters that it considers of vital national importance.[54] As a consequence, although member governments occasionally have abstained rather than block an agreement, unanimity in decision making has been the fundamental rule for the Council of Ministers. However, in May 1982, when Britain invoked its vital interest in the Council in order to block the annual price increases under the CAP, the nine other member states rejected the British veto and adopted the increase in farm prices with a qualified majority vote.

Insistence on qualified majority vote was further emphasized at the European Council meeting held in Luxembourg in December 1985.[55] Whether this means that the 1966 Luxembourg arrangement is dead and the EEC Treaty provisions regarding qualified voting have been fully resuscitated is uncertain. Our view is that vital national interests will again be invoked on future issues by the more powerful member states such as France and Britain if it suits their overall purposes or, alternatively, if a powerful political constituency is involved, such as the very influential and politically astute farmers of Western Europe.

The bargaining that preceded the conclusion of the Maastricht Agreement on Political and Economic Union of 1991 and the subsequent arguments lasting into the fall of 1993 about its ratification seem to support this prediction. Hence, it remains essential that the Commission's proposals on most types of decisions have to be formulated in such a way that they are acceptable to most, if not all, member states in order to have a reasonable chance for approval. This means that these proposals must search for the lowest common denominator, which reduces the role of the Commission and lowers its ability to represent truly the overall interests of the EC, despite the fact that the president of this body at the time, Jacque Delors of France, had proven to be an energizing leader for the EC.

Regardless of the circumstances, the Commission can still make a major contribution to the final decision of the Council. Because of its usually superior technical knowledge of all aspects of the situation with which the Council is faced, it can propose a package deal that may not fully satisfy all participants and all the interests of the member states, but may nonetheless represent an acceptable compromise. Especially after marathon sessions of bargaining, often lasting around the clock, a compromise submitted by the Commission may look very attractive, and an ultimate decision by the Council will be achieved.

In terms of the decision-making locus, this is a clear case where the formal procedures of the EEC Treaty, specifying balanced collaboration between the Commission and the Council with an eventual tilt in power to the former, have not been maintained in practice. Rather, the decision-making locus has shifted to some degree to control by the member governments, although nominal decision making continues to be carried out within the EC institutions; moreover, through the SEA, the European Parliament (EP) has gained slightly more influence. However, attempts to remedy what has been called the "democratic deficit" in the decision-making procedure of the EC by increasing substantially the power of the Parliament remain basically a failure because little change in this direction was accomplished in the proposed Maastricht Agreement on European Union. (This is discussed further in Chapter 5.) There are hopes for a review in 1996 when a more "democratic" constitution for a European Union could be developed. Meanwhile, decisions taken in the Council are characterized by a large amount of secrecy, and very little of the preceding discussion is made public for reporting by the news media.

The Andean Common Market (ANCOM): Defeat of a Fragile Decision-Making Approach. After it had become clear in the second half of the 1960s that LAFTA was not living up to the expectations of most of the member states (see Chapter 2), the dissatisfaction was especially pronounced among the

Andean states (Colombia, Chile, Ecuador, Peru, Bolivia, and Venezuela). One aspect of this dissatisfaction was the growing sense among these states that they were simply trading dependence on extraregional states for dependence on the Big Three states of LAFTA: Brazil, Mexico, and Argentina. For example, during the 1960s, Brazil, Mexico, and Argentina enjoyed increasing proportions of intraregional trade, especially among manufactured products, much of which was simply diverted trade from the smaller states of LAFTA that otherwise would have gone outside the region.

Interlocked with this growing perception of diverted dependence was the sense that the costs and benefits of LAFTA integration were not being shared equally among all members.[56] With no controls on foreign investment or distribution of industrialization, the Big Three, with already partially developed economies, were able to attract more capital investment and benefited more than the other members from the majority of industrial agreements.

In order to seek more rapid developmental gains and, at the same time, to counter Brazil's push for regional political leadership, the Andean states began to look for a new framework. The resulting Cartagena Treaty of 1969 establishing the Andean Common Market (ANCOM) represented a compromise among the Andean states regarding national development policies. Among the less developed countries of Bolivia, Ecuador, and Peru, the basis for development was perceived to be joint industrial planning. The prime movers of the Andean Pact (Chile and Colombia) focused on the developmental stimulus of trade liberalization and pushed for swifter movement toward free trade in the region rather than within LAFTA. Working from a shared conception of regionalism as a developmental tool, the Cartagena signatories opted to include both positions in order to get ANCOM off the ground.

Organizationally, there are two main institutions within the Andean Group, the Commission and the Junta. The Commission consists of one representative from each member state; it is charged with key decision making and the implementation of proposals. However, the power of the Commission is hampered by three provisos. First, the Commission (unlike the EC Commission) meets only three times a year, and not continuously. Second, decision making is hampered by the voting rules. Although most decisions, including the annual budget, are approved by a two-thirds majority, some matters are subject to veto by any state. The latter include treaty amendments, the approval of regional development plans, and the acceleration of trade liberalization. Moreover, Bolivia and Ecuador can veto the free circulation of certain commodities of special interest to them, although they were supposed to move immediately to full trade.[57] Last, since the Commission has no independent grant of authority, decisions are not automatically binding on the member states, but rather must be ratified and made a part of the legal code of each member.

The second institution, and the one that is most involved with both planning and executing policy within ANCOM, is the three-person Junta of technocrats, which is appointed by the Commission. It is the Junta, acting in the role of a secretariat, that formulates and proposes policies for the Commission. Moreover, the Junta carries out the decisions of the Commission and acts as a pressure group within the Pact to stimulate regional cooperation.

Functionally, the Cartagena Treaty presented an almost perfect expression of the economic thought promoted by the UN Economic Commission for Latin America (ECLA). Regional development was based on a three-pronged approach: trade liberalization, sectoral development programs, and control of private foreign investment. An Andean Development Corporation was established to function as the development financing arm of ANCOM. Unlike the negotiation approach taken by LAFTA, trade liberalization plans were written into the Cartagena Treaty. Regarding external trade, the Cartagena agreement called for the Andean states to reach agreement on a common minimum external tariff structure to be implemented gradually by member states from 1977 to 1980. Regarding internal trade, the members were committed to automatic gradual reductions of most tariffs, with Bolivia and Ecuador granted possibilities for delays in implementation.

To take advantage of the potential size of the market, the Cartagena Treaty called for the rationalization (or sectoralization) of industrial planning on a regionwide basis and Sectoral Programs of Industrial Development (SPIDs) were set up for this purpose.

The decision concerning the treatment of foreign capital, known as Decision 24, was adopted by the Commission in December 1970. This was a policy designed to limit the impact of foreign private investment on national economies, as well as to control existing foreign capital investments. The first broad element of Decision 24 was the classification of industries based on the mixture of capital investment: a company with less than 51 percent investment by native capital was considered to be a foreign firm, a company with between 51 percent and 80 percent local capital and under local management control was considered mixed, and a firm with 80 percent or more local capital participation was considered to be a local firm. The second, and perhaps the most controversial, aspect was the divestment requirement imposed on foreign capital. Foreign-owned corporations were given fifteen years in Chile, Colombia, and Peru, and twenty years in Bolivia and Ecuador to transfer capital holdings to local investors.[58] The third aspect of Decision 24 involved the limitations placed on new investments within the region. Outside of limited opportunities in industry, there was little occasion for new investment in other sectors of the economies.

It is noteworthy that the Cartagena Treaty provided for the creation of a regional judicial body: the Andean Court of Justice. How much influence the Court had on development activities in the ANCOM region is uncertain, but what is significant is simply that by this time, three regional organizations had established courts: the East African Community (to be discussed later in this chapter), ANCOM, and ECOWAS.

During the early years of its existence, ANCOM seemed to be a very successful IGO. By December 1971, Decision 24 had been accepted by all the member states. Venezuela, which had participated in the ANCOM negotiations, finally joined the Pact in 1973. Last, agreement was reached on the first two SPIDs for the region: in August 1972 on metalworking and metallurgy (except automobiles), and in September 1974 on petrochemicals.[59, 60] However, the Chilean notice of withdrawal in late 1976 almost immediately weakened the faith placed in ANCOM by the remaining members.

The Protocol of Lima, which was issued after a summit meeting in November 1976, made changes throughout the ANCOM action program. The target for full tariff-free regional trade was extended from 1985 until 1989, and the negotiation of the common external tariff was extended. The Protocol also made sweeping changes that gutted many of the key provisions of Decision 24. Tourism and agro-industry in Bolivia and Ecuador (countries which, with Chile, had been the chief agitators for reform) were exempted from the divestiture provision. Levels of profit remittance were raised from 14 percent to 20 percent, with the implication that each member could set them higher if it preferred.

Following issuance of the Protocol of Lima, integration within ANCOM continued to decline. The industrial development program for the automobile industry, which was signed in June 1977 after three years of negotiations, was scuttled by Peru in only two months. Furthermore, the new deadlines for trade liberalization, which were set in Lima in 1976, were extended even further at summit meetings in Arequipa in 1978, Cartagena in 1979, and Sochogota, Colombia, in 1981.

One important lesson can be learned from the decline of ANCOM following the heady days of the early 1970s. A fragile decision-making approach within the central institutions will only work properly if there is enthusiastic support for the integration experiment that a regional IGO has been commissioned to carry out. Once the original consensus of the member states begins to crumble, the central decision-making process is likely to be fatally wounded.

Part of the breakup of the consensus was due to changes in the regimes of the member states. Indeed, only Colombia and Venezuela have experienced fairly stable civilian governments since the Cartagena Treaty was signed, and they have been the strongest and most consistent advocates of salvaging the organization. On the other hand, the changes in the regimes in the remaining member states (with the consequent restructuring of national interests) have, more than anything, played havoc with the development of ANCOM as a viable regional integration scheme. The early successes of ANCOM came as a result of shared perceptions regarding dependence and development. With a changeover in regimes came a break in this consensus, and changed interests of the member states have led them away from the organizational structure and along different paths to development. The withdrawal of Chile in 1976 is a reflection of these changes.

In 1984, Ecuador, Colombia, and Peru became increasingly dissatisfied with the implementation of Decision 24 and pushed for liberal reform. Indeed, Ecuador threatened to withdraw from ANCOM unless quick action would be forthcoming. In terms of ANCOM's 1985 work program, major emphasis was placed on agricultural modernization, improving the quality of rural output, and disseminating modern farming techniques: objectives that might enhance the members' economies.

The East African Community (EAC): Asymmetry in Cooperation. Disenchantment with the EAC, in fact, resulted in the complete disintegration of a regional IGO whose performance was viewed by some of its members as increasingly unacceptable; in fact, as harmful to national interests. The three member states—Kenya, Uganda, and Tanzania—inherited an extensive integrative framework when they gained independence from Britain in the early 1960s. After an initial flurry of activity directed at moving from shared services to political amalgamation immediately following independence, the East African experience became a long slow process of movement toward total disintegration and declining output implementation. Fifteen years after independence, this culminated in complete disarray, with two member states, Uganda and Tanzania, engaged in full-scale war and the shared borders of all three states virtually closed. More recently, the member governments, especially those of Tanzania and Kenya, have become more friendly, due in part to economic necessities, and there has been some movement to reestablish EAC ties, although political tension continues to exist between Uganda and Kenya.

The history of integration in East Africa dates back to the turn of the twentieth century.[61] Although the colonies of Kenya and Uganda were run rather autonomously through the British Colonial Office, joint services were established early on. In 1902, rail service between Kenya and Uganda was placed under a common authority. A joint currency for the two colonies was established in 1905; a postal union, in 1911; and a customs union, in 1917. In the 1920s and 1930s, Tanganyika (the former name of Tanzania) was gradually merged into the common services network. It joined the customs union in 1923 and, in 1933, became a member of the postal union [62]

Following World War II, the British government gave the various common services a central governing organization. This resulted, in January 1948, in the establishment of the East African High Commission, consisting of the governors of the three colonies and serving as the executive authority for all the common services. Additionally, a central legislature was planned that would consist of representatives from the three colonies, as well as a regional customs and excise department to administer the customs union and a regional railways and harbors administration. Importantly, for the first time, the common services were placed under a single legal umbrella. With independence approaching, the London Conference of June 1961, which was attended by representatives of the three colonies and Britain, changed both the name and structure of the colonial arrangements, and the East African Common Services Organization (EACSO) was formed. The High Commission was replaced by a High Authority, which included the colonial governors of the three states; they were replaced by the heads of state as each of the three members became independent. A forty-five-member central legislative assembly was established to decide on the budget and other legal aspects of EACSO and held its first meeting in May 1962.[63, 64]

The reorganization of the common services into EACSO reflected more than mere disgruntlement over the management by the British Colonial Office and the desire of soon-to-become independent states to manage their own affairs. The creation of EACSO reflected as well the movement for the creation of a political federation within the region. As early as 1959, Julius K. Nyerere of Tanganyika endorsed the East African High Commission as a basis for the political federation of the region following independence. In March 1961, the political parties in Kenya expressed approval of the idea of federation of the three colonies and, in August 1961, they established a special committee in the Legislative Council to begin studying the problems of federation.[65]

The idea of an East African Federation gained momentum and, in June 1963, the heads of state of the three East African states agreed in Nairobi to establish such a federation by the end of that year. However, no consensus was possible concerning the details. Although Kenya and Tanganyika agreed on the necessity of a federal foreign policy and federal citizenship rather than national foreign policies and national citizenships in the federation, Uganda adamantly opposed both these propositions. It "was not prepared to lose its identity as a sovereign member of the international community and was particularly anxious to retain its separate representation in the United Nations."[66] Other intractable problems were the location of the capital and the division of powers, both between the two houses of parliament that were envisioned and between the federation and the constituent states.[67]

With federation having become a dead issue, interest turned toward the creation of an IGO to handle economic integration. To move ahead with this concept, there was a need to address the concrete issue of economic imbalance within the region. This was done during a meeting in Kampala, Uganda, in May 1964. Since colonial days, Kenya had been the leading economic power within the region, enjoying greater industrialization than the other two states and a near constant trade surplus with its partners. The agreement reached at Kampala specified that new industries would henceforth be allocated among the three states at a ratio of five (for Tanzania) to two (for Uganda) to one (for Kenya) in an effort to redress the imbalanced development.[68] Additionally, the agreement called for measures to adjust trade imbalances among the three.[69] Agreement on the economic restructuring of the region, however, proved to be as ephemeral as federation. Kenya withdrew its support for allocation when local investors announced plans to build an automobile plant similar to one that had been allocated in Tanzania. In the end, Kenya did not ratify the Kampala Agreement, and it was never implemented in the region.[70]

Faced with increasing disintegration, the heads of state again met in Mombassa in September 1965. After Kenya made a veiled threat to pull out of EACSO, the other member states went along with the Kenyan suggestion to revamp the current common services arrangement, and a nine-person commission was appointed to study the economic and political problems of the region. The report was finally delivered to the three heads of state; it formed the basis for the East African Community (EAC) which was inaugurated in December 1967.

Under the EAC, the services generating their own operating funds (such as the railways and harbors administration, the post and telecommunications administration, and East African Airways) were converted into corporations owned by the Community. Furthermore, the headquarters of the EAC was decentralized. Headquarters for the airline and the rail corporation remained in Nairobi. The harbors corporation was moved to Dar-es-Salaam, Tanzania, and the post and telecommunications corporation was relocated in Kampala, Uganda. The headquarters of the Community itself, including the customs union and the Common Market, was established in Arusha, Tanzania.

The new EAC also made provisions for more balanced regional development through two new provisions: the East African Development Bank and the transfer tax system. Rather than attempting to allocate new industries, the Bank was to be a means of providing incentives for new investment in Tanzania and Uganda.

The transfer tax system was created to correct the trade imbalances among the three states. From immediately after independence until the eventual collapse of the Community, Kenya maintained a massive trade surplus with the other two member states. The transfer tax system allowed deficit states (Tanzania and Uganda) to impose taxes on the types of goods imported from surplus states that they either already produced or were expecting to produce within three months. The taxes were seen as a temporary measure to protect infant industries and were to be phased out within fifteen years from the inception of the EAC.[71]

Soon after the EAC and its complex organizational and decision-making framework had been put into effect, disintegrative strains began to reemerge in East Africa. In July 1970, the East African University was dismembered and separate universities were established in each of the member states. Very severe strains were placed on the Community after the coup in Uganda in January 1971, when Idi Amin ousted Prime Minister Milton Obote. Following the coup, President Juluis Nyerere announced that Tanzania would not recognize the new regime.

In 1971, Uganda closed its border with Tanzania, and in response, Tanzania refused entry to Ugandans who were employed by the EAC offices in Arusha and Dar-es-Salaam. Things then went from bad to worse. In 1977, Tanzania permanently closed its border with Kenya. The curtain fell on the EAC in June 1977, when Kenya announced its formal withdrawal from the EAC and recalled its personnel from Arusha. Uganda and Tanzania attempted to keep the Community alive, but in August they announced that they, too, were withdrawing personnel.[72] In January 1978, the three ex-partners appointed Victor Umbricht, a UN official, to act as the arbitrator in the division of assets of the defunct Community.

A major problem with which the three states were never able to come to grips was the question of correcting the asymmetric interdependence that existed among the three. Uganda and Tanzania, the two deficit states, viewed Kenya as exploiting the common services and the Community for its own benefit and practicing subimperialism in the region. Kenya, on the other hand, felt that, as the most prosperous of the three states, it was forced to carry a disproportionate burden in the Community.[73]

The case of East Africa demonstrates that, under certain conditions, nation-states may decide to disengage from a network of regional cooperation, as embodied in an IGO, and allow it to atrophy. Apart from perceptions of unequal costs and benefits, different economic and foreign policy perspectives play important roles. Soon after independence, the three East African states began to approach common problems—and especially the transcendant problem of economic asymmetry—from divergent outlooks. Where Kenyan linkages were drawn to the more developed states of Western Europe, the Commonwealth, and the United States, and the development of an economy linked with the industrial West, Tanzanian linkages followed ideological trails to the more radical states of southern Africa, such as Zambia and Mozambique, and to the Peoples' Republic of China and members of the Soviet bloc. Uganda's problems arose from serious domestic controversies and conflicts that aggravated the economic difficulties arising from the economic asymmetries existing in the region. All these divergencies resulted in regional conflict rather than regional cooperation in East Africa. As Raymond Copson remarked, "Regional cooperation in East Africa became the victim of conflict rather than a force to limit conflict."[74]

OUTPUT IMPLEMENTATIONS

An important question to be explored in more detail relates to the tools that an IGO can use to implement decisions and the degree of effectiveness of the implementation method. Several methods are available to IGOs; the constituent treaties specify which method can be employed in particular circumstances and not all methods are permitted for all IGOs. In many cases, agencies or bureaucracies (both public and private) of member states must be used by IGOs to implement decisions and policies.

Member states that are concerned that the balance between national and IGO policymaking should favor their governments may not consider effectiveness of implementation to be the most desirable objective, since it may undermine national prerogatives. The history of disarmament and arms control negotiations bears eloquent witness to this observation. Even in low-politics issue areas, states may have only a limited interest in seeing the functionalist logic work too successfully unless the tasks to be performed by the IGO institutions are completely beyond the reach of their capabilities or are perceived as relatively unimportant.

The least circumscribed method for IGO output implementation is the dissemination of information. The effectiveness of this method depends on the issue area. The more technical and less political the subject or issue area, the better chances for this method's effectiveness, and for its acceptance by IGO member states. Information on health matters or agricultural production by the FAO or the WHO are cases in point. On the other hand, the use of UN agencies to disseminate such political information as conditions of apartheid in South Africa or the plight of the Palestinians in the Israeli-controlled Occupied Territories has aroused resistance and opposition.

A recommendation, which is normally nonbinding, is a method through which an IGO can move things forward. Especially if the same recommendation is approved by an important body such as the General Assembly, it can have a decisive effect on world public opinion. Opponents will be pushed into a corner when the same recommendation is passed with increasing majorities, and it will take a strongly held view for a member state to remain in the opposition year after year. The votes recommending the expulsion of South Africa from the General Assembly, if not from UN membership entirely, and the recommended sanctions against Israel to punish that state for the annexation of the Golan Heights are indicative of the problem.

Directives authorizing IGOs to issue an enforceable order are not frequent. The UN Charter's Chapter VII grants the Security Council such authority, but five UN member states have veto rights in the Council. Furthermore, the use of Article 19 of the Chapter to compel the financing of peacekeeping operations authorized by the Security Council has not been successful. In the EC system, however, directives as implementing tools for policy decision are used more often, and in most cases, member governments comply.

While directives, wherever authorized, are addressed to the member governments, a very few IGOs are empowered to implement policies with *regulations* (ordinances) that are directly binding on member states without positive implementing legislation or decrees by the national parliaments or executive administrations (rule-creating decisions). The prominent examples of this type of output implementation are the ECSC and EEC. In this kind of legal situation, the member governments and the nongovernmental actors must keep a very watchful eye on the entire IGO decision-making process in order to assure that their major interests are protected and their various national policy goals enhanced as much as possible. Indeed, in some cases, member governments may be anxious to frustrate completely the IGO implementation process if they are dissatisfied with a decision. The Iraq attitude after losing the Gulf War and continued Serbian expansion through the use of force into neighboring territories reveal the difficulty of implementing IGO decisions. The dissolution of the East African Community illustrates this point.

IMPLEMENTATION EVALUATION

The evaluation of the implementation of IGO decisions is largely an unexplored field, although in the domestic policy area, a fairly extensive literature has built up during the last few years.[75] At the heart of the evaluation of decision or policy implementation is the notion of causality. A decision that requires implementation is expected to have a particular causal effect. If the intended effect is achieved, implementation has been successful; if the effect is not achieved and, perhaps, the outcome of the attempted implementation is quite different from what the decision makers had intended to accomplish, something may have gone awry with the implementation process or the goals chosen for implementation may be unrealistic or inappropriate. What are some of the pertinent variables on which evaluation research should focus in order to determine, on a comparative, cross-national basis, the reasons for failures of IGO decision-making and policy implementation processes?

The dependent variable in such an evaluation is *implementation effectiveness*. A decision or policy is effectively implemented according to the degree to which the decision or policy goals are realized within the specified time period and within the budget allocated for this purpose.

The independent variables can be divided into three clusters.[76] The first cluster is concerned with aspects of the IGO subsystems consisting of: *the nature of the political structure; political culture; and economic characteristics of the member states*. Implementation of IGO decisions and policies, in most cases, requires the assistance of member state agencies. Hence, these variables are very relevant for an evaluation of implementation processes. With respect to culture, public opinion may be crucial: what are the attitudes of various target groups in the IGO member states regarding particular IGO goals and programs? Among the economic characteristics, the rates of inflation and unemployment in different member states are likely to affect the effectiveness of the implementation processes.

The second cluster of variables focuses on bureaucratic particularities. How strong is an IGO institution's commitment to a goal or program, and how high is the implementing state agency's priority to realize pertinent IGO decisions and policies? How well has the particular IGO policy whose implementation is being evaluated been funded compared with other IGO and national policies and programs? What are the levels of bureaucratic expertise and relevant experiences of the IGO civil service involved in implementation? How extensive and how centralized or decentralized is this authority, especially if state agencies are the prime implementors?

The third cluster of variables deals with *operational* problems. Since many IGO decisions and programs affect different groups in the member states, questions arise about the degree of support given by these groups and their willingness to participate in individual IGO-sponsored programs. Collaboration of local administrative subdivisions and political party organizations may be a salient element for the effectiveness of program and policy implementation, while nonsupportive target groups and antagonistic political forces strengthen the potential for delays and cost overruns in the implementing process. Some of these issues will become apparent in the discussion that follows in Chapter 5.[77]

NOTES

1. David Easton, *A Framework for Political Analysis* (Englewood Cliffs, NJ: Prentice-Hall, 1965). Other input-out models of decision making placing special emphasis on cybernetics are also useful.

2. Quoted in D. W. Bowett, *The Law of International Institutions,* (New York: Praeger, 1963), p. 326.

3. Articles 1, 5, 15, and 16 of the Covenant.

4. Bowett, *International Institutions,* p. 327.

5. Ibid.

6. Articles 148(2), EEC Treaty; 118(2), EURATOM Treaty; and 28(4) ECSC Treaty, as amended. See also Clive Archer, *Organizing Western Europe* (Serenoska, Kent, UK: Edward Arnold, 1992).

7. Grenville Clark and Louis B. Sohn, *World Peace through Law,* 2nd rev. ed. (Cambridge, MA: Harvard University Press, 1960), pp. 20–23, 25–31.

8. See Robert W. Cox and Harold K. Jacobson, eds., *The Anatomy of Influence* (New Haven, CT: Yale University Press, 1973), p. 12.

9. For more details, see ibid., pp. 9–11.

10. Charles A. Duffy and Werner J. Feld, "Whither Regional Integration Theory?" in *Comparative Regional Systems,* ed. Werner J. Feld and Gavin Boyd (New York: Pergamon Press, 1980), pp. 497–522. There is a growing literature discussing spillover effects, not only as pointed out by functionalists and neofunctionalists, but also as identified by regime theorists as regards the post-Cold War period and multilateralism. See, for example, the special issue on multilateralism of *International*

Organization 46 (Summer 1992). Many of the arguments concerning the Law-of-the-Sea Treaty, both pro and con, revolve around the question of locus of decision making.

11. Leon N. Lindberg and Stuart A. Scheingold, *Europe's Would-Be Polity* (Englewood Cliffs, NJ: Prentice-Hall, 1970), pp. 68–70.

12. Ibid., p. 71, Table 3.1.

13. John Worrall, "UN Watch on Environment Gets Lonelier," *Christian Science Monitor,* January 12, 1982, p. 5. See also William S. Broomfield, "Climbing toward the Earth Summit," *Christian Science Monitor,* April 28, 1992, p. 19.

14. Johan Kaufmann, *United Nations Decision Making* (Rockville, MD: Sijthoff and Noordhof, 1980), p. 73.

15. Ibid., pp. 90–92.

16. The following pages are drawn from John W. McDonald, Jr., "The North-South Dialogue and the United Nations" (Occasional Paper of the Institute for the Study of Diplomacy, Georgetown University, Edmund A. Walsh School of Foreign Service), pp. 17–22.

17. For a detailed discussion of the World Food Conference, see Thomas G. Weiss and Robert Jordan, *The World Food Conference and Global Problem Solving* (New York: Praeger, 1976). See also chapter 5 of this text.

18. For a complete discussion of this dialogue, see Harold K. Jacobson and Dusan Sidjanski, eds., *The Emerging International Economic Order: Dynamic Processes, Constraints, and Opportunities* (Beverly Hills, CA: Sage, 1982).

19. Weiss and Jordan, *World Food Conference,* p. 4. Examples of using conferences to focus on special regional or development issues are, respectively, the 1984 Second International Conference on Assistance to African Refugees; in 1989 the Conference for Central American Refugees and for Indo-Chinese Refugees; and the 1990 World Conference on Education for All: Meeting Basic Learning Needs.

20. For a review of the somewhat tortured progress of the negotiations between North and South, see Robert S. Jordan, "Why an NIEO: The View from the Third World," in Jacobson and Sidjanski, *International Economic Order.* See also George A. Codding, "Influence in International Conferences," *International Organization* 35 (Autumn 1981), 715–24.

21. Regarding the action by GATT's director-general Wyndham White at the end of the Kennedy Round negotiations, see Werner J. Feld, *The European Community in World Affairs* (Boulder, CO: Westview Press, 1982), p. 184.

22. For a discussion of a package-deal attempt at a single negotiating text and at consensus, see Mohamed El Baradei and Chloe Garvin, *Crowded Agendas, Crowded Rooms: Institutional Arrangements at UNCLOS III: Some Lessons in Global Negotiations,* Policy and Efficacy Studies no. 3 (New York: United Nations Institute for Training and Research, 1981).

23. For somewhat similar definitions, see Thomas Hovet, Jr., *Bloc Politics in the United Nations* (Cambridge, MA: Harvard University Press, 1960), p. 31; and Jack C. Plano and Robert E. Riggs, *Forging World Order* (New York: Macmillan, 1967), p. 148. See also Weiss and Jordan, *World Food Conference,* p. 27, for a discussion of bloc voting definitions in UN conferences; for a discussion of caucusing within conferences, see p. 110.

24. For a discussion of the role of groups, see Kaufmann, *United Nations Decision Making,* p. 87.

25. See the following series of studies by Jack E. Vincent: *The Caucusing Groups of the United Nations: An Examination of Their Attitudes toward the Organization* (Stillwater: Oklahoma State University Press, 1965); "National Attributes as Predictors of Delegate Attitudes at the United Nations," *American Political Science Review* 62 (September 1968): 916–31; "The Convergence of Voting and Attitude Patterns at the United Nations," *Journal of Politics* 31 (1969): 952–83; "An Analysis of Caucusing Group Activity at the United Nations," *Journal of Peace Research* 1 (1970): 133–50; "An Analysis of Attitude Patterns at the United Nations," *Quarterly Journal of the Florida Academy of Sciences* 32 (1969): 185–209; "Generating Some Empirically Based Indices for International Alliance and Regional Systems Operating in the Early 1960's," *International Studies Quarterly* 15 (1971): 465–525; "Predicting Voting Patterns in the General Assembly," *American Political Science Review* 65 (June 1971): 471–98; and "Testing Some Hypotheses about Delegate Attitudes in the United Nations and Some Implications for Theory Building," Research Report no. 52, Dimensionality of Nations Project, University of Hawaii (1971). We discuss the general tendencies of a state toward international organization in chapters 1 and 2.

26. Arend Lijphart, "The Analysis of Bloc Voting in the General Assembly," *American Political Science Review* 57 (December 1963): 902–17. Among the works cited by Lijphart are M. Margaret Ball, "Bloc Voting in the General Assembly," *International Organization* 5 (February 1951): 3–31; John H. Houston, *Latin America in the United Nations,* United Nations Studies no. 8 (New York: Carnegie Endowment for International Peace, 1956); F. H. Soward, "The Changing Balance of Power in the United Nations," *Political Quarterly* 28 (October–December 1957); Robert E. Riggs, *Politics in the United Nations: A Study of United States Influence in the General Assembly,* Illinois Studies in the Social Sciences no. 41 (Urbana: University of Illinois Press, 1958); Geoffrey Goodwin, "The Expanding United Nations, I—Voting Patterns," *International Affairs* 36 (April 1960); and Roderick C. Ogley, "Voting and Politics in the General Assembly," *International Relations* 2 (April 1961).

27. Thomas J. Hovet, *Bloc Politics in the United Nations* (Cambridge, MA: Harvard University Press, 1960): 910.

28. Lijphart, "Analysis of Bloc Voting," p. 910.

29. Hayward R. Alker, Jr., "Dimensions of Conflict in the General Assembly," *American Political Science Review* 58 (September 1964): 642–57.

30. Bruce M. Russett, "Discovering Voting Groups in the United Nations," *American Political Science Review* 60 (June 1966): 327–39.

31. Factor analysis is a rather common (but involved) technique, with the most frequently employed variation termed *R-analysis,* in which every variable is correlated to every other variable using the product-moment correlation coefficient (Pearson's rho). R-analysis is thus a data-reduction technique: those variables that show high correlations among themselves and very low correlation with other variables are seen as pointing to a single underlying dimension of factor. The factors themselves are uncorrelated with each other. Q-analysis treats the states as variables and the roll calls themselves become observations. If the matrix is factor-analyzed, the correlations identify states with similar voting patterns and the factors point to voting groups or blocs.

32. See the series of studies by Jack E. Vincent cited in note 25 above.

33. Jack E. Vincent, "An Application of Attribute Theory to General Assembly Voting Patterns and Some Implications," *International Organization* 26 (Summer 1972): 576.

34. See Inis L. Claude, Jr., *Swords into Plowshares,* 4th ed. (New York: Random House, 1973); and Stephen Goodspeed, *The Nature and Function of International Organization,* 2nd ed. (New York: Oxford University Press, 1967), pp. 148–49. For a general discussion, see Indar Rikhye and Kjell Skjelsbaek, eds., *The United Nations and Peacekeeping: Results, Limitations, and Prospects* (New York: St. Martin's Press, 1991). See also Sir Colin Crowe, "Some Observations on the Operation of the Security Council Including the Use of the Veto," in *Paths to Peace: The U.N. Security Council and Its Presidency,* ed. Davidson Nicol (New York: Pergamon Press, 1981); and Sydney D. Bailey, *The Procedure of the U.N. Security Council* (Oxford: Clarendon Press, 1988).

35. For details see Goodspeed, *International Organization,* p. 149.

36. Ibid. A more general discussion can be found in Adam Roberts and Benedict Kingsbury, eds., *United Nations, Divided World: The UN's Roles in International Politics* (New York: Oxford University Press, 1988).

37. Claude, *Swords into Plowshares,* p. 143. See also Leon Gordenker, *The U.N. Secretary General and the Maintenance of Peace* (New York: Columbia University Press, 1967), especially part 4; and Arthur S. Lall, ed., *Multilateral Negotiation and Mediation: Instruments and Methods* (New York: Pergamon Press, 1985).

38. For a more optimistic view, see G. R. Berridge, *Return to the UN: UN Diplomacy in Regional Conflicts* (New York: St. Martin's Press, 1991).

39. Articles of Agreement as amended, Articles 24 and 27, in *The International Monetary Fund 1945–1965: Twenty years of International Monetary Cooperation* (Washington: IMF, 1969), *vol. 3: Documents,* pp. 504–5; and Susan Strange, "IMF: Monetary Managers," in Robert W. Cox and Harold K. Jacobson, *The Anatomy of Influence* (New Haven, CT: Yale University Press, 1973), pp. 263–97, n. 4, p. 264.

40. Article 4 (d).

41. Arthur S. Banks and William Overstreet, eds., *The Political Handbook of the World 1981* (New York: McGraw-Hill, 1982)
p. 655.

42. Ibid., p. 656.

43. Article 3 of the Declaration concerning Aims and Purposes of May 10, 1944.

44. Article 3, section 5, ILO Constitution.

45. Article 7, ibid.

46. The points made in these paragraphs are drawn from "The United States and the International Labor Organization, Twenty-Sixth Report of the Commission to Study the Organization of Peace," December 1979, Introduction.

47. This information is drawn from the ILO entry in Banks and Overstreet, *Political Handbook of the World, 1981.*

48. *Organization of Peace,* p. 76.

49. Ibid.

50. ILO's formal complaint procedures can also be invoked by employers' and workers' organizations in two ways. First, delegates to the ILO Conference are competent to lodge complaints charging a member state with failure to give effect to a labor convention ratified by that member. Such complaints can be made by workers' and employers' delegates against their own governments. The complaint process can result in the convening of a Commission of Enquiry empowered to make findings of fact and law to the government involved. Second, under the ILO Freedom of Association procedure, workers' and employers' organizations are permitted to raise complaints concerning the infringements of trade union rights. Such

complaints are referred to the Governing Body's Committee on Freedom of Association and may result in the convening of a Fact-finding and Conciliation Commission with powers similar to those of a Commission of Enquiry. Again, complaints of this nature may be raised by an employers' or workers' organization concerning actions of its own government. Ibid., pp. 75–76.

51. These comments and the observations that follow are drawn from an information statement, "US Re-entry into the ILO," published in February 1980 by the Bureau of Public Affairs, U.S. Department of State. The U.S. withdrawal and reentry in the ILO is also discussed in Robert S. Jordan, "Boycott Diplomacy: The U.S., the U.N., and UNESCO," *Public Administration Review* 144, no.4 (July/August 1984): 283–91.

52. When decisions require a qualified majority for their adoption, 45 votes (considering their weighted value) are necessary for adoption. Moreover, the concurring votes of at least 6 member states are required for a favorable decision.

53. For an exhaustive study of the CPR, see Dimitri Tsikouris, "Institution of the Permanent Representatives of the Member States of the European Community" (Unpublished M.A. thesis, University of New Orleans, 1981).

54. For details, see John Lambert, "The Constitutional Crisis 1965–66," *Journal of Common Market Studies* 6 (May 1966): 195–228.

55. *Agence Europe Bulletin,* May 20, 1982; and the *Times* (London), December 5, 1985, p. 7.

56. Kevin C. Kearns, "The Andean Common Market: A New Thrust of Economic Integration in Latin America," *Journal of Inter-American Studies and World Affairs* 14 (May 1972): 228–29.

57. See Edward S. Milensky, "From Integration to Developmental Nationalism: The Andean Group 1965–1971," *Inter-American Economic Affairs* 25 (Winter 1971): 79, 85.

58. For details, see Ralph A. Diez, "The Andean Common Market: Challenge to Foreign Investors," *Columbia Journal of World Business* 6 (July-August 1971): 23.

59. *New York Times,* August 26, 1972.

60. *New York Times,* September 6, 1975.

61. Carl G. Rosberg and Aaron Segal, "An East African Federation," *International Conciliation* 543 (May 1963): 5. For more detailed analyses of regional integration in East Africa prior to independence, see Robert I. Rotberg, "The Federation Movement in British East and Central Africa, 1889–1953," *Journal of Commonwealth Political Studies* 2 (May 1964): 141–60; and Joseph S. Nye, Jr., *Pan-Africanism and East African Integration* (Cambridge, MA: Harvard University Press, 1965), pp. 86–94.

62. Tanganyika, which had formerly been German territory, became a League of Nations mandate administered by Great Britain following World War I. Tanganyika and Zanzibar were merged in April 1964 into the United Republic of Tanganyika and Zanzibar. In October 1964, the name Tanzania was adopted.

63. Joseph S. Nye, Jr., "East African Economic Integration," *Journal of Modern African Studies* 1 (December 1963): 479.

64. *New York Times,* May 23, 1962, p. 3.

65. *New York Times,* August 14, 1961, p. 3.

66. J. H. Proctor, "The Effort to Federate East Africa: A Post Mortem," *Political Quarterly* 37 (January-March 1966): 54.

67. Ibid., pp. 52–53.

68. Apolo Robin Nsibambi, "Political Committment and Economic Integration: East Africa's Experience," *African Review* 2 (June 1972): 199.

69. John Ravenhill, "Regional Integration and Development in Africa: Lessons from the East African Community," *Journal of Commonwealth and Comparative Politics* 17 (November 1979): 236.

70. Ibid., p. 237.

71. See Phillip Ndegwa, "Transfer Taxes Are a Challenge—Not an obstacle," *East Africa Trade and Industry* 13 (July 1967): 25–28.

72. Richard Hodder-Williams, "Changing Perspectives in East Africa," *World Today*, May 1978, p. 166.

73. Agrippah T. Mugomba, "Regional Organizations and African Underdevelopment: The Collapse of the East African Community," *Journal of Modern African Studies* 16 (June 1978): 263.

74. Raymond W. Copson, "African International Politics: Underdevelopment and Conflict in the Seventies," *Orbis* 22 (Spring 1978): 231.

75. See, for example, David Nachmias, *Public Policy Evaluation* (New York: St. Martin's Press, 1979).

76. This discussion draws on the conceptualizations developed by James D. Slack. See "The Cross-National Analysis of Implementation Effectiveness" (Paper presented at the 1979 Annual Meeting of the Southern Political Science Association, Gatlinburg, TN, November 1–3, 1973).

77. Kaufmann, *United Nations Decision Making,* discusses many of these questions.

5 IGO INTERACTIONS WITH MEMBER STATES AND OTHER IGOs: THE PURSUIT OF DOMESTIC AND FOREIGN POLICY GOALS AND ATTEMPTS AT COLLECTIVE SECURITY

When we discussed in Chapter 2 the genesis of IGOs, we stressed that these organizations are the creatures of their member states, and are established for the basic purpose of achieving objectives and carrying out functions perceived by the prospective member governments to be in some way beyond the reach of their national capabilities. Hence, IGOs are *instruments of policy* for member governments, whose aspirations and expectations ride on the appropriate task performance of the IGOs created or joined by them. Inevitably, member governments make cost-benefit calculations regarding the usefulness of their IGOs; they want to retain their influence in, and perhaps exercise control over, these IGOs. Decidedly, they do not want to slide into the position of Goethe's Sorcerer's Apprentice, who, after having magically transformed an old broom into an efficient water carrier, loses complete control over his creation and is unable to stop its persevering, untiring activities.

The desire to minimize the loss of freedom in national policy-making and to guide, if not control, the task performance of IGOs permeates the relations between member governments and international institutions. This is the case in universal organizations such as the United Nations, its specialized agencies, and other multilateral units such as UNCTAD and GATT, as well as in such regional organizations as the EC. The desire for influence is especially pronounced in such international financial organizations as the IMF, the World Bank, and regional development banks.

The influence of individual member states on the activities of IGOs varies and may change over time. For example, the influence of the United States in various bodies of the United Nations had steadily declined over the course of the Cold War, while that of the developing countries, in coalition with the Soviet-led socialist bloc, increased until the late 1980s and early 1990s. With the end of the Cold War, however, Washington was able to dominate the Security Council in order to form a coalition in pursuit of its foreign policy goals toward the Gulf region, and again in its humanitarian efforts to assist the starving population in Somalia and toward establishing democratic government in Haiti. In the EC, the influence of France on policy-making has waned somewhat, while that of Germany has increased. In ECOWAS, Nigeria has been the dominant member, although the Ivory Coast has not been comfortable with this.

For a systematic analysis of the relationship between member states and IGOs, a number of specific questions have been formulated that can serve as useful criteria for comparison.

IGOs AS INSTRUMENTS OF NATIONAL POLICIES

To what extent, and for which domestic and foreign policy goals, do national decision makers consider IGOs to be useful instruments of policy implementation? The answer will, of course, depend very much on the interests (security, economic, political, technological, or humanitarian) pursued by national governments which led to their participation in the IGO in the first place. It also depends on the competences and powers conferred on particular IGOs.

The United States has long complained, for example, that its contributions to the UN budget have not rewarded it with commensurate influence. This was one of the reasons given by the Reagan administration for withholding the U.S. contribution of $330 million for the 1988 budget year pending various personnel actions and budgetary reforms. As of April 1992, the United States owed $410 million out of a total owed by the member states of $1.2 billion. It is worthwhile, therefore, to note the degree and nature of U.S. interactions with two members of the UN family—UNESCO and FAO—in the following illustrative cases.

The U.S. Withdrawal from UNESCO: An Illustrative Case

The Changing UNESCO Idea. We pointed out in the introduction to this chapter that the member states want to use central institutions and specialized units as instruments to achieve their particular goals. Sometimes the goals of a particular member state may not be considered vital enough compared to the prevailing conceptions of the state's national interests. The case of the U.S. withdrawal from UNESCO illustrates this point.

The UNESCO constitution was adopted in November 1945 in London by the representatives of twenty governments. Its stated purpose was for "contributing to peace and security by promoting collaboration among the nations through education, science, and culture in order to further universal respect for justice, for the law, and for the human rights and fundamental freedoms which are affirmed for the peoples of the world, without distinction of race, sex, language or religion."[1]

Such a vision of the future grew out of the destruction and desperation caused by World War II. The so-called West had experienced two great wars and had suffered atrocities on a scale that, up to then, had been unimaginable. As a reaction to the destruction and carnage, the victors believed that an IGO should be created, not only to decide how to salvage the West's cultural and intellectual heritage, but also to explore the sources of conflict, whether interpersonal or international, that had confounded the earlier expectations that industrialization would enhance the human experience rather than debase it. The revolutionary dimension of UNESCO was the idea that "since wars begin in the minds of men, it is in the minds of men that defenses of peace must be constructed."[2]

The expectation was that, through the proper use of education, science, and culture, conditions inclining toward peace instead of conflict would flow out of human interactions. Not unexpectedly, UNESCO has been grappling with the practical meaning and functions of this expectation ever since. There have been two main interpretations as to how peace could be achieved. The first calls for UNESCO's programs to work directly for the promotion of peaceful conditions by studying conflict and by using education, science, and culture to promote efforts and methods of conflict resolution. The second calls for international cooperation by using UNESCO's designated fields of responsibility for development of the educational, scientific, and cultural structures within the member states, thereby indirectly promoting or maintaining peace.

The first, more intellectual interpretation of UNESCO's mandate characterized the early, or more Western-dominated, years of the organization, while the second, more operational interpretation has characterized the more recent, postcolonial period. It is this second interpretation that gave rise to the U.S. desire to withdraw from the organization. One observer classified the problem in the form of four questions:

> 1) Is UNESCO intended to be a political instrument committed to the task of bringing into existence some kind of world order? 2) Should UNESCO be completely non-political in the orientation of its program? 3) In its own technical sphere, should UNESCO be merely a clearing house of information or should it initiate research and undertake actions . . . designed to secure certain specified results? 4) What is the nature of priorities that should be established in order to minimize waste and frustration and maximize the achievement of tangible, measurable results?[3]

Changing Conceptions of Nationalism and Internationalism. By the 1970s, and the virtual tripling of the membership of the United Nations and its specialized agencies, the orientation of international activities had been redirected, from rebuilding and reconstructing after the devastation of World War II to providing programs of economic and social development for the emerging "Third World," which was composed primarily, but not exclusively, of newly independent states. This, together with the wealth provided by OPEC, gave this so-called Third World majority, as expressed through the Group of 77, a significant voice in the politics of international organizations.

One of the results of this newfound influence was a collective call for a New International Economic Order (NIEO) that would bring about a reordering of international priorities and resources to favor the disadvantaged Third World. The essence of the dispute that engulfed UNESCO was how to reconcile the new nationalistic (and apparently anti-Western) demands of the Third World with the more pro-Western liberal democratic traditions of the First World (industrialized states) that appeared to be threatened.[4]

One observer noted that "The Second World War had three profound effects on the international scene in general: a) it created a bipolar world; b) it made interdependence the hallmark of the post-war world; and c) it extended the scope and field of action of diplomacy to the entire planet."[5] The fact of interdependence in economic terms had engendered resistance to interdependence in social and cultural areas. However, as a consequence of World War I, the humanities and social sciences were being harnessed to the cause of nationalism as World War II approached. Inexorably, both economics and culture had become part of the politics of diplomacy; through the imperative of first World War II and then the Cold War, the natural sciences had already become irretrievably politicized, especially to fuel the nuclear arms race. Interdependence and nationalism would have to learn to coexist.

Opposition of the United States to the New World Information and Communication Order (NWICO). The immediate flash point of the UNESCO crisis, paradoxically, stemmed from the U.S. success in making "communication" a part of UNESCO's program of work. Communication or information had become, through technological inventiveness, increasingly a means to leap over nationalistic barriers. In fact, when UNESCO's constitution was being negotiated, the United States had pressed for the inclusion of the phrase, "all means of mass communication" as one of the ways to advance UNESCO's purposes.[6] More immediate factors were the declining economic growth in the West, which was partly brought on by sharply rising oil prices, and the very high rates of inflation that followed the 1979 oil price rise that had been successfully implemented through OPEC.

Thus, by the early 1980s, American policy toward UNESCO was experiencing basic perceptual problems. Within the Reagan administration, a powerful group of policymakers contended that UNESCO had become unacceptably "politicized." They pointed to anti-Israeli actions taken by

UNESCO's governing body, the General Conference, and also to the fact that a Soviet national had been appointed to a high position in the Secretariat.[7] The African member states at this time were supporting the Arab member states against Israel because of Arab oil power and monetary influence and as a "display of solidarity."[8] Furthermore, as far as the administration was concerned, there was criticism of the lack of clear program priorities and widespread bureaucratic inefficiencies that presumably led to wasteful spending. The director-general, Amadu M'Bow of Senegal, was accused of leaning toward the Third World coalition and favoring the Socialist bloc (i.e., the "Second World").

However, the major contentious issue was over the so-called New World Information and Communication Order (NWICO). Not only the United States, but also other Western member states, and in particular Britain, had deeply suspected the motives of the Third World majority which advocated proposals for the flow of communication that appeared to compromise the principle of a free press. The problem, from the Third World viewpoint, was that the "free flow" was dominated by the major Western news services, and in particular, those of the United States, Britain, and France. Because of this, it was believed that the news reflected Western values and perceptions at the expense of non-Western cultures. This looked dangerously like neocolonialism, which meant an invasion of national sovereignty. In other words, the internationalism of information was running up against the nationalistic sensitivities of the Third World majority in UNESCO—and in the UN system as a whole.

All this was encapsulated by the Media Declaration adopted by the General Conference on November 22, 1978. The Declaration called for a "free flow and a wider and better balanced dissemination of information[;] . . . a new equilibrium and greater reciprocity in the flow of information" and for "the mass media to contribute effectively . . . to the establishment of a more just and equitable international economic order" (here referring to the NIEO). The Declaration went on to mention protection "in the exercise of their functions [for] . . . journalists and other agents of the mass media," by way of "guaranteeing them the best conditions for the exercise of their profession."[9] It stressed or recognized the importance of "the exercise of freedom of opinion, expression and information" as "part of human rights and fundamental freedoms," and the freedom of journalists to these ends. States were called on to help the mass media in developing countries to procure "adequate conditions and resources enabling them to gain strength and expand."

Although initially the United States and the West in general had supported the declaration, by the time the Reagan administration took office, UNESCO had come under increasing attack from American newspapers and wire services over concerns that any hint of controlling the movement of journalists could result in press censorship or other forms of governmental control or intimidation. It was not lost on the journalistic community that governments interested in suppressing or controlling the news within their countries would have as much interest in an international policy that included the registration of journalists as would governments that tolerated a free press and would view such registration as a protection of journalists within a country from circumstances where personal security might be a serious problem. This is an example of the increasing misconceptions between the West and the Third World.[10] However, the fact is that the advent of direct satellite communication that would transcend, or escape from, the control of the state energized the debate over a NWICO. Third World states feared the possibility of a type of communications imperialism, while the United States and several other Western states focused on the need for a "free flow" of information. The Media Declaration became the ideological and political focal point against which the Reagan administration based its campaign for withdrawal from UNESCO.[11]

The Steps toward, and Justification for, Withdrawal. From October 1982 to withdrawal, the Heritage Foundation, a Washington-based, politically conservative think tank with great influence in the Reagan administration, published five papers that were critical of UNESCO. The Foundation first called for the termination of American funding, and then for withdrawal. This is an example of how an NGO can directly influence government policy. Somehow, the expectation was that world politics should stop at the door of IGOs, thus ignoring the fact that they are international *governmental* organizations, but at the same time, the Foundation expected that the United States should have the dominant voice in these organizations. The linkage, of course, was that the scale of assessments and contributions should reflect the degree and nature of which member states' national policies should prevail in a multilateral forum. (This debate is still present, as apparent in the post-Cold War Security Council's attempts to engage in peacekeeping, peacemaking, and peacebuilding worldwide on an unprecedented scale.)

On December 28, 1983, Secretary of State George Shultz gave notice of the U.S. intention to withdraw from UNESCO, effective December 31, 1984. This was the one-year notice required by the UNESCO constitution. The letter stated that certain "trends in the policy, ideological emphasis, budget and management of UNESCO were detracting from the Organization's effectiveness" and that actions taken at the 22nd General Conference to reverse the trends were not sufficient to justify the United States remaining in UNESCO. Although Director-General M'Bow was commended for his efforts, Shultz concluded that the United States should work toward achieving the initial goals of UNESCO from outside the Organization.

Two months after the notice, the Department of State released a U.S.-UNESCO policy review prepared by the Department's Bureau of International Organization Affairs which set out basic political goals termed "policies and criteria":

—"reassert American leadership in multilateral affairs;

—implement a budgetary policy of zero net program growth and significant absorption of non-discretionary cost increases for the first half of the decade;

—obtain adequate U.S. representation within the secretariats of multilateral agencies;

—reduce the financial burden imposed on all participants by an excessive number of lengthy international conferences [often dominated by the Group of 77];

—advocate a role for the private sector in international organization affairs."[12]

The Report continued by criticizing UNESCO's work in disarmament studies and in collective rights of peoples as "extraneous" to the Organization's mandate. UNESCO was also criticized as expressing "hostility toward the basic institutions of a free society" and having "the most unrestrained budgeting expansion in the United Nations system." However, the Report concluded that American efficacy in dealing with UNESCO's organizational problems, as well as its access to international scientific, educational, and cultural activities, would greatly decrease in the event of withdrawal.[13] Moreover, the State Department admitted that withdrawal would lessen, rather than increase, American influence over the actions of the Soviet Union in UNESCO. Nonetheless, the Report failed to endorse remaining in UNESCO.

With the notice of withdrawal given, UNESCO began evaluating reform of the Secretariat without cutting programs. However, the type of reform demanded by the United States was not possible within a one-year notice of withdrawal period. Many of the changes requested were structural in nature and would have required more time to implement (assuming they would have been deemed beneficial to the Organization). The immediate effect of the withdrawal—the sharp cut in funds—imposed on the Organization the need to prioritize its programs, and also to seek compensatory sources of funding from primarily non-Western states.

Conclusions. The basic situation as regards membership has not yet changed, even with the advent of a new director-general, Frederico Mayor, from Spain, who has virtually dropped the NWICO matter and has worked assiduously to meet the other concerns of the United States. A report by the Government Accounting Office (GAO), presented to a joint hearing of the House Science and Foreign Affairs subcommittee on June 25, 1992, cited progress by UNESCO in meeting management and budgetary conditions, including the reform of hiring and management practices, the streamlining of program activities, a significant reduction of UNESCO's assessed budget since 1984, and adherence to the zero-growth principle advocated by the United States. However, the GAO did not characterize these reforms as sufficient for American reentry, and it made additional reform recommendations.[14]

As indicated above, when the United States withdrew, three complaints were cited: mismanagement, budgetary growth, and a political atmosphere that it deemed hostile to itself. In the post-Cold War period, it would appear that all three conditions had been met. However, at the hearing, the Assistant Secretary of State for International Organization Affairs also implied a fourth condition: a change in the culture of UNESCO. The Clinton Administration, in contrast, undertook in 1993 a broad review of U.S. policy toward UNESCO and concluded that "the work of the revitalized UNESCO is so important that the U.S. needs to be a part of it."[15] Whether this results in concrete steps to rejoin remains to be seen.

Thus, one of the UN's most important specialized agencies, in terms of the involvement of NGOs and their influence on priority setting and policy-making, could not withstand the hostility of United States, whose own political system and national culture considers NGOs of all kinds as an integral part. Furthermore, even when UNESCO moved from majority voting to consensus formation in its collective decision-making, the often-outvoted United States still would not agree to play by these rules which favored the minority of Western states over the Third World majority. The cost-benefit calculation of membership still weighed in favor of continued withdrawal, although the original motivations were virtually either fulfilled or had passed from the international scene with the end of the Cold War. With ideology as a determinant of policy disappearing in the politics of international organizations, it would appear that UNESCO could be seen as providing an important outlet, not only for American foreign policy goals, but also for American political values.[16]

The Capacity of the FAO to Deal with the Food Issue: An Illustrative Case

Even though the World Food Conference (WFC), held in Rome in 1974, was considered one of the most successful of the global conferences of the 1970s, its long-term effect outside the U.S. system may not have been as important as the changes on the system itself. This is because global institutions are marginal in their ability to influence directly national decisions on food issues. INGOs also are increasingly playing a role in matters concerning food, hunger, malnutrition, and so forth as the illustrative case on Somalia in Chapter 6 reveals. The seeds of a globally organized food regime have been cast on the stony soil of sovereignty. As two skeptical scholars put it:

> The World Food Conference set about proliferating new food institutions, as constitutionally impotent as ever, but within the explanation that the older ones don't

work. Needless to say, if some institutions could work, propensities to pathological behavior in the global food system might be controlled. But, then, the pathologies result, after all, precisely from the fact that the current regime is distinctly inhospitable to the notion of "working international organizations."[17]

Even if states were committed to eradicating hunger as a first priority, the commitment would be irrelevant in the absence of a comprehensive analysis and plan of action that treated food behavior as if it were a global system. In fact, most of the efforts of the FAO and other UN agencies have taken a global view of food issues. The Freedom from Hunger Campaign of FAO, the World Food Program (WFP), the Indicative Plan of UNCTAD and the World Food Council (WFC) were all institutional as well as programmatic efforts within the United Nations System at a relatively comprehensive global approach. Along the same lines, those persons or institutions that concentrated on international food markets or commodities agreements could lay claim to a global perspective. Since production of surplus food is concentrated in a few states and separated from the hungry by geographic and political barriers, there are significant advantages to looking "from the top down," as it were.[18]

What made the World Food Conference significant was the fact that, in 1972, the total global production of food fell for the first time since World War II, a startling reduction of some 33 million tons. Since food output must expand at the rate of about 25 million tons annually to keep abreast of increases in population, the lack of approximately 60 million tons was felt, resulting in short supplies and increased prices. Although the 1973 harvest represented a good recovery from 1972, the main problem was that the biggest increases (in the Soviet Union and the Far East) did nothing to replenish the depleted stocks of the main cereal exporters. The world's margin of security against starvation dropped from ninety-six days in early 1972 to only twenty-six days by mid-1973 (and remains precarious in the 1990s, as evidenced by the starvation throughout Africa). The sense of crisis in food and agricultural matters was heightened by the deteriorating trade position of developing countries, galloping worldwide inflation, and a fourfold increase in the price of petroleum and fertilizers.[19]

Because of this critical situation, the Fourth Conference of the Heads of State of Non-Aligned Nations, which met in Algiers on September 5–9, 1973, urged that a joint, emergency conference of the FAO and UNCTAD should be convened at the ministerial level. In the opinion of these leaders of developing countries, the serious food shortages confronting vast areas and populations of the world necessitated a program of international cooperation. An important impetus for a high-level international discussion of food problems came on September 24, 1973. Then U.S. Secretary of State Henry Kissinger proposed that a world food conference under UN auspices be convened as rapidly as possible to mobilize all the resources of the international community to maintain adequate food supplies.

It is interesting to note that FAO perceived Kissinger's proposal as vital if the meeting were to have a chance of succeeding. An internal policy memorandum, for instance, noted:

> The most important positive feature of this proposal is that it has come from the United States in a major policy statement and the United States would therefore remain interested in the success of the Conference. In the past 25 years almost all important proposals for international food reserves—in one form or another or for a longer term international food aid policy—were thwarted because the United States has not been prepared to accept greater international control of its food and food aid policy. We cannot of course jump to the conclusion that this proposal constitutes a major shift in the United States policy but the fact remains that Henry Kissinger, with his unorthodox approach to international diplomacy, has made this proposal and it therefore offers at least some scope for some major initiatives.[20]

As the specialized agency whose mandate was food and agriculture, the reaction of FAO's biennial conference in Rome on November 10–29, 1973, was of vital importance. Recognizing that the United Nations itself, as well as the Secretariat, could best generate the political momentum to sustain such a conference, the FAO welcomed the effort under UN auspices and recommended that the proposed conference should focus on the resolution of food problems within the larger context of overall economic development. Echoing this point, in an address to ECOSOC, then FAO Director General A. H. Boerma pointed out that constraints on agriculture are constraints on development, and went on to identify the most important ones. Weather topped the list, followed closely by the failure of governments to "accord sufficient priority to agriculture and rural areas in general. More than any other sector, agriculture has suffered from a lack of sustained political will and commitment on the part of governments."[21] Land tenure systems and poverty were also high on Boerma's list; both are intimately related to the stability, if not the survival, of any Third World regime.

On February 1, 1974, in spite of U.S. reservations, Sayed Ahmed Marei of Egypt was named secretary-general of the World Food Conference. Shortly thereafter, the first session of the Preparatory Committee (PREPCOM), open to all governments and recognized observers, was held at UN headquarters in New York on February 11–15. ECOSOC, on May 15, 1974, took note of the PREPCOM in Resolution 1840 (LVI) and decided to convene the World Food Conference in Rome on November 5–16. Before the historic meeting occurred, two more sessions of the PREPCOM were held, in Geneva from June 4 to 8 and in Rome from September 23 to October 4.

From a macro-organizational perspective, the Seventeenth Session of the FAO Conference was extremely important. It provided an interesting example of a bureaucratic structure reacting to outside pressure. The formal

U.S. proposal—subsequently supported in the General Assembly by well-known international figures such as Algerian President Houari Boumedienne and West German Chancellor Willy Brandt—could be interpreted as a call for immediate action and an indirect criticism of past performances of IGOs concerned with food problems. This global awakening did not go unnoticed at FAO headquarters in Rome. Although many FAO officials saw the proposal for a conference as an excellent opportunity to use the politicians' preoccupation with the immediacy of the situation to get them to finally implement programs to combat long-standing problems, other officials reported that they, along with Director-General Boerma, were perturbed by the prospect that new activities on food might detract from FAO's image and mandate. The call for a food conference under UN (rather than FAO) auspices was indeed interpreted by some as a criticism of FAO's past performance. FAO supported Marei for secretary-general of the Conference because it was thought that he would be more amenable to FAO. As it turned out, however, this was not necessarily the case.[22]

Clearly, the international system was in a period of profound transformation. One of the symptoms of that transformation was the perception that institutions and arrangements rooted in the world of the 1950s and 1960s no longer worked in the 1970s and 1980s. Nonetheless, global institutions like the new World Food Council (WFC) and the International Fund for Agricultural Development (IFAD), as well as the old FAO, continue to serve two vital functions.[23]

First, they provide an intelligence capability for decision makers. Gathering and analyzing statistics, developing some expertise in advising policymakers on successful strategies for dealing with local problems, or wooing potential donors (a prime purpose of both the FAO staff and the Consultative Group on Food Production and Investment, which is composed of the World Bank, FAO, and the UN Development Program) is not a dramatic enterprise. However, if policies are to be implemented at any level that actually increases the amount of food on people's tables, it is a necessary one.

Second, in our opinion, if a new global consensus does arise, it will do so only through a quasi-dialectical process of confrontation, bargaining, and compromise, replete with symbolic appeals, posturing, and rhetoric. International institutions provide an established, focused, and continuing arena within which the politics of food can be played out. Not surprisingly, the arenas themselves become issues, as the pattern of events surrounding the 1974 World Food Conference illustrate. Institutional reform and restructuring make sense when changes can be measured against a criterion of efficiency and the issues are competitive means to a given end. Disagreement about basic goals cannot be dealt with by debating alternative programs of work or reorganizing the management of agencies. The exercise of influence, as in the case of the global issue of food, did bring about new international institutions and a renewed (even if limited) commitment to reduce hunger.

In the 1990s (as mentioned) widespread starvation in Africa remained a dominant FAO concern, and the WFC and IFAD became deeply involved in the problem. INGOs have also been playing a significant role in the food issue, as revealed in the discussion in Chapter 6 on the U.S.-UN humanitarian relief intervention in Somalia in 1992–1993. Also, in the middle of 1991, FAO also began analyzing food production systems in Eastern Europe, where food reserves had recently been falling.

MEMBER GOVERNMENTS' INFLUENCE ON IGO DECISIONS

The two preceding cases highlight the various interests of member governments for the exercise of influence on UNESCO and FAO operations. In more general terms, what means are available to member governments to influence the input and output of the decision-making processes in individual IGOs? A variety of possibilities come to mind. On the formal level, *participatory and representational* mechanisms are available to shape inputs and outputs, such as *governing councils* and *conferences*. These may take the form of shaping particular IGO policies, recommendations, and resolutions, or even legal, binding pronouncements. For example, the EC Council of Ministers, which is composed of those ministers of the member states designated by or drawn from the relevent ministry deemed competent to deal with a particular issue before the Council, has a major role in influencing inputs and in shaping the decisional output. In other words, the ministers actually participate in various phases of the decision-making process. In the same manner, members of the European Parliament (EP), the legislative assembly in the institutional framework of the EC, participate in the decisions of this body. Votes in the EP conceivably can be used to promote the goals of the member states.

Another form of representational mechanism is the *permanent missions* of the member states accredited to the United Nations. The staffs of these diplomatic missions represent the viewpoints of their respective governments and, therefore, are in a position to promote the national policies of their governments within the various UN organs and bodies. They also promote the policies of their governments among themselves outside the multilateral structure of the UN.[24]

On the informal level, *personal contacts* and other kinds of *interface between national and IGO bureaucracies* can be used to influence the IGO decision-making process in the direction of objectives sought by one or more member governments. So-called corridor deals during sessions of the General Assembly and similar organs and committee meetings, as well as during various UN-sponsored conferences, come to mind. Even if carefully organized, these contacts may not always be successful, however. The perceptions held by national civil servants or by their IGO counterparts are likely to play an important role, and, to a lesser degree, so are the images of specific national bureaucracies formed in the minds of the international civil servants. While IGO officials, especially those in higher positions, may provide (appropriately at times, but at other times inappropriately) important channels for the attainment of member states' goals, it should be noted that informal contacts between IGO and national government officials also can be used in the other direction: to persuade policymaking bureaucrats in the member states of the merits of IGO policy proposals.

Informal interactions also can take place between national and international INGOs and IGO institutions, often with the aim of influencing IGO decision making in accordance with interest group goals and, at times, converging national objectives of member states. (This is discussed further in Chapter 6.) Interest groups pursue goals in a wide variety of issue areas, including economic development, humanitarian, religious, ethnic, and arms control and disarmament matters. Therefore, depending on the particular goals pursued, all types of IGOs are perceived as useful targets.

Multilevel Bargaining between IGO Institutions and Member States: The European Regional Development Fund (ERDF)

The aim of member governments to influence IGO decisions is not confined to universal IGOs. National efforts to influence decisions are also exerted in regional IGOs. The structuring of regional development policies in the EC and the creation and operation of the European Regional Development Fund (ERDF) are prime examples of the bargaining on the European, national, and subnational levels to influence the nature and direction of EC policies.

The establishment of the ERDF was approved by the EC Council of Ministers in March 1975 for a three-year experimental period following two years of intensive and often bitter discussion among all the parties involved. The ERDF was subsequently renewed after the three-year period and then enlarged at subsequent intervals. However, initial approval came only after several earlier unsuccessful attempts by the Commission to institute a common regional policy. The initial resources allocated to the Fund were very modest, and many member states looked on it as primarily a quid pro quo for cooperation in other areas of Community activity. As Helen Wallace points out, it was felt that the creation of the new Fund "would allow for budgetary transfers that would ease, even cancel out, unfavorable financial commitments incurred on other common policies."[25]

The negotiations over the establishment of the ERDF took place within the decision-making framework of the EC but were dominated by serious controversies among the member governments, particularly between Britain and West Germany. Moreover, different ministries in the national capitals got into the act, trying to promote their own institutional interests through suggestions as to how their governments should respond to repeated, though different, Commission policy proposals. Finally, subnational units such as the West German states (*Länder*), Italian regional governments, and Scotland and Wales in Britain had particular interests in regional development that they were anxious to pursue while EC development policies were discussed and formulated.

Historically, the basic tenets of an EC regional policy had been under consideration for several years, but the formulation of such a policy did not become a major issue until the Summit Conference that was held in Paris in October 1972. This conference was particularly important because the EC was to gain three new members in 1973—Ireland, Britain, and Denmark, the first two of which had serious regional problems. In addition, the negotiations about the Fund came at a time when questions were raised about the effective management of the EC budget and about which priorities should be assigned to EC expenditures.

After some inconclusive attempts, the Commission presented proposals for a regional policy based on the following guidelines:

1. Community regional policy cannot be a substitute for the national regional policies which Member States have been conducting for many years. It must complement them with the aim of reducing the main disparities across the Community.
2. Since overconcentration of economic activity in some regions is a major social and economic problem which tends to become more and more acute, the Community, as well as giving aid to the poorer regions, should seek agreement between the Member States on common policies to reduce concentration in the congested regions.
3. If Community regional policy is to be successful, it requires not only new incentives but coordination of the various common policies and financial instruments that exist at Community level with a view to their improved utilization for regional objectives.
4. The principal vehicle for mobilizing Community resources as a complement to actions presently carried out in the Member States should be the Regional Development Fund. The assistance of the Fund should be devoted entirely to the medium and long term development of the less developed and declining regions within the Member States, with the aim of bringing about self-sustaining growth.
5. The Fund will have to concentrate its expenditures very largely in those regions that are the most in need in relation to the Community as a whole. In other words, there must be standards to ensure that the means available to the Fund are used in a manner quite independent of any criterion of *juste retour*. . . . The acceptance of this principle will be an important test of Community solidarity.[26]

However, in proposing to go beyond assistance to the hard core of neglected areas and to take into consideration the accommodation of members' national interests and goals, the Commission gave the impression of "being a watering can . . . sprinkling a little in everyone's direction" so that no member government would oppose it.[27] It based its position on the expanding suburban sprawl; substandard, overcrowded, and insufficient housing; growing commuter traffic congestion; and pollution of the air and water. Therefore, affluent areas as well as poorer regions were to be beneficiaries.

The amount of the Fund was originally set at 1.3 billion UAs (units of account) to be expended over three years. The West German government was to supply 30 percent of the total and the French, 20 percent. Neither the British nor the Italians considered the size of the Fund sufficient. The Germans, on the other hand, thought the amount too high and the distribution formula unacceptable. Their position was that only the poorer countries should benefit and that Britain, Denmark (for Greenland and the Faroe Islands), Ireland, and Italy should draw the same net figure. Regions eligible for aid should be those with a gross national product that was at least 10 percent lower than the Community average. Under the German proposal, France would not have benefited at all from the Fund, nor would the Netherlands, Belgium, or Luxembourg. The French opposed the idea of not being able to draw from the regional purse for their less developed areas, and later a compromise was drafted, leaning toward concentration on the most needy regions. This was accepted at the December 1974 Summit Conference.[28]

How effective has the ERDF been in improving the economies of the depressed regions, and what are the likely EC development policies of the future? First, the gap between the richer and the poorer regions has widened instead of narrowing. The ratio between the richest regions and the poorest regions was 2.9:1 in 1970, while at the end of the decade, it had risen to 4.0:1.[29] This development occurred despite the fact that the annual size of the Fund quadrupled from 1975 to 1980. Obviously, the policy had not at that time attained its intended purpose.

Second, questions were raised as to whether the national quota system, which controls 95 percent of the ERDF expenditures, may have been responsible for the Fund's poor record in helping the poorer regions. Of these expenditures, 74 percent went into improvements to infrastructure, leaving only 26 percent for industrial projects.[30] Assuming that the strict adhesion to the quota system was indeed harmful to the achievements of an effective regional development policy, the Commission recommended new policy outlines in July 1981. In a memorandum published at that time, the following points were stressed:

1. The Commission noted the urgent need for the EEC to reverse the trend of increasing regional differences, which had been in evidence since the common market was first founded.

2. ERDF funds should be concentrated more on regions that lag far behind the EEC average (rather than base aid on national averages) so as to give ERDF aid greater impact.
3. The ERDF's top priority should be to create new jobs, taking due account of population trends and the fact that there will be less mobility between regions than in the past. (This is not, in itself, a negative factor since the EEC must work to prevent overconcentration of economic activity in certain areas that are already well provided for, which merely puts outlying regions even further behind.)
4. The Community should make the most of local development potential in the regions that need assistance: manpower, of course, as well as alternative sources of energy, and latent industrial potential, especially in small- and medium-scale industries.
5. Coordination of the different EEC instruments should be improved and strengthened, and a guarantee should be given that EEC aid is to match national efforts and not replace them.[31]

Although the Commission did not suggest the complete elimination of quotas, only states with extensive regional economic problems were to be allocated quotas, and these were to be increased. It is important to note that future total quota allocations of the Fund were reduced to 80 percent from 95 percent, providing considerably larger amounts of money to nonquota projects.

The basic rationale for the Commission's enlargement of the nonquota portion of the ERDF seemed to make sense. Problem regions at times straddle the territories of several countries and do not necessarily coincide with assisted areas, as defined by member states for their own national assistance to troubled areas. Moreover, multiannual programs can be developed that may have a much more significant impact on the poorest regions than annual projects that are often poorly integrated.

There were voices of support for this new approach from the EP, but there were also rumblings of opposition from the chambers of commerce and industry groups. It is noteworthy that permanent observers from the German *Länder,* as well as from Scotland and Wales, were installed in Brussels, and that these observers injected themselves in regional issues. The regions, of course, seek to exert influence on the national governments as well as to interact among themselves in an effort to enhance their particular interests.

In 1986, the Fund reached 2.3 billion UAs, and while this may not have been adequate for a Community of twelve states, it represented progress that was generally in keeping with the member states' objectives.

In 1988 it was decided to double the size of ERDF over five years in conformity with Article 23 of the Single European Act (SEA) which had been adopted the previous year. Special efforts are being made to help through this fund the newest members of the Community—Greece, Portugal and Spain, whose economies are weaker than the more senior EC members (except Ireland). Indeed, by 1990, the Fund had already attained 5.4 billion UAs and, hence, was well on its way to fulfilling its function of "participating in the development and structural adjustment of regions whose developing is lagging behind, and in the conversion of declining industrial regions" (Article 130c amended, EEC Treaty).

The preceding pages demonstrate the significant influence that domestic politics can have in the issue area of regional development and on the relation between the Community institutions and the member states, as well as on the direction and content of policy formulation and, perhaps also, implementation. Obviously, to evolve a truly rational, common policy has been extremely difficult. Compromises to satisfy the interests of various groups, subnational units, and national governmental agencies are a continuing part of the policymaking process that is further compounded by a shifting and unpredictable global economy. The *retour juste* continues to be a persisting concern in the minds of national leaders. Nevertheless, progress has been made on the multilateral IGO policy level, and this progress, involving ever-larger dispensations of financial aid, is likely to strengthen the legitimacy of the EC institutions. In the longer term, the economic conditions of the aid recipients may be improved and the gap between the rich and poor regions of Western Europe narrowed, if not closed. As for the progress achieved, considerable credit must be given to the Commission, whose patience and persistence, coupled with a measure of flexibility, essentially achieved its original goal for the ERDF.

Thus, we see evidence in this case that, in spite of differing perceptions and objectives on the part of the member states, central IGO institutions can evolve compromises for policies that are eventually accepted and that are in line with the fulfillment of important IGO objectives. At the same time, member governments are satisfied with the IGO performance when they see the enhancement of their own national interests.

THE ROLE OF COALITIONS IN IGO INTERACTIONS

To what extent are transgovernmental, interbureaucratic, and transnational coalitions formed to enhance member states' goals? Coalitions may be formed: (1) by national governments exclusively; (2) by national bureaucracies, either entirely from member states or, in exceptional circumstances, with selected segments of IGO bureaucracies; or (3) between interest groups, working in some cases with national bureaucrats or even leaders of member governments. Interest groups may also seek to work with IGO officials if that may enhance the achievement of their objectives.

The Group of 77 is a prime example of a governmental coalition that interacts with several IGOs, and the national bureaucracies of the members of this Group are more likely than not to cooperate to achieve their various goals. In certain instances, IGO bureaucracies of such development-oriented agencies of the United Nations as UNCTAD, UNDP, or UNIDO are mandated to work with governmental and nongovernmental coalitions. The negotiations regarding the UN Code of Conduct for Transnational Corporations, which began in 1974 under the general auspices of ECOSOC and have continued through the present, albeit without success, illustrate different attempts at such coalition formation (as discussed Chapter 7). Interest groups in the advanced industrial states actively solicited the cooperation and support of the officials of the UN Centre on Transnational Corporations (CTC), which was established to provide administrative support and research, for these negotiations.

In the search for coalition partners, member governments of an IGO may seek the support of a third state. For example, during the early years of the ECSC and the EEC, the support of the United States for regional integration was sought by the member states of the two Communities; this support was given with enthusiasm and contributed to a large degree to the initial success of the EC. IGOs as formal coalition structures may also be employed by member governments to influence the decision-making process in another IGO. This is happening in regard to attempts to curtail or stop the warfare in the former Yugoslavia with, to differing degrees, the UN, UNHCR, NATO, EC, CSCE, and WEU all being involved according to the interests of their various member states. The institutionalized practices for external policy coordination all play a role.

Another aspect of coalition building is the fact that states are members of many IGOs; overlapping membership may mean overlapping interests, but this may not necessarily be so. Nonetheless, this makes it possible for states to expand their communication channels and instruments for the promotion of their national policies. The creation of an EFTA-EC connection in regard to trade relationships is an example.

Intergovernmental and IGO Effectiveness—European Political Cooperation (EPC): An Illustrative Case

While it is frequently contended, with justification, that increased intergovernmental interaction among IGO member states tends to undermine the effectiveness of the central IGO institutions, there are areas where intergovernmentalism might strengthen particular functions of these institutions. This was the case with European Political Cooperation (EPC), a foreign-policy coordinating mechanism established by the EC member states during the 1970s.

The constituent treaties of the EC contain provisions for the formulation of selected external policies and for relations with other IGOs, but the full acceptance and use of these provisions has been slow and often troublesome.

Undoubtedly, the EEC Treaty has the most extensive provisions, including the creation of common commercial policies toward nonmember states and the conclusion of association agreements with third states. Although a number of these agreements have been signed since the early 1960s and progress has been made in the formulation of EEC commercial policies, many Western Europeans have expressed the desire to see their states speak with one voice in international affairs. As a consequence, efforts have been made to devise other means to produce common foreign policies on the part of the member states.

As a result of these efforts, an alternative structure outside the EC decision-making framework, as specified in the three treaties, was created to coordinate the foreign policies of the EC member states. The EPC structure had only very loose, poorly defined ties to the EC system. Its origins were in the Fouchet Plans which were elaborated in 1962 by a committee of diplomats chaired by Christian Fouchet, then the French ambassador to Denmark. The basic idea of the Fouchet Plans (there were two somewhat different proposals made by the committee) was the creation of a council at the level of heads of state and government that was to meet every four months and, acting by unanimity, to coordinate foreign and defense policy. To assist the council and to prepare policy proposals, an intergovernmental European political commission, perhaps in the form of a permanent secretariat, was to be established. It was to be composed of senior officials in the national foreign services and to be located in Paris. Although a chance for success seemed to exist in the early stages of the negotiations on the essentially Gaullist draft treaty for policy coordination, no synthesis between the divergent positions of France and the other EC partners was achieved.

In 1969, initiatives were again launched to find new paths for the construction of some kind of European union. One of these initiatives was the creation of a committee composed of high foreign ministry officials of the member states under the chairmanship of Vicomte Etienne Davignon of the Belgian Foreign Ministry. The results of the deliberations of the Davignon Committee were published on July 20, 1970. In accordance with this report, the foreign ministers began to schedule joint meetings every six months. A conference of heads of state and government could also be called when crucial issues justified such a meeting.

To prepare the sessions of the foreign ministers, a special committee was created composed of the political directors of the foreign ministries, to which were added in 1973 their counterparts from Britain, Ireland, and Denmark. In 1981, a member was added from Greece, and in 1986, one member was added from Spain and one from Portugal. This Political Committee was to meet at least four times a year, but actually it has met more often. Subordinate to this Committee are working groups and groups of experts entrusted to investigate particular problems and recommend possible solutions. The chairmanship and the venue for their sessions is rotated according to whichever country chairs the EC Council of Ministers, whose presidency changes every six months.

The Committee considers important questions of foreign policy; the member governments can suggest any issue for consideration that may pertain to general foreign policy problems or to such matters as monetary affairs, energy, and security. Whenever the work of this committee impinges on the competences and activities of the EC, the Commission is requested to submit its own position on the matter under consideration and is invited to send a representative.

The foreign policy coordination activities of the EPC are supplemented by periodic sessions of staff members held in the embassies of the member states. The commercial counselor of the embassy of the member state that holds the presidency of the Council of Ministers at a particular time prepares a report on these meetings. These reports are addressed to the president of the Council and are also distributed to the permanent representatives in Brussels and to a number of national governmental agencies. If no objections are raised by a member government within eight days, a copy of this report is furnished to the Commission. Policy coordination meetings have also been held at the United Nations.

The emergence of the EPC as an important factor in the formulation of common foreign policies pitted several organizational and bureaucratic groups against each other, since both intrabureaucratic (i.e., international civil servants) and interbureaucratic (i.e., national ministries) coalitions work in EC foreign policy-making. Some kind of liaison between the EPC structure and the Council is now also envisaged through ad hoc groups of senior civil servants of the foreign and other ministries on matters affecting EC affairs.[32]

Whatever the bureaucratic interplay and its effect on the morale of the "Eurocracy," the range of activities of the staff of the EPC that might lead to common action is impressive:

1. An average of some one hundred communications are transmitted every week over a common telex system called COREU.
2. More than 100 sessions of common working groups are scheduled, composed of national diplomats who analyze important international problems.
3. Political Committee meetings are held twice a month to exchange information about the work and operations of the various foreign ministries that are relevant to EPC. A crisis procedure exists that will assure meetings of the Committee within forty-eight hours.
4. Representation of the member states at international conferences and in IGOs is carried out by one delegation.[33]

As a result of the EC's particular external policy competences and the EPC mechanism, third states have become aware that their own foreign policy developments must take into serious consideration both processes; moreover, in order to influence the foreign policies of the EC member states, the foreign ministries of third states should know as much as possible of what is happening in the EPC deliberations on various international issues. The United States has been especially sensitive to this and was particularly concerned with events and policies during the Yom Kippur War in October 1973 and the initiation of the Euro-Arab dialogue in 1974. To satisfy U.S. concerns, a compromise agreement was concluded among the foreign ministers of the EC states making it possible for the United States to participate in EPC deliberations prior to a final decision by the EC foreign ministers, provided a member state desires consultation with Washington on a particular issue and the remaining member states agree to that procedure. If unanimity about the invitation of such consultation cannot be attained, then contacts and consultations with the United States may be conducted only on a bilateral basis.[34] This arrangement has worked well and seems to have satisfied all parties.

An Evaluation. The achievements of EPC have been mixed. The EPC has played an important role in responding to the breakup of Yugoslavia, although the final judgment in the solution of this crisis remains unresolved. The EC Commission participated vigorously and effectively in the deliberations on economic issues and contributed materially to shaping the common stand regarding sanctions ultimately taken by the member states. An EC negotiator, Lord Owen of Britain, has worked alongside a UN negotiator, in attempting to bring a negotiated peace to the region.

Consultations between the United States and the EPC members regarding the creation of the Conference on Security and Cooperation in Europe (CSCE) were carried out within the framework of NATO. Washington accepted the leading role of the EC Nine in the preparation of the CSCE negotiations as far as nonmilitary matters were concerned; and, as a consequence, the Final Act of Helsinki carried the imprint of conclusions reached in the EPC deliberations.[35] Clearly, this is an example of effective policy harmonization of both the member states and the EC proper, although the specific competences of the latter were not directly involved.

Another major foreign policy effort in which the EPC mechanism was used jointly with the EC external relations system is the Euro-Arab dialogue which was initiated in 1975 and continues. The delegation for the EC and its member states is led by the government chairing the EPC and by the Commission president or his representatives.[36] The Arab League states have wanted to conclude a comprehensive preferential trade agreement with the EC and to have economic assistance and tariff preferences that had been extended to Israel suspended. However, this has been rejected consistently by the EC institutions and may soon be moot.[37]

Other major issues in which EPC has been involved include the invasion of Afghanistan in 1979, about which their suggestions were not taken seriously, and the Falklands crisis of 1982, in which EPC and the EC institutions worked closely in the imposition of trade sanctions on Argentina.[38] During the Persian Gulf crisis in 1990–1991, EPC also played an important role by producing joint foreign policy statements and coordinated responses, although the interests of the member states were sometimes at variance, and security issues, outside of EPC, became important.

Conclusions. While it is obviously in the nature of the EC that its external policies should concentrate mostly on economic issues, it is equally evident that the EPC has been concerned mainly with selected political matters such as turmoil in Cyprus and Afghanistan and some aspects of CSCE. Hence, while EPC complemented the external activities of the EC, it has served as a fully harmonizing agent for overall policy only insofar as it draws the Commission into deliberations on a particular issue. Nevertheless, some long-range benefits for the operations of the EC institutions may flow from the operations of the EPC mechanism. This mechanism and the EC external policymaking process operate side by side in a useful, pragmatic manner. Even though at present no particular integrative effect can be observed, in fact, EPC may have strengthened intergovernmentalist trends in the relations between the member states and the EC institutions, and thus, the EPC may become a building block for developing the necessary preconditions for integrative forward movement. Meanwhile, the aspirations of many Western Europeans to see their region speak with one voice in international affairs have received a strong boost from the EPC operations. This trend is also reflected in Article 30 of the Single European Act (SEA), which provides a legal basis for EPC as the means and endeavor to formulate and implement a European foreign policy.

Decisions on policy *formulations* are made by unanimity, but there is hope that policy *implementation* decisions by the EC Council of Ministers may be made in the future by a qualified majority. A small EPC secretariat is now established in Brussels in the Council of Ministers building.

In terms of IGO task performance, EPC, with its new permanent secretariat, has strengthened the Commission's effectiveness in commercial policy formulation and implementation. From the member states' point of view, the EC has become a more important instrument of national policy through the EPC coordination effort, but the range of foreign policy activities has not expanded. This perception of the member states with respect to handling their foreign policy activities is not unique. As James M. McCormick and Young W. Kihl have shown, the conduct of foreign affairs through IGOs by their member states did not increase overall until the end of the Cold War, despite the rising number of these organizations since World War II. They were used only selectively as instruments for gaining foreign policy objectives.[39] That situation appears to be changing in the contemporary period of economic interdependence linked to peacekeeping, peacemaking and peacebuilding.

INTER-IGO RELATIONS

An intriguing question is whether relations among IGOs may also be affected by the attempts of member governments to use, and perhaps to manipulate, the operations of one IGO in order to influence the activities and policies of another IGO for the purpose of enhancing national interests. In some cases, the form and scope of inter-IGO relations are stipulated in the constituent treaties. For example, the EEC Treaty contains a number of provisions prescribing this organization's formal relations with the United Nations, the Council of Europe, and other IGOs (Articles 229–231). Although these relations under international law are between the IGOs as a result of their recognized legal personalities, it is quite conceivable that, in political terms, they may well be influenced, and perhaps shaped, to varying degrees by the interests pursued by some or all of the member states of the interacting organizations.[40] That is more likely to be the case in relations among IGOs within a particular region, such as between the EC and the Council of Europe, the OAU and the UN Economic Commission for Africa, or NATO and the OECD. In relations between units of the UN family, administrative and bureaucratic considerations (e.g., budget concerns) may play a more significant role, but economic and political concerns may also induce the member states to exert some influence on interunit relationships that they might perceive to be in the interests of the entire membership.[41] The close collaboration in peacekeeping and peacemaking, involving threats to the peace on humanitarian grounds, has brought about the direct involvement of the Security Council with many UN agencies and activities, such as UNHCR, UNICEF, UNDP, and IAEA.

The European Community in the United Nations

Member states of IGOs frequently employ coalition strategies in order to influence the decision-making process, especially if the states concerned already belong to another relatively cohesive IGO. The institutionalized practices for external policy coordination by the EC member states in the General Assembly are a good example of this coalition formation behavior. Whatever issue may come up in the United Nations (as pointed out earlier in this chapter), the EC member states, as a coalition, attempt to coordinate their approach in order to promote their particular national objectives.

On the whole, the EC member states have attempted to coordinate their approach in order to promote their particular national objectives. They realize that only through coordination will they be able to exert a measure of influence in UN bodies.

What is revealed is the use of an IGO (the United Nations) as an instrument for the pursuit of national policies by the member states of another IGO (the EC). The EC is used as the core for coalition formation, with national and EC civil servants playing important roles through the EPC mechanism. However, it is important to note that the EC coordination efforts have not led to a special relationship between the EC and the United Nations, although interbureaucratic contacts between EC and UN civil servants may well have been intensified.

Collective Security and Conflict Resolution: An Inter-IGO Issue

Regionalism Rediscovered. Following a vigorous debate in San Francisco over the merits of universalism versus regionalism, both concepts were incorporated in the United Nations Charter.[42] (A copy of the UN Charter is reprinted as Appendix B to this volume.) By virtue of the authority given to the Security Council in Chapters VI and VII and Article 2, paragraph 7, universalism came out on top. However, in Chapter VIII, a role was also envisaged, though not too precisely, for "regional arrangements or agencies for dealing with such matters relating to the maintenance of international peace and security as are appropriate for regional action." The lack of precision is evident in the very terms "regional arrangements" and "appropriate." Both terms were left undefined. The terms "collective security" and "conflict resolution" are used broadly here, encompassing the Charter aims—"the maintenance of international peace and security" and "pacific settlement of disputes," as well as the powers derived from the Charter for "peacekeeping" and "peacemaking."[43]

The basic idea of Chapter VIII was (1) for member states to "make every effort to achieve pacific settlement of local disputes through such regional arrangements or by such regional agencies before referring them to the Security Council," and (2) for the Security Council "to encourage the development of pacific settlement of local disputes through such regional arrangements or by such regional agencies either on the initiative of the states concerned or by reference from the Security Council," and "where appropriate [to] utilize such regional arrangements or agencies for enforcement action under its authority."

The Cold War prevented the development of a close relationship between the Security Council and existing regional arrangements. The Security Council itself was paralyzed by the veto, and regional arrangements were used, in the words of Inis Claude, "as jurisdictional refuges, providing pretexts for keeping disputes out of U.N. hands."[44] The major antagonists of the Cold War, the United States and the Soviet Union, were unwilling to permit Security Council involvement in regional conflicts in which they were respectively implicated. In such instances, they much preferred the friendlier jurisdiction of a regional organization to that of the Cold War–dominated Security Council. Beginning with the Guatemala case in 1954 through the Cuban complaint against the United States in 1962, that of Panama in 1964, and the Americans' sending of troops into the Dominican Republic in 1965 (all matters that came up before the Security Council), the United States successfully insisted that these matters belonged in the OAS and not in the Security Council.[45] In similar fashion, the USSR denied the Security Council's competence to deal with the suppression of the Hungarian uprising in 1956 and the 1968 Soviet intervention in Czechoslovakia, contending that these matters were properly the concern of the "socialist community" bound together in the Warsaw Pact. Clearly, regional organizations were used by each superpower as instruments for hegemonic supremacy in a region and not as agencies for broader collective security and conflict resolution.

One of the consequences of the Gulf Crisis is a strong feeling among many that the peace and security provisions of the Charter are finally being implemented. Along with this feeling has come renewed interest in Chapter VIII of the Charter. Although the Security Council's handling of Iraq's invasion of Kuwait has been hailed by many as a demonstration, at long last, that the United Nations is functioning according to the original intent of the Charter, a noticeable unease with the action has also been evident, particularly regarding the precedents set for the future of collective security. Former Foreign Minister Eduard A. Shevardnadze of the Soviet Union typified this concern when he stated:

> The example of the action of the coalition forces in the Persian Gulf demonstrates the need for further improving the functioning of the U.N. Security Council. No single country, not even as powerful and rich as the United States, can or has the right to play the role of global policeman. No one country, even the smallest and weakest, would agree with the idea of restraining the violators of order in the world if the restraining were done by a single power.[46]

The attention given to the involvement of regional arrangements in collective security is part of a search on the part of scholars and practitioners to improve the functioning of the Security Council and the system for collective security and conflict resolution.

Defining "Regional Arrangements or Agencies." The definition of a region has persistently troubled social scientists.[47] How is a region to be determined: geopolitically, culturally, ideologically, or economically? The Charter does not delineate the regions of the world, nor does it establish criteria to which regional organizations should conform. An ideal definition of a region that was advanced a generation ago by a leading political scientist reads: "[A region] must cohere in many respects—in many transactions and commodities, in the flow of labor, management and capital, in economic structure, in education, in culture, in science, in politics, in intermarriage and migration, and in still other ways."[48] This ideal concept of the region has been achieved rarely and is certainly not the criterion by which regions are measured in the United Nations. However, it is instructive to keep this notion in mind in assessing the problems that arise in trying to implement the idea of regionalism in the United Nations.

At first glance, it would appear very plausible to deal with threats to the peace initially at the local regional level prior to elevating it to an international dispute before the United Nations. Why make an international case of an issue if it could be dealt with locally? Local regional actors can be expected to have a better understanding of local issues; problems can be handled, so to speak en famille, without the intrusion of extraneous players.

More than two decades ago, Inis Claude raised "a cautionary 'it ain't necessarily so' in response to the proposition that organized action operates best within regional groupings." He noted that "interregional affinities may be offset by historically rooted intraregional animosities, and geographical proximity may pose dangers . . . rather than collaborative possibilities which [states] wish to exploit in regional privacy."[49] This situation has changed little with the passage of time; in fact, it has been exacerbated. Because all states within a region are not necessarily compatible, regional groupings often lack the degree of internal cohesion needed for them to play a peacekeeping and conflict resolution role.

Moreover, regional groupings are not made up of equal partners, except in the juridical sense that they are all sovereign states. Some states are certainly more powerful economically and militarily, and hence, politically as well. Further complicating this inequality is the introduction of nuclear arms into a number of regions and its almost inevitable consequence: a competitive, regional nuclear balance of terror. Since nuclear deterrence strategy leads to heightened tensions, the outlook is dim for progress toward effective regional security arrangements in a number of regions in which nuclear arms are a factor.

Under these circumstances, are regional organizations in a position structurally to undertake the responsibility of playing a leading role in the area of peace maintenance and conflict resolution? Do they have the necessary political will? If we are to judge the capacity of regional organizations to play a peace-preserving role by recent experience, the answer is problematical. In the post-Cold War period, a number of situations arose that have involved regional agencies:

1. Iraq-Kuwait—the Arab League and the Gulf Cooperation Council (GCC);
2. Central America—OAS;

3. Liberia—OAU and ECOWAS;
4. Cambodia—ASEAN;
5. Somalia—the Arab League, the Islamic Conference, and OAU;
6. Yugoslavia—EC (partially NATO, WEU)

Unfortunately, regional peacekeeping efforts have not yet been successful, and several of them are on the brink of failure.

As in Liberia, the conflicts in Central America were basically civil wars but were marked by "cross-border guerrilla warfare, a situation where the internal conflict in some countries tended to spill over into neighboring countries and embitter their relations."[50] Alvaro De Soto, the secretary-general's special representative in Central America, has explained why the United Nations rather than the OAS became the instrument for settlement:

> Report to regional organizations or to the United Nations is optional. There is no obligation to resort first to a regional organization and then, in the event of failure, to the world organization. In the case of Central America, the United Nations and the Secretary-General were the preferred vehicles because an extraregional dimension was involved.[51]

The UN involvement in the four other cases listed above came about essentially because the regional organizations were unable to act. The existence of harsh political tensions within a region combined with a lack of resources and experience often create intractable obstacles to the exercise of leadership by the regional body. It was not the furtive influence of extraneous powers that prevented each of the regional agencies from assuming responsibility but rather, internal political configurations and weaknesses that provided the stubborn impediments.

The absence of clout should not automatically rule out a potential role for regional bodies. Chapter VIII of the Charter did not envisage "regional arrangements and agencies" functioning in the area of collective security and conflict resolution on their own. They were expected to work in conjunction with the Security Council, but the relationship is ambiguous.

The initially projected role for "regional arrangements or agencies" as part of the original UN Charter's structure for international conflict resolution and the maintenance of international peace is still to be defined and worked out. Oscar Schachter points out that "at San Francisco the U.N. Security Council was perceived as a forum of last resort when states were unable to resolve conflicts between them through the peaceful means listed in Chapter VI or through regional instrumentalities."[52] This concept was recently reiterated by Australia's Deputy Secretary of Foreign Affairs and Trade, Michael J. Costello, who emphasized "the importance of regional organizations in preventing and ameliorating disputes before they get to the level of the Security Council.[53] Until now, things have not worked out this way.

A New Road Ahead? Now that the Cold War is over, debate over the utility of regional arrangements and agencies in the pursuit of collective security and conflict resolution has entered a new phase. Even those who welcomed the "coming of age" of the United Nations in the Security Council's handling of Iraq's aggression felt somewhat uncomfortable about it because a number of pertinent provisions of the Charter were not used. Together with the critics of the Security Council's action in the Gulf Crisis, they came away with the feeling that in this post-Cold War period, it was time to look more carefully at all the provisions of the Charter regarding collective security, namely, agreements between member states and the Security Council on contingency forces, as called for in Article 43; resurrection of the Military Staff Committee; and delineating a clearer role for regional arrangements and agencies in the maintenance of international peace and security in relationship with the Security Council, in accordance with Chapter VIII. (Figure 5.1 details UN peacekeeping activities in the years 1987–1992.)

Does this mean that the renewed interest in the role of regional arrangements in the UN system for collective security and conflict resolution is misplaced? It probably does, if the expectation is that regional organizations can step in now and relieve the Security Council of some of the responsibility in the field of collective security and conflict resolution. At the same time, it must also be recognized that the new world order is only in the process of being shaped. It should be noted that the secretary-general has been asked by the Security Council to suggest ways in which regional arrangements might play a role in the new security arrangements. Certainly, the freedom of regional agencies to engage in enforcement actions is restricted by the Charter, since these can be undertaken only with the authorization of the Security Council. However, "resort to regional agencies or arrangements" is one of the means included in Article 33 of Chapter VI as a route to the pacific settlement of a dispute.

Since assuming office at the beginning of 1992, Secretary-General Boutros Boutros-Ghali has been confronted with a number of thorny disputes in which both the United Nations and regional organizations have been involved. These include Yugoslavia, Nagorno-Karabakh, and Somalia. In talking about these issues, the secretary-general has raised a number of interesting propositions regarding the synergistic roles of regional organizations and the United Nations in the area of conflict resolution. Boutros-Ghali believes, first, that it is better that local disputes be solved in a local or a regional framework; second, that through the regional organizations, the United Nations can implement certain sanctions against an aggressor; and third, that a desirable division of labor has emerged between regional organizations and the United Nations, in that the former pursue the political aspects of a problem (i.e. peacemaking), while the UN mandate is limited

Figure 5.1
Peacekeeping Activities: Number of Operations Deployed and their Annual Cost, 1987–1992

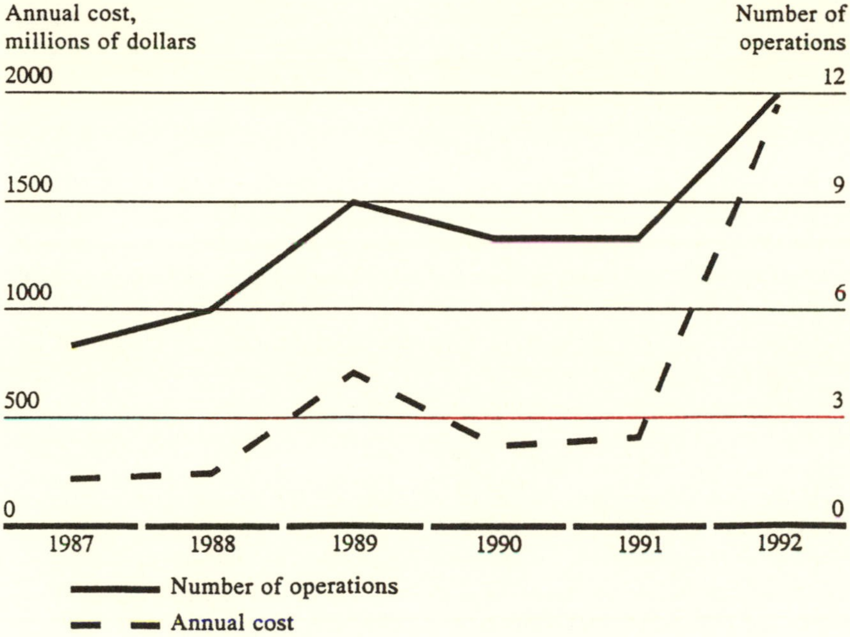

Source: United Nations, *Report of the Secretary-General on the Work of the Organization* (GA Doc. A/47/1, September 11, 1992).

to peacekeeping operations to maintain the cease-fire. Fourth, since the UN may be overtaxed by the very many conflicts it may be called on to deal with, regional organizations should be encouraged "to help us in the solution of the problem."[54] The secretary-general expanded his thoughts on regional organizations in a speech delivered in May 1992 in Washington:

> The United Nations has never claimed that it alone can carry out peace-keeping operations . . . [but] the United Nations is by far the most experienced peace-keeper. It is more likely, perhaps, to be seen as having the impartiality which is an essential condition for successful peace-keeping, and it has worked out structures for establishing, financing and managing such operations. It was thus inevitable that the international community should turn to the United Nations when the end of the Cold War increased the demand for peace-keeping. But the demand has not become such that I believe that the United Nations must share the work with others. A multipolar world should be led by a multiplicity of institutions. . . . It is therefore logical that an effort should be made to "decentralize" the responsibilities for peace-

keeping and peace-making that today are continuously being entrusted to the United Nations. The regional organizations are the obvious candidates for larger roles. . . . The problem at present is that the regional organizations have almost no experience and lack the necessary structures and procedures, and most of them are in an even worse financial condition than the United Nations. I am, however, convinced that the regional organizations must be helped to carry a larger share of the burden in peace-making as well as in peace-keeping. . . . Their involvement will in turn serve to promote the democratization of international relations.[55]

The secretary-general's expressions are obviously indicative of greater interest in the use of regional machinery, and also of awareness of the great difficulties inherent in any such undertakings. At this time, the future of regional arrangements and agencies in the area of peace and security is, to say the least, uncertain. Clearly, they are not an immediate panacea for the misgivings over the current state of affairs in the Security Council. Further involvement of regional agencies in this area is a long-time proposition. Key to this is the Security Council's willingness to share responsibility, on the one hand, and the capacity and willingness of the regional organizations to assume these responsibilities.

The confluence of a regional IGO with the UN in peacekeeping and peacemaking can be seen in the ECOWAS case study in Chapter 3, and in the situation in Bosnia-Herzegovina, discussed above. In the latter case, the reluctant authorization of the NATO Council, prodded by the U.S., to authorize the UN Secretary-General to employ NATO air power not only to protect UN peacekeeping forces, but also to frustrate the Bosnian Serbian attempt to capture Sarajevo, represents a milestone in inter-IGO cooperation.

CONCLUSIONS

The post-Cold War period has witnessed a greater interest in linking regional conflicts with the UN. However, it also has linked humanitarian concerns with security concerns (see Figure 5.2). Thus, the interaction with national domestic and foreign policy goals with IGOs is significantly increasing. Increasingly, as the various conflicts persist and new ones appear, IGOs are involved as possibly a "last resort" to the failure of the state itself. This appears to be the case, for example, in Afghanistan, Somalia, and possibly Cambodia.

Partly for these reasons, there is a heightened interest on the part of states of all sizes and political characteristics in joining IGOs that can assist them in achieving their economic and security goals. The creation of the North Atlantic Cooperation Council (NACC) as a means to embrace the states of the former Soviet Union and Soviet bloc in some systematic relationship with the stable states of the Alliance is a case in point, as is the desire of

Figure 5.2
Peacekeeping Forces and Observer Missions, 1948–1992

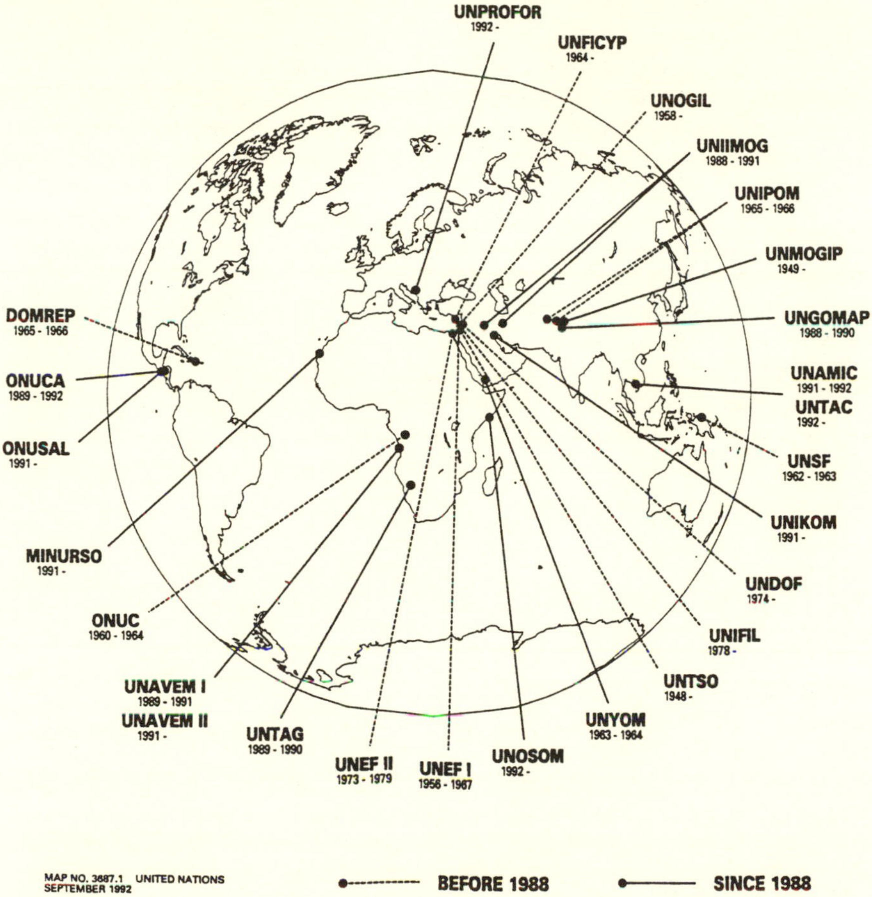

Source: United Nations, *Report of the Secretary-General on the Work of the Organization* (GA Doc. A/47/1, September 11, 1992).

many of these states to join the EC. Finally, as discussed in Chapter 7, the proliferation of regional free-trade organizations is testimony to the perception that economic interdependence is a global and regional fact of international life.

In contrast, the circumstances that motivate a state to withdraw from an IGO appear more and more circumscribed, for the reasons discussed above. Nonetheless, that option always remains a possibility and, therefore, should not be ignored.

NOTES

1. UNESCO Constitution, Article 1—Purposes and Functions.

> UNESCO's special function is to remind the rest of the U.S. system as well as its Member-States that most major problems (of population, environment, development itself) have a more than economic dimension; that they involve more than one part of human experience, that value-implications, the social and individual costs of programmes, are to be put in balance. (Richard Hoggart, *An Idea and Its Servants: Unesco from Within* [New York: Oxford University Press, 1978], p. 164.)

2. UNESCO Constitution, Preamble. In today's perspective, the word *men*, which was doubtless used in a generic sense, would probably have not been used; instead, the term *people* would likely have been chosen as more gender-neutral.

3. T. V. Sathyamurthy, *The Politics of International Cooperation: Contrasting Conceptions of UNESCO* (Geneva: Librairie Droz, 1964), pp. 207–8.

4. Ibid, p. 16. To be more precise, the bloc that composed the Third World and was known as the Group of 77 itself grew out of the Non-Aligned Movement (NAM) of the Cold War circumstances of the 1950s. It gained parliamentary strength in the UN system when decolonization virtually tripled the membership. As Lawrence Finkelstein put it, the Group of 77 was "the instrument for concerting objectives, policies, and tactics among the [developing states] with respect to the rules and structure of international economic relations." Lawrence Finkelstein, ed., *The United States and International Organization: The Changing Setting* (Boston: MIT Press, 1969), p. 21.

5. Houshang Ameri, *Politics and Process in the Specialized Agencies of the United Nations* (Aldershot, UK: Gower Publishing Co., 1982), p. 126. For a post-Cold War view, see Pierre Hassner, "Beyond Nationalism and Internationalism," *Survival,* Vol. 35, No. 2 (summer 1993), pp. 49–65.

6. See Walter H. C. Laves and Charles A. Thomson, *UNESCO: Purpose Progress Prospects* (Bloomington: Indiana University Press, 1957).

7. In 1974 the PLO and the OAU were granted Observer status and two anti-Israeli resolutions were passed; one accused Israel of altering archeological treasures, and the other asked the director-general (who happened to be the first black African to hold the post) to withhold assistance to Israel. Many of the anti-Israeli sentiments were fueled by the 1975 UN General Assembly Resolution which equated Zionism with racism. The resolution was repealed by an overwhelming vote of the General Assembly on December 16, 1992.

8. Nihal Singh, *The Rise and Fall of UNESCO* (Calcutta: Allied Publishers, 1987), p. 69.

9. UNESCO, *New Communication Order 9: Historical Background of the Mass Media Declaration* (Paris: UNESCO, n.d.), pp. 127–30. The declaration's full title was "Declaration on Fundamental Principles Concerning the Contribution of the Mass Media to Strengthening Peace and International Understanding, to the Promotion of Human Rights and to Countering Racialism, Apartheid and Incitement to War."

10. For example, a conference of Western news organizations held in Talloires, France, criticized the New-World Information and Communication Order (NWICO) as giving UNESCO "the power to regulate the flow of news and in-

formation around the world [by] transform[ing] the press into an instrument of government." The conference was organized by a pro-Western lobby, the World Press Freedom Committee (WPFC), whose purpose was "monitoring and opposing the threats they perceived as emanating from UNESCO and the proponents of the NWICO." Edward S. Herman, "U.S. Mass Media Coverage of the U.S. Withdrawal from Unesco," in *Hope and Folly: The United States and UNESCO,* ed. William Preston, Jr., Edward S. Herman and Herbert I. Schiller (Minneapolis: University of Minnesota Press, 1989), pp. 208–10. See also Robert S. Jordan, "Boycott Diplomacy: The U.S., the U.N., and UNESCO," *Public Administration Review* 44, no. 4 (July-August 1984), pp. 283–291.

11. The subject for UNESCO was not, by any means, new. As examples: Resolution 4.301, which the General Conference adopted in 1970, considered "that information should play an important part in furthering international understanding and co-operation in the interests of peace and human welfare . . . [and] affirmed the inadmissibility of using information media for propaganda on behalf of war, racialism and hatred among nations"; in 1972, the General Conference adopted resolution 4.113, reaffirming resolution 4.301 and called on the director-general "to prepare and submit . . . a draft declaration concerning the fundamental principles governing the use of the mass information media with a view to strengthening peace and international understanding and combating war propaganda, racialism and apartheid." Also in 1972, a "Declaration of Guiding Principles on the Use of Satellite Broadcasting" was adopted.

12. "U.S./UNESCO Policy Review," U.S. Department of State, February 27, 1984, p. 1.

13. One consequence of the American withdrawal was the curtailing of access by many International Scientific and Professional Associations (ISPAs) to American scientific activities through UNESCO. ISPAs are forums for organizing and maintaining cross-national contact among their respective national memberships. It was because of this networking that many ISPAs disapproved of the U.S. withdrawal, although much bilateral interaction continues.

14. These paragraphs are drawn from a 1992 report contained in the *Interdependent,* Vol. 18, no. 2 (summer 1992), published by the United Nations Association of the United States.

15. See "U.S. Reviewing Return to UNESCO," the *Interdependent,* Vol. 19, No. 2, (Summer 1993). As the article reported: "While the administration's interagency review found that UNESCO had met all U.S. conditions and that reentry was in the national interest, it called for delaying the U.S. return until the fall of 1995. At that time the payment of U.S. arrearages to the United Nations and other international organizations will be completed, freeing up funds already in the International Organization account to pay UNESCO dues." (Ibid., p. 4). A 1993 report by a study panel of the UNA-U.S.A., *Schooling for Democracy: Reinventing UNESCO for the Post-Cold War World,* helped to change official attitudes. See also "Richard S. Williamson and Jeffrey Laureuti, "Rebuild Defences of Peace by Rejoining UNESCO," *The Christian Science Monitor,* July 5, 1993, p. 18.

16. This illustrative case draws with permission on the unpublished master's thesis, by Paul Sanchez-Navarro, *Multinationalism vis-a-vis the National Interest: An Assessment of the Withdrawal from UNESCO of the United States and Great Britain,* University of New Orleans, 1990. It can be compared with the discussion of the U.S. withdrawal and return to the ILO in chapter 4.

17. Donald Puchala and Raymond Hopkins, "Toward Innovation in the Global Food Regime," *International Organization,* Vol. 32 (Summer 1978), p. 624. These paragraphs are drawn from David N. Balaam and Michael J. Carey, *Food Politics: The Regional Conflict* (Montclair, NJ: Allanheld, Osmun, 1981), pp. 190–200.

18. Balaam and Carey, *Food Politics*, p. 202. Also Henry Nau, "The Diplomacy of World Food: Goals, Capabilities, Issues and Arenas," *International Organization,* 32 (Summer 1978), p. 780.

19. These paragraphs are drawn from Thomas G. Weiss and Robert S. Jordan, *The World Food Conference and Global Problem Solving* (New York: Praeger, 1976), pp. 10–12.

20. Quoted in Ibid., p. 11.

21. Quoted in Balaam and Carey, *Food Politics,* p. 199. The entire reference to Director-General Boerma is from p. 199. The remainder of this discussion is from Weiss and Jordan, op. cit., p. 12.

22. These paragraphs are drawn from Weiss and Jordan, *The World Food Conference,* pp. 13–14. Since then, however, FAO has taken several initiatives that have won international recognition. Among them are the Global Information and Early Warning System (GIEWS) that drew attention to Africa's food crisis and the World Food Security compact. See Peta Fitzpatrick, "Candidates Vie for Top FAO Post," the *Interdependent,* Vol.19, No. 2 (Summer 1993), p. 5. The fact that the former Soviet Union was not a member of FAO was an important reason for going to the United Nations.

23. These paragraphs are drawn from Balaam and Carey, *Food Politics,* pp. 203–4.

24. See Johan Kaufmann, *United Nations Decision Making* (Rockville, MD: Sijthoff and Noordhoff, 1980), esp. ch. 6.

25. Helen Wallace, "The Establishment of the Regional Development Fund: Common Policy or Pork Barrel" in *Policy-Making in the European Community* ed. Helen Wallace, William Wallace and Carole Webb (New York: Wiley, 1977), pp. 137–63.

26. Quoted in "Report on the Regional Problems in the Enlarged Community," Supplement 8/73, *Bulletin of the European Communities* (Brussels).

27. *Die Zeit,* December 14, 1973.

28. *Agence Europe Bulletin,* January 25, 1974; January 26, 1974; November 1, 1974; December 12, 1974. It is interesting that France managed to obtain at least a small portion of the funds disbursement (15 percent), while even West Germany received 6.4 percent.

29. *Agence Europe Bulletin,* December 4, 1980.

30. *Economist,* October 24, 1981, p. 38.

31. *Agence Europe Bulletin,* July 16, 1981.

32. G. Bonvincini, "Der Dualismus zwischen EPZ and Gemeinschaft," in *Der Europaische Politische Zusammenarbeit,* ed. Reinhardt Rummel and Wolfgang Wessesls (Bonn: Europa Union Verlag, 1978), pp. 89–90.

33. For greater detail, see Wolfgang Wessels, "New Forms of Foreign Policy in Western Europe," in *Western Europe's Global Reach,* ed. Werner J. Feld (New York: Pergamon Press, 1980), pp. 12–29; and *Agence Europe Bulletin,* October 16, 1981.

34. For details, see Beate Kohler, "Die Europaisch-Amerikanischen Beziehunger-Die EPZ als Vehikel der Emanzipation?" in Rummel and Wessels, *Zusammenarbeit,* pp. 167–88.

35. For details, see Goetz von Groll, "The Helsinki Consultation," *Aussenpolitik*

24 (1973): 123–29; and "The Geneva Final Act of the CSCE," *Aussenpolitik* 26 (1975): 247–69.

36. EC Commission, *Ninth General Report* (Brussels: EC, 1975), pp. 260–61.

37. *Agence Europe Bulletin,* October 27, 1977; November 7/8, 1977.

38. *Agence Europe Bulletin,* April 13/14, 1982.

39. James M. McCormick and Young W. Kihl, "Intergovernmental Organizations and Foreign Policy Behavior: Some Empirical Findings," *American Political Science Review* 73 (June 1979): 494–504.

40. Article 51 of the UN Charter is cited by the North Atlantic Treaty Organization (NATO) and was cited as well by the now-defunct Warsaw Treaty Organization, but this was almost entirely pro forma. In the post-Cold War period, with its emphasis on regional conflicts, this article may come to have more direct relevance.

41. Charles W. Kegley and Eugene R. Wittkopf, *American Foreign Policy* (New York: St. Martin's Press, 1979), p. 34.

42. This section is extracted and edited, with permission, from Benjamin Rivlin, "Regional Arrangements and the UN System for Collective Security and Conflict Resolution: A New Road Ahead?" *International Relations* (London) 11, no. 2 (August 1992): 95–110. The citations that follow are from the article. According to Francis O. Wilcox, the question of "the relative merits of regionalism and globalism in international organization . . . generated as much heat as any other issue at San Francisco in 1945 with the possible exception of the veto." Francis O. Wilcox, "Regionalism and the United Nations," *International Organization* 19 (Summer 1965): 789.

43. Strictly construed, "collective security is exclusively a means of deterring aggression and for reversing its consequences when deterrence fails." Tom J. Farer, "The Role of Regional Collective Security Arrangements," in *Collective Security in a Changing World,* Occasional Paper no. 10 (Brown University, Thomas J. Watson, Jr., Institute for International Studies, Providence, RI, 1992), p. 41.

44. Inis L. Claude, Jr., "Implications and Questions for the Future," *International Organization* 19 (Summer 1965): 843.

45. In the case of the Dominican Republic, the United States acquiesced to pressure from some Latin American states and accepted a Security Council resolution (SC Res. 203, May 14, 1965) that called for a strict cease-fire and invited the Secretary-General to report to the Council on the situation.

46. Eduard A. Shevardnadze, "Working Together," Occasional Paper no. 7 (Brown University, Thomas J. Watson, Jr., Institute for International Studies, Providence, RI, 1991), p. 21.

47. Karl Deutsch wrote: "For the political scientist the definition of a region is considerably more difficult than the definition of a rose was to Gertrude Stein. We cannot simply say, 'A region is a region is a region.' " Karl W. Deutsch, *Nationalism and its Alternatives* (New York: Knopf, 1969), p. 93.

48. Ibid., p. 102.

49. Inis L. Claude, Jr., *Swords into Plowshares* 4th ed. (New York: Random House, 1971), p. 105.

50. See chapter 3 of this text for a complete discussion of the role of ECOWAS in the Liberian civil war.

51. Alvaro de Soto, "Case Study: The Peace Process in Central America," (Paper presented at the Singapore Symposium, "The Changing Role of the United Nations

in Conflict Resolution and Peace-Keeping," sponsored jointly by the Institute of Policy Studies of Singapore and the UN Department of Public Information, with the support of the governments of Singapore and Japan, Singapore, March 13–15 1991).

52. Oscar Schachter, "Authorized Uses of Force by the United Nations and Regional Organizations," in *Law and Force in the New International Order,* ed. Lori Fisler Damrosch and David J. Scheffer (Boulder, CO: Westview Press, 1991), pp. 86–87.

53. Michael J. Costello, "The Contribution of Regional Arrangements in Promoting Peace and Security" (Paper presented at the Singapore Symposium, "Changing Role"), p. 52.

54. See transcripts of Secretary-General Boutros Boutros-Ghali's press conferences of March 19, 1992, SG/SM/4718; and April 10, 1992, SG/SM/4727/Rev.1. See also Boutros Boutros-Ghali, "Empowering the United Nations," *Foreign Affairs,* Vol. 72, No. 5 (Winter 1992/93), pp. 89–102.

55. "From Peace-Keeping to Peace-Making," Ninth Annual David M. Abshire Lecture (Washington, DC: Center for Strategic and International Studies, May 13, 1992). See also Adam Roberts, "The United Nations and International Security," *Survival,* Vol. 35, No. 1 (Summer 1993), PP. 3–30.

6 ACCESS TO IGO DECISION MAKING: THE ROLE OF INTERNATIONAL NONGOVERNMENTAL ORGANIZATIONS (INGOs) AND OTHER LINKS TO IGOs

In this chapter we will examine the methods of direct access to IGO decision making that are available to individuals and groups that do not represent governments and are not composed of governments. The entire question of access to decision making has seen a radical transformation during the last few years. This is as much due to the end of the Cold War as to other factors presently at play in the international system. For example, the notion of collective security now embraces not only political/economic responsibilities (in addition to the Cold War notion of political/security "high politics"), but also human rights and environmental and humanitarian responsibilities.

In fact, the use of multilateral means to deal with conflicts of all kinds is now recognized as legitimate for collective security and, in the case of individual state interests, as falling within the range of a country's "national security" concerns.

Furthermore, international nongovernmental organizations (INGOs) are now heavily involved in activities that give them unparalleled access to international organizations; in fact, in some instances, the work of IGOs could not go forward without the participation of INGOs. This is indeed a sharp departure from the recent past.

ACHIEVEMENT OF INGO GOALS

The decision as to whether to establish an INGO must take into consideration a careful calculation of benefits and costs regarding the potential for attaining the goals that are viewed as essential in advancing the organization's particular interests. When it comes to attaining goals that embrace human rights or environmental or humanitarian concerns, these calculations can be very difficult to assess. For example, the dramatic increase in refugee populations (as a consequence of both manmade and natural disasters) renders the prospect of achieving any kind of clear resolution of these issues problematical at best.

Nonetheless, a primary goal of all INGOs is access to IGO decision making, either through influencing the member governments' policies in regard to IGO issues or through influencing the IGO itself. Even though it might appear that this latter attainment potential is small because INGOs lack the attributes of sovereignty and are inherently quite different from nation-states, the nature of the issue areas now confronting the international system has resulted in greater access. No better example can be seen than the efforts of inspection teams to monitor Iraq's compliance with Security Council resolutions, wherein specialists composing these teams are drawn from INGOs as well as from governments and the IAEA. Another, more direct example is the deep involvement of the ICRC, the Cooperative for American Relief Everywhere (CARE), and other humanitarian INGOs working alongside both IGOs and individual states to ameliorate the consequences of widespread starvation brought on by drought and civil conflict in Somalia, the Sudan, and southern Africa.

The notion of benefits vis-à-vis interdependence costs (first discussed in Chapter 2) is useful because INGOs pursue various interests, just as states do. If the attainment potential of a national nongovernmental organization (NGO) can be enhanced through contacts and action on the international level, including consultative status with selected IGO bodies, then the decision about organizing above the national level is likely to be positive.

The judgment as to whether to participate in IGO activities can be affected by the perceived usefulness of different strategies to achieve the NGO's international, national, or even subnational goals. These strategies can be broken down into three groups:

1. To call for and insist on the formulation of appropriate policies by national governments and/or IGOs or, if possible, to institute such policies through INGOs themselves, with the explicit or tacit authorization (or at least with the assurance) of noninterference by governments. When "national security" overlaps with "collective security" in human rights, environmental, or humanitarian endeavors, the degree of host country noninterference becomes a crucial measure of the capability of INGOs to carry out their mandates. A host government, warring factions or even self-appointed vigilante groups (in the case of ethnic civil conflict) may develop obstructionist tactics when transnational policies are introduced without their advance knowledge, or when these are imposed on them.
2. To promote, modify, or oppose existing policies and policy goals of global and regional IGOs in accordance with INGO objectives. There has been real confusion about this in regard to post-Cold War peacekeeping. When governments

intervening under a UN mandate resort to peacemaking, this is a different dimension concerning the use of force.

3. To support, modify, or oppose existing policies and policy goals of national governments in accordance with INGO objectives. The U.S. attitude toward the abortion (or population control) policies of other countries under the Reagan and Bush administrations ran contrary to the goals of such INGOs as the International Planned Parenthood Federation. The illustrative case on the UN Conference on Environment and Development (UNCED) which follows also illustrates that governmental policies and the goals of INGOs do not always converge.

The aims included in items 2 and 3 are likely to be functions of the specific objectives encompassed by the first category, but this is not necessarily the case when it comes to general, often ideological or religious-centered, goals. It is also quite conceivable that a particular INGO will support specific IGO goals but oppose national goals of a particular government, especially where human rights and environmental or humanitarian concerns are involved. Therefore, IGOs and national governments may perceive an individual INGO as alternately either friendly or hostile depending on rapidly shifting circumstances.[1]

INGO INFLUENCE ON DECISION MAKING

The diverse nature of INGOs and the huge differences in their organizational attributes make it difficult to assess their overall influence on national governments, IGOs, and such other nongovernmental actors as religious, ethnic, or even paramilitary groups.[2] Clearly, many INGOs do not possess great financial resources and, therefore, their impact on the policy-making of national governments and IGOs is likely to be minimal. Nevertheless, governments at times perceive INGO activities as an infringement of national sovereignty, especially, for example, when human rights or humanitarian and environmental issues are involved.

In evaluating the effect of INGO activities on governmental policy-making, it is perhaps useful to distinguish among them. The first distinction refers to *the nature of the group's action.* One category of INGOs bases its capabilities on technical expertise, as for example, the International Organization for Standardization, the International Planned Parenthood Federation, Save the Children, the Sierra Club, and Amnesty International. Other categories exert influence by leading and representing large segments of the public through the creation of various societies. In the latter category are trade union federations and religious organizations, which pursue objectives based on widespread interests that are usually self-selected, or the Red Cross and Red Crescent Societies.

Another useful distinction derives from *the fields in which they are active.*

One group operates in areas of major concern to national governments, such as industry (including arms transfers and environmental degradation), commerce, finance, food aid, and technology, while a second category is concerned with essentially noneconomic matters, such as sports, religious affairs, cultural activities, and so forth. Since the first group has more influence on the policies of individual states, its impact on national government decision makers is likely to be greater than that of the second group, and the reactions of the governments are likely to be more severe. It is also significant that the number of INGOs that belong to the first group, especially those concerned with development or economic-related matters, has been growing generally more rapidly than the number in the second group.

A third distinction refers to the *states in which they carry out their transnational activities*. As a general rule, economically developed, pluralistic states have many more INGOs operating in their midst than do developing countries. This is one reason why many states view INGOs with some suspicion: they are seen as pro-Western. However, Western INGOs have played a more central—even crucial—role in ameliorating human suffering in post-Cold War ethnic warfare.

We may conclude, generally at least, that the effects of INGOs on policymaking are more pronounced in the industrially advanced states with pluralistic political systems, while interest groups concerned with economic, social (including human rights), and humanitarian affairs are likely to have a greater impact than those in other fields. It is fair to assume that the more the demands and objectives of INGOs support the high-priority goals of governmental actors and national decision-making elites, the greater are the prospects of successfully influencing the international or transnational policymaking process. This is discussed in the illustrative case on UNCED which follows. This also is illustrated by the shifting fortunes of those INGOs concerned with human rights according to the priorities of successive U.S. presidents, the leaders of the other Western advanced industrial states, and states embroiled in civil or ethnic strife.

There is another aspect of transnational INGO activity that deserves to be mentioned, particularly as it has minimal political implications for national governments. This aspect relates to INGO activity that may provide much-needed assistance outside the normal realm of governmental concern without suggesting any kind of patronage. In such cases, national policymakers may consider it useful to adopt a policy of noninterference and to let INGOs act as their informal agents in achieving worthwhile, though low-priority, goals. This has occurred on many occasions when visible activity at the governmental level might have been impossible in the context of existing relations. A hospital built on the edge of a desert in Africa through the efforts of an INGO can bring comfort and health to the surrounding villages without the government of the recipient state having to sacrifice

Table 6.1
General Support Goals of INGOs

	Percent Response
To improve communication between members in the special field of the organization so that they can do a better job.	87%
To promote general cooperation and friendship between the members.	79
To let members know each other so that they have contacts in other countries for travel, correspondence, and so forth.	56
To work for social and economic development in the world.	51
To improve general cooperation and friendship between all human beings.	48
To work for peace between all nations and peoples in the world.	45

Source: Kjell Skjelsbaek, "A Survey of International Non-governmental Organizations," *International Associations* (May 1974): 267–70.

any of its declared international positions. When a central, effective government has been weakened or is virtually nonexistent, INGOs increasingly step in and assume some of the economic, social, and humanitarian functions for which governments are normally responsible. The examples of Cambodia, Angola, Nicaragua, Somalia, Afghanistan, and Bosnia come to mind. For this reason alone, INGOs have been able to operate and to achieve some measure of success in such humanitarian activities as providing child care, medical aid, food, and educational benefits in states that would have been reluctant to be exposed to any appearance of a limitation on their freedom of action in the international community, even to obtain these much-needed benefits.

The general support goals pursued by INGOs for the achievement of their particular objectives can be gleaned from responses to a detailed questionnaire sent to 2,196 organizations in 1974 by the International Peace Research Institute in Oslo. More than 800 INGOs returned completed questionnaires. Based on the responses, a rank ordering of six general support goals according to their relative frequency is presented in Table 6.1. These goals reflect the emphasis placed by INGOs on transactional flows and the potential of interdependence.

The creation of INGOs by itself is, of course, not sufficient to exert the necessary influence for successful goal attainment. This requires organizational effectiveness and adequate resources of individual INGOs to spread their message. In this respect, we need to examine two ways in which nongovernmental groups gain systemic direct access to IGO decision making.

SYSTEMIC DIRECT ACCESS

Access of INGOs to the UN System

For the United States the constitutional right of a citizen to petition the government for redress of a grievance or to influence governmental action is a domestic expression of the INGO tradition. It is thus no great leap conceptually to embrace the notion that groups of citizens can petition their governments concerning their governments' participation in an IGO and, by extension, petition the IGO itself. In fact, this was clearly set forth in Article 71 of the UN Charter, which provided:

> The Economic and Social Council may make suitable arrangements for consultation with nongovernmental organizations which are concerned with matters within its competence. Such arrangements may be made with international organizations and, where appropriate, with national organizations after consultation with the member of the United Nations concerned.

These words, according to one author, are humble and couched in "rather condescending terminology," and thus envisaged an insignificant, or at best a peripheral, role for INGOs in relation to the overall activities of the United Nations.[3] More than eight hundred INGOs have consultative status, which is divided into three categories.

Category I: Organizations that are concerned with most of the activities of the Council and can demonstrate to the satisfaction of the Council that they have marked and sustained contributions to make to the achievement of the objectives of the United Nations (with respect to international, economic, social, cultural, educational, health, scientific, technological and related matters, and to questions of human rights), and are closely involved with the economic and social life of the peoples of the areas they represent and whose membership, which should be considerable, is broadly representative of major segments of population in a large number of countries.

Category II: Organizations that have a special competence in, and are concerned specifically with, only a few of the fields of activity covered by the Council, and that are known internationally within the fields for which they have, or seek, consultative status.

Roster: Other organizations that do not have general or special consultative status but which the Council or the secretary-general of the United Nations, in consultation with the Council or its Committee on Non-Governmental Organizations (CONGO) considers can make occasional and useful contributions to the work of the Council, or its subsidiary bodies, or other UN bodies, within their competence.[4]

A grant of consultative status entitles the organization to propose agenda items for consideration by the Council or its subsidiary bodies (Category I), attend meetings (Categories I and II and Roster), submit written statements (Categories I and II and Roster), and be granted hearings (Categories I and II).[5]

These formal provisions have not, however, resulted in an expansion of the influence of INGOs in the work of ECOSOC. This is because ECOSOC itself has not played the role in the UN system that was envisaged for it. The rapid expansion of UN membership resulted in a greater interest in using the General Assembly—where all member states are equal in voting rights—rather than ECOSOC to deal with economic and social matters.

A further discouraging feature with respect to INGO influence has been the failure of the restructuring effort of the UN system to restore ECOSOC to a position of genuine influence. The fault lies with the developing states that have preferred to use the General Assembly as their primary forum, thus bypassing ECOSOC.[6] The developing states have preferred the General Assembly's Second (economic and financial) and Third (social, humanitarian, and cultural) Committees over ECOSOC. This development began in the 1960s and accelerated in the 1970s. As one observer summarized it:

ECOSOC was among the first of the Third World's targets. With the arrival of close to two score members from Africa the Council came under heavy attack. It was called completely unrepresentative of the total United Nations membership and a tool of the rich. One African delegate proclaimed in public session that his chief purpose in serving on the Economic and Social Council was to destroy it. In 1964–65, the effectiveness of the Council was severely impaired. A majority of the LDCs reinterpreted Chapters IX and X [of the Charter] as vesting all responsibilities for economic and social matters in the General Assembly. They denied that the Council had any real function or power, particularly to coordinate programs and activities.[7]

In 1979, at the 34th Session of the General Assembly, an attempt was made to restore some vitality to ECOSOC. It was proposed that ECOSOC's membership should be expanded by amending the Charter, thus making it representative of the total membership. No action was taken on this recommendation. Consequently, influencing either ad hoc conferences (e.g., the Stockholm Conference on the Human Environment and others that were held in the 1970s) or continuing conferences (e.g., the General Assembly) became strong goals for both national and international NGOs. In fact, the level of interest of INGOs regarding their participation in IGO conference activities was generally and dramatically enhanced after the 1972 Stockholm Conference, in which participation went beyond those INGOs in the traditional consultative status to include a broader spectrum of NGO activity. Grass-roots organizations concerned with all aspects of environmental issues gained valuable experience operating as public interest groups at that conference.[8] This activity was expanded further at the Rio Conference (UNCED) in 1992, which can be gleaned from the illustrative case on that topic later in this chapter.

Some INGOs view themselves as single-issue–oriented. They concentrate on a particular issue over many years and have drawn to them persons with a particular commitment to that issue. One of the reasons for this orientation is the efficiency achieved by an INGO that concentrates on a single issue rather than risking dissipating its scarce volunteer and other resources on a wider range of issues. It is not uncommon around the United Nations to encounter INGO representatives who are trying to make the point that their particular issue is pivotal to all others, but this may not necessarily be so. Most issues that are taken up through conferences are interrelated with other issues to the extent that mutually reinforcing coalitions of INGOs often prove more effective. Recognizing this, an International Coalition for Development Action (ICDA) was created in the late 1970s to enhance the effectiveness of INGOs in ad hoc conferences.

In any event, the relations of the United Nations and its specialized agencies with INGOs—which are based usually on specific provisions of their constituent instruments, rules of procedures, and resolutions—are diverse, even though the general principles and objectives of consultative relationships are basically similar. On the basis of parallel legal provisions, the various specialized agencies have established consultative relations with those different sets of INGOs that are particularly relevant to their work.

In general, the main purposes for the consultative and cooperative arrangements within the UN system are to: (1) secure advice and technical cooperation from competent INGOs, (2) enable organizations that represent important elements of public opinion in many states to express their views, and (3) advance the objectives of the UN system through promotional activities and projects of INGOs. In broad terms, to acquire consultative status, INGOs should be: (1) particularly interested in matters within the competence of the UN body or agency concerned, (2) able and willing to make an effective contribution to the achievement of its objectives, and (3) internationally recognized and broadly representative of interested groups in a substantial number of states. However, the specific requirements for classifying INGOs and the corresponding privileges and obligations are far from uniform.

Like ECOSOC, several specialized agencies—particularly the ILO, FAO, and UNESCO—classify INGOs into three consultative categories; however, the other agencies and activities maintain an undifferentiated list of INGOs in consultative status. Among the relevant economic and social bodies under the General Assembly, only the Advisory Committee of the

UNHCR applies the ECOSOC classification in its relations with INGOs; UNCTAD, UNIDO, UNEP, UNICEF, and UNDP maintain, so far, single lists of INGOs. In all cases, a distinction is made between the INGOs on the official list and those not having consultative status; nonetheless, each organization maintains informal working relations.

The classification of INGOs in the UN family takes two forms. The first form, which is based on the scope of INGO activities relative to the competence of a UN body or agency, has been adopted by ECOSOC, UNHCR, ILO, and FAO. It distinguishes INGOs possessing a wide-ranging interest from those with a specialized interest, and both types from those with a more limited or occasional interest in the work of a UN body or agency. The second form, which is used by UNESCO, takes into account the capacity for, and record of, effective contribution to the achievement of the agency's objectives. In accordance with the extent and quality of its contribution, an INGO with a mutual information status (category C) may be promoted after two years to the information and consultative status (category B), and eventually to the consultative and associate status (category A), with each promotion involving greater privileges and obligations.

The third category of INGOs, which is included on a special list prepared by the Secretariat, normally maintains relations with a UN agency that are limited to the exchange of relevant information and documentation, attendance at certain meetings, and, occasionally upon request, the preparation of specific studies or papers and the circulation of short statements within a subsidiary body. There is little difference among agencies in their relations with INGOs in the liaison category. However, in the first two categories (representing general and specialized consultative status), the diversity of agency practices is considerable. For the second category of INGOs, ECOSOC allows modest privileges in addition to those of the liaison category, including oral statements on a major subject not covered by a subsidiary body. For the first category, ECOSOC allows, in addition, the privilege to suggest, through ECOSOC's INGO Committee, items for its provisional agenda and the right to make an expository statement. In contrast, UNESCO's first two categories may give advice and assistance regarding its studies and may contribute by their activities to the execution of its programs, but, significantly, they also may receive from UNESCO financial aid in the form of either subventions or contracts for conducting their activities. In addition, the INGOs in the first category are closely associated with the various stages of planning and execution of relevant UNESCO activities and assist in the efforts to promote international coordination among related INGOs.

The striking features of other agencies' relations with INGOs pertain to the cooperative arrangements that go beyond the consultative system. Because of its tripartite nature, ILO provides employees and labor representatives with ample opportunity for official participation in decision making.

In cooperation with major INGOs having large-scale technical assistance programs, it carries out development projects to promote the cooperative movement, the rights of women and young workers, occupational safety, and vocational training. FAO's Freedom from Hunger Campaign/Action for Development (FFH/AD), which operates through a network of INGOs and national committees, serves to stimulate a critical awareness of development issues and to promote the involvement of people in their own development. Based on local and national initiatives, the FFH/AD represents dynamic nongovernmental programs of education and action with the technical support of the FAO Secretariat.

A major task of fund-raising is undertaken by voluntary agencies associated with the programs of UNICEF and the UNHCR. Those INGOs perform a major role in developing public understanding of emergency needs and in helping to carry out field projects. The promotion of basic health services provided by church and other nongovernmental groups complements significantly the efforts of WHO and member governments.

According to a survey, the external technical assistance provided by INGOs to low-income states in 1973 was estimated to be over $1 billion. As a number of those INGOs are now moving toward longer-term technical assistance in addition to their huge grants of relief assistance, the UNDP has set up procedures for mutual consultation and the effective coordination of activities at the field level. The purpose is to benefit from the full potential of INGO direct contribution to development in harmony with the priorities and projects of IGOs and national governments. In other words, direct access into the IGO system by INGOs in support of development is now encouraged by IGOs.

Access of INGOs to Other IGOs

While the United Nations and its various specialized and other agencies embrace the largest number of INGOs in consultative status, other non-UN IGOs, such as the Council of Europe and the OAS, also have adopted similar relationships with INGOs.

The EC has seen an increasing number of INGOs that are composed mostly of nongovernmental organizations in the member states. These so-called Eurogroups (there are approximately seven hundred)—the best known of which are the Committee of Professional Agricultural Organizations (COPA), the Union of Industries of the European Community (UNICE), and the European Trade Union Confederation (ETUC)—have easy access to the Commission and its extensive advisory committee system. Recently, the Eurogroups have become interested in presenting their views to members of the EP, although the power of the EP to promote their demands is still rather limited.

INGO Access to the IGO Political Dialogue

Direct access to UN activity that can aid INGOs in furthering sensitive political and security national interests has been attained only recently. Two issue areas that reveal just how this access has come about are human rights, an issue that is very sensitive in a national political sense, and disarmament, which impacts on perceptions of national security.

Human Rights as an Issue Area. Since the end of World War II, there has been a great proliferation in INGOs, as already noted. They have challenged, not only the power of governmental elites to control international events, but also the right of all governments to define exclusively international issues.

Indeed, one major explanation for the emergence of human rights as a major issue for IGOs during recent decades lies in the increasing number and influence of INGOs acting transnationally for the promotion and defense of those rights. Simultaneous with this has been the diffusion of literacy and education, with increasing numbers of people at the base of society becoming conscious of the fact that poverty (the denial of economic human rights) and repression (the denial of political human rights) are not immutable facts of nature. As people on all continents have begun to demand social justice, their voices have been amplified by INGOs in solidarity with their aspirations. The communications revolution—especially that involving the mass media—has meant that gross violations of human rights, even in a remote area, cannot for long be covered up or locally contained. Those who feel they are oppressed can internationalize their struggle through appeals to international forums or international public opinion. Thus, IGOs are frequently the arenas in which human rights issues come to be defined, while INGOs serve as the instrumentality through which demands for change are expressed.

It was the gas chambers of the Third Reich, along with a very intensive lobbying effort by INGOs, that enabled human rights to be inscribed into the Charter of the United Nations. As Theo van Boven, former Director of the UN Division of Human Rights, observed in his remarks at the opening of the Thirty-Sixth Session of the Commission on Human Rights (1980), the human rights provisions of the UN Charter, and the express mention of the Commission in Article 68 thereof, was "the result of the insistence of nongovernmental organizations and individuals at the San Francisco Conference. It is a matter of record that had it not been for the determined role played by these organizations and individuals, the place assigned to human rights in the Charter might have been less pronounced." With respect to promotion of the cause of human rights, the record of the last fifty years has been impressive. Human rights law is highly developed at the universal level and is evolving at the regional level. Many states have incorporated whole sections of the Universal Declaration into their national constitutions, and some have made the effort to bring national law into line with international standards. IGOs have been particularly instrumental in this process, although credit must also be given to INGOs that have often stimulated or encouraged the process, as with Amnesty International's role in the elaboration of the UN Declaration of the Protection of All Persons Against Torture and Other Cruel, Inhuman, and Degrading Treatment or Punishment, (1979); the role of the International Committee of the Red Cross in developing the 1977 Protocols to the Geneva Conventions; and the role of the antiapartheid movement in drafting the Convention on the Suppression and Punishment of the Crime of Apartheid, 1973. Nonetheless, even if international human rights law now exists, implementing a human rights regime is still a distant objective.

This is partly because of disagreement over whether political rights take precedence over economic and social rights. This was fiercely debated at the 1993 UN World Conference on Human Rights held in Vienna, with neither set of protagonists prevailing, but also with both sides compromising. Human rights were still defined as universal and individual, but at the same time it was acknowledged that there are differences in historical, cultural, and religious backgrounds among states. Unfortunately, however, the debate weakened the desire of the conference participants to establish a new post of UN Commissioner for Human Rights, similar to that of the UNHCR. Such a post would bring both focus and definition to the concept of human rights, and would become an agency for ferreting out and punishing gross violations.

By and large, the actors in the forefront of monitoring the status of human rights have been INGOs: international human rights INGOs like Amnesty International, the International Committee of the Red Cross, the International Commission of Jurists, the International Human Rights Law Group, and the Anti-Slavery Society; church organizations such as the Human Rights Office of the National Council of Churches in the United States and the Vicariate of Solidarity in Chile; professional associations such as the Clearinghouse on Science and Human Rights of the American Association for the Advancement of Science and the Committee to Review the Abuse of Psychiatry for Political Purposes of the World Psychiatric Association; numerous national civil liberties organizations, such as the Scottish Council Liberties; a myriad of support groups, such as the Argentine Human Rights Committee, and the Friends of the Filippino People; and, occasionally, ad hoc special peoples' tribunals, such as the Bertrand Russell Tribunals on U.S. war crimes in Vietnam, human rights violations in Latin America and West Germany, and the projected tribunal on genocide against indigenous peoples. The Secretary-General submitted a draft statute for a "war crimes" tribunal to the Security Council in 1993, in response to international outrage over the vicious warfare in the former Yugoslavia. Such a tribunal would raise for INGOs as well as IGOs, a host of thorny issues involving accountability under the Geneva Conventions, violations of the laws and customs of war, and genocide and crimes against humanity. It would also offer some humanitarian possibilities, such as, for example, punishment for crimes, including rape, against women and children.

Perhaps the most important functions performed by INGOs have been those involving information gathering, evaluation, and dissemination, for without information on the status of human rights observance and on the nature and context of human rights violations, there is little hope for the protection of human rights.

With respect to human rights enforcement, both INGOs and IGOs, as well as governments, have performed some additional and vital functions. They have, through statements and other actions, expressed solidarity with the oppressed; they have also, through a wide variety of different mechanisms, performed an advocacy function, actively taking up the case of the oppressed in the mass media, in international forums, and through bilateral diplomatic channels. For INGOs, this has frequently involved lobbying of either their own government or of others. For governmental authorities, this has involved attempts at conciliation and mediation and, sometimes, the application of economic or political sanctions. The various policy options open to INGOs concerned with the promotion and protection of human rights depend, of course, on the nature and source of threats that are perceived, and there exist very different perceptions concerning the causes of human rights violations. As mentioned earlier, in 1993 a UN World Conference on Human Rights was convened in Vienna to examine how to facilitate the implementation of standards. The scope of the Conference embraced the following objectives, which were largely achieved in spite of the aforementioned disagreement over the concept of "human rights" itself, and in particular whether the term expressed universal—or transcendent—principles, or rather whether they were culturally-derived and situational in character.

1. To review and assess progress in the field of human rights since the adoption of the Universal Declaration of Human Rights, identifying obstacles to progress and the ways in which they can be overcome;
2. To examine the relation between development and the enjoyment of all economic, social, and cultural rights, as well as civil and political rights, recognizing the importance of creating the conditions that will allow peoples everywhere to enjoy these rights, as set out in the international covenants on human rights;
3. To examine ways and means to improve the implementation of existing human rights standards and instruments;
4. To evaluate the effectiveness of the methods and mechanisms used by the United Nations in the field of human rights;
5. To formulate concrete recommendations for improving the effectiveness of UN activities and mechanisms in the field of human rights through programs aimed

at promoting, encouraging, and monitoring respect for human rights and fundamental freedoms; and

6. To make recommendations for ensuring the necessary financial and other resources for the UN activities that are designed to promote and protect human rights and fundamental freedoms.

In the realm of women's rights as such, the conference considered the appointment of a Special Rapporteur on Violence Against Women, called on the UN to strengthen the Convention on the Elimination of All Forms of Discrimination Against Women, and urged the UN to integrate women's rights in all of its activities.

In summary, there has been a flowering of INGOs dedicated to the promotion and protection of internationally recognized human rights, and these have succeeded in attracting co-interest groups (labor unions, professional associations, and churches) into the struggle. Amnesty International, which was organized in 1961, not only received the Nobel Peace Prize in 1977 but has become a virtual worldwide movement of individuals and groups dedicated to the abolition of torture, prolonged political detention without trial, and the death penalty. Thus, if there has been regional collaboration between dictatorial regimes to quell opposition (as in the Southern Cone or in Southern Africa), there has also been increasing regional cooperation between those groups that are dedicated to the protection of human rights. It seems hard to imagine that anything, short of nuclear disaster, can diminish the growing influence of INGOs in advocating and defending human rights, not only by influencing governments directly, but also by doing so indirectly by gaining access to the IGO political dialogue.

The primary organs are the UN General Assembly, and the fifty-three-member Commission on Human Rights report on Special Rapporteurs on summary or arbitrary executions, torture, and religious intolerance.They have reported on violations in such countries as Afghanistan, Cuba, El Salvador, Iran, Iraq, Burma, and Haiti. Additionally, there are working groups on enforced or involuntary disappearances and arbitrary detention.

Furthermore, there is an Economic and Social Rights Committee that reports to ECOSOC, and independent supervisory committees composed of expert members who monitor compliance of the six principal human rights treaties of the United Nations. These are:

—International Covenant on Civil and Political Rights: Human Rights Committee (eighteen members).

—International Covenant on Economic, Social and Cultural Rights: Committee on Economic, Social and Cultural Rights (eighteen members).

—International Convention on the Elimination of All Forms of Racial Discrimination (CERD; eighteen members).

—Convention against Torture and Other Cruel, Inhuman or Degrading Treatment or Punishment: Committee on Torture (CAT; ten members).

—Convention on the Rights of the Child (CRC; ten members).

—Convention on the Elimination of All Forms of Discrimination Against Women (CEDAW, twenty-three members).

Disarmament as an Issue Area. Even before the United Nations was organized, during the era of the League of Nations, INGOs were active in disarmament affairs.[9] INGOs had a large role in the disarmament conference during the 1930s in Geneva. In the 1950s, some INGOs in ECOSOC went beyond economic and human rights issues and tried to relate to the disarmament deliberations in the General Assembly and related organs. In the late 1960s, Quakers and others formed the Special INGO Committee on Disarmament at Geneva. This brought together INGOs in Western and Eastern Europe that were concerned with problems of war and peace, especially arms limitation in the Eighteen-Nation Disarmament Committee (ENDC) meeting in Geneva. In 1973, a sister INGO Committee on Disarmament was formed at UN headquarters in New York. Here, INGOs observed the work of the General Assembly's First Committee on disarmament issues and also other General Assembly bodies devoted to disarmament.

General Assembly resolutions on disarmament have occasionally referred to INGOs, but mostly for distribution of disarmament studies or information. Nonetheless these resolutions indirectly recognized a role for INGOs in disarmament. On the other hand, an ad hoc committee on the review of the role of the United Nations in the field of disarmament that was convened in 1976 could have been an occasion for forty-two member states to explore the role of INGOs in this area. Despite a sympathetic chairperson, Inga Thorsson of Sweden, the committee soon realized that the climate was not favorable for any real discussion of the role of INGOs, let alone any recommendation. One reason for this lack of action was that some developing and socialist states were critical of INGOs within ECOSOC for speaking out against human rights violations, and thus tended at the time to be against all INGOs.

Consequently, the first significant opportunity for INGOs within the UN system in the field of disarmament came at the Special Session on Disarmament of the General Assembly in 1978 (and during its preparations). The status that this event gave INGOs in the field of disarmament provided for a higher level of subsequent involvement. When the preparatory committee for the Special Session on Disarmament first met in 1977, INGOs were already actively working with some friendly governments to assure an INGO role in the preparatory work as well as in the Special Session itself. In May 1977, the second meeting of the preparatory committee formally welcomed INGOs to observe and participate in its work. A table was provided for the distribution of INGO statements, and the UN Secretariat issued a periodic index of such statements.

INGOs around the world prepared for the Special Session. Some worked educationally within their organizations. Some INGOs formed national coalitions to urge their foreign offices to prepare initiatives. A great number of national, regional, and even international seminars and conferences were held, some involving diplomats. The informal activities of INGOs during the five-week Special Session were intensive. Several thousand representatives of INGOs from all continents converged on UN headquarters. The INGO Committee on Disarmament (at UN headquarters) organized a Disarmament Information Center in a storefront opposite the United Nations. The committee also published thirty-three issues of *Disarmament Times,* an independent newspaper in an edition of five thousand copies. There were also major demonstrations, rallies, vigils, sit-ins, and forums.

As a result of the enhancement of the role of INGOs at the Special Session, various UN bodies welcomed INGOs as observers and, in some cases, their written statements were indexed (for example, by the Disarmament Commission). The then-new Committee on Disarmament (CD) at Geneva, like its several predecessors since 1962, opened its galleries to INGOs. Ad hoc committees of the General Assembly on disarmament continued to be open to INGOs. Moreover, the second review conference of the Nuclear Non-Proliferation Treaty in 1980, as with the first in 1975, was open to INGOs, as are subsequent review conferences.

When the preparatory committee for the second Special Session was formed in 1980 (and even before), INGOs began consulting to ascertain how they could again play a role: if possible, an increased one. At the first meeting of the committee, the chairman, Ambassador Alu Adeniji of Nigeria, declared: "The Committee might follow the practice of the first Special Session on disarmament, which had decided that such representatives [INGOs] should be present at meetings of the Committee and that they should provide the Secretariat with lists of communications received [on] research in the field of disarmament."[10] INGOs worked, worldwide, to help make the second Special Session on disarmament a success, despite the bleak political climate.

Directing our attention to another important aspect of arms control, in 1991 the Third Review Conference of the Parties to the Convention on the Prohibition of the Development, Production and Stockpiling of Bacteriological (Biological) and Toxic Weapons and on Their Destruction took place. The conference resulted in the strengthening of confidence-building and verification measures.

At the European regional level, a CSCE Forum on Security Cooperation was given a mandate at the July 1992 CSCE summit meeting in Helsinki to undertake new arms control negotiations, devise new conflict prevention measures, and conduct an ongoing dialogue on security building. Such

NGOs as the Stockholm International Peace Research Institute (SIPRI) have played active roles in focusing interest on these matters.

Another aspect of disarmament has been efforts to control arms transfers. In 1992, the General Assembly approved the creation of a UN conventional arms registry to record information supplied by member states on their arms imports and exports in the preceding year. Special interest by the five permanent members of the Security Council has been directed at controlling destabilizing transfers of conventional weapons, weapons of mass destruction, and associated technologies into the Middle East. Countervailing this development has been persistent arms sales by the United States (over 50 percent of all sales in 1992), and by the CIS states.

If governments have often not been cooperative, the INGOs themselves have often not taken advantage of the opportunities that some of their leaders have eked out for them. INGOs consist not only of organizations that specialize in disarmament, but general purpose organizations (e.g., religious, vocational, and national). Some of the latter also want to do their share to enhance disarmament. However, neither type of INGO has been particularly active in observing, or lobbying, at the United Nations for those issues where disarmament and development coincide. There was, however, an International Conference on the Relationship between Disarmament and Development held in 1987 from which came a recommendation that a portion of resources released by disarmament be allocated to social and economic development.

INGO Access to Conference-Related IGO Activities

We should note, however, that there are issue areas other than that of disarmament that have involved INGOs in IGO conference decision making. Conferences, whether ad hoc or continuing, provide great opportunities for INGOs to influence international policy-making. However, results of a succession of UN conferences appear to reveal both the limitations and the potential of multilateral decision making. As one observer commented in discussing the tenth anniversary of the Stockholm Conference:

> There is no likelihood of a repeat performance of the Stockholm conference, which was financed by governments; and in any case the conference did not directly create public awareness *do novo*. Stockholm was able to focus existing interest and then to amplify it, thus encouraging and lending respectability to many other citizen action groups which were perhaps short of confidence, impetus and material until then. In the end the net result was more public interest—but it was created by indirect pumping. It will not be done twice.[11]

However, the illustrative case that follows indicates otherwise. Nonetheless, there has emerged among INGOs an increasingly critical view of the UN Secretariat's apparent inability to repeat the Stockholm success at other conferences, and a growing despondency about the role of certain states that appear to be working against the use of multilateral means to deal with global problems. Since the end of the Cold War, however, the former Eastern European bloc states have not been among them. In contrast, the CIS states have been resisting strong international environmental pollution control measures.

There is also an increasing concern felt by INGOs that they should not become trapped into the UN agenda. They resent the temptation to work on particular issues merely because these are the issues inscribed on an official conference agenda. An example of an INGO departure from an official agenda occurred at the Eleventh Special Session of the General Assembly on Economic Issues, held in New York during August and September 1980, when INGOs focused on the role of transnational corporations in development because they felt that this issue was not adequately addressed on the official agenda.

Another interesting development is that INGOs are spending as much time lobbying media representatives at intergovernmental conferences as they are lobbying the official delegates, thereby acquiescing in the political cliché that what is said is not as important as how it is reported or portrayed to the public (whether governmental or otherwise). Many INGOs come to intergovernmental conferences or to the General Assembly sessions with press accreditation for local newspapers or radio stations. They file reports and mix with the press corps. For example, of a team of approximately forty people working with the International Coalition for Development Action (ICDA) at UNCTAD V in Manila, two-thirds had press accreditation and were writing stories and sending radio reports back to their capitals.

Toward the end of the 1970s, INGOs seemed to be doing more than merely recasting and redefining the various agendas of the conference activities; they were concerned mostly with the economic and social issues commonly termed the New International Economic Order (NIEO). INGOs are continuing to pursue independent paths or strategies that could possibly enhance realization of some of these economic and social goals. However, the problem of global recession in the early 1990s did very little to alter the negative mood among the industrialized states, even though global awareness of such issues as human rights, refugees, control of the spread of nuclear weapons or fissionable material, and the environment is steadily being enhanced through the conferencing mechanism.

As it has become more and more evident that many of the issues that separate the industrial states from the developing states are not going to be resolved either easily or soon through multilateral means, INGOs may find it more useful to concentrate their efforts on educating and sensitizing general public opinion and on lobbying at the national centers of power. Unless there is a change in this situation, the 1990s will perhaps witness the increased formation of national NGO coalitions. Many of the points raised above are illustrated in the following cases on UNCED and on the Somalia relief operation.

INGO Activities at the 1992 UN Conference on Environment and Development (UNCED): An Illustrative Case

At the beginning of the 1970s, many INGOs were represented at IGO conferences by individuals or by very small groups. There had been some coordination among INGOs up to a point; but it was not until the Stockholm Conference (1972), the World Population Conference in Bucharest (1974), the World Food Conference in Rome (1974), and the World Conference on Agrarian Reform and Rural Development (1979) that the role of INGOs at single-issue global conferences was enhanced.[12]

The presence and activities of INGOs at these conferences helped to ensure that central issues were not ignored. INGOs accomplished this through publications, newsletters, conferences, and even lobbying. INGOs also can affect the deliberations and outcomes of IGO conferences by influencing national parliamentarians and governmental representatives through "networking." The United Nations Conference on Environment and Development (UNCED), called the Earth Summit, held in Rio de Janeiro in the summer of 1992 provides a successful illustration of these two forms of access to IGO decision making.

The Preparatory Committee (PREPCOM). A very important series of PREPCOM conferences was held before the Earth Summit. These PREPCOMS were organized by Maurice Strong, the UNCED secretary-general. Strong, a Canadian, had a long history of involvement in environmental projects and the UN system. He was the first Director of the United Nations Environment Programme (UNEP), after having played a major role in the 1972 UN Conference on the Human Environment, held in Stockholm. Strong also has been involved in the business world, having been the president of the Canadian national oil company, PetroCanada. Because of his expertise in bringing together the business world and environmentalists, Strong was seen as a natural leader in organizing PREPCOM meetings, as well as UNCED itself. The PREPCOMs were seen as stepping-stones toward the Conference in Rio, with each succeeding session of information transfer defining more clearly the general themes. Ambassador Tommy Koh of Singapore was the chairman for each of the PREPCOMs.

The first session was held in Nairobi in August 1990 and was followed by PREPCOM 2 eight months later in Geneva. The main difference between PREPCOMs 1 and 2 was the transition from analyzing environmental issues to developing strategies of action. By the time PREPCOM 3 was held in

August 1991 in Geneva, there was more agreement on the environmental issues to be discussed in Rio and how they would be implemented. Finally, PREPCOM 4 in March 1992 in New York brought all the issues together.

An important aspect of the PREPCOMs was the involvement of INGOs. If INGOs wanted to be heavily involved in the Rio Conference in June, then they were likely to be involved in the PREPCOMs as well. Many different organizations saw this not only as an opportunity to get involved in the historic Earth Summit, but also as a means of being included in future international conferences as well. For example, for the first time, the American Society of International Law (ASIL) sought NGO status in order to obtain Observer status at the UNCED. Starting at the last PREPCOM held in March, and through to the last days of the Earth Summit in June, the ASIL was allowed two observers to attend the meetings. In all, more than 1,200 NGOs were accredited as observers to the Plenary and Main Committee sessions.[13]

To provide a closer relationship, the United Nations gave many INGOs consultative status with the Economic and Social Council (ECOSOC). This gave INGOs, such as the World Conservation Union and the Sierra Club, the right to attend meetings, submit written statements, and testify before ECOSOC. They can even, under certain circumstances, propose agenda items for ECOSOC consideration.[14]

Maurice Strong also felt that NGOs would have important and long-lasting effects on the outcome of the conference. During the non-governmental Global Forum, the UNCED "counterconference," he encouraged all NGOs to participate both in educating people from around the world and in influencing governments and businesses on environmental concerns. Strong and his Danish wife, Hanna Strong, entertained many INGOs at their ranch in the hills above the Rio Centro Convention Center. Hanna even went so far as to set up a new INGO, Earth Restoration Corps, which will function similarly to the Peace Corps.

The importance of NGOs at the Earth Summit did not go unnoticed by the United Nations, as illustrated in the following statement:

> For its part, the UN system should initiate a process, in consultation with NGOs, to review formal procedures for their involvement at all levels including policy design, decision making, implementation and evaluation of programs. The UN system should also review its financial and administrative support to NGOs, as well as the extent and effectiveness of NGO involvement in implementing projects and programs of the UN.[15]

The Global Forum. The main focus of NGO activity at the Rio Summit was the '92 Global Forum. This so-called counterconference consisted of many NGOs, INGOs, environmentalists, scientists, and other individuals from around the world. They gathered in the Flamengo Park area, Rio's downtown convention center, and many auditoriums around the city. For INGOs, the INGO Forum was one of the most important events at the Global Forum. Through this outlet they were able to convene daily to discuss current UNCED issues.[16] In all there were 7,892 NGOs from 167 countries at the Global Forum between June 3 and 14.[17]

Throughout the twelve-day conference, many INGOs set out to influence the international press corps. They accomplished this through a variety of activities: from producing their own model treaties, to issuing declarations of ethical principles and an earth charter and staging rock concerts and marches. They also handed out many books and pamphlets relating to global conservation.[18] INGOs had such a great effect on the media that the perception of the conference as reported in the press coverage reflected a new, broader notion of the interaction of environmental and developmental concerns. For example, William Reilly, head of the U.S. Environmental Protection Agency, observed, "The two weeks of intense press coverage and attention really encouraged people everywhere to take this seriously."[19]

By the time the 1992 UNCED was drawing to a close, the INGOs had agreed on many proposals that they felt would have a lasting effect on the global community. For example, they called for alternatives to the way in which the World Bank handled grass-roots organizations and local enterprises.[20] It was felt that the Bank, while helping to develop poor countries, was ignoring environmental concerns. The INGOs' influence was revealed when the Bank released its annual report in September 1992, in which it vowed to help its borrowing developing states reform their environmental policies and to advise borrowing states through a series of conferences, to be partly financed by a "Global Environmental Facility," set up as a joint enterprise between the World Bank and the United Nations.[21]

INGOs also proposed that the General Agreement on Tariffs and Trade (GATT) be replaced with the more fair (to the developing states) International Trade Organization (ITO).[22] Such an organization was originally promoted following World War II by John Maynard Keynes. The ITO was to work with the International Monetary Fund (IMF) in fighting unfair trading practices such as discriminatory pricing and business cartels. After the Earth Summit, INGOs hoped that the ITO could be revamped to help improve trade between the developing states and the industrialized states.[23]

In order to focus multilateral lending and other aid policies on environmental conditions, many INGOs felt that they needed a more direct influence in IGO decision making. They proposed that eleven international financial institutions, including the United Nations, be democratized.[24] It was thought that the best way to change these organizations was by influencing the process of decision making. For example, if the General Assembly adopted a weighted voting system based on member countries' populations, the developing states might have more influence in the international arena.

In addition to proposing such changes to the international organizational system, many INGOs wanted to improve the way in which people are educated about environmental issues: for example, by retraining economists to increase their knowledge of environmental concerns.[25] They wanted to increase economists' awareness of sustainable development: the idea that economic growth need not be sacrificed for environmental reforms.

INGOs wanted not only to influence these economists, but also to educate the average citizen. They hoped to promote this "citizen awareness" through the use of the mass media. At the Global Forum, a plan was proposed for a global NGO TV satellite channel that would demonstrate successful environmental organizations at work.[26]

The INGOs' Influence on Parliamentarians. Environmental INGOs worked hard to sway national parliaments toward practicing environmentalism both before and during UNCED. Besides focusing at the Conference on drawing the attention of governments to important facts and figures and on drawing up plans of their own that they hoped would be adopted by IGOs later on, INGOs also set out to influence the parliamentarians attending the Conference. It was very important that these legislators be influenced because, after all, they would be the ones who would be instrumental in enacting environmental legislation in their respective states.

A large number of legislators from around the world attended the Global Summit during the UNCED, especially the two-day Parliamentarians Earth Summit. This forum, which was headed by Japanese businessman Akio Matsumura, was held at the Palacio Tiradentes House of Deputies in downtown Rio. Here the legislators were able to discuss global environmental problems with INGO representatives.[27]

INGOs also played a major role in influencing national legislators prior to the Earth Summit. Through the use of the mass media, INGOs encouraged them to attend both the UNCED and the parallel Global Forum. Through the use of television, newspapers, magazines, and radio, INGOs were able to rally citizens support for the environmental cause, and thereby, pressure was put on their governmental leaders.[28]

The best example of INGOs influencing citizens occurred in the United States. Public opinion surveys conducted by the Americans Talk Issues Foundation of Washington, D.C., found that Americans were more aware of such bio-related issues as the economy, the environment, energy, and international security than were their political leaders.[29] Because the UNCED was held during an election year, many U.S. legislators took notice of the surveys and attended the Global Forum. One of the most prominent of these was Senator (and future Vice President) Albert Gore of Tennessee. Gore chaired the U.S. Senate delegation at the UNCED and also the Subcommittee on Science, Technology, and Space of the Senate Commerce Committee. He was a good candidate for these chairs because of his lifetime involvement in the environmental movement. He has written many books on environmental concerns and has been involved in many environmental legislative acts.[30]

Gore believed that in a post-Cold War world, environmental concerns would become one of the main elements of foreign policy everywhere. He felt that the UNCED was the starting point for recognizing this. Both before and after the Earth Summit, Gore criticized the Bush administration's environmental policies. For example, he asserted that the White House environmental record had "been a disgraceful performance, the single worst failure of political leadership I have seen in my lifetime."[31]

President George Bush was finally persuaded to briefly come to Rio, albeit reluctantly. For many months before the UNCED was held, it had appeared that Bush would not attend because he did not want to be part of an agreement which he felt would not be in the interests of both the American environment and the economy.[32] Many people from around the world viewed Bush as an "Uncle Scrooge," citing the fact that he refused to sign the Convention on Biological Diversity.[33] Bush objected to financing and other clauses in the convention because he felt they would hurt the U.S. economy.[34]

On the other hand, President Bush did not totally project a negative posture. For example, he offered an unspecified amount of money to help states inventory their species on the assumption that if this were known, the rates of extinction could be reduced. He also pledged $25 million to help countries with their greenhouse gas emissions, and $150 million to help protect the world's forests. Finally, Bush called for an international conference later that year to discuss environmental progress.[35]

Global Forum: An Appraisal. The Global Forum, the UNCED counter-conference, was considered a success even though it had major problems. The main problem it faced was the fact that there were too many people attending and not enough money. All kinds of people showed up, from environmentally conscience politicians to those on "the fringe," and from leaders of important environmental organizations to "party-seekers." The hundreds of thousands of people who congregated in Rio placed great strains on the Global Forum's budget. Less than halfway through the conference, the Forum was experiencing a deficit of over $2 million. However, many different groups came to its rescue: individuals, INGOs, and governments all helped in supporting the Forum.[36]

As mentioned before, the NGOs at the Global Forum were able to bypass the official governmental rhetoric of the UNCED and, instead, to work on the major issues that led to the alternative treaties. For the first time, many American environmentalists were able to communicate with colleagues from the developing world. Each gained great insights into the other's ideologies. This NGO networking was seen as one of the greatest successes of the Forum.[37]

This networking also took place between NGOs and parliamentarians both before and during the conference. At the PREPCOMs, NGO representatives would spend much of their time in the halls and in meetings influencing Earth Summit delegation members. For example, representatives of American NGOs would discuss issues at breakfast meetings with the members of the U.S. delegation, and members of the congressional delegation participated in question-and-answer sessions with NGO representatives at the Global Forum.[38]

The successful networking that took place led Secretary-General Maurice Strong to make the following observation at the closing of the Conference:

> [UNCED had been] a profoundly important human experience from which none of us can emerge unchanged. . . . The world will not be the same after this Conference. Diplomacy will not be the same. The United Nations will not be the same. And prospects for our earth cannot—must not be the same.[39]

The 47th UN General Assembly. At the forty-seventh UN General Assembly, the United Nations remained committed to ending environmental degradation around the world. Its main goal was to create a new international agency to hear complaints against governments that misuse the environment. The idea of this environmental agency, which became known as the "Sustainable Development Commission," was born at the Earth Summit.[40]

The Sustainable Development Commission will be modeled after the UN Human Rights Commission (UNHRC), which is located in Geneva. That is, like the UNHRC, this commission will have no legal power to coerce governments to improve their environmental policies. Instead, the Commission will encourage member states to comply with the pledges they made at the Earth Summit. They hope to accomplish this goal through disclosure and by motivating governments to implement their pledges. NGOs, private individuals, the media, and Commission investigators will be responsible for informing the Commission which states continue to abuse their environment. In addition, governments will be encouraged to submit reports to the Commission on what steps they are taking to meet the plans that were proposed in Rio.[41]

Conclusion. The Global Forum served three major functions for INGOs that would not have been possible at the Earth Summit itself. First, INGOs learned how to increase their networking capabilities by overcoming such obstacles as differences in language, culture, and wealth. Second, the Forum provided an opportunity for many INGOs to express opinions that are sometimes either ignored or suppressed in their host countries. Third, it established a set of norms to promote more effective transnational coordination of INGO activities.[42]

The networking that took place between INGOs at the Global Forum proved to be very important in producing two major products. The first was the Business Council on Sustainable Development's book, *Changing Course: A Global Business Perspective on Development and the Environment.* The book examines, in thirty-eight different case studies, successful business opportunities through sustainable development. The second major product was the many alternative treaties that began to be drafted at the PREPCOMs and were concluded at the Global Forum. These treaties ranged from INGO commitments of action to denunciations of present governmental policies.[43]

By the time UNCED ended, networking by INGOs succeeded in persuading the delegations to adopt and recommend the following proposals for endorsement by the General Assembly: the Rio Declaration on Environment and Development, "Agenda 21," a "Statement of Principle on the Management, Conservation and Sustainable Development of All Types of Forests," the Convention on Climate Change, and the Convention on Biological Diversity.[44]

In the aftermath, the Convention on Biological Diversity has received official support in the U.S., with the advent of the Clinton administration, and in fact has been signed. Furthermore, in June 1993, the UN Commission on Sustainable Development—created to translate the environmental accords into action—had a surprisingly non-confrontational first session, due in part to the changed attitude of the U.S. For example, the U.S. now was willing to work with the Group of 77 on how to transfer to the developing states technology aimed at improving the environment.

Redefining Security: Somalia and the 1992 Famine Crisis—Domestic Dissolution and IGO-INGO Intervention: An Illustrative Case

Early in 1991 the United Nations had withdrawn from Somalia because the country was considered too dangerous, and, until the fall of 1992, the United Nations had played a very small role in helping to stop the starvation in Somalia. However, for months many international relief organizations (NGOs) had tried to get food to the famine-stricken country. However, they themselves had been subjected to looting, bribery, and armed attack. Finally, in October 1992, the Security Council agreed to send in a minimum of 500 Pakistani soldiers to help protect relief organizations, such as CARE, the International Committee of the Red Cross (ICRC), Save the Children Foundation, and Oxfam. However, these troops, which in any event were slow in arriving, proved to be of little help because of the lack of support from many of the Somali clans, especially General Aidid's Habr Gedir. Also, one of the terms of reference for the UN peacekeeping force composed of Pakistanin troops was to fire only if fired upon, which severely restricted the Pakistanis' ability to protect relief operations effectively. According to one Western diplomat in Nairobi, Aidid was "still the big frog in the pond" and as long as he opposed the UN presence, "food still remains power."[45]

Many NGO and IGO relief organizations felt that the only way to end the civil war was to deprive the fighters of their chief incentive to continue fighting by making food plentiful as well as accessible. Andrew Natsios, assistant administrator for the Bureau for Food and Humanitarian Assistance of the U.S. Agency for International Development (USAID), was appointed by President Bush as special coordinator for Somali relief in the summer of 1992. He spoke for many when he said that the international community "must break the vicious cycle in Somalia in which food equals money, a commodity so valuable it is being obtained at gunpoint." Consequently, the United States established a six-point relief strategy:

1. Sell food to Somali merchants to drive down prices;
2. Provide free food through feeding stations or soup kitchens, primarily targeted at displaced populations in urban areas;
3. Provide free dry food in bulk quantities to those with no resources in remote villages;
4. Enhance security, relying on UN peacekeeping troops;
5. Decentralize food distribution sites away from urban areas; and
6. Make more stable areas, such as northeast Somalia, self-sufficient once again by providing seeds and tools, rehabilitating animal herds, reconstructing wells, and starting up hospitals using the money obtained from the sale of food.[46]

The problem with the American relief plan was that it lacked the support of the United Nations. While many NGOs continued their attempts to deliver food, the United Nations was temporarily involved in bickering. Secretary-General Boutros Boutros-Ghali blamed the Security Council for inaction; the Security Council, in turn, faulted him for his delay in presenting a plan of action that the Council had requested.[47] Finally, after months of finger pointing, the United Nations, under pressure from the international and NGO community and spurred on by the media, decided to take action. One factor was the accusation by Secretary-General Boutros-Ghali in July 1992 (which was repeated thereafter) that the West was preoccupied with the European "rich white man's war" in Yugoslavia while ignoring starvation in "poor non-white Somalia."[48]

Attempts by Humanitarian NGOs and INGOs to Solve the Problem. Long before there was a UN presence, the NGO relief organizations had been highly successful at getting food to Somali ports, but they had been just as unsuccessful as the United Nations at distributing the food throughout Somalia. Most of these organizations had rushed in without clear aims, without analyzing real needs, and without any desire to coordinate their efforts, and each had its own ideas of how to stop the suffering.[49] CARE, for example, believed the solution was simply more food, assuming that even if the looters would take much of the food, sooner or later, if enough were shipped in, some would eventually reach the starving people.[50] In contrast, the ICRC, not accepting CARE's "trickle-down" theory, believed that the answer was to make the food less attractive to the looters by delivering it on the spot to the needy and cooking it in soup kitchens.[51] Other organizations used food that contained great nutritional value but was so unappetizing that only starving people who required the nourishment would consider eating it.

Another reason for the difficulty encountered by relief organizations in carrying out their mission was the lack of a national bureaucratic and logistical infrastructure. Because of this lack of authority, the NGOs, over time, began to establish their own infrastructure. The Southern Air Transport, which delivered much of the food for the relief agencies, helped them organize a collaborative working relationship among themselves, including a system of security signals to ensure safe landings into the airfields. A flag on the end of the runway was one method agreed on by the NGOs involved to signal safe conditions.[52] The CARE organization's approach was to develop a "food for work" program, according to which thousands of Somalis would be employed to repair a network of canals connected to the Juba and Schebele rivers. Philip Johnston, president of CARE, felt that this would be just a start, estimating that it would take Somalia ten to twenty years to rebuild its transportation infrastructure.[53] The ICRC hoped to improve the political climate by persuading clan elders to curb the activities of their armed gangs.[54]

Although all the NGOs involved were highly motivated, by December 1992 they had accomplished very little because of the persistent looting and general banditry. Even though they hired armed Somalis for protection, some of these "technicals" had turned against those they were supposed to protect. Therefore, many NGOs felt that they needed more reliable armed protection, preferably provided by UN troops.

As mentioned earlier, the United Nations had withdrawn its support from the Horn of Africa early in the civil war. Most NGOs had been reluctant to criticize the United Nations publicly for fear of damaging their relations; but some UN officials themselves, at first privately and then publicly, complained that the organization was mishandling the situation. An unidentified UN official was quoted as saying that "Somalia is the greatest failure of the U.N. in our time."[55]

UNHCR had remained surprisingly absent during most of the Somali crisis, which turned out to be a major mistake, not only for its reputation, but also for the thousands of starving Somalis who had desperately needed UNHCR's support. An example of such neglect was found in the village of Dolo. Dolo is a small village straddling Somalia and Ethiopia and the home for many Somali refugees. By late summer 1992, the village had a population of 80,000 displaced persons and, at one point, a death rate of 50 a day. However, UNHCR remained absent, arguing that its presence would only attract additional refugees. If it had not been for the relief agency, *Doctors without Borders-Holland,* many of the hundreds of people arriving daily would not have survived.[56] Nicolas Bwakira, the UNHCR director for Africa, said that his agency wanted to do more to help the Somalis, but many UNHCR relief personnel were forced to evacuate because of the violence. "We've had 15 UNHCR officials killed in that country [Somalia] in less than a year. We're not going to start people back there until there is a political solution," Bwakira explained.[57]

UNICEF personnel also faced danger from local armed bandits while they were delivering aid; in the city of Kismayu on November 23, 1992, UNICEF relief agents were attacked at the local airport. A UNICEF passenger plane, while taxiing to takeoff, was stopped by more than a dozen teenage gunmen. If it were not for another group of armed youths who ambushed the first group, the plane would never have been able to take off. Carl Howorth, a UNICEF logistics officer, said, "[The attack was] like many other ones, it was economically motivated," describing it as a normal skirmish.[58]

Multilateral Peacekeeping and Humanitarian Aid. Finally, the international community became tired of these "normal skirmishes." With food piling up on the docks and increasing numbers of relief agencies under attack from bandits, the international community set out to bring an end to the massive starvation in Somalia. A multilateral UN-authorized force, headed by the United States, was established on December 3, 1992, with the unanimous approval of the Security Council. The resolution called for the United States to take the lead in helping to deliver food to the starving, while at the same time not getting involved in the internal clan politics and warfare. The U.S. mission was to secure the Somali ports and airports, open supply routes, establish protected feeding centers, and prevent bandits from robbing the food intended for the starving Somalis.[59]

Conclusion. In President Bush's address to the nation on December 4, 1992, he assured the American people that "Operation Restore Hope" was not open-ended and that it was strictly humanitarian. This is significant because it marked one of the first times that the United States was willing to risk members of its armed forces in a possible conflict that appeared not to be in the "vital" national interest of the United States. This humanitarianism was seen as a bridge to respond to the unfortunate consequences of both the civil war and the drought.

Although it may have been a humanitarian mission, it was not without risk. The U.S. armed forces had been involved in several other humanitarian operations since the end of the Cold War; they distributed food and set up shelters in Bangladesh, helped the people of south Florida after Hurricane Andrew, and patrolled the streets of Los Angeles after the racial riots. However, Somalia was different: it was neither a traditional war zone nor a strictly humanitarian operation, and this ambiguity worried many officials. A senior U.S. Army planner commented that in operations like Somalia, "there is a chance of a higher U.S. casualty rate than there is in situations where we can use decisive force."[60] Soon after the arrival of the troops, General Aidid and President Ali Mahdi met in Mogadishu for a "peace conference": the first time they had met in over a year since they had joined forces to overthrow the Barre government. They called on their clan members to drop all arms and assist in the feeding of the starving. In any event, a UN-mounted operation in mid-1993 to disarm General Aidid's followers, confiscate his arms caches, and capture him, disrupted any negotiating efforts and in addition it created disagreement within the UN coalition as to whether using force in this way will bring stability. The INGOs and humanitarian IGOs involved did not think it would. Their opinion appeared to be borne out when, after some loss of life, the United States decided to cease active military attacks in October 1993, and declared that it would withdraw by April 1994. Secretary General Boutros-Ghali along with the heads of OAU, the Arab League, and the Organization of the Islamic Conference appealed to African and Arab states to contribute troops and money.

The military operation in Somalia has been unique because it has represented another example of how, in the post-Cold War era, the line between high politics and low politics was becoming blurred. The high politics of political/military affairs was intersecting the low politics of economic/social/environmental concerns. Would it now be the responsibility of the United Nations to intervene in other parts of the world in order to rescue helpless peoples from their own civil disorder as well as to construct some form of political or governing order? Where else in the world would the likelihood of similar conditions arise? The Sudan, Angola, Mozambique, Haiti and Zaire instantly come to mind.[61]

SUMMARY AND CONCLUSIONS

It is quite clear that, although not as "open" as either INGOs or parliamentarians would like, IGO decision making is moving in that direction. Issue areas that are perceived as global are increasingly becoming the concern of "peoples" (see the Preamble to the UN Charter) as well as of governments (see the Charter itself). How this concern is being expressed, in an age of sophisticated communications and information transfer, has aroused frustration, and even cynicism, because the contemporary international political system, of which INGOs increasingly are playing a part, has been adapting only slowly and with reluctance to respond either to "globalism" or to "particularism." However, with the blurring of the post-Cold War distinction between "high" and "low" politics, the mutual interaction of IGOs and INGOs forms an essential component of an emerging multilateralism, as the integrity and legitimacy of the state to have itself viewed as the building block of the contemporary international political system is challenged.

Global ad hoc conferences, and conferencing in general, as this chapter suggests, have been utilized by INGOs to gain access to IGO decision making. IGO decisions can be viewed as a form of legislative decision-making or in some cases international legislation. INGOs, by using networking techniques whereby the activities of national bodies are coordinated at the international level or by forming coalitions at the international level to influence governments or each other, are coming to play an increasingly important role in framing and articulating the issue areas of IGO decision making. In fact, for many issue areas (e.g., those concerned with the environment, population, renewable energy, harnessing science and technology for development, hunger and malnutrition, disease prevention and control, and arms control and disarmament), INGOs are now essential adjuncts of IGOs. Patterns of IGO-INGO cooperation in responding to the needs of these issue areas have led to a heightened interest in the potential of international regimes as a technique of multilateralism that can minimize both the national particularism of IGOs and fears of excessive supranationalism. This point is examined in the following chapter.

NOTES

1. Werner J. Feld, "The Impact of Nongovernmental Organizations on the Formulation of Transnational Policies," *Jerusalem Journal of International Relations* 2 (Fall 1976): 8. For an illustration of the interaction of INGOs with IGOs in a post-Cold War conflict, see Larry Minear et al., *United Nations Coordination of the International Humanitarian Response to the Gulf Crisis, 1990–1992,* Occasional Paper no. 13 (Brown University, Thomas J. Watson Institute for International Studies, Providence, RI: 1992).

2. Ibid. The following paragraphs were drawn from Feld, "Transnational Policies," pp. 87–89.

3. Robert Fenaux, "The Transnational Family of Associations (INGOs) and the New World Order," *Transnational Associations* 4 (1978): 194.

4. For a fuller description, see Ylter Turkmen, "The Role of the Non-Governmental Organization within the United Nations System," *Transnational Associations* 2 (1978): 81–83. See also the UNITAR Conference Report by Berhanykun Andemicael and Elfan Rees, *Non-Governmental Organizations in Economic and Social Development* (New York: United Nations Institute for Training and Research, 1975).

5. This section is drawn from Johan Kaufmann, *United Nations Decision Making* (Rockville, MD: Sitjhoff and Noordhoff, 1980), p. 93.

6. For background, see Robert S. Jordan, "Why a NIEO? The View from the Third World," in *The Emerging International Economic Order: Dynamic Processes, Constraints, and Opportunities,* ed. Harold Jacobson and Dusan Sidjanski (Beverly Hills, CA: Sage, 1982). See also John P. Renninger, *ECOSOC: Options for Reforms,* Efficacy and Policy Studies no. 4 (New York: UNITAR, 1981).

7. Quoted in Walter R. Sharp, *The United Nations Economic and Social Council* (New York: Columbia University Press, 1969), p. 205.

8. For a summary of the varieties of impacts of INGOs and IGOs, see Anthony J. N. Judge, "Assessing the Impact of International Associations," *Transnational Associations* (October 1978): 435–40. For a definition and discussion of NGOs, see Werner Feld, *Nongovernmental Forces and World Politics* (New York: Praeger, 1972), pp. 175–209.

9. This section is excerpted from the article by Homer A. Jack, "The Expanding Role of NGOs in the UN Disarmament Debate," *Development* 1 (1982): 62–64.

10. Ibid., p. 64.

11. *Development Forum,* June 1981, p. 9.

12. See chapter 4 for a discussion of "conferencing." Edward J. Mikulenka, a graduate student at the University of New Orleans, assisted in the preparation of this case, drawing in part on a graduate seminar paper that reported on UNCER, by Ernesto Gomez, also a graduate student.

13. "ASIL Observers Report on UN Conference on Environment and Development," *ASIL Newsletter,* August/September 1992, p. 6.

14. See the article by Robert Livernash, "The Growing Influence of NGOs in the Developing World," *Environment* 34, no. 5 (June 1992) pp. 12–20, 41–43; Further references include Maurice F. Strong, "Preparing for the UN Conference on Environment and Development," *Environment,* 33, no. 5 (June 1991): 5, 39; Stephen Collett, "PrepCom 3: Preparing for UNCED," *Environment,* 34, no. 1 (January/February 1992): 3–5, 45.

15. *The Global Partnership for Environment and Development* (New York: United Nations, April 1992), p. 99.

16. Livernash, "Growing Influence of NGOs." For more on the Global Forum, see Brad Knickerbocker, "Alternative Earth Summit Gives Voice to Grass Roots," *Christian Science Monitor,* June 8, 1992, p. 3; Brook Larmer, "Earth II: Tune In, Turn On and Tap Out," *Newsweek,* June 15, 1992, p. 32; Walter Russel Mead, "Not Beyond the Fringe: Global Forum Sets Agenda for Future," *Los Angeles Times,* June 14, 1992, p. M2; and Joel Achenbach, "Counter-Summit Goes Broke—But Goes On," *Washington Post,* June 5, 1992, p. A42.

17. Eugene Linden, "Rio's Legacy," *Time,* June 22, 1992, p. 44.

18. Hazel Henderson, "At Rio NGO's Were Again Out in Front," *Christian Science Monitor,* June 25, 1992, p. 19.

19. "Delegates Take Home Three Pacts to Aid Earth," *Times-Picayune* (New Orleans), June 15, 1992, pp. A5, 19.

20. Henderson, "NGOs Out in Front."

21. "World Bank Vows to Weigh Environmental Effect of Projects," *New York Times,* September 21, 1992, p. A7.

22. Henderson, "NGOs Out in Front."

23. Jeffrey E. Garten, "Lord Keynes Had It Right the First Time," *New York Times,* November 5, 1989, p. F3.

24. Henderson, "NGOs Out in Front."

25. Ibid.

26. Ibid.

27. Ibid.

28. Ibid.

29. Ibid.

30. For more on Al Gore and his views on the environment, see his *Earth in the Balance: Ecology and the Human Spirit* (Boston: Houghton Mifflin, 1992); "A Failure of Nerve?" *Audubon,* May/June 1992, pp. 88, 99 (excerpted from Steve Lerner, *Beyond the Earth Summit of Sustainable Development* [Common Knowledge Press, 1992]).

31. Ibid. p. 90. Comments like this one against the Bush administration probably constitute one of many reasons why Bill Clinton picked Gore as his running mate in the 1992 presidential election.

32. "Bush Undecided about Earth Summit," *Christian Science Monitor,* April 23, 1992, p. 8.

33. The Convention on Biological Diversity is a legally binding treaty to protect endangered plant and animal species. See "Delegates Take Home Three Pacts," pp. A4, 19. President Clinton subsequently signed it.

34. Ibid.

35. Sharon Begley, "And Now, the Road from Rio," *Newsweek,* June 22, 1992, p. 46. Many people felt that President Bush's contributions to the Earth Summit did not live up to the responsibilities of the world's largest economy. See, for example, Linden, "Rio's Legacy," pp. 44–45.

36. The Global Forum was short of money even before the conference began. The Brazilian government contributed $1 million two weeks before the start of the Earth Summit. See Larmer, "Earth II," p. 32. During the Global Forum, many microphones were turned off due to unpaid bills and many European governments had to come to the rescue. See Mead, "Not Beyond the Fringe," p. M2. Money also came from other sources. The Global Forum's co-organizers, Tony Gross and Warren Lindner, even held a press conference midway through the two-week fair to gain support. It was reported that at the end of the conference, a hat was passed around to collect money. See Achenbach, "Counter-Summit Goes Broke," p. A42.

37. Janet Maughan, "The Road from Rio," *Ford Foundation Report* 23 (2) (Summer 1992): 13–16.

38. Ibid.

39. UN Department of Public Information, "United Nations Conference on Environment and Development" (United Nations Press Release, New York, June 16, 1992), p. 1.

40. Paul Lewis, "Revived Debate about Ecology Likely at U.N.," *New York Times,* September 16, 1992, pp. A1, A6.

41. Ibid.

42. Peter M. Haas, Marc A. Levy, and Edward A. Parson, "Why Should We Judge UNCED's Success?" *Environment* 34, no. 8 (October 1992): p. 30. See also "Follow-up UN Conference on Environment and Development," *UN Chronicle* 29, no. 3 (September 1992): pp. 59–67.

43. For a description of some of the alternative treaties agreed on by NGOs at the Global Forum, see Edward A. Parson, Peter M. Haas, and Marc A. Levy, "A Summary of the Major Documents Signed at the Earth Summit and the Global Forum," *Environment* 34, no. 8 (October 1992): 35–36.

44. See UN Department of Public Information, "United Nations Conference on Environment and Development" (Press Release, New York, June 16, 1992), p. 2.

For more on Agenda 21, see "The Earth Summit," *UN Chronicle* 39, no. 2 (June 1992): 40–63.

45. Robert M. Press, "Somali Clans Take Up Arms against Looter," *Christian Science Monitor,* October 29, 1992, p. 3.

46. Andrew Natsios, "Feeding Somalia," *Christian Science Monitor,* September 11, 1992, p. 18.

47. "Force for Humanity," *Times* (London), August 6, 1992, p. 11.

48. "U.N. Vows to Step Up Aid Efforts," *New York Times,* September 13, 1992, p. 20.

49. "Somalia: The Politics of Hunger," *Africa Confidential,* September 25, 1992, p. 3.

50. Jonathan Stevenson, "Food for Naught," *New Republic,* September 21, 1992, p. 14.

51. Ibid.

52. Julius Alexander, "Creating a Country's Infrastructure," *Air Cargo World,* November 1992, p. 32.

53. Robert M. Press, "Small Signs of Renewal in Somalia," *Christian Science Monitor,* September 29, 1992, p. 5.

54. Alex de Waal and Rankiya Omaar, "Lessons of Famine," *Africa Report* (September-October 1992), p. 63.

55. Julie Flint, "UN Crisis over West's 'Tyranny'," *Observer,* August 2, 1992, p. 11.

56. Rakiya Omaar, "In the Village of the Dead," *Observer,* August 2, 1992, p. 20.

57. John Parry, "UN Aide Faults West on Refugee Policies," *Washington Post,* August 20, 1992, p. A21.

58. Thomas Wagner, "Armed Teens Halt Takeoff, Rob UN Relief Workers," *Times-Picayune* (New Orleans), November 24, 1992, p. A10.

59. Michael R. Gordon, "UN Backs Somalia Force; Bush Promises a Quick Exit But Pentagon Is Less Sure," *New York Times,* December 4, 1992, p. A6.

60. David Wood, "GIs May Be in Danger without Decisive-force Rule," *Times-Picayune* (New Orleans), December 3, 1992, p. A16. For a comparable analysis, see Minear et al., *United Nations Coordination.*

61. One change was the commitment in July 1993 of German combat troops to the Somalian operation—the first such commitment since World War II. Other German forces had helped in distribution of relief supplies. All troops will still be assigned non-combat roles. This case was prepared with the assistance of Edward J. Mikulenka, a graduate student at the University of New Orleans.

7 INCIPIENT REGIMES AND MULTILATERALISM: A MIDDLE WAY BETWEEN UNIVERSALISM AND NATIONALISM?

The concept of international regimes was discussed briefly in Chapter 1, where we suggested that this could be a useful in gaining an understanding of the manifold interactions that are found in the international arena. We also pointed out that, while IGOs and regimes can pursue common goals through various cooperation management arrangements, those addressed by regimes typically are more narrow, often dealing only with one important single issue. Furthermore, regime structures are less formal and more fluid than those of IGOs, and they are more likely to adjust to new or changing conditions.

In a world characterized by growing interdependence, international regimes may become increasingly useful for governments that want to solve common problems and pursue complementary purposes without subordinating themselves to hierarchical systems of control.[1]

IGOs can provide the legal setting for international regimes. For example, the ICAO (an IGO), in cooperation with an INGO, the International Air Transport Association (IATA), has established regimes for international flights. A regional IGO, the Andean Common Market (discussed in Chapter 4), set up an international investment regime through the well-known Decision 24. More significant, within the Law-of-the-Sea Treaty, which is now still undergoing ratification, a regime called the Enterprise was proposed to ensure the access of the developing countries to the benefits of deep-seabed exploitation. In the post-Cold War new international world "dis-order," regimes are increasingly being utilized to deal with large-scale and dangerous concentrations of armaments of all kinds.

At times IGOs may attempt to establish regimes or regimes may be established through treaties containing provisions for self-enforcement, or the IGOs may, themselves, be means to ensure enforcement of the treaties themselves, but often, in any case, major difficulties can arise because of disagreements among the member or signatory states. There follows here a more systematic look at the characteristics of international regimes, dealing with both political/security and political/economic matters.

As Robert Keohane puts it, international regimes should not be interpreted as elements of a new international order beyond the nation state. Rather, they should be understood as arrangements motivated by self-interest, in which state sovereignty is likely to be an important factor.

ORIGINS

One path to the establishment of an international regime is the *contractarian* track.[2] Governmental, and sometimes nongovernmental, actors, in cooperating on a particular task or activity, meet for the explicit purpose of negotiating a contract or convention setting forth the details of a regime to accomplish the task or perform the activity in question. The Conventional Armed Forces in Europe Treaty (CFE) is a possible example of an incipient regime. In 1990, as a part of the treaty arrangement, NATO created a "Verification Coordinating Committee" to coordinate among the member states the implementation of this treaty and related disarmament and arms control agreements. These inspections have been carried out, involving forces and installations in thirty states and utilizing either national units or teams composed of inspectors from several states. Furthermore, the "Cooperating Partners" of the NATO Cooperation Council—which is composed of the former Soviet bloc states and the post-Soviet CIS states—have also been brought into the implementation procedures.[3]

A much larger effort in terms of the participation of states, yet following basically the same contractual pattern, is the drawn-out negotiations for a Law-of-the-Sea Treaty which (as mentioned) set up a regime—the Enterprise—for the mining of the deep-seabed on behalf of the vast majority of the signatory states that do not possess the technology to exploit the minerals of the deep-seabed. When it becomes operative, the Enterprise will have quasi-taxing power over, as well as a claim on, the transfer of technology on the mining activities of the technology-possessing states (see Figure 7.1). These are principally the United States, Britain, and Germany.

However, the best example of an operative regime is probably the Antarctica Treaty of 1959, whose original signatory states numbered only twelve. The purpose has been to prevent the installation of nuclear weapons in this region of the world. The inspection and verification system of the International Atomic Energy Agency (IAEA), which was created in the late 1960s as a consequence of the conclusion of the Nuclear Nonproliferation Treaty (NPT), may also fall into this category. In fact, the IAEA's powers

Figure 7.1
Seabed Exploration Regime Map

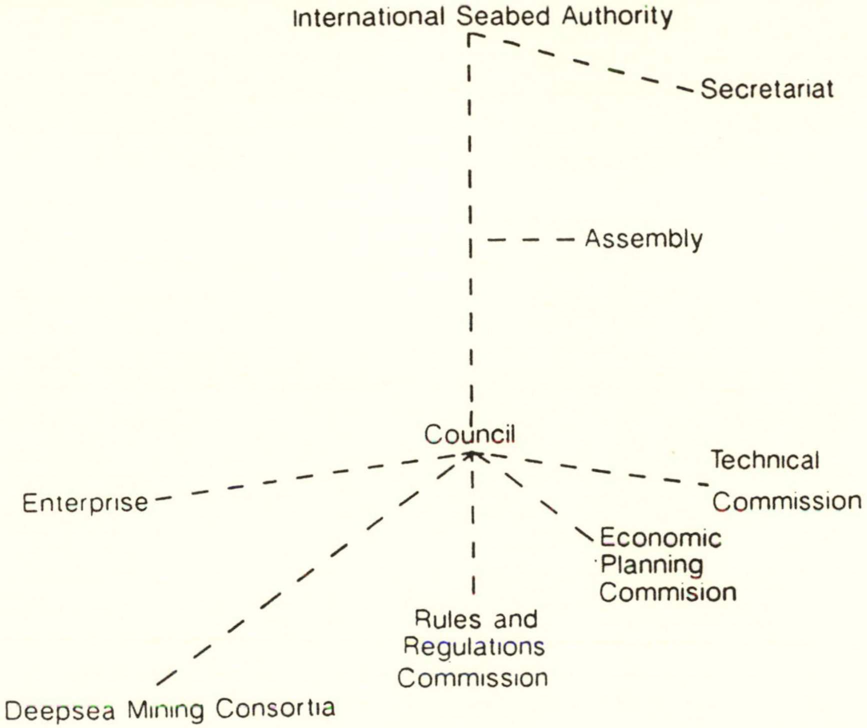

are being strengthened to enhance the "transparency" of possibly offending states, such as Iraq. (This is discussed further later in the chapter.)

An agreement on a contractual basis for a regime might not always yield the benefits promised. The text of the contract or a convention may be cast in ambiguous language that is designed to obscure the basic conflicts of the parties to the agreement. Obligations may have been accepted by one party without a true intention to comply. In all cases, issues and issue areas may be linked, or package deals may be proposed and accepted that are reflections of coalitional and bargaining dynamics rather than actual agreements on the integrated objectives to be attained. Additions or amendments to the agreements establishing a regime may be made over a period of time without the parties always keeping in mind their subordinate conception of shared objectives. In summary, problems may be built into regimes, the extent of which will emerge only as the regime enters into sustained operation. The case of the European Monetary System (EMS), discussed below, is illustrative of such a development.

A second type of regime origin is the *evolutionary* approach. Under this concept, regimes evolve from widespread practice over time, through which international institutions may develop, and rules that were temporary or provisional take on the character of customary law. Regimes concentrating on the exploration of marine resources, including fisheries, have often followed this pattern. Regimes evolve as a consequence of a dramatic unilateral action taken by a state that subsequently is accepted by other states on a de facto (and, perhaps later, on a de jure) basis. The post-1945 regime for the outer continental shelves is an example of such a pattern.

A third possibility for the creation of a regime can be characterized as the *piecemeal* process. States may reach agreement on one or more components of a regime but, for a variety of reasons, they may not be able to obtain comprehensive consensus. Alternatively, they may hope that such a consensus will be found later as a consequence of task expansion or spillover. An example of the piecemeal approach is the slow and arduous creation of the EMS. The UN Code of Conduct for TNCs (discussed later) might also be placed in this category. Other examples of the piecemeal approach include the regional fisheries regimes in the North Atlantic and Pacific (ICNAF) and International North Pacific Fisheries Convention (INPFC). In some cases, the piecemeal approach may be transformed into the evolutionary approach. This might be the case, for example, with the code of conduct for TNCs.

During the period of regime formation, the capabilities of the participating states, as well as the specific functions attributed to the regime, are likely to determine the nature of the regime's activities. However, once the regime becomes relatively well organized, constraints on it become increasingly important. As Robert Keohane and Joseph Nye point out: "Regimes are established and organized in conformity with distributions of capabilities, but subsequently the relevant networks, monies, and institutions will themselves influence actors' abilities to use these capabilities."[4] Control over outcomes will then depend on voting power, ability to form coalitions, and influence in elite networks.

RIGHTS, RULES, AND COHERENCE

Regime participants have rights and obligations regardless of whether they are governmental or nongovernmental actors. How the rights can be exercised and how the obligations must be carried out is stipulated by the rules and procedures of the regime. Some regimes emphasize central planning and provide detailed rules governing the actions of individual member states. The deep-seabed mining regime, as proposed in the UN Conference on the Law-of-the-Sea (UNCLOS), falls into this category. Other regimes tend to follow a laissez-faire philosophy, and their rules are less restrictive, leaving the participants a measure of discretion as to cooperation and goal attainment, as illustrated in the OECD Guidelines for TNCs.

Coherence refers to the degree to which elements of an international regime are internally consistent.[5] Especially when regimes have several goals, the rights and obligations of the participants must show a high degree of coherence, with a careful determination of the trade-offs between the goals and expectations of the regime members. Otherwise, conflicts and contradictions arise, as exemplified between general use rights for marine resources and the specific right vested in adjacent coastal states to exclude outsiders from offshore activities that could impinge on their rights. It is highly desirable, therefore, that a state's sovereign interest and the obligations imposed by the rules of an international regime be carefully weighed, and the relationship spelled out as precisely as possible.

ORGANIZATIONAL FEATURES

Although international regimes characteristically have fewer organizational arrangements and institutional features than IGOs, effective task achievement is usually enhanced by explicit organizational arrangements, especially concerning budgetary requirements, physical facilities, and personnel staffing. Of course, considerable variations in organizational arrangements exist; the proposed seabed mining organization is highly complex, whereas the EMS structure is relatively limited. As Oran Young points out, even where a need for explicit organization is apparent, instead of creating their own autonomous arrangements, international regimes may make use of international institutional structures that were created for other purposes or were associated with a more comprehensive authority.[6] For example, the EMS relies heavily on the institutions and personnel of the EC to attain its goals; the NPT regime could not achieve its purpose without the use of the UN-related IAEA; and a future regime on the code of conduct for TNCs could not carry out its monitoring task without the UN Secretariat. On the other hand, deep-seabed mining as an object of a regime, as has been proposed by the majority of the UNCLOS negotiating states, requires a vast institutional organizational framework.

Some of the reasons for endowing international regimes with rather extensive organizational arrangements include the collection and distribution of revenues, the need to conduct continuous research, the monitoring of activities to ensure compliance with regime rules, and the settlement of disputes.[7] Again, the proposed seabed regime provides a good example of all these organizational aspects. However, less complex regimes, such as the various regimes regulating fisheries; arms control and disarmament measures, such as those in the CFE Treaty (CFE) mentioned above; or confidence-building measures (CBMs) developed within the Conference on Security and Cooperation in Europe (CSCE) and other treaties dealing with aspects of conventional and nonconventional weapons also show the need for some of the actions enumerated above.

Organizational arrangements also help in setting forth the clearly defined procedures that would be required to assure the appropriate regime performance and the attainment of regime goals. Carefully thought-out procedures can avoid much of the conflict potential inherent in all regimes, assure more effective collaboration with respect to the issue or issue areas for which the regime has been created, and guide the task performance of the bureaucracy of the regime and its member states.

When such organizational and institutional arrangements are devised, some critical questions, which are shared by IGOs, must be answered. How much authority should be conferred on the organizational structure? What should be the extent of discretion given to the institutional leadership? How much autonomy should the organization have vis-à-vis other centers of authority within the global or regional international system? How is the organization to be financed and staffed? The answers to these questions are likely to affect the quality of task performance and the benefits of, or losses to, the members or participants of the regime. Some expectations will be disappointed as a direct result of the nature and shape of the organizational arrangements and, therefore, certain organizational features may well be hotly contested throughout the operation of the regime. This will become quite apparent in the cases presented below.

POLICY INSTRUMENTS

As in all organizations, policy instruments must be chosen carefully to attain intended regime goals. Examples of such instruments are the introduction or relaxation of restrictive business practices in TNC operations, depending on the overall goal of the code-of-conduct regime; the nondiscriminatory treatment on the transfer of technology by members of a regime; the introduction of stringent accounting standards for TNCs; the regulation for the issuance of mining licenses or permits in a deep-seabed regime; the conditions under which the EMS can make currency exchange-rate adjustments; and the verification by IAEA of Security Council Resolutions vis-à-vis Iraq in the wake of the 1991 Gulf War.

If regimes lack explicit organizational arrangements, new policies may not be adopted unless all members agree. However, it is conceivable that some powerful government, supported by nongovernmental entities, may take unilateral actions to force an issue to which other members of the regime subsequently conform.[8] An example is the U.S.-British-French enforcement of "no-fly" zones over northern and southern Iraq, to protect, respectively, Kurdish and Shiite minorities. This can happen in TNC codes of conduct, and it has occurred in ICAO/IATA air-fare regimes. Such actions may also be taken to redefine the contents of regime rights and rules in order to adjust the regime operations to new conditions; for example, if important EMS members should experience serious currency problems, unilateral actions to force the EMS regime to change the currency relationships may be a way to proceed and obtain the modification of the rules. This occurred in 1992–1993 when Britain, Italy, and Ireland responded to speculative pressures on their currencies as a consequence of persistently high interest rates in Germany.

REGIME TRANSFORMATION

Even after international regimes have fully developed, they are unlikely to become static structures. Since all regimes are created to attain goals that benefit their members politically, economically, or in terms of their perceived security needs, they tend to undergo transformation in response to changes in these environments. Hence, the content of rights and rules may be changed and procedures may be altered with respect to choice and compliance mechanisms.

Oran Young distinguishes three types of pressure for regime transformation.[9] First, there can be *fundamental changes in the nature of the activity for which an international regime was established,* for example, a change in the consumption pattern of a particular species of fish that would require modifying the content of marine fisheries regimes, a major breakthrough in technology for a transfer of technology regime, or an arms control regime. Second, pressures for change may be generated because of *dissatisfaction with the benefits and costs of a particular regime* by one or more regime members or secondary participants. The various changes in the Law-of-the-Sea Treaty and especially the introduction of the 200-mile economic zone have not pleased all the negotiating states, and pressures for further changes are inevitable, as witness the refusal in 1982 of the United States to sign the draft treaty. The third kind of pressure is to *rationalize a regime that has grown ambiguous or contradictory in the course of its evolution.*

If regime rules contain procedures for amendment, adjustments may be made, but the ease with which amendments may be carried out depends to some extent on the stringency of the amendment procedures and the willingness of the dissatisfied regime members to abide by them. If vital national interests are perceived to be at stake and the concerned government disposes of sufficient political power or economic resources, it may withdraw, at least temporarily, from the regime unless its wishes are accommodated. In such a case, the whole regime may be threatened with collapse unless some relevant organizational or substantive adjustments are accepted by the other regime participants. The currency crisis in 1992–1993 in the EMS is a good example. It is possible that the NPT regime may need to be adjusted by treaty to admit new members in order to bring to bear the conditions of START I and other arms control restraints on beneficiaries of the post-Cold War proliferation of nuclear and ballistic missile technology.

To offer greater insights into the creation and operation of regimes, and especially the often difficult circumstances surrounding these processes, the following cases have been selected for a more in-depth discussion: the operation of the European Monetary System (EMS), the GATT-based trade regime, the NPT nonproliferation regime, and the possibilities for a UN-sponsored TNC regime.

The European Monetary System (EMS)

Although well-intentioned, the EC Council decision to embark on the first stage of the EMU was delayed until details could be worked out in the intergovernmental conferences working up a basis for European union, which is currently embodied in the Maastricht Agreement of December 1991. It should be noted that the Single European Act of 1987 provided an initial legal foundation for EMU. An important reason for the delay was the official devaluation of the U.S. dollar in August 1971 (the so-called Smithsonian Agreement), formalizing a continued weakness of the dollar on world currency markets. Another reason was the inability of the member states to impose some kind of discipline on their currencies in the face of the turbulent climate of the financial markets everywhere.

The Snake. In anticipation of the Community's enlargement by three (Britain, Denmark, and Ireland), the EC Council passed a resolution in March 1972 that introduced a somewhat broader currency coordination system, with an exchange rate limit of ±2.25 percent.[10] Based on this resolution, the Committee of Governors of the Central Banks, meeting in Basel, Switzerland, agreed on the arrangements for the "snake in the tunnel," which was designed to stabilize exchange rates within an overall agreed upon range of the member states, especially in regard to cross-rates with the dollar.

Two important differences characterized the new plan. First, the wider variation of ±2.25 percent on either side of the dollar exchange rate formed the walls of a tunnel. The snake was formed by the strongest and weakest currencies in the EC vis-à-vis the dollar. In a sense, the EC currencies formed a joint float, or snake, which stayed within the walls of a tunnel formed by the maximum fluctuation around the par value of the dollar. Second, the use of the dollar as an intervention currency was minimal. Primary intervention in exchange markets was to take place with the currencies of the member states. Theoretically, the stronger-currency states would purchase the weaker currencies in the EC to maintain the integrity of the snake. The dollar was to be used as an intervention currency only when it was needed to keep the joint float of EC currencies stable against the fluctuation of the dollar.[11] Not only did this lessen the impact of the dollar on the economies of the member states, but it effectively established a stable snake-to-dollar parity.[12]

The snake in the tunnel did not fare much better than its predecessor.

Before actual accession to the EC, Britain had agreed, as had Ireland and Denmark, to join the snake arrangement. However, under intense speculative pressure, on June 23, 1972, Britain took the pound out, followed by the Irish pound. Four days later, Denmark also opted out of the arrangement, but was able to rejoin the snake in October 1972 after speculation on the kroner relaxed. The lira, the other chronically weak currency in the EC, was withdrawn by Italy following the second devaluation of the dollar in February 1973.[13] The attitude of France toward the snake varied. The franc remained in the snake until January 1974, but from then through July 1975, it dropped out because the French government came to prefer a fixed exchange rate. France briefly reentered the snake from July 1975 to March 1976 and then reentered in 1978.[14]

Following the withdrawal of Italy, and more so after the French departure, the snake-in-the-tunnel arrangement began to change in form and substance. The devaluation of the dollar in February 1973 and continued speculation thereafter forced the abandonment of the tunnel, even though the snake continued as a joint float of European currencies. West Germany offered reserve assets to the smaller states (Benelux and Denmark) which continued in the snake in order to maintain the joint float.

Transition to the EMS. It was obvious by 1978 that the monetary coordination arrangements, as reflected by the snake devices, were insufficient to satisfy the economic needs and goals of the major participants; a different organizational and functional framework was required to attain some measure of monetary stability within the EC. West Germany wanted to eliminate recurring upward pressures on the deutsche mark (DM) which tended to damage its export business, and France was eager to assure, as much as possible, fixed currency exchange rates. Hence, French and German proposals called for the creation of a new system of monetary cooperation in Europe.[15] At the next meeting of the European Council—in Brussels, in December 1978—a resolution was introduced that called for the creation of the EMS. The EC Commission, acting on this resolution, "confirmed that the EMS had been set up as a Community instrument, and that it would be fully involved in operating the new scheme."[16] The EMS began operations on March 13, 1979. As conceived, the EMS has two main components: the European Currency Unit (ECU)—along with the Exchange Rate Mechanism (ERM)—and the credit mechanisms.

The ECU is a multifunctional device for EC monetary transactions. Primarily, it serves as the common denominator for member currencies. That is, the exchange rates of member states' currencies are pegged to fluctuation margins of ±2.25 percent vis-à-vis the ECU, with the exception of the lira and the Irish pound which, because of structural weaknesses in the economies of Italy and Ireland, are allowed a fluctuation of ±6.00 percent.

Besides its role as the common denominator, the ECU has another important purpose in the EMS: it serves as the threshold of divergence. When a currency's exchange rate with the ECU reaches 75 percent of its maximum deviation in either direction from par (±1.6875 percent from par), it is a signal for consultation among the central banks of member states and intervention in exchange markets to stem revaluative or devaluative tendencies. This brings into play the ERM, which may result in national currencies leaving the EMS, as happened in September 1992 with respect to the British pound, the Danish kroner, and the Italian lira. In mid-1993, speculation against the French franc brought the EMS's ERM virtually to its knees. With the exception of the German mark and the Dutch guilder, the other currencies in the EC were allowed to fluctuate by as much as 15% above and below the currency grid previously set, thus effectively bringing about a revaluation.

This freeing of the valuation of the EC's currencies from the mark also meant decoupling their economies from Germany's, and in particular from the German policy of maintaining high interest rates. Lower interest rates hopefully will stimulate their economies out of the stalled depression which had brought high unemployment and attendant political pressures, especially concerning "foreign workers." But the price for this dramatic development may be the capacity of the EC to create a common political and monetary union in the foreseeable future. The formerly stable exchange rate within the EMS between the mark and the franc had symbolized the strength of the German-French alliance, which had been a cornerstone for any EC aspirations for such a union.

The second major component of the EMS consists of two credit mechanisms: a short-term credit facility of 14 billion ECUs and a medium-term facility of 11 billion ECUs. These mechanisms, which are administered by the European Monetary Cooperation Fund (EMCF), were created as a part of the EMS for maintaining the values of member currencies experiencing balance-of-payments difficulties and speculation in exchange markets. Funding for these facilities has come from the member states, who have deposited 20 percent of their gold reserves and 20 percent of their dollar reserves with the EMS in exchange for equivalent amounts of ECUs. Short-term credit is available for up to three months to remedy short-term deficits in the balance of payments; medium-term assistance is available for periods of two to five years. Both forms of aid become available when a member state's currency reaches its threshold of divergence away from the ECU. Obviously, these mechanisms have proven inadequate to forestall speculation.

In addition to its short-term goal of minimizing exchange rate fluctuations on a day-to-day basis, the EMS was perceived by many Europeans as having favorable long-term implications for greater integration within the EC. In terms of the policies of member states, it was hoped that the EMS, particularly through its consultative arrangements, would lead to increased convergence among the economic policies of member states, especially through its use as an instrument to ease inflation and unemployment.[17] For the future, the ECU has been cast as a possible reserve currency to replace the fluctuating dollar as a means of maintaining international liquidity, not just for the EC, but for the rest of the world as well.[18]

Nonetheless, following the Single European Act (SEA) of 1987, the members of the EC are still fully committed to evolve an Economic and Monetary Union (EMU). Stage one of the EMU began on July 1, 1990, and the British pound sterling entered the ERM on October 1, 1990, which left outside the ERM only the Greek currency. Stage two is still expected to begin on January 1, 1994, but this may not be possible; also this date should signify the establishment of a European Central Bank. The difficulties (mentioned earlier) concerning keeping all the currencies in the snake do not bode well for the future. In stage three, a common currency for all member states may be put in place sometime in 1999, although this goal may not be achievable either.

EMS Problems. The regime institutions for the EMS lack the specificity and comprehensiveness of, for example, the prospective seabed regime; the major institutional roles are divided between the EC and the member states. The Commission plays the most important managerial part in the EC structure; a much lesser role is assigned currently to the EMCF, although with the successful operation of the EMS, the credit mechanisms under the control of the EMCF can become very significant. Whenever the EMF is installed, it is likely to have greater authority than is exercised presently by the EMCF. In the member states, the central banks have most of the influence on the operation of the EMS, and their power is likely to exceed that of the Commission if conflicts between member states should arise. The national finance ministries also have a voice in the EMS operation. Thus, there is an institutional division of labor that may create problems for EMS goal attainment. Even then, however, the rules and the procedures of the regime accepted by the participants may be jettisoned whenever new turmoil in the EC financial markets should break out, as occurred in 1992.

As far as the future task performance of the EMS is concerned, it should be noted that some of the current problems of the EMS were not foreseen in 1978, when the rules and obligations of the regime members were negotiated. Nor was it possible then to recognize impediments to the creation of the EMF, although the history of the EC should have been a warning that the pursuit of perceived national interests by member governments tends to outweigh the recognition or attainment of the common interest.

The consistent support of the French franc by the German DM, thus linking the two currencies closely together even in the face of the 1992 devaluations referred to above, points up the centrality of the Franco-German connection in this area of the EC's activities, as in almost all others. It is France and Germany's shared perception of interests—or costs and benefits—that still lies at the heart of any possible monetary union, whether accomplished in stages, as is recommended by some observers in the face of reluctance for full integration by such states as Ireland, Britain and Denmark, and hence favoring some revisions (or negotiated "exceptions" or "side agreements") to the Maastricht Agreement, or whether accomplished with the eventual wholesale installation of a common monetary union.

The GATT-Based Trade Regimes

During the mid-1960s, an international trade regime—centered on GATT and based on the principles of reciprocity, liberalization, and nondiscrimination—functioned successfully, and world trade since 1950 increased more rapidly than world production.[19] Led by the United States and the EC, the trade regime was highly institutionalized, with explicit rules and widespread membership. As a result of the "Kennedy Round" of negotiations concluded in 1967 and the "Tokyo Round" completed in Geneva in 1983, tariffs were lower in 1983 than in the mid-1960s. At the same time, however, the regime lost much of its effectiveness. National controls on trade, sometimes under the guise of international policy, proliferated for a wide variety of manufactured goods, and trade wars were threatened between prominent members of the regime. An example of this was the conflict between the United States and the EC in the second part of 1986, when Washington imposed a 200 percent duty on a number of EC processed-food items in retaliation for losses of American agricultural exports caused by the entry of Spain and Portugal into the EC in January of 1986, and by the consequent effects of the CAP. This conflict was finally settled after highly confrontational discussions early in 1987.[20]

On September 20, 1986, at Punta del Este, Uruguay, representatives of the regime member states launched a new round of multilateral trade negotiations with the hope of overcoming the protectionist trends that were visible, not only in the U.S. Congress, but in other countries as well. Claims had been made by business circles and members of Congress that the regime had lost its usefulness and that the dispute settlement procedures were not working anymore; in sum, that GATT was out of date.[21]

Clearly, changes had become even more evident by the end of the 1980s, when time after time, efforts to conclude the Uruguay Round have foundered: mostly due to the inability of the United States and the EC to agree on what constitutes "dumping" and what constitutes fair pricing in various commodities (Japan has also been involved in this issue); in addition, the thorny issue of agricultural price subsidies, as between American and European agricultural goods, has not been resolved. However, the regime survives even as the major powers have evaded in various ways GATT's rules, as well as disagreeing among themselves.

One consequence of these extended GATT negotiations among 103 member states has been the proliferation of regional trade agreements involving far fewer states, thus making agreements easier to obtain. There are mixed views about whether these regional agreements help or hinder GATT. One view is that if they contain the antiprotectionist clauses reflective of GATT rules, then they are not a direct threat, and in a practical sense, regional free-trade deals are better than no deals at all. In any event, the spread of these other free-trade arrangements is gaining momentum, and this creates a potential for more regimes.

In the Western Hemisphere, the five Andean states of Colombia, Ecuador, Bolivia, Peru, and Venezuela have agreed to form a free trade area; Chile made treaties in 1991 with Argentina and Mexico, and is negotiating with Venezuela and Costa Rica; and Canada and the United States have signed a North America Free Trade Agreement including Mexico.[22] *Mercosur,* signed in 1991 among Argentina, Brazil, Paraguay and Uruguay, has already been discussed in Chapter 4. Also in 1991 EFTA and the EC created a free-trade area, and in 1992 Sweden and the Baltic states of Estonia, Latvia, and Lithuania set up a free-trade area, as did ASEAN in the same year. In the latter case, Vietnam and Laos have expressed interest in joining ASEAN.

The Nuclear Nonproliferation Regime and Its Spinoffs

The purpose of the nuclear nonproliferation regime is to enhance global security by preventing the spread of nuclear-weapon production capabilities to states that do not possess such capabilities. With the collapse of the Soviet Union, four new nuclear powers were created out of one: Russia, Ukraine, Belarus, and Kazakhstan. Under the accords creating the Commonwealth of Independent States (CIS), all the nuclear weapons are to be concentrated in Russia and disposed of under appropriate START and other agreements. There is an urgency in dealing with nonproliferation because the technology to build nuclear arms is spreading rapidly. Not only is the example of Iraq only too plain, but the persistent efforts of Iran, Pakistan, and North Korea, for example, are not to be ignored. The transfer of various nuclear-related technologies from such "haves" as China and Russia, and even the illegal transfer from the United States, France or Britain, along with the sale of plutonium from, for example, France to Japan, openly challenge the capacity of the regime to accomplish its purpose.

The regime is based on two pillars. One is the Nuclear Nonproliferation Treaty (NPT) of 1968, which went into effect in March 1970; with over 140 parties, it has the largest number of adherents of any arms control agreement. The NPT has three major goals: (1) to prevent the further spread of nuclear weapons; (2) to foster peaceful nuclear cooperation under safeguards; (3) to encourage negotiations to end the nuclear arms race with a view to general and complete disarmament.[23] Under the treaty, nuclear weapon states are obligated not to assist any non–nuclear weapon state to acquire nuclear explosive devices. Correspondingly, non–nuclear weapon states that are party to the treaty are obligated not to manufacture or otherwise acquire such devices.

The treaty provides for the International Atomic Energy Agency (IAEA), created in 1957, to apply international safeguards, including on-site inspections, to all nuclear material in the peaceful programs of non–nuclear weapon states. The treaty also obligates the parties to require IAEA safeguards on nuclear materials and certain equipment exported to non–nuclear weapon states. The safeguard system helps to verify compliance, and it is designed to detect and deter the diversion of nuclear material from peaceful uses to nuclear explosive devices. Review conferences are held every five years, with the most recent having taken place in 1990. In 1995, the treaty calls for a conference to decide whether to extend the treaty indefinitely beyond its initial twenty-five-year duration or to extend it only for a fixed period or periods. There seems little doubt that an extension of some kind will be agreed on, especially since in the post-Cold War period, the issues confronted by the treaty and the IAEA have become even more urgent than before.

The IAEA grew out of President Dwight D. Eisenhower's Atoms for Peace Program, and, as mentioned above, it has been entrusted with the administration of a system of international safeguards. The aim of the safeguards has been to prevent the diversion of fissionable materials from civilian to military purposes. However, as discussed in Chapter 5, IAEA has taken on new importance as a means, following the Gulf War between Iraq and a UN coalition, to monitor compliance with Security Council Resolutions aimed at discovering and destroying Iraq's nuclear weapons capability. This has meant giving the Agency the right to inspect on-site suspected installations, thus ensuring "transparency" in regard to this important matter.

Negotiations for the creation of the IAEA and the safeguards system were long and difficult because there were important political, economic, and strategic considerations involved.[24] The basic aim of the short treaty was to obligate states not to develop or aid in the development of nuclear weapons or explosives. In addition, nonweapon states were to agree to put all their peaceful nuclear facilities under safeguard, including those set up through domestically generated technology. On the other hand, nonweapon states were promised access to the technology they needed for peaceful nuclear purposes, as well as information on the potential benefits of peaceful nuclear explosions. The final trade-off involved the nuclear-capable states assisting the nonweapon states in the application of nuclear energy for peaceful purposes, in return for which the latter were required to accept national safeguards and international inspections imposed on them by the former. Nonweapon states were required to file regular, detailed reports on their nonmilitary nuclear activities with the IAEA, and to permit international inspectors to visit their nuclear facilities in order to verify these reports. The initial acceptance of IAEA safeguards was slow and halting, but gradually, the program has been implemented to a considerable degree, as pointed out above in regard to the Security Council and Iraq.

The NPT was negotiated within the framework of the UN disarmament effort, but the main actors were the United States and the Soviet Union; bilateral negotiating procedures were also used in order to reach agreement.[25] A complement to the NPT is its regional counterpart in Latin America, the Treaty of Tlatelolco. It seeks to set up a nuclear weapons–free zone (NWFZ) in that region, and thereby helps to strengthen the international regime by emphasizing the same interest as symbolized by the NPT. Antarctica has also been declared a nonnuclear region by treaty.

Spinoffs from the NPT are the Nuclear Suppliers Group (NSG), located in London, in which the major suppliers come together to discuss guidelines for nuclear commerce to reduce competition that might undermine safeguards obligations; the International Nuclear Fuel Cycle Evaluation (INFCE), which brought together in Vienna 66 states and organizations, including suppliers and consumers along with a number of states that had not signed the NPT; and the Missile Technology Control Regime (MTCR). The MTCR is the only multilateral missile nonproliferation regime, and was formed in April 1987. It is neither an international agreement nor a treaty, but rather a voluntary arrangement among states sharing a common interest in arresting missile proliferation. The regime consists of common export policy guidelines applied to a common list of controlled items, thus seeking to limit the spread of missiles and unmanned air vehicles and delivery systems capable of carrying at least a 500-kilogram payload for at least 300 kilometers.[26] Since the regime is not a treaty but rather a means of establishing "guidelines," all states are free to participate if they wish. More recently, the Chemical Weapons Convention (CWC) was negotiated, which also includes sanctions against violating states and a "strong and forthright" verification regime, including challenge inspections.[27]

These various incipient or actual regimes, stemming from the NPT initiative, have made a significant contribution to international stability by establishing a normative presumption against proliferation and by creating procedures for verifying national intentions. Nonetheless, the issue of discrimination between nuclear weapon states and nonweapon states (and their accompanying technologies and/or possession of enriched uranium) remains a continuing dilemma, even if safeguards may be regarded as "beneficial necessities."[28]

The UN Code of Conduct for the TNCs: A Future Regime?

Unlike the established regimes discussed above, the UN code of conduct for transnational corporations (TNCs) is still in the negotiating stage. Better known until a few years ago as multinational corporations or simply multinationals, TNCs have evoked sharply different reactions to their operations, which may span a few states or be carried out worldwide. Many observers in the Western industrial states look at TNCs as "good fairies" that enhance the standards of living in states where they establish subsidiaries by providing greater opportunities for employment; promoting the building of infrastructure facilities, including schools and hospitals; and strengthening the host government's balance of payments.

One of the reasons for the proliferation of regional free-trade arrangements is to enhance the transnationals' marketing potential within a region. However, many developing countries look on TNCs as "devils" that exploit natural resources and labor in their states, engage in restrictive business practices, impose their will on host governments through the sheer magnitude of their economic and financial activities, and seek to influence the governments of the states where they are headquartered, to the disadvantage of the host country's interests.

It is difficult to determine the correct view of TNCs, as nothing in the world of business and finance is entirely white or black. In the post-Cold War world, however, with its emphasis on market-oriented economic reforms, nearly every state—including the remaining communist giant, China—is welcoming the TNCs in order to take advantage of the possibilities of technology transfer as well as skills.

The United Nations became involved in TNC activities in 1972 when ECOSOC appointed a group of eminent persons to study the role of TNCs and their impact on development.[29] Following the delivery of the study group's report, UN Secretary-General Kurt Waldheim established the Commission on Transnational Corporations in the fall of 1974; its tasks included the elaboration of a code of conduct for TNCs. The Commission was to be assisted by a UN Centre on Transnational Corporations (CTC), which was established in 1975.

The first Commission meeting was held in March 1975, during which the initial organizational steps were taken toward the formulation of a code. Other Commission meetings were held at least once a year, with the substantive work on the code carried out by working groups that met much more frequently. As of this writing, the code had not been completed because deep disagreements on major points of principle were unable to be bridged.

Initial Positions. The enormity of the task can best be seen by the initial positions taken by the Group of 77 and the five leading industrial states (the United States, Britain, France, West Germany, and Italy) during the Commission meeting in 1976. There were twenty-one main areas of concern with respect to TNCs that were listed by the Group of 77, including:

—Lack of adjustment by TNCs to the legislation of the host states in the matters, inter alia, of foreign investment and policies concerning credit exchange, fiscal matters, prices and commercial matters, industrial property, and labor policies;

—The negative attitude of TNCs toward the renegotiation of original concessions when this is considered necessary by the government of the state;

—The refusal of TNCs to accept the exclusive jurisdiction of domestic law in cases of litigation;

—Direct or indirect interference in the internal affairs of host states by TNCs;

—Requests by TNCs to governments of the home state to intercede with the host government by means of political or economic initiatives in support of their private interests;

—Obstruction by TNCs of the efforts of the host state to assume its rightful responsibility and exercise effective control over the development and management of its resources, in contravention of the accepted principle of permanent sovereignty of states over their natural resources;

—Imposition of excessively high prices for imported technology without any adaptation to local conditions;

—Failure of TNCs to promote research and development in host states; and

—Imposition of restrictive business practices, inter alia, on affiliates in developing states as a price for technical know-how.

The industrial states listed twenty-three areas of concern that they wanted taken into consideration in the formulation of the code, including:

—The extent to which host state legislation and regulations may discriminate, either in favor of or against TNCs as compared to domestic enterprises, in the treatment of enterprises on the basis of whether such enterprises are under foreign control;

—The extent to which expropriation of properties undertaken for public purposes related to internal requirements of the countries concerned are nondiscriminatory in application and are accompanied by prompt, adequate, and effective compensation; and

—The role played by TNCs and governments in the transfer of technology to host states, including the type of technology involved and the conditions that may be imposed by TNCs and governments.[30]

Negotiation Problems. It was decided early in the deliberations that the code would consist of six chapters: (1) Preamble and Objectives; (2) Definitions; (3) Major Principles and/or Issues Related to the Activities of Transnational Corporations; (4) Principles and/or Issues Relating to the Treatment of Transnational Corporations; (5) Legal Nature and Scope of the Code; and (6) Implementation. To overcome the differences in positions, the group turned its attention first to Chapters 1, 3, and 4, whose subject matters contained more common elements and appeared to have greater prospects for compromises than Chapter 2 and, especially, Chapter 5, where the gap between opposing positions was very wide.

The basic method of operation in the group's deliberations was to set forth the principle or issues involved with respect to each item for the code, identify the elements in which agreement existed, list other points raised by some group members, and add commentaries of a legal or organizational nature, concerning, for example, whether a particular code provision should be in one or another chapter. The discussion was initially postponed on issues that had been dealt with in other forums, such as transfer of technology (UNCTAD), employment and labor (ILO), and corrupt practices (ad hoc working group). Without doubt, this approach, although slow, was systematic, useful, and effective.

The first major attempt at producing an annotated code elaborated by the Commission staff was published in January 1978. It showed an initial, although modest, convergence of viewpoints between the developed and developing countries.

A further significant step was taken by the working group at its September 1978 meeting, when it authorized its chairman to draft formulations for a future code that would attempt to consolidate the discussions to date. These formulations were a tremendous step forward toward agreement on the actual articles. However, it should be noted that the formulations did not commit the delegations in any way. Since the legal nature of the code had not been agreed on and, therefore, specific commands to the parties involved would have been inappropriate, the word *should* instead of *shall* was used throughout the formulations. This suggested that the formulations were primarily a basis for deliberations rather than a definitive draft for a code.

After seventeen sessions of the working group, each lasting a minimum of two weeks, considerable progress had been made by early 1982 in narrowing the conceptual, legal, and factional gaps between the Western developed states and the Group of 77. On restrictive business practices, a separate agreement was reached within UNCTAD in 1980, and on employment and labor issues a tripartite declaration that was acceptable to all parties was formulated within the framework of the ILO. However, in some issue areas, agreement remained very difficult and quite elusive.

With respect to jurisdiction and sovereignty, including the concept of permanent sovereignty over natural resources, the Group of 77 delegates had taken a hard stand. Moreover, they have displayed a high level of solidarity on all issues, despite the fact that their interests have begun to diverge. The reason is that such states as Mexico, Brazil, and Singapore have reached a more advanced level of economic development and sophistication than many of the very poor states in Africa and Central America.

If the code were adopted in the form of a multilateral treaty, it would entail ratification by each UN member state according to that state's constitutional system, which could be a long process. The provisions of the code addressed to TNCs and their subsidiaries would most likely be incorporated into the national legal systems of those states adhering to the multilateral treaty. The provisions, therefore, could be enforced in the national courts. For situations in which the codes are embodied in international instruments other than a treaty (for example, a declaration passed by the General Assembly), enforcement would be through appeals to fairness and justice as well as sanctions such as unfavorable public opinion (black lists), or some other type of adverse measures by other states or even TNCs. Consultation mechanisms among governments, conducted within the UN framework, may also be useful to ensure adherence to the code.

The code of conduct exercise has shown that there are some common interests between TNCs and host states, despite their many differences, especially the fact that one represents the Western industrialized states and the other consists primarily of developing states. It is also necessary to point out that in the period since the CTC was created, many developing states have themselves become major industrialized states in their own right, thus blurring somewhat the original distinctions between negotiating parties. In addition, with the creation of free-trade zones, or areas, the movement of factories to the labor force is accelerating: a major issue, for example, for the NAFTA as well as the EC. Nonetheless, it is not inconceivable that those articles of the code where agreement has been possible may constitute a basis for the rules of an incipient regime.

SUMMARY AND CONCLUSIONS

Several commonalities and differences can be noted in the international regimes discussed in this chapter. All have an organizational framework for task performance, but the specificity of functions assigned to the various organs and their size varies considerably. Indeed, only the seabed regime has specifically designed organs, and all rules and procedures are carefully delineated. In the EMS regime, the main IGO organ used for task performance has many other functions that, in the overall context of the EC, are more important than the EMS management task. Only the EMCF (later replaced by the EMF) is especially designed to support the EMS. Similarly, the national organs—the central banks and financial institutions—are borrowed from the EMS task performance. Nonetheless, the rules and procedures for the EMS seem to be quite clear.

As for the international trade regime, GATT plays a central managerial role, and its principles, rules, and procedures are at the heart of the regime. Although successful at first, doubts have been voiced about progress in the future as strong tendencies toward protectionism are visible within important regime member states. Nonetheless, new efforts to reinvigorate the bases of the regime may be succeeding depending on the outcome of the Uruguay Round of negotiations instituted in 1986.

The main institution in the NPT regime, the IAEA (although it is not specifically designed for the regime, and, in fact, is related to the UN structure) expends many of its resources on task performance, that is, inspection and verification activities. INFCE plays mainly a supporting role.

The regime rules are clear; however, since the regime activities are deeply involved in high-stakes international politics and can affect critically the vital interests of the participating states, pressure may develop for modifications in the regime to accommodate the national aspirations of middle powers close to the nuclear-weapon threshold. The linking of nuclear weapons, ballistic missiles, and plutonium and waste disposal with chemical and biological weaponry is producing strengthened regime patterns. In addition, with the end of the Cold War, even conventional arms control efforts, as reflected in the CFE arrangements as well as more general efforts at grappling with massive arms concentrations and transfers, are embracing regime principles.

The prospective TNC code of conduct regime also will need to borrow heavily from the existing UN structure for its task performance, although regional IGOs and some INGOs, such as the International Chamber of Commerce, can aid in its complex management. This means that, at present, only the CTC possesses special capabilities to perform the regime tasks, and its activities have now been incorporated within the Secretariat; other institutions will have to acquire full familiarity and expertise with the code of conduct before the overall management can become truly effective. If agreement on the code of conduct is reached, the rules will be explicit, though subject to legal and administrative interpretation. Considering the vast field that the operation of the world's TNCs constitutes, this could cause a bottleneck in any attempts to limit TNC activities. Pressures for future rule changes will be exerted and, depending on the political and economic power of the units desiring such changes, the rules are likely to be modified.

The preceding discussion highlights the usefulness of the regime concept as an important construct for both defining and managing the attainment of objectives in the international arena by governmental and nongovernmental actors. At the same time, it also makes understandable the search for new conceptualizations in the international regime area pursued by many international relations scholars and reflected in the scholarly literature.

Although regime theory has continued to arouse interest, as the international system configures and reconfigures in the wake of the Cold War, another theoretical approach to understanding the way that IGOs interact with states and with INGOs is attracting attention. This approach is somewhat loosely termed *multilateralism*. Economic activities, at least as far as Europe is concerned, have tended to adopt the theoretical formulation known as functionalism (as discussed in Chapter 2). Functionalism contemplated—if not measured—the extent of the transference of specified activities (i.e., sectoral) from the national to the supranational levels. Regimes clearly can play a part in this process.

We think it is fair to say that as long as the two superpowers preferred to pursue their respective security policies ("high politics") with an almost obsessive focus on each other, any serious contemplation that military power would be transferred during the Cold War by either superpower, within their respective alliance systems, from national control to multilateral (or multinational) control was unlikely. Suggestions that this might have been possible, as, for example, over the possession and use of nuclear weapons, inevitably foundered on grounds of national interest. The provisions of the North Atlantic Treaty made it explicit that a "national recourse" was always an option for a state to "opt out" of NATO crisis activity if the state viewed participation as not in its national interest. The same has been true for UN peacekeeping/peacemaking.

Nonetheless, it should also be pointed out that any alliance relationship—i.e. multilateralism—affects notions of the member-states' interests that over time might weaken nationalistic tendencies toward unilateralism. NATO is still searching for a function that transcends simply calculations of respective national interests. The June 1993 meeting of the NATO foreign ministers in Athens, where the European allies agreed to join the U.S. in providing air cover for UN peacekeepers in Bosnia, provides an inter-IGO role for NATO

It is, nonetheless, not implausible to contemplate that the formation of security regimes in the post-Cold War period could be a reflection of a tendency toward multilateralism which originated during the Cold War. Each of the incipient or functioning regimes discussed in this chapter presumably also possesses this potential. (This is also discussed in Chapter 3.) What makes the multilateralism approach relevant today is that it is being viewed as leading, in and of itself, to the further institutionalization of the international system.[31]

NOTES

1. Robert O. Keohane, *After Hegemony: Cooperation and Discord in the World Political Economy* (Princeton, NJ: Princeton University Press, 1984), p. 63.

2. The typology of regime origins in these paragraphs follows Oran Young, "International Regimes: Problems of Concept Formation," *World Politics* 32 (April 1980): 349–51.

3. See NATO Press Release (93)6, "NATO Seminar with Partner Countries on Cooperation in CFE Treaty Implementation," January 22, 1993. Approximately 450 inspections were conducted during the Treaty's baseline validation period of July-November 1992.

4. Robert O. Keohane and Joseph S. Nye, *Power and Interdependence. World Politics in Transition* (Boston: Little Brown, 1977), p. 55.

5. Young, "International Regimes," p. 343.

6. Ibid., p. 344.

7. Regimes would perhaps benefit from direct taxing authority. In addition to the proposals for revenue sharing in the proposed Law-of-the-Sea (LOS) Treaty,

see Eleanor B. Steinberg and Joseph A. Yager, *New Means of Financing International Needs* (Washington, DC: Brookings Institution, 1978).

8. Young, "International Regimes," pp. 346–47.

9. Ibid., p. 351.

10. "Resolution of the Council and of the Representatives of the Governments of the Member States of 21 March 1972 on the Application of the Resolution of 22 March 1971 on the Attainment of Stages of Economic and Monetary Union in the Community" (OJ No. C 38/3 of 18.4.1972) in *Compendium,* pp. 33–34.

11. Gunter Wittich and Masake Shiratori, "The Snake in the Tunnel," *Finance and Development* 10 (June 1973), pp. 10–12; see also Ranier Hellman, *Gold, the Dollar, and the European Community: The Seven Year Monetary War* (New York: Praeger, 1979), pp. 24–26.

12. Joanne Salop, "Dollar Intervention Within the Snake," *IMF Staff Papers* 24 (1977), pp. 64, 76.

13. Hellman, *Gold,* pp. 26–29; Loukas Tsoukalis, "Is the Relaunching of Economic and Monetary Union a Feasible Proposal?" *Journal of Common Market Studies* 15 (June 1977): 26–29.

14. Hellman, *Gold,* pp. 44–45.

15. EC *Bulletin* (6–1978), pt. 1.5.2.

16. EC *Bulletin* (12–1978), pt. 1.1.3.

17. Geoffrey Denton, "European Monetary Co-operation: The Bremen Proposals," *World Today* 34 (1978): 445. See also Lawrence Ingrassia and Peter Gumbel, "Changing the Rules: Europe's Money Moves May Pave the Way to Rise in the Global Economy," *The Wall Street Journal,* August 3, 1993, p. 1.

18. This view is already evident since the EC *Bulletin,* besides quoting exchange rates for member state currencies, also quotes exchange rates for the ECU with other major currencies.

19. For details, see the *New York Times,* January 18, 1987.

20. Delegations of the Commission of the EC, *A Letter from Europe,* no. 35 (September 24, 1986).

21. See Robert Keohane, *After Hegemony: Cooperation and Discord in the World Political Economy* (Princeton, NJ: Princeton University Press, 1984), p. 189.

22. Keith Bradsher, "As Global Talks Stall, Regional Trade Pacts Multiply," *New York Times,* August 23, 1992, p. 5.

23. Information presented in this section is drawn from U.S. Department of State, *Fact Sheet: Nuclear Non-Proliferation Treaty* (Washington, DC: Bureau of Public Affairs, July 11, 1991).

24. For a detailed discussion of the problems, see "Nuclear Proliferation: Breaking the Chain," special issue, George H. Quester, ed., *International Organization* 35 (no. 1, Winter 1981). IAEA is an autonomous IGO with its own governing body, but it provides the General Assembly with annual reports and carries out special duties at the direction of the Security Council. IAEA has furthered research in, and development of, nonmilitary uses of nuclear technology. It has also worked to establish safeguards against the illegal use of nuclear materials and to establish and uphold health and safety standards in industries and installations employing such materials. See Julie Jones, "Big Job for Little-Known Atomic Agency," *Interdependent,* August–September 1991, p. 3. For Iraq, the UN Special Commission was created to oversee the elimination of weapons of mass destruction, working with other UN agencies

and various conferences. The Commission was assigned its duties in Security Council Resolution 687 of April 3, 1991.

25. Ibid., pp. 605–10.

26. This is drawn from U.S. Arms Control and Disarmament Agency, "Fact Sheet: The Missile Technology Control Regime (MTCR)," December 20, 1991.

27. U.S. Arms Control and Disarmament Agency, "Fact Sheet: Fact Sheet on Chemical Weapons Initiative," May 13, 1991. There is also the "Australia Group," which was formed in 1984 as a result of chemical weapons (CW) use in the Iran-Iraq War. The members meet twice a year in Paris, in an informal capacity with no charter or constitution. The group has established common export controls for chemical and biological weapons nonproliferation purposes, and it periodically issues warnings concerning chemical-biological warfare (CBW) proliferation. There is also the review conference procedures of the Convention on the Prohibition of the Development, Production and Stockpiling of Bacteriological (Biological) and Toxic Weapons and on their Destruction (BWC), which was signed in 1972 and entered into force on March 26, 1975.

28. Joseph S. Nye, "Maintaining a Nonproliferation Regime," *International Organization* 35 (Winter 1981): 15–38. Related to these incipient or actual CBW and nuclear weapons regimes is the UN's effort to obtain "transparency" in conventional armaments. Given the increasing level of ethnic and related conflicts occurring as an aftermath of the end of the Cold War and the dissolution of the Soviet Union, the following UN General Assembly Resolution is only too apropos:

> The General Assembly[,] . . . *Recognizing* the importance of the prevention of the proliferation of nuclear weapons and other weapons of mass destruction. 1. *Recognizes* that an increased level of openness and transparency in the field of armaments would enhance confidence, promote stability, help States to exercise restraint, ease tensions and strengthen regional and international peace and security; [and] . . . *Requests* the Secretary-General to establish and maintain at United Nations Headquarters in New York a universal and non-discriminatory Register of Conventional Arms, to include data on international arms transfers as well as information provided by Member States on military holdings, procurement through national production and relevant policies. (UNGA Doc. A/C.1/46/L.18/Rev. 1 as amended, November 13, 1991)

29. For details, see Werner J. Feld, *Multinational Corporations and U.N. Politics* (New York: Pergamon Press, 1980), pp. 35–48.

30. Ibid., pp. 60–64.

31. Abstract to the article by Steve Weber, "Shaping the Postwar Balance of Power: Multilateralism in NATO," *International Organization* 46 (symposium issue on multilateralism) (Summer 1992). See also Pierre Hassner, "Beyond Nationalism and Internationalism," *Survival* 35, no. 2 (Summer 1993): pp. 49–65.

8 THE QUALITY OF IGO TASK PERFORMANCE: PAST, PRESENT, AND FUTURE

It seems self-evident that the quality of an IGO's task performance determines its success or failure in terms of the expectations that the founding fathers of the organization had in mind and that led to its establishment in the first place. It is also obvious that the circumstances, both national and international, that prevailed at the time when the creation of the IGO was considered are likely to change with time. Tremendous changes have taken place in the political, economic, and physical environment of the world arena since the end of World War II, and these changes are reflected in relations within and among the states of the world. The move from the bipolar to the multipolar world, of which the United States is the only remaining global military power, is only the latest example. No wonder, then, that the turbulence of these post-Cold War changes has also affected IGOs and their task performance, and, indeed, has produced new conditions (sometimes better and sometimes worse) for the activities and effectiveness of INGOs as well, in the pursuit of their particular interests.

The initial enthusiasm associated with the creation of practically every IGO starts to diminish within a relatively short time and, with this development, its task performance begins to suffer. In many cases, this initial enthusiasm was fed by ideological fervor. In the case of the United Nations, it was originally the vision of a world without devastating war; then the ideal was self-government for colonial peoples and territories accompanied by economic and social improvement and the reform of international trade and commerce, followed in the late 1970s by concern over human rights. During the Cold War, looming over everything was the specter of devastating nuclear war. Nonetheless, the prospects of a world community, and perhaps eventually a world government evolving through the United Nations, captivated large numbers of people the world over.

Similarly, it was an integrated Western Europe, centered around Franco-German cooperation and avoiding the recurring hostilities of the past, that had captivated the people in that region and had made them strive during the Cold War for a "United States of Europe." It was in this climate of opinion that the ECSC was born, although, as noted earlier, other and narrower short-range motivations also played a role. These motivations had their origins in the various foreign policy considerations of the prospective member states, including indirect control over a Germany that might seek revenge for its defeat and dismemberment. Finally, various sources of ideological support, couched in economic terms and stimulated by ECLA, formed the genesis of LAFTA and the CACM and may lead eventually to *Mercosur* (discussed in Chapter 4), which could encompass all of Latin America in a common market, to complement a possible North American Free Trade Area (NAFTA).

Foreign policy goals were also on the minds of the statesmen who laid the groundwork for the United Nations. This new IGO was clearly seen as a potential instrument of national policy; indeed, national interests have played a significant part in the creation of *all* IGOs. It is largely for this reason that task performance begins to lag in almost all IGOs as well, including certain security-oriented organizations, except perhaps those IGOs whose major functions were primarily technical (e.g., the UPU or ICAO). In fact, security IGOs have not performed well; the demise of SEATO and the Central Treaty Organization (CENTO) makes this clear, and the OAU and OAS have had their share of problems. However, it appears that the more technical the nature of IGOs, the greater is the likelihood that their task performance will remain adequate and, moreover, that they will successfully adapt themselves to changing conditions. ICAO, UNHCR, UNICEF, and IAEA appear to be prime examples in support of this assertion.

What are the major reasons for the stagnation, or lag in task performance, of IGOs that have mainly economic and/or political objectives?

One important cause for the uneven quality of IGO task performance is essentially political. States that looked to IGOs to shore up or supplement their national capabilities and resources militarily, economically, or politically tend to become apprehensive about the gradual loss or dilution of their national prerogatives that membership in these organizations required. The French withdrawal from the NATO military structure and the Spanish conditional participation in NATO are examples, as is the reluctance of Britain and Denmark to embrace full monetary union in the EC. Especially during periods of economic stress, governments prefer national over multinational solutions for economic problems with serious political implications for the governmental leadership. National solutions are sought in spite of the fact that, from purely national points of view, common IGO-administered policies might be not only desirable, but also essential.

In the developing countries, the leaders of the newly independent states usually have been faced with the enormous effort of nation building, so they have tended to employ short-term self-serving or self-enriching stopgap measures whereby they can reap immediate benefits for themselves or their own states, rather than longer-range solutions that might be found through IGOs and that will benefit all states in a region. The difficulty that ECOWAS has experienced in peacekeeping in Liberia is an example; the failure of the East African Community is another example of how short-term national prerogatives overcame the prospective advantages of long-term multilateral benefits. This is one of the reasons why the task performance of regional IGOs, up to now, rarely has been consistently successful. The difficulty the EC has experienced in the early 1990s in transforming itself from a customs union to a complete economic, monetary and political union, is the best example available. The redistribution of costs and benefits from the wealthier (i.e., northern) to the poorer (i.e., southern) member states—and to regions within them—has created great stress at times to the EC, as has the issue of farm subsidies.

Another cause for lagging task performance, which is also political in nature, is disappointment of IGO member governments that the hoped-for utilization of the IGO structure for the promotion of their foreign policy goals either did not materialize or became increasingly difficult and frustrating. The latter is one reason for the disenchantment of the United States with the United Nations during the Cold War, and this has had, overall, a negative impact on UN task performance, although some budgetary reforms have been launched and Washington's attitudes have become much more positive, albeit skeptical, in the 1990s. The U.S. attitude toward the ILO and UNESCO and the Group of 77's attitude toward GATT can also be mentioned. The use of the veto by the Permanent Members of the Security Council (and not just the United States and the USSR) contributed during the Cold War to a decline in the effectiveness of the UN's peacekeeping and peacemaking efforts, including the prestige of the secretary-general.

A third cause for undermining, and perhaps completely destroying, the task performance of an IGO is the perception of member governments and the people in the member states that the distributions of benefits received through the IGO and the costs incurred are inequitable. In most cases, the member governments rebel against paying these costs and, as a consequence, regional IGOs such as LAFTA, the CACM, and other IGOs in the developing countries have not been successful. The issue of disparity of benefits and costs among the member states (as pointed out earlier) was a major reason for the collapse of the East African Community. It remains to be seen if the conflict in the former Yugoslavia and the efforts at peacebuilding in Somalia and Cambodia will bring about a reassessment of the costs and benefits of multinational intervention. The dangers in intervening to force a cessation of hostilities in civil ethnic conflict appear, however, to be perceived worth the risk when weighed against the humanitarian costs. The example of the U.S.-led multinational interventions in the Persian Gulf against Iraq dramatically, if perhaps temporarily, transformed the perceived effectiveness of the United Nations as an instrument, not only of peacekeeping, but also of peacemaking. Furthermore, as inauspicious as it may seem, the United Nations is continuing efforts at peacebuilding in El Salvador, Nicaragua, Angola, Cambodia, Afghanistan, Somalia, Mozambique, and, perhaps in the not-too-distant future, Zaire.

Obviously, cost-benefit calculations by member governments have a bearing on IGOs in economically developed areas as well. The early evolution of the European Regional Development Fund (ERDF) illustrates this problem in the EC. Increasing national economic egotism has tended to exacerbate this issue. It should be noted, however, that economic IGOs are not the only ones to suffer from perceptions of unfavorable cost-benefit calculations by member states. Security and political IGOs may also be regarded as imposing too heavy a burden on particular member states. The WTO is a case in point: the burdens of a nuclear arms race, coupled with maintaining large standing armies, became, by the late 1980s, intolerable for the Soviet Union.

A fourth cause harming IGO task performance may be an increasing trend toward resorting to "intergovernmentalism" which, in effect, bypasses the IGO decision-making process as laid out in the constituent treaties. Under such circumstances, cooperative activities between member states are carried out and results achieved through national channels rather than through the IGO machinery. European Political Cooperation (EPC) is an excellent example of such intergovernmentalism among the EC states, but this attitude has invaded other issue areas for which the EC institutions were to be primarily responsible and has adversely affected task performance. In NATO, the Franco-German military cooperation is an example that created pressure from Britain in particular to link this cooperation to NATO planning. U.S. unilaterial actions in Somalia and Haiti could come to reflect actions leading to intergovernmentalism rather than multiculturalism.

Intergovernmentalism is a problem not only for the EC, but also for any IGO except, perhaps, organizations exclusively dealing with technical matters. It tends to undermine the morale of IGO international civil servants, who see competing organizational arrangements blunting their own organizational arrangements and bureaucratic goals. All this is aggravated by frequently unfavorable perceptions of international bureaucracies which are prevalent, not only among national civil servants who work with IGO officials, but also among the public, especially in the advanced industrial member states.

Finally, the task performance of IGOs may be adversely affected by a waning enthusiasm for political and economic world organization in general. In the minds of most people, the nation-state remains the focus of their loyalty and support; it retains the highest level of legitimacy, and nationalism (patriotism) persists as a virtue, both morally and instrumentally. Even though, with the end of the Cold War, more parochial sentiments have reasserted themselves which threaten to undermine the territorial and, in particular, multi-ethnic integrity of the national state, nonetheless, the state still remains the cornerstone (or building block) of the evolving international system. It may be, as well, that the increased formations of regimes and other types of interstate interactions (such as those suggested by the term *multilateralism*) will create new types of international institutions.

Furthermore, the proliferation of INGOs, in support of economic, social, and humanitarian endeavors, widens even further the definition of IGO activities. Their involvement in post-Cold War humanitarian activities alongside IGOs and multinational military forces posits the evolution of new methods of dealing with what are perceived as global—or transcendent—issue areas. Environmental problems, refugees, health issues, human rights, arms transfers, drug trafficking, terrorism (whether state-sponsored or not), and "ethnic cleansing" are examples.

What, therefore, does the future hold for IGO task performance? There is no clear indication that the factors and trends outlined in the preceding pages are likely to change radically, although the data for 1991–1992 show a decline of total numbers of IGOs compared with 1980. Regional IGOs, whose numbers are increasing (as discussed in this text), are not immune to the problems besetting all IGOs. Moreover, whether there will be a further dramatic proliferation of specialized agencies or other universal or regional IGOs in the UN family is difficult to predict. Certainly the United States and other industrial states will very likely continue to oppose further bureaucratic/institutional proliferation. Instead, new functions will likely be assigned to existing units, as the provisions for the implementation of the resolutions (or "plan of action") of recent UN conferences reveals. The strengthening of IAEA's "intrusive" authority in monitoring UN Security Council resolutions is another example. On the other hand, international regimes may well continue to be formed as needs arise to fulfill specific limited goals through cooperative ventures by states with the participation of transnational corporations and other INGOs. INGOs will thus continue to play their useful roles, and in participating actively in peacekeeping/humanitarian activities, they will become more involved in post-Cold War high politics. They will also continue to pressure for more formal access to the political deliberative bodies of those IGOs that are concerned with their interests and goals. Networking among IGOs and INGOs will help to further both roles.

In our view, this somewhat uneven balance between pessimism and optimism is realistic, as far as the world community is concerned. While there may be more cooperation than conflict among international and transnational actors and worldwide conflagration may thereby be avoided, the international arena will continue to be characterized by the pursuit of national interests and national egoisms, alongside ethnic and religious particularism, and the common interests of humankind are likely to be compromised as a result. Not to be discounted, however, are countervailing "globalist" forces that are building up and that cut across particularisms of all sorts, perhaps finding their analytical expression in multinationalism. In such a scenario, IGOs, working at times with and through INGOs, can play a "genteelizing" role by fulfilling human needs and aspirations wherever they are allowed to do so.

Finally, not to be neglected is the power of the media to create a sense of global concern at all levels of the international system, thus bringing an awareness to publics everywhere that did not exist prior to this period in time. Whether this enhanced awareness will change human values and human behavior cannot be foretold.

APPENDIX A

MEMBERSHIP OF THE UN AND ITS SPECIALIZED AND RELATED AGENCIES

MEMBERSHIP OF THE UNITED NATIONS AND ITS SPECIALIZED AND RELATED AGENCIES

ORGANIZATION[a]	UN[b]	FAO	GATT	IAEA	IBRD	ICAO	IDA	IFAD	IFC	ILO	IMF	IMO	ITU	UNESCO	UNIDO	UPU	WHO	WIPO	WMO
Members[c]	179	161[d]	104[e]	114[f]	172[g]	171[h]	146[i]	147[j]	148[k]	157[l]	173[m]	137[n]	167[o]	171[p]	158[q]	176[r]	179[s]	127[t]	160[u]
COUNTRIES																			
Afghanistan	1946	x		x	x	x	x	3	x	x	x		x	x	x	x	x		x
Albania	1955	x		x	x	x	x	3	x		x		x	x	x	x	x	x	x
Algeria	1962	x	(e)	x	x	x	x	2	x	x	x	x	x	x	x	x	x	x	x
Angola	1976	x	(e)		x	x	x	3	x	x	x	x	x	x	x	x	x	x	x
Antigua and Barbuda	1981	x	x		x	x		3	x	x	x	x	x	x			x		x
Argentina	1945	x	x	x	x	x	x	3	x	x	x	x	x	x	x	x	x	x	x
Armenia	1992				x	x					x			x	x	x	x		
Australia	1945	x	x	x	x	x	x	1	x	x	x	x	x	x	x	x	x	x	x
Austria	1955	x	x	x	x	x	x	1	x	x	x	x	x	x	x	x	x	x	x
Azerbaijan	1992				x					x	x		x	x					
Bahamas	1973	x	(e)		x	x			x	x	x	x	x	x	x	x	x	x	x
Bahrain	1971	x	(e)		x	x				x	x	x	x	x	x	x	x		x
Bangladesh	1974	x	x	x	x	x	x	3	x	x	x	x	x	x	x	x	x	x	x
Barbados	1966	x	x		x	x		3	x	x	x	x	x	x	x	x	x	x	x
Belarus	1945			x	x					x	x		x	x	x	x	x	x	x
Belgium	1945	x	x	x	x	x	x	1	x	x	x	x	x	x	x	x	x	x	x
Belize	1981	x	x		x	x	x	3	x	x	x	x	x	x	x	x	x		x
Benin	1960	x	x		x	x	x	3	x	x	x	x	x	x	x	x	x	x	x
Bhutan	1971	x			x	x	x	3			x		x	x	x	x	x		
Bolivia	1945	x	x	x	x	x	x	3	x	x	x	x	x	x	x	x	x		

ORGANIZATION	UN	FAO	GATT	IAEA	IBRD	ICAO	IDA	IFAD	IFC	ILO	IMF	IMO	ITU	UNESCO	UNIDO	UPU	WHO	WIPO	WMO
COUNTRIES (cont.)																			
Bosnia and Herzegovina	1992																x		
Botswana	1966	x	x		x	x	x	3	x	x	x		x	x	x	x	x		x
Brazil	1945	x	x	x	x	x	x	3	x	x	x	x	x	x	x	x	x	x	x
Brunei	1984	x	(*e*)			x						x	x			x	x		x
Bulgaria	1955	x		x	x	x			x	x	x	x	x	x	x	x	x	x	x
Burkina Faso	1960	x	x		x	x	x	3	x	x	x		x	x	x	x	x	x	x
Burundi	1962	x	x		x	x	x	3	x	x	x		x	x	x	x	x	x	x
Cambodia	1955	x	(*e*)	x	x	x	x	3		x	x	x	x	x		x	x		x
Cameroon	1960	x	x	x	x	x	x	3	x	x	x	x	x	x	x	x	x	x	x
Canada	1945	x	x	x	x	x	x	1	x	x	x	x	x	x	x	x	x	x	x
Cape Verde Islands	1975	x	(*e*)		x	x	x	3	x	x	x	x	x	x	x	x	x		x
Central African Republic	1960	x	x		x	x	x	3	x	x	x		x	x	x	x	x	x	x
Chad	1960	x	x		x	x	x	3		x	x		x	x	x	x	x	x	x
Chile	1945	x	x	x	x	x	x	3	x	x	x	x	x	x	x	x	x	x	x
China	1945	x		x	x	x	x	3	x	x	x	x	x	x	x	x	x	x	x
Colombia	1945	x	x	x	x	x	x	3	x	x	x	x	x	x	x	x	x	x	x
Comoro Islands	1975	x			x	x	x	3	x	x	x		x	x	x	x	x		x
Congo	1960	x	x		x	x	x	3	x	x	x	x	x	x	x	x	x	x	x
Costa Rica	1945	x	x	x	x	x	x	3	x	x	x	x	x	x	x	x	x	x	x
Côte d'Ivoire	1960	x	x	x	x	x	x	3	x	x	x	x	x	x	x	x	x	x	x
Croatia	1992					x						x		x	x	x	x		
Cuba	1945	x	x	x		x		3		x		x	x	x	x	x	x	x	x
Cyprus	1960	x	x	x	x	x	x	3	x	x	x	x	x	x	x	x	x	x	x
Czechoslovakia	1945	x	x	x	x	x	x		x	x	x	x	x	x	x	x	x	x	x
Denmark	1945	x	x	x	x	x	x	1	x	x	x	x	x	x	x	x	x	x	x
Djibouti	1977	x			x	x	x	3	x	x	x	x	x	x	x	x	x		x
Dominica	1978	x	(*e*)		x		x	3	x	x	x	x		x	x	x	x		x
Dominican Republic	1945	x	x	x	x	x	x	3	x	x	x	x	x	x	x	x	x		x
Ecuador	1945	x		x	x	x	x	3	x	x	x	x	x	x	x	x	x	x	x
Egypt	1945	x	x	x	x	x	x	3	x	x	x	x	x	x	x	x	x	x	x

El Salvador	1945	x	x	x	x	x	x	3	x	x	x	x	x	x	x	x	x	x	x
Equatorial Guinea	1968	x	(*e*)		x	x	x	3	x	x	x	x	x	x	x	x	x		
Estonia	1991	x		x	x	x				x	x	x		x		x			
Ethiopia	1945	x		x	x	x	x	3	x	x	x	x	x	x	x	x	x		x
Fiji	1970	x	(*e*)		x	x	x	3	x	x	x	x	x	x	x	x	x	x	x
Finland	1955	x	x	x	x	x	x	1	x	x	x	x	x	x	x	x	x	x	x
France	1945	x	x	x	x	x	x	1	x	x	x	x	x	x	x	x	x	x	x
Gabon	1960	x	x	x	x	x	x	2	x	x	x	x	x	x	x	x	x	x	x
Gambia	1965	x	x		x	x	x	3	x		x	x	x	x	x	x	x	x	x
Georgia	1992				x						x			x			x		
Germany[v]	1973	x	x	x	x	x	x	1	x	x	x	x	x	x	x	x	x	x	x
Ghana	1957	x	x	x	x	x	x	3	x	x	x	x	x	x	x	x	x	x	x
Greece	1945	x	x	x	x	x	x	1	x	x	x	x	x	x	x	x	x	x	x
Grenada	1974	x	(*e*)		x	x	x	3	x	x	x		x	x	x	x	x		
Guatemala	1945	x	x	x	x	x	x	3	x	x	x	x	x	x	x	x	x	x	x
Guinea	1958	x			x	x	x	3	x	x	x	x	x	x	x	x	x	x	x
Guinea-Bissau	1974	x	(*e*)		x	x	x	3	x	x	x	x	x	x	x	x	x	x	x
Guyana	1966	x	x		x	x	x	3	x	x	x	x	x	x	x	x	x		x
Haiti	1945	x	x	x	x	x	x	3	x	x	x	x	x	x	x	x	x	x	x
Honduras	1945	x			x	x	x	3	x	x	x	x	x	x	x	x	x	x	x
Hungary	1955	x	x	x	x	x	x		x	x	x	x	x	x	x	x	x	x	x
Iceland	1946	x	x	x	x	x	x		x	x	x	x	x	x		x	x	x	x
India	1945	x	x	x	x	x	x	3	x	x	x	x	x	x	x	x	x	x	x
Indonesia	1950	x	x	x	x	x	x	2	x	x	x	x	x	x	x	x	x	x	x
Iran	1945	x		x	x	x	x	2	x	x	x	x	x	x	x	x	x		x
Iraq	1945	x		x	x	x	x	2	x	x	x	x	x	x	x	x	x	x	x
Ireland	1955	x	x	x	x	x	x	1	x	x	x	x	x	x	x	x	x	x	x
Israel	1949	x	x	x	x	x	x	3	x	x	x	x	x	x	x	x	x	x	x
Italy	1955	x	x	x	x	x	x	1	x	x	x	x	x	x	x	x	x	x	x
Jamaica	1962	x	x	x	x	x		3	x	x	x	x	x	x	x	x	x	x	x
Japan	1956	x	x	x	x	x	x	1	x	x	x	x	x	x	x	x	x	x	x
Jordan	1955	x		x	x	x	x	3	x	x	x	x	x	x	x	x	x	x	x
Kazakhstan	1992				x		x				x			x		x			

ORGANIZATION	UN	FAO	GATT	IAEA	IBRD	ICAO	IDA	IFAD	IFC	ILO	IMF	IMO	ITU	UNESCO	UNIDO	UPU	WHO	WIPO	WMO
COUNTRIES (cont.)																			
Kenya	1963	x	x	x	x	x	x	3	x	x	x	x	x	x	x	x	x	x	x
Democratic People's Republic of Korea	1991	x		x		x		3				x	x	x	x	x	x	x	x
Republic of Korea	1991	x	x	x	x	x	x	3	x	x	x	x	x	x	x	x	x	x	x
Kuwait	1963	x	x	x	x	x	x	2	x	x	x	x	x	x	x	x	x		x
Kyrgyzstan	1992				x		x			x	x			x			x		
Laos	1955	x			x	x	x	3	x	x	x		x	x	x	x	x		x
Latvia	1991	x			x	x	x			x	x		x	x	x	x	x		
Lebanon	1945	x		x	x	x	x	3	x	x	x	x	x	x	x	x	x	x	x
Lesotho	1966	x	x		x	x	x	3	x	x	x		x	x	x	x	x	x	x
Liberia	1945	x		x	x	x	x	3	x	x	x		x	x	x	x	x	x	x
Libya	1955	x		x	x	x	x	2	x	x	x	x	x	x	x	x	x	x	x
Liechtenstein	1990			x									x			x		x	
Lithuania	1991	x			x	x				x	x		x	x		x	x	x	
Luxembourg	1945	x	x	x	x	x	x	1	x	x	x	x	x	x	x	x	x	x	x
Madagascar	1960	x	x	x	x	x	x	3	x	x	x	x	x	x	x	x	x	x	x
Malawi	1964	x	x		x	x	x	3	x	x	x	x	x	x	x	x	x	x	x
Malaysia	1957	x	x	x	x	x	x	3	x	x	x	x	x	x	x	x	x	x	x
Maldives	1965	x	x		x	x	x	3	x		x	x	x	x	x	x	x	x	x
Mali	1960	x	(*e*)	x	x	x	x	3	x	x	x		x	x	x	x	x	x	x
Malta	1964	x	x		x	x		3		x	x	x	x	x	x	x	x	x	x
Marshall Islands	1991				x	x			x		x						x		
Mauritania	1961	x	x		x	x	x	3	x	x	x	x	x	x	x	x	x	x	x
Mauritius	1968	x	x	x	x	x	x	3	x	x	x	x	x	x	x	x	x	x	x
Mexico	1945	x	x	x	x	x	x	3	x	x	x	x	x	x	x	x	x	x	x
Federated States of Micronesia	1991					x											x		
Moldova	1992				x	x				x	x			x			x		
Mongolia	1961	x		x	x	x	x		x	x	x		x	x	x	x	x	x	x

Morocco	1956	x	x	x	x	x	x	3	x	x	x	x	x	x	x	x	x	x	x
Mozambique	1975	x	x		x	x	x	3	x	x	x	x	x	x	x	x	x		x
Myanmar (Burma)	1948	x	x	x	x	x	x	3	x	x	x	x	x	x	x	x	x		x
Namibia	1990	x	(*e*)	x	x	x		3	x	x	x		x	x	x	x	x		x
Nepal	1955	x			x	x	x	3	x	x	x	x	x	x	x	x	x		x
Netherlands	1945	x	x	x	x	x	x	1	x	x	x	x	x	x	x	x	x	x	x
New Zealand	1945	x	x	x	x	x	x	1	x	x	x	x	x	x	x	x	x	x	x
Nicaragua	1945	x	x	x	x	x	x	3	x	x	x	x	x	x	x	x	x	x	x
Niger	1960	x	x	x	x	x	x	3	x	x	x		x	x	x	x	x	x	x
Nigeria	1960	x	x	x	x	x	x	2	x	x	x	x	x	x	x	x	x		x
Norway	1945	x	x	x	x	x	x	1	x	x	x	x	x	x	x	x	x	x	x
Oman	1971	x			x	x	x	3	x		x	x	x	x	x	x	x		x
Pakistan	1947	x	x	x	x	x	x	3	x	x	x	x	x	x	x	x	x	x	x
Panama	1945	x		x	x	x	x	3	x	x	x	x	x	x	x	x	x	x	x
Papua New Guinea	1975	x	(*e*)		x	x	x	3	x	x	x	x	x	x	x	x	x		x
Paraguay	1945	x		x	x	x	x	3	x	x	x		x	x	x	x	x	x	x
Peru	1945	x	x	x	x	x	x	3	x	x	x	x	x	x	x	x	x	x	x
Philippines	1945	x	x	x	x	x	x	3	x	x	x	x	x	x	x	x	x	x	x
Poland	1945	x	x	x	x	x	x		x	x	x	x	x	x	x	x	x	x	x
Portugal	1955	x	x	x	x	x		3	x	x	x	x	x	x	x	x	x	x	x
Qatar	1971	x	(*e*)	x	x	x		2		x	x	x	x	x	x	x	x	x	x
Romania	1955	x	x	x	x	x		3	x	x	x	x	x	x	x	x	x	x	x
Russia[w]	1945			x	x	x	x			x	x	x	x	x	x	x	x	x	x
Rwanda	1962	x	x		x	x	x	3	x	x	x		x	x	x	x	x	x	x
St. Kitts and Nevis	1983	x	(*e*)		x		x	3			x			x	x	x	x		
St. Lucia	1979	x	(*e*)		x	x	x	3	x	x	x	x		x	x	x	x		x
St. Vincent	1980	x	(*e*)		x	x	x	3			x	x	x	x	x	x	x		
San Marino	1992					x				x	x		x	x		x	x		
Sao Tome and Principe	1975	x	(*e*)		x	x	x	3		x	x	x	x	x	x	x	x		x
Saudi Arabia	1945	x		x	x	x	x	2	x	x	x	x	x	x	x	x	x	x	x
Senegal	1960	x	x	x	x	x	x	3	x	x	x	x	x	x	x	x	x	x	x
Seychelles	1976	x	(*e*)		x	x		3	x	x	x	x		x	x	x	x		x
Sierra Leone	1961	x	x	x	x	x	x	3	x	x	x	x	x	x	x	x	x		x
Singapore	1965		x	x	x	x			x	x	x	x	x			x	x	x	x
Slovenia	1992			x		x				x				x	x	x	x		

ORGANIZATION	UN	FAO	GATT	IAEA	IBRD	ICAO	IDA	IFAD	IFC	ILO	IMF	IMO	ITU	UNESCO	UNIDO	UPU	WHO	WIPO	WMO
COUNTRIES (cont.)																			
Solomon Islands	1978	x	(*e*)		x	x	x	3	x	x	x	x	x			x	x		x
Somalia	1960	x			x	x	x	3	x	x	x	x	x	x	x	x	x	x	x
South Africa[y]	1945		x	x	x	x	x		x		x		x				x	x	x
Spain	1955	x	x	x	x	x	x	1	x	x	x	x	x	x	x	x	x	x	x
Sri Lanka	1955	x	x	x	x	x	x	3	x	x	x	x	x	x	x	x	x	x	x
Sudan	1956	x		x	x	x	x	3	x	x	x	x	x	x	x	x	x	x	x
Suriname	1975	x	x		x	x		3		x	x	x	x	x	x	x	x	x	x
Swaziland	1968	x	(*e*)		x	x	x	3	x	x	x		x	x	x	x	x	x	x
Sweden	1946	x	x	x	x	x	x	1	x	x	x	x	x	x	x	x	x	x	x
Syria	1945	x		x	x	x	x	3	x	x	x	x	x	x	x	x	x		x
Tajikistan	1992																x		
Tanzania	1961	x	x	x	x	x	x	3	x	x	x	x	x	x	x	x	x	x	x
Thailand	1946	x	x	x	x	x	x	3	x	x	x	x	x	x	x	x	x	x	x
Togo	1960	x	x		x	x	x	3	x	x	x	x	x	x	x	x	x	x	x
Trinidad and Tobago	1962	x	x		x	x	x	3	x	x	x	x	x	x	x	x	x	x	x
Tunisia	1956	x	x	x	x	x	x	3	x	x	x	x	x	x	x	x	x	x	x
Turkey	1945	x	x	x	x	x	x	3	x	x	x	x	x	x	x	x	x	x	x
Turkmenistan	1992				x						x								
Uganda	1962	x	x	x	x	x	x	3	x	x	x		x	x	x	x	x	x	x
Ukraine	1945			x	x					x	x		x	x	x	x	x	x	x
United Arab Emirates	1971	x	(*e*)	x	x	x	x	2	x	x	x	x	x	x	x	x	x	x	x
United Kingdom	1945	x	x	x	x	x	x	1	x	x	x	x	x		x	x	x	x	x
United States	1945	x	x	x	x	x	x	1	x	x	x	x	x		x	x	x	x	x
Uruguay	1945	x	x	x	x	x		3	x	x	x	x	x	x	x	x	x	x	x
Uzbekistan	1992				x		x				x						x		
Vanuatu	1981	x			x	x	x		x		x	x	x		x	x	x		x
Venezuela	1945	x	x	x	x	x		2	x	x	x	x	x	x	x	x	x	x	x
Vietnam	1977	x		x	x	x	x	3	x	x	x	x	x	x	x	x	x	x	x
Western Samoa	1976	x			x		x	3	x		x		x	x		x	x		
Yemen	1990[z]	x	(*e*)		x	x	x	3	x	x	x	x	x	x	x	x	x	x	x
Yugoslavia	1945	x	x	x	x	x	x	3	x	x	x	x	x	x	x	x	x	x	x
Zaire	1960	x	x	x	x	x	x	3	x	x	x	x	x	x	x	x	x	x	x
Zambia	1964	x	x	x	x	x	x	3	x	x	x		x	x	x	x	x	x	x
Zimbabwe	1980	x	x	x	x	x	x	3	x	x	x		x	x	x	x	x	x	x

[a] The following abbreviations are used: UN – United Nations; FAO – Food and Agriculture Organization; GATT – General Agreement on Tariffs and Trade; IAEA – International Atomic Energy Agency; IBRD – International Bank for Reconstruction and Development; ICAO – International Civil Aviation Organization; IDA – International Development Association; IFAD – International Fund for Agricultural Development; IFC – International Finance Corporation; ILO – International Labour Organisation; IMF – International Monetary Fund; IMO – International Maritime Organization; ITU – International Telecommunication Union; UNESCO – United Nations Educational, Scientific and Cultural Organization; UNIDO – United Nations Industrial Development Organization; UPU – Universal Postal Union; WHO – World Health Organization; WIPO – World Intellectual Property Organization; WMO – World Meterological Organization.

[b] Dates are those of each member's admission to the United Nations.

[c] Totals for all columns beginning with FAO include non-UN members.

[d] The 161 members of FAO include the following not listed in the table: European Community, Switzerland, Tonga. The FAO also has one associate member: Puerto Rico.

[e] The 104 contracting parties to GATT include the following not listed in the table: Hong Kong, Macao, Switzerland. The 25 states marked (*e*) in the table (plus Kiribati, Tonga, and Tuvalu, which are not listed) are territories to which GATT applied before independence and which now as independent states maintain de facto application of the Agreement pending final decisions as to their commercial policies.

[f] The 114 members of IAEA include the following not listed in the table: Holy See (Vatican City State), Monaco, Switzerland.

[g] The 172 members of IBRD include the following not listed in the table: Kiribati, Switzerland, Tonga.

[h] The 171 members of ICAO include the following not listed in the table: Cook Islands, Kiribati, Monaco, Nauru, Switzerland, Tonga.

[i] The 146 members of IDA include the following not listed in the table: Kiribati, Switzerland, Tonga.

[j] The 147 members of IFAD are divided into three categories: (1) developed states, (2) oil-producing states, and (3) developing states. Members include the following not listed in the table: Switzerland (1), Tonga (3).

[k] The 148 members of IFC include the following not listed in the table: Kiribati, Switzerland, Tonga.

[l] The 157 members of ILO include the following not listed in the table: Switzerland.

[m] The 173 members of IMF include the following not listed in the table: Kiribati, Switzerland, Tonga.

[n] The 137 members of IMO include the following not listed in the table: Monaco, Switzerland. The IMO also has two associate members: Hong Kong and Macao.

[o] The 167 members of ITU include the following not listed in the table: Holy See (Vatican City State), Kiribati, Monaco, Nauru, Switzerland, Tonga.

[p] The 171 members of UNESCO include the following not listed in the table: Cook Islands, Kiribati, Monaco, Switzerland, Tonga, Tuvalu. UNESCO also has three associate members: Aruba, British Virgin Islands, Netherlands Antilles.

[q] The 158 members of UNIDO include the following not listed in the table: Switzerland, Tonga.

[r] The 176 members of UPU include the following not listed in the table: Holy See (Vatican City State), Kiribati, Monaco, Nauru, Netherlands Antilles, Overseas Territories of the United Kingdom, Switzerland, Tonga, Tuvalu. South Africa was expelled in 1984.

[s] The 179 members of WHO include the following not listed in the table: Cook Islands, Kiribati, Monaco, Switzerland, Tonga. WHO also has two associate member: Puerto Rico, Tokelau.

[t] The 127 members of WIPO include the following not listed in the table: Holy See (Vatican City State), Monaco, Switzerland.

[u] The 160 members of WMO include the following not listed in the table which maintain their own meteorological services: British Caribbean Territories, French Polynesia, Hong Kong, Netherlands Antilles, New Caledonia, Switzerland. South Africa's membership has been suspended since 1975.

[v] German Democratic Republic and Federal Republic of Germany admitted separately to the UN in 1973; merged as Federal Republic of Germany in 1990.

[w] Russia assumed the seat formerly held by the Union of Soviet Socialist Republics following the USSR's dissolution on December 8, 1991.

[y] In addition to expulsion from the UPU, certain of South Africa's rights of membership in ICAO, IAEA, ITU, UPU, WHO, WIPO, and WMO have been suspended or restricted.

[z] Merger of the two Yemens; the former Yemen Arab Republic joined the UN in 1947 and the former People's Democratic Republic of Yemen in 1967.

Source: Arthur S. Banks, ed., *Political Handbook of the World, 1992*, (Binghamton, NY: CSA Publications, 1992), pp. 1071–1074.

APPENDIX B

CHARTER OF THE UNITED NATIONS

We the Peoples of the United Nations Determined

to save succeeding generations from the scourge of war, which twice in our lifetime has brought untold sorrow to mankind, and

to reaffirm faith in fundamental human rights, in the dignity and worth of the human person, in the equal rights of men and women and of nations large and small, and

to establish conditions under which justice and respect for the obligations arising from treaties and other sources of international law can be maintained, and

to promote social progress and better standards of life in larger freedom,

And for These Ends

to practice tolerance and live together in peace with one another as good neighbors, and

to unite our strength to maintain international peace and security, and

to ensure, by the acceptance of principles and the institution of methods, that armed force shall not be used, save in the common interest, and

to employ international machinery for the promotion of the economic and social advancement of all peoples,

Have Resolved to Combine Our Efforts to Accomplish These Aims.

Accordingly, our respective Governments, through representatives assembled in the city of San Francisco, who have exhibited their full powers found to be in good and due form, have agreed to the present Charter of the United Nations and do hereby establish an international organization to be known as the United Nations.

Chapter I
Purposes and Principles

ARTICLE 1. The Purposes of the United Nations are:

1. To maintain international peace and security, and to that end: to take effective collective measures for the prevention and removal of threats to the peace, and for the suppression of acts of aggression or other breaches of the peace, and to bring about by peaceful means, and in conformity with the principles of justice and international law, adjustment or settlement of international disputes or situations which might lead to a breach of the peace;

2. To develop friendly relations among nations based on respect for the principle of equal rights and self-determination of peoples, and to take other appropriate measures to strengthen universal peace;

3. To achieve international cooperation in solving international problems of an economic, social, cultural, or humanitarian character, and in promoting and encouraging respect for human rights and for fundamental freedoms for all without distinction as to race, sex, language, or religion; and

4. To be a center for harmonizing the actions of nations in the attainment of these common ends.

ARTICLE 2. The Organization and its Members, in pursuit of the Purposes stated in Article 1, shall act in accordance with the following Principles.

1. The Organization is based on the principle of the sovereign equality of all its Members.

2. All Members, in order to ensure to all of them the rights and benefits resulting from membership, shall fulfil in good faith the obligations assumed by them in accordance with the present Charter.

3. All Members shall settle their international disputes by peaceful means in such a manner that international peace and security, and justice, are not endangered.

4. All Members shall refrain in their international relations from the threat or use of force against the territorial integrity or political independence of any state, or in any other manner inconsistent with the Purposes of the United Nations.

5. All Members shall give the United Nations every assistance in any action it takes in accordance with the present Charter, and shall refrain from giving assistance to any state against which the United Nations is taking preventive or enforcement action.

6. The Organization shall ensure that states which are not Members of the United Nations act in accordance with these Principles so far as may be necessary for the maintenance of international peace and security.

7. Nothing contained in the present Charter shall authorize the United Nations to intervene in matters which are essentially within the domestic jurisdiction of any state or shall require the Members to submit such matters to settlement under the present Charter; but this principle shall not prejudice the application of enforcement measures under Chapter VII.

Chapter II
Membership

ARTICLE 3. The original Members of the United Nations shall be the states which, having participated in the United Nations Conference on International Organization at San Francisco, or having previously signed the Declaration by United Nations of January 1, 1942, sign the present Charter and ratify it in accordance with Article 110.

ARTICLE 4. 1. Membership in the United Nations is open to all other peace-loving states which accept the obligations contained in the present Charter and, in the judgment of the Organization, are able and willing to carry out these obligations.

2. The admission of any such state to membership in the United Nations will be effected by a decision of the General Assembly upon the recommendation of the Security Council.

ARTICLE 5. A Member of the United Nations against which preventive or enforcement action has been taken by the Security Council may be suspended from the exercise of the rights and privileges of membership by the General Assembly upon the recommendation of the Security Council. The exercise of these rights and privileges may be restored by the Security Council.

ARTICLE 6. A Member of the United Nations which has persistently violated the Principles contained in the present Charter may be expelled from the Organization by the General Assembly upon the recommendation of the Security Council.

Chapter III
Organs

ARTICLE 7. 1. There are established as the principal organs of the United Nations: a General Assembly, a Security Council, an Economic and Social Council, a Trusteeship Council, an International Court of Justice, and a Secretariat.

2. Such subsidiary organs as may be found necessary may be established in accordance with the present Charter.

ARTICLE 8. The United Nations shall place no restrictions on the eligibility of men and women to participate in any capacity and under conditions of equality in its principal and subsidiary organs.

Chapter IV
The General Assembly

COMPOSITION

ARTICLE 9. 1. The General Assembly shall consist of all the Members of the United Nations.

2. Each Member shall have not more than five representatives in the General Assembly.

FUNCTIONS AND POWERS

ARTICLE 10. The General Assembly may discuss any questions or any matters within the scope of the present Charter or relating to the powers and functions of any organs provided for in the present Charter, and, except as provided in Article 12, may make recommendations to the Members of the United Nations or to the Security Council or to both on any such questions or matters.

ARTICLE 11. 1. The General Assembly may consider the general principles of cooperation in the maintenance of international peace and security, including the principles governing disarmament and the regulation of armaments, and may make recommendations with regard to such principles to the Members or to the Security Council or to both.

2. The General Assembly may discuss any questions relating to the maintenance of international peace and security brought before it by any Member of the United Nations, or by the Security Council, or by a state which is not a Member of the United Nations in accordance with Article 35, paragraph 2, and, except as provided in Article 12, may make recommendations with regard to any such questions to the state or states concerned or to the Security Council or to both. Any such question on which action is necessary shall be referred to the Security Council by the General Assembly either before or after discussion.

3. The General Assembly may call the attention of the Security Council to situations which are likely to endanger international peace and security.

4. The powers of the General Assembly set forth in this Article shall not limit the general scope of Article 10.

Article 12. 1. While the Security Council is exercising in respect of any dispute or situation the functions assigned to it in the present Charter, the General Assembly shall not make any recommendation with regard to that dispute or situation unless the Security Council so requests.

2. The Secretary-General, with the consent of the Security Council, shall notify the General Assembly at each session of any matters relative to the maintenance of international peace and security which are being dealt with by the Security Council and shall similarly notify the General Assembly, or the Members of the United Nations if the General Assembly is not in session, immediately the Security Council ceases to deal with such matters.

Article 13. 1. The General Assembly shall initiate studies and make recommendations for the purpose of:

a. promoting international cooperation in the political field and encouraging the progressive development of international law and its codification;

b. promoting international cooperation in the economic, social, cultural, educational, and health fields, and assisting in the realization of human rights and fundamental freedoms for all without distinction as to race, sex, language, or religion.

2. The further responsibilities, functions and powers of the General Assembly with respect to matters mentioned in paragraph 1(b) above are set forth in Chapters IX and X.

Article 14. Subject to the provisions of Article 12, the General Assembly may recommend measures for the peaceful adjustment of any situation, regardless of origin, which it deems likely to impair the general welfare or friendly relations among nations, including situations resulting from a violation of the provisions of the present Charter setting forth the Purposes and Principles of the United Nations.

Article 15. 1. The General Assembly shall receive and consider annual and special reports from the Security Council; these reports shall include an account of the measures that the Security Council has decided upon or taken to maintain international peace and security.

2. The General Assembly shall receive and consider reports from the other organs of the United Nations.

ARTICLE 16. The General Assembly shall perform such functions with respect to the international trusteeship system as are assigned to it under Chapters XII and XIII, including the approval of the trusteeship agreements for areas not designated as strategic.

ARTICLE 17. 1. The General Assembly shall consider and approve the budget of the Organization.

2. The expenses of the Organization shall be borne by the Members as apportioned by the General Assembly.

3. The General Assembly shall consider and approve any financial and budgetary arrangements with specialized agencies referred to in Article 57 and shall examine the administrative budgets of such specialized agencies with a view to making recommendations to the agencies concerned.

VOTING

ARTICLE 18. 1. Each member of the General Assembly shall have one vote.

2. Decisions of the General Assembly on important questions shall be made by a two-thirds majority of the members present and voting. These questions shall include: recommendations with respect to the maintenance of international peace and security, the election of the non-permanent members of the Security Council, the election of the members of the Economic and Social Council, the election of members of the Trusteeship Council in accordance with paragraph 1(c) of Article 86, the admission of new Members to the United Nations, the suspension of the rights and privileges of membership, the expulsion of Members, questions relating to the operation of the trusteeship system, and budgetary questions.

3. Decisions on other questions, including the determination of additional categories of questions to be decided by a two-thirds majority, shall be made by a majority of the members present and voting.

ARTICLE 19. A Member of the United Nations which is in arrears in the payment of its financial contributions to the Organization shall have no vote in the General Assembly if the amount of its arrears equals or exceeds the amount of the contributions due from it for the preceding two full years. The General Assembly may, nevertheless, permit such a Member to vote if it is satisfied that the failure to pay is due to conditions beyond the control of the Member.

PROCEDURE

ARTICLE 20. The General Assembly shall meet in regular annual sessions and in such special sessions as occasion may require. Special sessions shall be convoked by the Secretary-General at the request of the Security Council or of a majority of the Members of the United Nations.

ARTICLE 21. The General Assembly shall adopt its own rules of procedure. It shall elect its President for each session.

ARTICLE 22. The General Assembly may establish such subsidiary organs as it deems necessary for the performance of its functions.

Chapter V
The Security Council

COMPOSITION

ARTICLE 23. 1. The Security Council shall consist of eleven [1] Members of the United Nations. The Republic of China, France, the Union of Soviet Socialist Republics, the United Kingdom of Great Britain and Northern Ireland, and the United States of America shall be permanent members of the Security Council. The General Assembly shall elect six [2] other Members of the United Nations to be non-permanent members of the Security Council, due regard being specially paid, in the first instance to the contribution of Members of the United Nations to the maintenance of international peace and security and to the other purposes of the Organization, and also to equitable geographical distribution.

2. The non-permanent members of the Security Council shall be elected for a term of two years. In the first election of the non-permanent members, however, three shall be chosen for a term of one year. A retiring member shall not be eligible for immediate re-election.

3. Each member of the Security Council shall have one representative.

FUNCTIONS AND POWERS

ARTICLE 24. 1. In order to ensure prompt and effective action by the United Nations, its Members confer on the Security Council primary responsibility for the maintenance of international peace and security, and agree that in carrying out its duties under this responsibility the Security Council acts on their behalf.

2. In discharging these duties the Security Council shall act in accordance with the Purposes and Principles of the United Nations. The specific powers granted to the Security Council for the discharge of these duties are laid down in Chapters VI, VII, VIII, and XII.

3. The Security Council shall submit annual and, when necessary, special reports to the General Assembly for its consideration.

ARTICLE 25. The Members of the United Nations agree to accept and carry out the decisions of the Security Council in accordance with the present Charter.

ARTICLE 26. In order to promote the establishment and maintenance of international peace and security with the least diversion for armaments of the world's human and economic resources, the Security Council shall be responsible for formulating, with the assistance of the Military Staff Committee referred to in

[1] Expanded to fifteen members by Charter amendment in 1965.

[2] Ten elective members, five chosen each year, provided for by Charter amendment in 1965.

Article 47, plans to be submitted to the Members of the United Nations for the establishment of a system for the regulation of armaments.

VOTING

ARTICLE 27. 1. Each member of the Security Council shall have one vote.

2. Decisions of the Security Council on procedural matters shall be made by an affirmative vote of seven [3] members.

3. Decisions of the Security Council on all other matters shall be made by an affirmative vote of seven [4] members including the concurring votes of the permanent members; provided that, in decisions under Chapter VI, and under paragraph 3 of Article 52, a party to a dispute shall abstain from voting.

PROCEDURE

ARTICLE 28. 1. The Security Council shall be so organized as to be able to function continuously. Each member of the Security Council shall for this purpose be represented at all times at the seat of the Organization.

2. The Security Council shall hold periodic meetings at which each of its members may, if it so desires, be represented by a member of the government or by some other specially designated representative.

3. The Security Council may hold meetings at such places other than the seat of the Organization as in its judgment will best facilitate its work.

ARTICLE 29. The Security Council may establish such subsidiary organs as it deems necessary for the performance of its functions.

ARTICLE 30. The Security Council shall adopt its own rules of procedure, including the method of selecting its President.

ARTICLE 31. Any Member of the United Nations which is not a member of the Security Council may participate, without vote, in the discussion of any question brought before the Security Council whenever the latter considers that the interests of that Member are specially affected.

ARTICLE 32. Any Member of the United Nations which is not a member of the Security Council or any state which is not a Member of the United Nations, if it is a party to a dispute under consideration by the Security Council, shall be invited to participate, without vote, in the discussion relating to the dispute. The Security Council shall lay down such conditions as it deems just for the participation of a state which is not a Member of the United Nations.

Chapter VI
Pacific Settlement of Disputes

ARTICLE 33. 1. The parties to any dispute, the continuance of which is likely to endanger the maintenance of international peace and security, shall, first of all, seek a solution by negotiation, enquiry, mediation, conciliation, arbitration, judi-

[3] Changed to nine members by Charter amendment in 1965.
[4] Changed to nine members by Charter amendment in 1965.

cial settlement, resort to regional agencies or arrangements, or other peaceful means of their own choice.

2. The Security Council shall, when it deems necessary, call upon the parties to settle their dispute by such means.

ARTICLE 34. The Security Council may investigate any dispute, or any situation which might lead to international friction or give rise to a dispute, in order to determine whether the continuance of the dispute or situation is likely to endanger the maintenance of international peace and security.

ARTICLE 35. 1. Any Member of the United Nations may bring any dispute, or any situation of the nature referred to in Article 34, to the attention of the Security Council or of the General Assembly.

2. A state which is not a Member of the United Nations may bring to the attention of the Security Council or of the General Assembly any dispute to which it is a party if it accepts in advance, for the purposes of the dispute, the obligations of pacific settlement provided in the present Charter.

3. The proceedings of the General Assembly in respect of matters brought to its attention under this Article will be subject to the provisions of Articles 11 and 12.

ARTICLE 36. 1. The Security Council may, at any stage of a dispute of the nature referred to in Article 33 or of a situation of like nature, recommend appropriate procedures or methods of adjustment.

2. The Security Council should take into consideration any procedures for the settlement of the dispute which have already been adopted by the parties.

3. In making recommendations under this Article the Security Council should also take into consideration that legal disputes should as a general rule be referred by the parties to the International Court of Justice in accordance with the provisions of the Statute of the Court.

ARTICLE 37. 1. Should the parties to a dispute of the nature referred to in Article 33 fail to settle it by the means indicated in that Article, they shall refer it to the Security Council.

2. If the Security Council deems that the continuance of the dispute is in fact likely to endanger the maintenance of international peace and security, it shall decide whether to take action under Article 36 or to recommend such terms of settlement as it may consider appropriate.

ARTICLE 38. Without prejudice to the provisions of Articles 33 to 37, the Security Council may, if all the parties to any dispute so request, make recommendations to the parties with a view to a pacific settlement of the dispute.

Chapter VII
Action with Respect to Threats to the Peace, Breaches of the Peace, and Acts of Aggression

ARTICLE 39. The Security Council shall determine the existence of any threat to the peace, breach of the peace, or act of aggression and shall make recommendations, or decide what measures shall be taken in accordance with Articles 41 and 42, to maintain or restore international peace and security.

ARTICLE 40. In order to prevent an aggravation of the situation, the Security Council may, before making the recommendations or deciding upon the measures provided for in Article 39, call upon the parties concerned to comply with such provisional measures as it deems necessary or desirable. Such provisional measures shall be without prejudice to the rights, claims, or position of the parties concerned. The Security Council shall duly take account of failure to comply with such provisional measures.

ARTICLE 41. The Security Council may decide what measures not involving the use of armed force are to be employed to give effect to its decisions, and it may call upon the Members of the United Nations to apply such measures. These may include complete or partial interruption of economic relations and of rail, sea, air, postal, telegraphic, radio, and other means of communication, and the severance of diplomatic relations.

ARTICLE 42. Should the Security Council consider that measures provided for in Article 41 would be inadequate or have proved to be inadequate, it may take such action by air, sea, or land forces as may be necessary to maintain or restore international peace and security. Such action may include demonstrations, blockade, and other operations by air, sea, or land forces of Members of the United Nations.

ARTICLE 43. 1. All Members of the United Nations, in order to contribute to the maintenance of international peace and security, undertake to make available to the Security Council, on its call and in accordance with a special agreement or agreements, armed forces, assistance, and facilities, including rights of passage, necessary for the purpose of maintaining international peace and security.

2. Such agreement or agreements shall govern the numbers and types of forces, their degree of readiness and general location, and the nature of the facilities and assistance to be provided.

3. The agreement or agreements shall be negotiated as soon as possible on the initiative of the Security Council. They shall be concluded between the Security Council and Members or between the Security Council and groups of Members and shall be subject to ratification by the signatory states in accordance with their respective constitutional processes.

ARTICLE 44. When the Security Council has decided to use force it shall, before calling upon a Member not represented on it to provide armed forces in fulfilment of the obligations assumed under Article 43, invite that Member, if the Member so desires, to participate in the decisions of the Security Council concerning the employment of contingents of that Member's armed forces.

ARTICLE 45. In order to enable the United Nations to take urgent military measures, Members shall hold immediately available national air-force contingents for combined international enforcement action. The strength and degree of readiness of these contingents and plans for their combined action shall be determined, within the limits laid down in the special agreement or agreements referred to in Article 43, by the Security Council with the assistance of the Military Staff Committee.

ARTICLE 46. Plans for the application of armed force shall be made by the Security Council with the assistance of the Military Staff Committee.

ARTICLE 47. 1. There shall be established a Military Staff Committee to advise and assist the Security Council on all questions relating to the Security Council's military requirements for the maintenance of international peace and security, the employment and command of forces placed at its disposal, the regulation of armaments, and possible disarmament.

2. The Military Staff Committee shall consist of the Chiefs of Staff of the permanent Members of the Security Council or their representatives. Any Member of the United Nations not permanently represented on the Committee shall be invited by the Committee to be associated with it when the efficient discharge of the Committee's responsibilities requires the participation of that Member in its work.

3. The Military Staff Committee shall be responsible under the Security Council for the strategic direction of any armed forces placed at the disposal of the Security Council. Questions relating to the command of such forces shall be worked out subsequently.

4. The Military Staff Committee, with the authorization of the Security Council and after consultation with appropriate regional agencies, may establish regional subcommittees.

ARTICLE 48. 1. The action required to carry out the decisions of the Security Council for the maintenance of international peace and security shall be taken by all the Members of the United Nations or by some of them, as the Security Council may determine.

2. Such decisions shall be carried out by the Members of the United Nations directly and through their action in the appropriate international agencies of which they are members.

ARTICLE 49. The Members of the United Nations shall join in affording mutual assistance in carrying out the measures decided upon by the Security Council.

ARTICLE 50. If preventive or enforcement measures against any state are taken by the Security Council, any other state, whether a Member of the United Nations or not, which finds itself confronted with special economic problems arising from the carrying out of those measures shall have the right to consult the Security Council with regard to a solution of those problems.

ARTICLE 51. Nothing in the present Charter shall impair the inherent right of individual or collective self-defense if an armed attack occurs against a Member of the United Nations, until the Security Council has taken measures necessary to maintain international peace and security. Measures taken by Members in the exercise of this right of self-defense shall be immediately reported to the Security Council and shall not in any way affect the authority and responsibility of the Security Council under the present Charter to take at any time such action as it deems necessary in order to maintain or restore international peace and security.

Chapter VIII
Regional Arrangements

ARTICLE 52. 1. Nothing in the present Charter precludes the existence of regional arrangements or agencies for dealing with such matters relating to the maintenance of international peace and security as are appropriate for regional action, provided that such arrangements or agencies and their activities are consistent with the Purposes and Principles of the United Nations.

2. The Members of the United Nations entering into such arrangements or constituting such agencies shall make every effort to achieve pacific settlement of local disputes through such regional arrangements or by such regional agencies before referring them to the Security Council.

3. The Security Council shall encourage the development of pacific settlement of local disputes through such regional arrangements or by such regional agencies either on the initiative of the states concerned or by reference from the Security Council.

4. This Article in no way impairs the application of Articles 34 and 35.

ARTICLE 53. 1. The Security Council shall, where appropriate, utilize such regional arrangements or agencies for enforcement action under its authority. But no enforcement action shall be taken under regional arrangements or by regional agencies without the authorization of the Security Council, with the exception of measures against any enemy state, as defined in paragraph 2 of this Article, provided for pursuant to Article 107 or in regional arrangements directed against renewal of aggressive policy on the part of any such state, until such time as the Organization may, on request of the Governments concerned, be charged with the responsibility for preventing further aggression by such a state.

2. The term enemy state as used in paragraph 1 of this Article applies to any state which during the Second World War has been an enemy of any signatory of the present Charter.

ARTICLE 54. The Security Council shall at all times be kept fully informed of activities undertaken or in contemplation under regional arrangements or by regional agencies for the maintenance of international peace and security.

Chapter IX
International Economic and Social Cooperation

ARTICLE 55. With a view to the creation of conditions of stability and well-being which are necessary for peaceful and friendly relations among nations based on respect for the principle of equal rights and self-determination of peoples, the United Nations shall promote:

a. higher standards of living, full employment, and conditions of economic and social progress and development;
b. solutions of international economic, social, health, and related problems; and international cultural and educational cooperation; and
c. universal respect for, and observance of, human rights and fundamental freedoms for all without distinction as to race, sex, language, or religion.

ARTICLE 56. All Members pledge themselves to take joint and separate action in cooperation with the Organization for the achievement of the purposes set forth in Article 55.

ARTICLE 57. 1. The various specialized agencies, established by inter-governmental agreement and having wide international responsibilities, as defined in their basic instruments, in economic, social, cultural, educational, health and related fields, shall be brought into relationship with the United Nations in accordance with the provisions of Article 63.

2. Such agencies thus brought into relationship with the United Nations are hereinafter referred to as specialized agencies.

ARTICLE 58. The Organization shall make recommendations for the coordination of the policies and activities of the specialized agencies.

ARTICLE 59. The Organization shall, where appropriate, initiate negotiations among the states concerned for the creation of any new specialized agencies required for the accomplishment of the purposes set forth in Article 55.

ARTICLE 60. Responsibility for the discharge of the functions of the Organization set forth in this Chapter shall be vested in the General Assembly and, under the authority of the General Assembly, in the Economic and Social Council, which shall have for this purpose the powers set forth in Chapter X.

Chapter X
The Economic and Social Council

COMPOSITION

ARTICLE 61. 1. The Economic and Social Council shall consist of eighteen [5] Members of the United Nations elected by the General Assembly.

2. Subject to the provisions of paragraph 3, six [6] members of the Economic and Social Council shall be elected each year for a term of three years. A retiring member shall be eligible for immediate reelection.

3. At the first election, eighteen members of the Economic and Social Council shall be chosen. The term of office of six members so chosen shall expire at the end of one year, and of six other members at the end of two years, in accordance with arrangements made by the General Assembly.

[5] Expanded to twenty-seven members by Charter amendment in 1965.
[6] Changed to provide for the election of nine members each year by Charter amendment in 1965.

4. Each member of the Economic and Social Council shall have one representative.

FUNCTIONS AND POWERS

ARTICLE 62. 1. The Economic and Social Council may make or initiate studies and reports with respect to international economic, social, cultural, educational, health, and related matters and may make recommendations with respect to any such matters to the General Assembly, to the Members of the United Nations, and to the specialized agencies concerned.

2. It may make recommendations for the purpose of promoting respect for, and observance of, human rights and fundamental freedoms for all.

3. It may prepare draft conventions for submission to the General Assembly, with respect to matters falling within its competence.

4. It may call, in accordance with the rules prescribed by the United Nations, international conferences on matters falling within its competence.

ARTICLE 63. 1. The Economic and Social Council may enter into agreements with any of the agencies referred to in Article 57, defining the terms on which the agency concerned shall be brought into relationship with the United Nations. Such agreements shall be subject to approval by the General Assembly.

2. It may coordinate the activities of the specialized agencies through consultation with and recommendations to such agencies and through recommendations to the General Assembly and to the Members of the United Nations.

ARTICLE 64. 1. The Economic and Social Council may take appropriate steps to obtain regular reports from the specialized agencies. It may make arrangements with the Members of the United Nations and with the specialized agencies to obtain reports on the steps taken to give effect to its own recommendations and to recommendations on matters falling within its competence made by the General Assembly.

2. It may communicate its observations on these reports to the General Assembly.

ARTICLE 65. The Economic and Social Council may furnish information to the Security Council and shall assist the Security Council upon its request.

ARTICLE 66. 1. The Economic and Social Council shall perform such functions as fall within its competence in connection with the carrying out of the recommendations of the General Assembly.

2. It may, with the approval of the General Assembly, perform services at the request of Members of the United Nations and at the request of specialized agencies.

3. It shall perform such other functions as are specified elsewhere in the present Charter or as may be assigned to it by the General Assembly.

VOTING

ARTICLE 67. 1. Each member of the Economic and Social Council shall have one vote.

2. Decisions of the Economic and Social Council shall be made by a majority of the members present and voting.

PROCEDURE

ARTICLE 68. The Economic and Social Council shall set up commissions in economic and social fields and for the promotion of human rights, and such other commissions as may be required for the performance of its functions.

ARTICLE 69. The Economic and Social Council shall invite any Member of the United Nations to participate, without vote, in its deliberations on any matter of particular concern to that Member.

ARTICLE 70. The Economic and Social Council may make arrangements for representatives of the specialized agencies to participate, without vote, in its deliberations and in those of the commissions established by it, and for its representatives to participate in the deliberations of the specialized agencies.

ARTICLE 71. The Economic and Social Council may make suitable arrangements for consultation with non-governmental organizations which are concerned with matters within its competence. Such arrangements may be made with international organizations and, where appropriate, with national organizations after consultation with the Member of the United Nations concerned.

ARTICLE 72. 1. The Economic and Social Council shall adopt its own rules of procedure, including the method of selecting its President.

2. The Economic and Social Council shall meet as required in accordance with its rules, which shall include provision for the convening of meetings on the request of a majority of its members.

Chapter XI
Declaration Regarding Non-Self-Governing Territories

ARTICLE 73. Members of the United Nations which have or assume responsibilities for the administration of territories whose peoples have not yet attained a full measure of self-government recognize the principle that the interests of the inhabitants of these territories are paramount, and accept as a sacred trust the obligation to promote to the utmost, within the system of international peace and security established by the present Charter, the well-being of the inhabitants of these territories, and, to this end:

a. to ensure, with due respect for the culture of the peoples concerned, their political, economic, social, and educational advancement, their just treatment, and their protection against abuses;

b. to develop self-government, to take due account of the political aspirations of the peoples, and to assist them in the progressive development of their free political institutions, according to the particular circumstances of each territory and its peoples and their varying stages of advancement;

c. to further international peace and security;

d. to promote constructive measures of development, to encourage research, and to cooperate with one another and, when and where appropriate, with specialized international bodies with a view to the practical achievement of the social, economic, and scientific purposes set forth in this Article; and
e. to transmit regularly to the Secretary-General for information purposes, subject to such limitation as security and constitutional considerations may require, statistical and other information of a technical nature relating to economic, social, and educational conditions in the territories for which they are respectively responsible other than those territories to which Chapters XII and XIII apply.

ARTICLE 74. Members of the United Nations also agree that their policy in respect of the territories to which this Chapter applies, no less than in respect of their metropolitan areas, must be based on the general principle of good-neighborliness, due account being taken of the interests and well-being of the rest of the world, in social, economic, and commercial matters.

Chapter XII
International Trusteeship System

ARTICLE 75. The United Nations shall establish under its authority an international trusteeship system for the administration and supervision of such territories as may be placed thereunder by subsequent individual agreements. These territories are hereinafter referred to as trust territories.

ARTICLE 76. The basic objectives of the trusteeship system, in accordance with the Purposes of the United Nations laid down in Article 1 of the present Charter, shall be:

a. to further international peace and security;
b. to promote the political, economic, social, and educational advancement of the inhabitants of the trust territories, and their progressive development towards self-government or independence as may be appropriate to the particular circumstances of each territory and its peoples and the freely expressed wishes of the peoples concerned, and as may be provided by the terms of each trusteeship agreement;
c. to encourage respect for human rights and for fundamental freedoms for all without distinction as to race, sex, language, or religion, and to encourage recognition of the interdependence of the peoples of the world; and
d. to ensure equal treatment in social, economic, and commercial matters for all Members of the United Nations and their nationals, and also equal treatment for the latter in the administration of justice, without prejudice to the attainment of the foregoing objectives and subject to the provisions of Article 80.

ARTICLE 77. 1. The trusteeship system shall apply to such territories in the following categories as may be placed thereunder by means of trusteeship agreements:

a. territories now held under mandate;

b. territories which may be detached from enemy states as a result of the Second World War; and

c. territories voluntarily placed under the system by states responsible for their administration.

2. It will be a matter for subsequent agreement as to which territories in the foregoing categories will be brought under the trusteeship system and upon what terms.

Article 78. The trusteeship system shall not apply to territories which have become Members of the United Nations, relationship among which shall be based on respect for the principle of sovereign equality.

Article 79. The terms of trusteeship for each territory to be placed under the trusteeship system, including any alteration or amendment, shall be agreed upon by the states directly concerned, including the mandatory power in the case of territories held under mandate by a Member of the United Nations, and shall be approved as provided for in Articles 83 and 85.

Article 80. 1. Except as may be agreed upon in individual trusteeship agreements, made under Articles 77, 79, and 81, placing each territory under the trusteeship system, and until such agreements have been concluded, nothing in this Chapter shall be construed in or of itself to alter in any manner the rights whatsoever of any states or any peoples or the terms of existing international instruments to which Members of the United Nations may respectively be parties.

2. Paragraph 1 of this Article shall not be interpreted as giving grounds for delay or postponement of the negotiation and conclusion of agreements for placing mandated and other territories under the trusteeship system as provided for in Article 77.

Article 81. The trusteeship agreement shall in each case include the terms under which the trust territory will be administered and designate the authority which will exercise the administration of the trust territory. Such authority, hereinafter called the administering authority, may be one or more states or the Organization itself.

Article 82. There may be designated, in any trusteeship agreement, a strategic area or areas which may include part or all of the trust territory to which the agreement applies, without prejudice to any special agreement or agreements made under Article 43.

Article 83. 1. All functions of the United Nations relating to strategic areas, including the approval of the terms of the trusteeship agreements and of their alteration or amendment, shall be exercised by the Security Council.

2. The basic objectives set forth in Article 76 shall be applicable to the people of each strategic area.

3. The Security Council shall, subject to the provisions of the trusteeship agreements and without prejudice to security considerations, avail itself of the assistance of the Trusteeship Council to perform those functions of the United Nations under the trusteeship system relating to political, economic, social, and educational matters in the strategic areas.

ARTICLE 84. It shall be the duty of the administering authority to ensure that the trust territory shall play its part in the maintenance of international peace and security. To this end the administering authority may make use of volunteer forces, facilities, and assistance from the trust territory in carrying out the obligations towards the Security Council undertaken in this regard by the administering authority, as well as for local defense and the maintenance of law and order within the trust territory.

ARTICLE 85. 1. The functions of the United Nations with regard to trusteeship agreements for all areas not designated as strategic, including the approval of the terms of the trusteeship agreements and of their alteration or amendment, shall be exercised by the General Assembly.

2. The Trusteeship Council, operating under the authority of the General Assembly, shall assist the General Assembly in carrying out these functions.

Chapter XIII
The Trusteeship Council

COMPOSITION

ARTICLE 86. 1. The Trusteeship Council shall consist of the following Members of the United Nations:

a. those Members administering trust territories;

b. such of those Members mentioned by name in Article 23 as are not administering trust territories; and

c. as many other Members elected for three-year terms by the General Assembly as may be necessary to ensure that the total number of members of the Trusteeship Council is equally divided between those Members of the United Nations which administer trust territories and those which do not.

2. Each member of the Trusteeship Council shall designate one specially qualified person to represent it therein.

FUNCTIONS AND POWERS

ARTICLE 87. The General Assembly and, under its authority, the Trusteeship Council, in carrying out their functions, may:

a. consider reports submitted by the administering authority;

b. accept petitions and examine them in consultation with the administering authority;

c. provide for periodic visits to the respective trust territories at times agreed upon with the administering authority; and

d. take these and other actions in conformity with the terms of the trusteeship agreements.

ARTICLE 88. The Trusteeship Council shall formulate a questionnaire on the political, economic, social, and educational advancement of the inhabitants of each trust territory, and the administering authority for each trust territory within the competence of the General Assembly shall make an annual report to the General Assembly upon the basis of such questionnaire.

VOTING

ARTICLE 89. 1. Each member of the Trusteeship Council shall have one vote.

2. Decisions of the Trusteeship Council shall be made by a majority of the members present and voting.

PROCEDURE

ARTICLE 90. 1. The Trusteeship Council shall adopt its own rules of procedure, including the method of selecting its President.

2. The Trusteeship Council shall meet as required in accordance with its rules, which shall include provision for the convening of meetings on the request of a majority of its members.

ARTICLE 91. The Trusteeship Council shall, when appropriate, avail itself of the assistance of the Economic and Social Council and of the specialized agencies in regard to matters with which they are respectively concerned.

Chapter XIV
The International Court of Justice

ARTICLE 92. The International Court of Justice shall be the principal judicial organ of the United Nations. It shall function in accordance with the annexed Statute, which is based upon the Statute of the Permanent Court of International Justice and forms an integral part of the present Charter.

ARTICLE 93. 1. All Members of the United Nations are *ipso facto* parties to to the Statute of the International Court of Justice.

2. A state which is not a Member of the United Nations may become a party to the Statute of the International Court of Justice on conditions to be determined in each case by the General Assembly upon the recommendation of the Security Council.

ARTICLE 94. 1. Each Member of the United Nations undertakes to comply with the decision of the International Court of Justice in any case to which it is a party.

2. If any party to a case fails to perform the obligations incumbent upon it under a judgment rendered by the Court, the other party may have recourse to the Security Council, which may, if it deems necessary, make recommendations or decide upon measures to be taken to give effect to the judgment.

ARTICLE 95. Nothing in the present Charter shall prevent Members of the United Nations from entrusting the solution of their differences to other tribunals by virtue of agreements already in existence or which may be concluded in the future.

ARTICLE 96. 1. The General Assembly or the Security Council may request the International Court of Justice to give an advisory opinion on any legal question.

2. Other organs of the United Nations and specialized agencies, which may at any time be so authorized by the General Assembly, may also request advisory opinions of the Court on legal questions arising within the scope of their activities.

Chapter XV
The Secretariat

ARTICLE 97. The Secretariat shall comprise a Secretary-General and such staff as the Organization may require. The Secretary-General shall be appointed by the General Assembly upon the recommendation of the Security Council. He shall be the chief administrative officer of the Organization.

ARTICLE 98. The Secretary-General shall act in that capacity in all meetings of the General Assembly, of the Security Council, of the Economic and Social Council, and of the Trusteeship Council, and shall perform such other functions as are entrusted to him by these organs. The Secretary-General shall make an annual report to the General Assembly on the work of the Organization.

ARTICLE 99. The Secretary-General may bring to the attention of the Security Council any matter which in his opinion may threaten the maintenance of international peace and security.

ARTICLE 100. 1. In the performance of their duties the Secretary-General and the staff shall not seek or receive instructions from any government or from any other authority external to the Organization. They shall refrain from any action which might reflect on their position as international officials responsible only to the Organization.

2. Each Member of the United Nations undertakes to respect the exclusively international character of the responsibilities of the Secretary-General and the staff and not to seek to influence them in the discharge of their responsibilities.

ARTICLE 101. 1. The staff shall be appointed by the Secretary-General under regulations established by the General Assembly.

2. Appropriate staffs shall be permanently assigned to the Economic and Social Council, the Trusteeship Council, and, as required, to other organs of the United Nations. These staffs shall form a part of the Secretariat.

3. The paramount consideration in the employment of the staff and in the determination of the conditions of service shall be the necessity of securing the highest standards of efficiency, competence, and integrity. Due regard shall be paid to the importance of recruiting the staff on as wide a geographical basis as possible.

Chapter XVI
Miscellaneous Provisions

ARTICLE 102. 1. Every treaty and every international agreement entered into by any Member of the United Nations after the present Charter comes into force shall as soon as possible be registered with the Secretariat and published by it.

2. No party to any such treaty or international agreement which has not been registered in accordance with the provisions of paragraph 1 of this Article may invoke that treaty or agreement before any organ of the United Nations.

ARTICLE 103. In the event of a conflict between the obligations of the Members of the United Nations under the present Charter and their obligations under any other international agreement, their obligations under the present Charter shall prevail.

ARTICLE 104. The Organization shall enjoy in the territory of each of its Members such legal capacity as may be necessary for the exercise of its functions and the fulfilment of its purposes.

ARTICLE 105. 1. The Organization shall enjoy in the territory of each of its Members such privileges and immunities as are necessary for the fulfilment of its purposes.

2. Representatives of the Members of the United Nations and officials of the Organization shall similarly enjoy such privileges and immunities as are necessary for the independent exercise of their functions in connection with the Organization.

3. The General Assembly may make recommendations with a view to determining the details of the application of paragraphs 1 and 2 of this Article or may propose conventions to the Members of the United Nations for this purpose.

Chapter XVII
Transitional Security Arrangements

ARTICLE 106. Pending the coming into force of such special agreements referred to in Article 43 as in the opinion of the Security Council enable it to begin the exercise of its responsibilities under Article 42, the parties to the Four-Nation Declaration, signed at Moscow, October 30, 1943, and France, shall, in accordance with the provisions of paragraph 5 of that Declaration, consult with one another and as occasion requires with other Members of the United Nations with a view to such joint action on behalf of the Organization as may be necessary for the purpose of maintaining international peace and security.

ARTICLE 107. Nothing in the present Charter shall invalidate or preclude action, in relation to any state which during the Second World War has been an enemy of any signatory to the present Charter, taken or authorized as a result of that war by the Governments having responsibility for such action.

Chapter XVIII
Amendments

ARTICLE 108. Amendments to the present Charter shall come into force for all Members of the United Nations when they have been adopted by a vote of two thirds of the members of the General Assembly and ratified in accordance with their respective constitutional processes by two thirds of the Members of the United Nations, including all the permanent members of the Security Council.

ARTICLE 109. 1. A General Conference of the Members of the United Nations for the purpose of reviewing the present Charter may be held at a date and place to be fixed by a two-thirds vote of the members of the General Assembly and by a vote of any seven members of the Security Council. Each Member of the United Nations shall have one vote in the conference.

2. Any alteration of the present Charter recommended by a two-thirds vote of the conference shall take effect when ratified in accordance with their respective constitutional processes by two thirds of the Members of the United Nations including all the permanent members of the Security Council.

3. If such a conference has not been held before the tenth annual session of the General Assembly following the coming into force of the present Charter, the proposal to call such a conference shall be placed on the agenda of that session of the General Assembly, and the conference shall be held if so decided by a majority vote of the members of the General Assembly and by a vote of any seven members of the Security Council.

Chapter XIX
Ratification and Signature

ARTICLE 110. 1. The present Charter shall be ratified by the signatory states in accordance with their respective constitutional processes.

2. The ratifications shall be deposited with the Government of the United States of America, which shall notify all the signatory states of each deposit as well as the Secretary-General of the Organization when he has been appointed.

3. The present Charter shall come into force upon the deposit of ratifications by the Republic of China, France, the Union of Soviet Socialist Republics, the United Kingdom of Great Britain and Northern Ireland, and the United States of America, and by a majority of the other signatory states. A protocol of the ratifications deposited shall thereupon be drawn up by the Government of the United States of America which shall communicate copies thereof to all the signatory states.

4. The states signatory to the present Charter which ratify it after it has come into force will become original members of the United Nations on the date of the deposit of their respective ratifications.

ARTICLE 111. The present Charter, of which the Chinese, French, Russian, English, and Spanish texts are equally authentic, shall remain deposited in the archives of the Government of the United States of America. Duly certified copies thereof shall be transmitted by that Government to the Governments of the other signatory states.

IN FAITH WHEREOF the representatives of the Governments of the United Nations have signed the present Charter.

DONE at the city of San Francisco the twenty-sixth day of June, one thousand nine hundred and forty-five.

APPENDIX C

INTERNATIONAL ORGANIZATIONS BY TYPE (1992–1993); AND INTERNATIONAL ORGANIZATIONS BY YEAR AND TYPE (1909–1992)

TABLE 1. International organizations by type - 1992/93 edition

Types	Intergovernmental			Nongovernmental			Total	
	No.	% Type	% IGO	No.	% Type	% NGO	No.	% Total
CONVENTIONAL INTERNATIONAL BODIES								
A. Federations of international organizations	1	2.5	0.3	39	97.5	0.8	40	0.8
B. Universal membership organizations	34	7.4	11.9	426	92.6	9.1	460	9.2
C. Intercontinental membership organizations	36	4.4	12.6	774	95.6	16.5	810	16.3
D. Regionally oriented membership organizations	215	5.9	75.2	3457	94.1	73.6	3672	73.7
TOTAL "CONVENTIONAL"	286	5.7	100.0	4696	94.3	100.0	4982	100.0
OTHER INTERNATIONAL BODIES								
E. Organizations emanating from places, persons, other bodies	719	30.5	51.2	1641	69.5	21.1	2360	25.7
F. Organizations of special form	633	21.4	45.1	2325	78.6	30.0	2958	32.3
G. Internationally-oriented national organizations	52	1.4	3.7	3795	98.6	48.9	3847	42.0
TOTAL "OTHER"	1404	15.3	100.0	7761	84.7	100.0	9165	100.0
TOTAL Types A-G	1690	-	-	12457	-	-	14147	-

SPECIAL TYPES								
H. Dissolved or apparently inactive organizations	286	10.4	9.0	2469	89.6	16.8	2755	15.4
J. Recently reported bodies, not yet confirmed	184	14.0	5.8	1128	86.0	7.6	1312	7.3
K. Subsidiary and internal bodies	347	31.5	10.9	753	68.5	5.1	1100	6.1
N. National organizations	17	0.3	0.5	5068	99.7	34.4	5085	28.4
R. Religious orders and secular institutes	C	0	0	738	100.0	5.0	738	4.1
S. Autonomous conference series	86	15.5	2.7	468	84.5	3.2	554	3.1
T. Multilateral treaties and intergovernmental agreements	1789	100.0	56.1	0	0	0	1789	10.0
U. Currently inactive nonconventional bodies	479	10.4	15.0	4109	89.6	27.9	4588	25.6
TOTAL "SPECIAL"	3188	17.8	100.0	14733	82.2	100.0	17921	100.0
TOTAL ALL TYPES	4878	-	-	27190	-	-	32068	-

This table suggests different answers to the question "How many international organizations are there?"

1. Conventional intergovernmental organizations, for those who attach importance to the non-existence of international non-governmental organizations in terms of international law. (Multilateral treaties, Type T, might be added as closely related international "instruments".)
2. Conventional international bodies, both governmental and non-governmental, for those who attach importance to the existence of autonomous international bodies as a social reality.
3. Conventional bodies (Types A to D) plus special forms (Type F), for those who recognize the importance of organizational substitutes and unconventional form. (To the latter might be added conference series, Type S, and multilateral treaties, Type T, as forms of organization substitute.)
4. Conventional bodies (Types A to D), special forms (Type F), and religious orders (Type R), for those who accept the social reality of the latter as independent actors.
5. Conventional bodies (Types A to D), other international bodies (Types E to G), religious orders (Type R), and multilateral treaties (Type T), for those who are interested in the international impact of semi-autonomous and nationally-ties organizations. (Documentalists might also include inactive bodies, Type H, which figure in "authority lists" of international organizations.)

TABLE 2. International organizations by year and type (1909-1992)

	1909	1956	1960	1964	1968	1976	1981	1984	1985	1986	1987	1988	1989	1990	1991	1992
Year	1909	1956	1960	1964	1968	1976	1981	1984	1985	1986	1987	1988	1989	1990	1991	1992
Edition	(a)	6	8	10	12	16	19	21	22	23	24	25	26	27	28	29
CONVENTIONAL INTERNATIONAL BODIES (b)																
A. NGO	-	-	-	-	-	-	43	43	43	43	42	41	41	40	39	39
IGO	-	-	-	-	-	-	1	1	1	1	1	1	1	1	1	1
B. NGO	-	-	-	-	-	-	370	397	397	417	420	422	425	430	427	426
IGO	-	-	-	-	-	-	31	30	30	32	33	33	33	34	34	34
C. NGO	-	-	-	-	-	-	859	792	796	807	760	796	781	770	773	774
IGO	-	-	-	-	-	-	50	51	51	51	45	45	43	41	40	36
D. NGO	-	-	-	-	-	-	2991	3383	3440	3382	3013	3259	3374	3406	3381	3457
IGO	-	-	-	-	-	-	255	283	296	285	232	230	223	217	222	215
Total NGO	176	973	1255	1470	1899	2502	4265	4615	4676	4649	4235	4518	4621	4646	4620	4696
Total IGO	37	132	154	179	229	252	337	365	378	369	311	309	300	293	297	286
Total "convent."	213	1105	1409	1649	2128	2754	4602	4980	5054	5018	4546	4827	4921	4939	4917	4982
OTHER INTERNATIONAL BODIES (c)																
E. NGO (d)	-	-	-	-	-	-	1010	1285	1532	1710	1751	1996	2051	2129	1656	1641
IGO	-	-	-	-	-	-	384	643	705	729	722	751	778	796	763	719
F. NGO (e)	-	-	-	-	-	-	680	1209	958	1190	1380	1538	1807	1915	1970	2325
IGO	-	-	-	-	-	-	278	450	485	542	561	590	625	680	647	633
G. NGO (f)	-	-	-	-	-	-	3443	5577	6602	6969	7577	8273	5854	7518	7867	3795
IGO	-	-	-	-	-	-	40	72	64	59	55	52	8	87	87	52
Total NGO	-	12	13	248	678	2653	5133	8071	9092	9869	10708	11807	9712	11562	11493	7761
Total IGO	-	-	-	-	-	-	702	1165	1254	1330	1338	1393	1489	1563	1497	1404
Tl "other"	-	12	13	248	678	2653	5835	9236	10346	11199	12046	13200	11201	13125	12990	9165
Total A-G	213	1117	1422	1897	2806	5407	10437	14216	25400	16217	16592	18027	16122	18064	17907	14147

SPECIAL TYPES																
H. NGO (h)	-	-	-	-	741	1067	1393	1549	1528	1684	2172	2109	2138	2204	2323	2469
IGO	-	-	-	-	-	-	-	191	197	212	242	240	247	251	257	286
J. NGO	-	-	-	-	-	-	539	925	1175	792	1205	1341	1391	1023	941	1128
IGO	-	-	-	-	-	-	-	105	125	77	88	137	154	141	144	184
K. NGO	-	-	-	-	-	-	-	-	-	-	-	-	-	-	511	753
IGO	-	-	-	-	-	-	-	-	-	-	-	-	-	-	86	347
M. NGO (i)	-	-	-	-	-	-	-	888	-	-	-	-	-	-	-	-
IGO	-	-	-	-	-	-	-	34	33	-	-	-	-	-	-	-
N. NGO	-	-	-	-	-	-	-	-	-	-	-	-	-	-	-	5068
IGO	-	-	-	-	-	-	-	-	-	-	-	-	-	-	-	17
R. NGO (e)	-	-	-	-	-	-	-	605	599	652	688	690	683	683	753	738
IGO	-	-	-	-	-	-	-	0	0	0	0	0	0	0	0	0
S. NGO (e)	-	-	-	-	-	-	-	-	344	368	392	406	424	437	449	468
IGO	-	-	-	-	-	-	-	-	34	49	58	63	71	71	76	86
T. NGO	-	-	-	-	-	-	-	0	0	0	0	0	0	0	0	0
IGO	-	-	-	-	-	-	-	910	1419	1418	1620	1634	1663	1674	1767	1789
U. NGO (j)	-	-	-	-	-	-	1904	2961	3220	3515	3848	4033	1094	1779	2545	4109
IGO	-	-	-	-	-	-	-	72	106	140	240	262	222	329	441	479
Total NGO	-	-	-	-	741	1067	3836	6928	6866	7011	8305	8579	5730	6126	7522	14733
Total IGO	-	-	-	-	-	-	-	1312	1914	1896	2248	2336	2357	2466	2771	3188
Total	-	-	-	-	741	1067	3836	8240	8780	8907	10553	10915	8087	8592	10293	17921
Total all types	213	1117	1422	1897	3547	6474	14273	22456	24180	25124	27124	28942	24209	26656	28200	32068

(a) From "Annuaire de la Vie Internationale", published by the UIA prior to the Yearbook series.
(b) Early editions of the Yearbook covered only conventional international bodies. From 1976 to 1978 these were grouped into "Section A".
(c) Criteria were broadened in 1976 to permit inclusion of borderline cases in a new "Section B". In 1981 "Section A" was redefined as the current Types A to D, and "Section B" was redefined as the current Types E to H.
(d) From 1962 to 1972 NGOs created in relation to the EEC or EFTA communities were treated as "secondary entries".
(e) Religious orders were transferred from Section F to a new Section R in 1983. Conference series were transferred from Section F to the new Section S in 1985.
(f) From 1954 to 1964 only national NGOs with consultative status at ECOSOC were included. From 1966 other national NGOs were included, eventually justifying "Section B" from 1976 to 1978. In 1989 more radical criteria were applied to exclude apparently less active or less "international" bodies. In 1992 less "international" bodies were moved to a new "Type N"
(g) Up to 1974 the total number of "international NGOs" reported in various academic studies included those indicated in note (f)
(h) Included in "Section B" from 1976, and as "secondary entries" prior to that. Stricter criteria of continuing activity (applied from 1987) increased the proportion of bodies transferred to Types H and U.
(i) In 1981 included in Section F. Since 1985 again in Type F (only governmental enterprises).
(j) From 1981 to 1983 this section was only used for unconfirmed and untraceable bodies from the past. From 1984 this type is used to maintain an index trace on inactive bodies previously in Types E and F. From 1989 , only inactive bodies, previously in Types E and F, are included in this type.

Source: Union of International Associations, *Yearbook of International Organizations, 1992/93* 10th ed., vol 2: Geographic Volume (New York: G.G. Saur, 1992/93), pp. 1610–1611.

BIBLIOGRAPHICAL REFERENCES

Abi-Saad, Georges, ed. *The Concept of International Organization*. Paris: UNESCO, 1981.

Amerasinghe, C. *Documents on International Administrative Tribunals*. Oxford: Clarendon Press, 1989.

Ameri, Houshang. *Politics and Process in the Specialized Agencies of the United Nations*. Aldershot, UK: Gower Publishing Co., 1982.

Archer, Clive. *International Organization*. 2nd ed. New York: Routledge, 1992.

———. *Organizing Western Europe*. Sevenoaks, Kent, UK: Edward Arnold, 1992.

Asanta, S. K. B. *The Political Economy of Regionalism in Africa: A Decade of ECOWAS*. New York: Praeger, 1986.

Atkins, G. Pope. *Latin American in the International Political System*. Boulder, CO: Westview Press, 1989.

Beigbeder, Yves. *Threats to the International Civil Service*. London: Pinter Publishers, 1988.

Bergsten, C. Fred, and Edward M. Graham. *The Globalization of Industry and National Governments*. Washington, DC: Institute for International Economics, 1993.

Berridge, G. R. *Return to the UN: UN Diplomacy in Regional Conflicts*. New York: St. Martin's Press, 1991.

Bodenheimer, Susanne J. *Political Union: A Microcosm of European Politics, 1960–1966*. Leyden, Holland: A. W. Sijthoff, 1967.

Bowett, D. W. *The Law of International Institutions*. New York: Praeger, 1963.

Bowker, Mike, and Robin Brown, eds. *From Cold War to Collapse: Theory and World Politics in the 1980s*. New York: Cambridge University Press, 1992.

Brown, Seyom. *International Relations in a Changing Global System: Toward a Theory of the World Polity*. Boulder, CO: Westview Press, 1992.

Cox, Robert W., and Harold K. Jacobson, eds. *The Anatomy of Influence*. New Haven, CT: Yale University Press, 1973.

Damrosch, Lori Fisler, and David J. Scheffer, eds. *Law and Force in the New International Order*. Boulder, CO: Westview Press, 1991.

Dembinski, Ludwik. *The Modern Law of Diplomacy*. Boston: Nijhoff and United Nations Institute for Training and Research, 1988.

De Palaeius Puyana, Alicia. *Economic Integration among Unequal Partners: The Case of the Andean Group*. New York: Pergamon, 1982.

Easton, David. *A Framework for Political Analysis*. Englewood Cliffs, NJ: Prentice-Hall, 1965.

Edwards, Michael and David Hulme, eds. *Making a Difference: NGOs and Development in a Changing World*. London: Earthscan, 1992.

Etzioni, Amitai. *Political Unification: A Comparative Study of Leaders and Forces*. New York: Holt, Rinehart and Winston, 1965.

Feld, Werner J. *Arms Control and the Atlantic Community*. New York: Praeger, 1987.

———. *The Future of the European Security and Defense Policy*. Boulder, CO: Adamantine Press, 1993.

Forsyth, David P. *Human Rights and World Politics*. 2nd. rev. ed. Lincoln: University of Nebraska Press, 1989.

Franck, Thomas. *Political Questions/Judicial Answers: Does the Rule of Law Apply to Foreign Affairs?* Princeton, NJ: Princeton University Press, 1992.

Frieden, Jeffrey A., and David A. Lake. *International Political Economy: Perspectives on Global Power and Wealth*. New York: St. Martin's Press, 1991.

Gardner, Richard, N. *Negotiating Survival: Your Priorities after Rio*. New York: Council on Foreign Relations, 1992.

Gauhar, Altaf, ed. *Regional Integration: The Latin American Experience*. Boulder, CO: Westview Press, 1985.

Gore, Al. *Earth in the Balance: Ecology and the Human Spirit*. Boston: Houghton Mifflin, 1992.

Graham, Norman A., and Robert S. Jordan. *The International Civil Service: Changing Role and Concepts*. New York: Pergamon Press, for the UN Institute for Training and Research, 1980.

Groom, A. J. R., and Paul Taylor, eds. *Functionalism: Theory and Practice in International Relations*. New York: Crane, Russak and Co., 1975.

Haas, Ernst B. *When Knowledge Is Power: Three Models of Change in International Organizations*. Berkeley: University of California Press, 1990.

Hammond, Grant. *Plowshares into Swords: Arms Races in International Politics*. Columbia: University of South Carolina Press, 1993.

Harf, James E., and B. Thomas Trout, eds. *The Politics of Global Resources*. Durham, NC: Duke University Press, 1987.

Harrelson, Max. *Fires All around the Horizon: The U.N.'s Uphill Battle to Preserve the Peace*. New York: Praeger, 1989.

Hoggart, Richard. *An Idea and Its Servants: UNESCO from Within*. New York: Oxford University Press, 1987.

Holmberg, Johan, ed. *Policies for a Small Planet, from the International Institute for Environment and Development*. London: Earthscan, 1992.

Hurrell, Andrew, and Benedict Kingsbury, eds. *The International Politics of the Environment*. Oxford: Clarendon Press, 1992.

Hurwitz, Leon. *The European Community and the Management of International Cooperation*. Westport, CT: Greenwood Press, 1987.

———, and Christian Lequesne, eds. *The State of the European Community: Policies,*

Institutions and Debates in the Transition Years. Boulder, CO: Lynne Rienner, 1991.

Imber, Mark F. *The USA, ILO, UNESCO, and IAEA*. New York: St. Martin's Press, 1990.

Jackson, Robert J., ed. *Europe in Transition: The Management of Security after the Cold War*. New York: Praeger, 1992.

Jacobson, Harold K., and Dusan Sidjanski, eds. *The Emerging International Economic Order: Dynamic Processes, Constraints, and Opportunities*. Beverly Hills, CA: Sage, 1982.

James, Alan. *Peacekeeping in International Politics*. New York: St. Martin's Press, 1990.

Jordan, Robert S., ed. *Dag Hammarskjöld Revisited: The U.N. Secretary-General as a Force in World Politics*. Durham, NC: Carolina Academic Press, 1983.

———, ed. *International Administration: Its Evolution and Contemporary Applications*. New York: Oxford University Press, 1971.

———. *Political Leadership in NATO: A Study in Multinational Diplomacy*. Boulder, CO: Westview Press, 1979.

Joyner, Christopher, and Sudhir K. Chopra, eds. *Antarctica and the Law of the Sea*. Dordrecht, Holland: Martinus Nijhoff Publishers, 1992.

———. *The Antarctic Legal Regime*. Boston: Martinus Nijhoff Publishers, 1988.

Kaufmann, Johan. *United Nations Decision Making*. Rockville, MD: Sijthoff and Noordhoff, 1980.

———, and Nico Schrijver. *Changing Global Needs: Expanding Roles for the United Nations System*. Hanover, NH: Academic Council on the United Nations System, Reports and Papers, 1990–5, 1990.

Keohane, Robert O. *After Hegemony: Cooperation and Discord in the World Political Economy*. Princeton, NJ: Princeton University Press, 1984.

———, and Stanley Hoffman, eds. *The New European Community: Decision-Making and Institutional Change*. Boulder, CO: Westview Press, 1991.

———, and Joseph S. Nye. *Power and Interdependence: World Politics in Transition*. Boston: Little Brown, 1977.

Krasner, Stephen D., ed. *International Regimes*. Ithaca, NY: Cornell University Press, 1983.

Kurbayashi, Tadao and Edward L. Miles, eds. *The Law of the Sea in the 1990s: a Framework for Further International Cooperation*. Honolulu: Law of the Sea Institute, University of Hawaii, 1992.

Lillich, Richard, ed. *Fact-Finding before International Tribunals*. Ardsley-on-Hudson, NY: Transnational Publishers, 1992.

Liu, F.T. *United Nations Peacekeeping and the Non-use of Force*. Boulder, CO: Lynne Rienner, 1992.

Lodge, Juliet, ed. *European Community and the Challenge of the Future*. New York: St. Martin's Press, 1989.

Loescher, Gil. *Refugee Movements and International Security*. Adelphi Papers 268. London: International Institute for Strategic Studies, Summer 1992.

McLaren, Robert L. *Civil Servants and Public Policy*. Waterloo, Ont., Canada: Wilfrid Laurier University Press, 1980.

Meron, Theodor. *Human Rights and Humanitarian Norms as Customary Law*. Oxford: Clarendon Press, 1989.

———. *Status and Independence of the International Civil Servant*. Leydon: Sijthoff and Noordhoff, 1981.

———. *The United Nations Secretariat: The Rules and the Practice*. Lexington, MA: Lexington Books, 1977.

Minear, Larry. *United Nations Coordination of the International Humanitarian Response to the Gulf Crisis, 1990–1992*. Occasional Paper no. 13. Providence, RI: Brown University, Thomas J. Watson Institute for International Studies, 1992.

———. *The Challenge of Famine Relief: Emerging Operation in the Sudan*. Washington, D.C.: The Brookings Institution, 1992.

Moon, Bruce E. ed. *The Political Economy of Basic Human Needs*. Ithaca, NY: Cornell University Press, 1992.

Nicol, Davidson, ed. *The United Nations Security Council: Towards Greater Effectiveness*. New York: United Nations Institute for Training and Research, 1982.

Nicoll, William, and Trevor C. Salmon. *Understanding the European Communities*. Savage, MD: Barnes and Noble, 1990.

Nuttall, Simon J. *European Political Co-operation*. Oxford: Clarendon Press, 1992.

Olson, Mancur. *The Logic of Collective Action: Public Goods and the Theory of Groups*. Cambridge, MA: Harvard University Press, 1971.

Packenham, Robert A. *The Dependency Movement: Scholarship and Politics in Development Studies*, Cambridge, MA: Harvard University Press, 1992.

Peterson, M. J. *The General Assembly in World Politics*. Boston: Unwin and Hyman, 1990.

Pitt, David, and Thomas George Weiss, eds. *The Nature of United Nations Bureaucracies*. London: Croon Helm, 1987.

Preston, William, Edward S. Herman, and Herbert I. Schiller. *Hope and Folly: The United States and UNESCO*. Minneapolis: University of Minnesota Press, 1989.

Purvis, Hoyt. *Interdependence: An Introduction to International Relations*. New York: Harcourt Brace Jovanovich College Publishers, 1992.

Renninger, John P. *ECOSOC: Options for Reform*. Efficacy and Policy Studies no. 4. New York: United Nations Institute for Training and Research (UNITAR), 1981.

———. *Multinational Cooperation for Development in West Africa*. New York: Pergamon Press, 1979.

Rikhye, Indar Jit, and Kjell Skjelsbaek, eds. *The United Nations and Peacekeeping: Results, Limitations, and Prospects*. New York: St. Martin's Press, 1991.

Roberts, Adam, and Benedict Kingsbury, eds. *United Nations, Divided World: The UN's Roles in International Politics*. New York: Oxford University Press, 1988.

Robertson, A. H. *Human Rights in the World: An Introduction to the Study of International Protection of Human Rights*. 3rd. ed. New York: St. Martin's Press, 1990.

Russett, Bruce, Harvey Starr, and Richard J. Stall, eds. *Choices in World Politics: Sovereignty and Interdependence*. New York: W. H. Freeman, 1989.

Schachter, Oscar, and Christopher C. Joyner, eds. *United Nations Legal Order*. Cambridge: Grotius Publications, 1993.

Singh, Nihal. *The Rise and Fall of UNESCO*. Calcutta: Allied Publishers, 1987.

Skolnikoff, Eugene B. *The Elusive Transformation: Science, Technology, and the Evolution of International Politics*. Princeton, NJ: Princeton University Press, 1993.

Spanier, John. *Games Nations Play*. 8th ed. Washington, DC: Congressional Quarterly Press, 1992.

Treverton, Gregory F., ed. *The Shape of the New Europe*. New York: Council on Foreign Relations Press, 1992.

Walt, Stephen M. *The Origins of Alliances*. Ithaca, NY: Cornell University Press, 1987.

Weiss, Thomas George, *International Bureaucracy*. Lexington, MA: D. C. Heath, 1975.

———. *The World Food Conference and Global Problem Solving*. New York: Praeger, 1976.

Whalley, John. *The Future of the World Trading System*. Institute for International Economics, 1993.

Wharton, William, ed. *Security Arrangements for a New Europe*. Washington, DC: National Defense University Press, 1992.

White, Lyman C. *International Non-Governmental Organizations*. New York: Greenwood Press, 1968.

White, N. D. *The United Nations and the Maintenance of International Peace and Security*. New York: St. Martin's Press, 1990.

INDEX

About the Authors

WERNER J. FELD is UNO Distinguished Professor Emeritus of Political Science, and Director of the Institute for Comparative Public Policy at the University of New Orleans. Dr. Feld is the author of numerous publications, including *American Foreign Policy: Aspirations and Reality* (1984), *Congress and National Defense* (with John K. Wildgen, 1985), *Arms Control and the Atlantic Community*, and *The Future of the European Security and Defense Policy* (1993). In addition, Dr. Feld is the author of more than sixty articles in various journals. He is currently Adjunct Professor at the Graduate School of International Studies, University of Denver.

ROBERT S. JORDAN is Research Professor of International Institutions, Professor of Political Science, and Senior Research Associate of the Eisenhower Center, at the University of New Orleans. He is serving in 1992–94 as Visiting Professor of International Relations at the U.S. Air War College. He is former Vice President of the International Studies Association and Chairman of its International Organization Section. He also has been Chairman of the section on International and Comparative Administration of the American Society for Public Administrations and an active member of the American Society of International Law. He has also published several books on International Politics.

LEON HURWITZ is Professor of Political Science at Cleveland State University. His previous books include *The Harmonization of European Public Policy: Regional Responses to Transnational Challenges* (1983), *The European Community and the Management of International Cooperation* (1987), and *The State of the European Community* (1991).